STAFF APPRAISAL AND STAFF MANAGEMENT IN SCHOOLS AND COLLEGES

A GUIDE TO IMPLEMENTATION

Editors: Brian Fidler and Robert Cooper

LONGMAN

In association with
The British Educational Management
and Administration Society

Published by Longman Industry and Public Service Management, Longman Group UK Limited, Westgate House, The High, Harlow, Essex CM20 1YR, UK.
Telephone (0279) 442601
Fax: (0279) 444501 Group 3 & 2

© British Educational Management and Administration Society, 1992

All rights reserved. No part of this publication may be reproduced, stored in a retrieval system, or transmitted in any form or by any means, electronic, mechanical, photocopying, recording or otherwise, without the prior permission of the Copyright owner.

First published 1992.

A catalogue record for this book is available from the British Library.

ISBN 0 582 067537

Typeset by EMS Phototypesetting, Berwick on Tweed
Printed and bound in Great Britain by
Biddles Ltd, Guildford and King's Lynn

Contents

	Page
Foreword by Derek Esp	vi
Acknowledgements	vii
Introduction – Brian Fidler and Bob Cooper	ix

Section 1 Concepts and Theory – Brian Fidler — 1

    1.1   Concepts and theory in staff appraisal and staff management — 1
    1.2   Experience of appraisal in non-educational organisations — 21
    1.3   Problems of appraisal in education — 27

Section 2   Staff Management and Appraisal — 39

    2.1   Staff management – **Bob Cooper** — 39
    2.2   Appraisal and staff development – **John West-Burnham** — 53
    2.3   Implementation of change – **Barry Mountford** — 66

Section 3   Appraisal Experience — 75

    3.0   Overall structure of the appraisal process – **Brian Fidler and Bob Cooper** — 75
    3.1   Experience from pilot schemes of staff appraisal in schools – **Brian Fidler** — 87

    3.2   Appraisal in primary schools — 92
    3.2.1 Tool for performance and professional development at St Edmunds RC School, Salford – **Peter Delaney** — 92
    3.2.2 Pilot appraisal scheme at Arnside National School, Cumbria – **Iain Johnston** — 101

3.3	*Appraisal in secondary schools*	113
3.3.1	First steps in appraisal at Emmbrook School, Berkshire – **Keith Barnes**	113
3.3.2	Developmental approach to appraisal at Birchwood Community High School, Cheshire – **Mike VaughanEdwards**	124
3.4	*Appraisal of head teachers*	134
3.4.0	Experience from pilot schemes of the appraisal of head teachers – **Brian Fidler**	134
3.4.1	Cumbria's experience: 'Not out of the woods': Dilemmas in the statutory appraisal of head teachers – **Vanessa Champion**	138
3.4.2	Salford's experience 1987-91 – **Dallas Hackett**	143
3.5	*Appraisal in further education colleges*	148
3.5.0	Experience from pilot schemes of appraisal in further education colleges – **Brian Fidler**	148
3.5.1	Staff appraisal at Barnet College – **Ian Duckett**	153
3.5.2	Professional and management development in Cheshire – **Kevin Quinlan**	163
3.6	*LEA appraisal schemes*	177
3.6.0	Experience of piloting staff appraisal in LEAs – **Brian Fidler**	177
3.6.1	Cumbria's experience – **Vanessa Champion**	180
3.6.2	Salford experience – **Dallas Hackett**	188
Section 4	**Processes of Appraisal**	198
4.1	Job descriptions and organisational structure – **Brian Fidler**	198
4.2	Observation of classroom teaching – **Chris Kyriacou**	218

4.3 *Interviewing*		232
4.3.0 Introduction to interviewing – **Bob Cooper**		232
4.3.1 Effective teacher appraisal interviews – **Keith Diffey**		238
4.3.2 Counselling interview – **Bob Cooper**		253
4.3.3 Target setting – **David Trethowan**		262

Section 5   Issues   271

    5.1   *Appraising management competencies –* **Bertie Everard**   271

    5.2   *Handling poor performers –* **Brian Fidler**   281

    5.3   *Performance related pay*   303

    5.3.0 Performance related pay in local government and public sector organisations: lessons for schools and colleges – **Brian Fidler**   303

    5.3.1 Experience of performance related pay in an education department – **David Cracknell**   316

    5.3.2 Performance related pay for head teachers and deputy heads – **David Turley**   327

Section 6   Overview and Action Plan   335

    6.1   *Overview and guide to the process –* **Brian Fidler and Bob Cooper**   335

    6.2   *Formulating an action plan –* **Bob Cooper and Brian Fidler**   349

Contributors   363

Notes   366

References   367

Index   377

Foreword

This second book on staff appraisal retains the basic approach of *Staff Appraisal in Schools and Colleges* but sets appraisal in the context of staff management. It takes account of the *Education (School Teacher Appraisal) Regulations 1991* and the *1991 National Framework for Appraisal in Further Education Colleges*.

Its publication is timely. Schools and colleges have to meet a target of implementation of appraisal for all staff by 1994. The 'mechanics' of appraisal may seem straightforward, but the implementation of a scheme which directly affects personal and professional development needs careful handling. The fears as well as the hopes of individual teachers are at the centre of any attempt to introduce an appraisal scheme.

In schools and colleges appraisal is set in the context of institutional development. It is not only to do with individual needs. Management, appraisers and appraisees need a shared understanding of what is intended and all need access to full information and training.

In this book the authors look at the underlying concepts and theories before going on to consider staff appraisal as part of staff management. There are new case studies drawn from schools and colleges as well as two examples of local education authority appraisal support structures. One section of the book analyses the skills of appraisal, including the writing of job descriptions, classroom observation, interviewing and target setting. Two forward looking sections consider the implications for appraisal of developments towards work based competencies, especially management competencies, and the introduction of performance related pay.

The first appraisal book in the BEMAS/Longman series was very popular. I hope that this second volume will prove to be equally popular with managers in schools and colleges, appraisers, and not least, those who are to be appraised. The success of any appraisal scheme depends upon the full commitment of all participants. A good scheme, well implemented will contribute greatly to individual professional development and to the increasing effectiveness of teams and of the whole institution.

Derek Esp
Chair, BEMAS Publications Committee
October, 1991

Acknowledgements

The inspiration for this book and the previous book *Staff Appraisal in Schools and Colleges* was two appraisal conferences which were put on by the Education Management Teachers' Committee of the British Educational Management and Administration Society in 1985 and 1986. The first conference studied appraisal experience in non-educational organisations and the second looked at developing practice in schools. We are grateful to the speakers and participants at those conferences for their contribution to our understanding of staff appraisal. In particular one of us (Brian Fidler) is indebted to one of the conference speakers, Nick Laycock of ICI Plant Protection Division, for an earlier talk at a 20 day school management course in which the positive attributes of staff appraisal and the organisational complexities of such a system were first made clear.

We wish to thank Derek Esp, Chair of BEMAS Publications Committee, for contributing the foreword.

Louise Birley, a Surrey primary headteacher, carried out research on job descriptions from which the example in section 4.2 is derived.

Finally we should like to thank the individual contributors to this volume who wrote and delivered their writings to a very demanding deadline. These accounts of practice in schools, colleges and LEAs were written in the Summer term 1991. They give a sense of realism to the appraisal process which is invaluable.

Brian Fidler *Robert Cooper*
University of Reading Citta di Castello, Italy

February 1992

Note – This book has attempted to use non-sexist language throughout. To prevent duplication of *his* and *her*, occasionally, although strictly grammatically incorrect, *their* has been used for a singular possessive.

Introduction

Brian Fidler and Robert Cooper

Context

This book develops the approach of *Staff Appraisal in Schools and Colleges* by locating staff appraisal within the process of staff management. We said there 'It will only succeed if it is seen to be an integral part of the existing management practice' (p.181). Others were somewhat slow to appreciate the significance of this and indeed accounts of much of the pilot work in LEAs have not greatly illuminated the implications of this. Perhaps, in part, this is because staff management in schools and colleges has not been adequately conceptualised and explained. This book is the first to give an account of staff management and to explain the place of staff appraisal within it.

Appraisal was mentioned in the Government White Paper *Teaching Quality* in 1983 mainly as a device which would allow LEAs to build up data on the capabilities of their teachers. The word had scarcely been mentioned in educational circles before that date although some schools were already practising a form of staff appraisal. From such beginnings the situation has developed rapidly. In the *1986 Education Act (no.2)* the Secretary of State took reserve powers which would allow him to impose an appraisal process by requiring local education authorities and others to ensure that the performance of teachers is regularly appraised in 'accordance with such requirement as may be prescribed'. And in the *Conditions of Service* (DES 1987) which were enforced on teachers there was a requirement to comply with an appraisal process 'within an agreed national framework'.

After DES-funded pilot work in six LEAs, a set of recommendations was published as a *National Framework* (DES, 1989). There followed a delay occasioned by changing Secretaries of State with different views on the speed with which a national scheme should be introduced. In July 1991 Kenneth Clarke, the then Secretary of State, established the regulations to introduce a national scheme (DES, 1991) and a timetable for implementation requiring all teachers to have completed their first appraisal by the end of the school year in 1995.

The *National Framework* and the statutory instrument containing the legal requirement have moved increasingly towards the managerial approach to staff appraisal proposed in *Staff Appraisal in Schools and Colleges*. The scheme, wherever possible, requires appraisal by those who 'already have management responsibility for the school teacher' (DES, 1991). Targets and development have to take account of institutional requirements and 'meet the needs of the school as well as those of individual appraisees' and there should be mutual support between appraisal and development planning. Indeed the *Regulations (SI 1511, 1991)* specifically give as the aims for appraisal

> Appraising bodies shall secure that appraisal assists—
> (a) school teachers in their professional development and career planning; and
> (b) those responsible for taking decisions about the management of school teachers (para 4(1))

Whilst it is clear that within a short time staff appraisal will be a regular feature of life in our schools and colleges, its exact form and purpose are still at a formative stage. The 1991 regulations provide a framework but it is anticipated that LEAs and individual schools will have scope to tailor their schemes within that framework. In formulating individual school schemes and preparing for implementation there is an increasing amount of useful material on which to draw.

Individual appraisal schemes have been implemented in a number of schools and colleges details of which have appeared in the literature (Bunnel (1987), Fidler & Cooper (1988), Bell (1988)). A number of LEAs including the six pilot schemes (Croydon, Cumbria, Newcastle, Salford, Somerset and Suffolk) have published material and an evaluation of the LEA pilot schemes (Bradley et al, 1989) and seven pilot FE College schemes (Lee, 1991) have also been published. The results of these activities will be of great interest to those in schools, colleges and LEAs who are currently contemplating the introduction of staff appraisal. Further guidance is available by studying practice in overseas educational systems which have a form of staff appraisal. Finally, there is the accumulated experience of operating staff appraisal in non-educational organisations – industry, commerce and other public services. It is the contention of this book that there is much to be learned from these sources which will be of great value to those for whom this book is written – *those in schools, colleges and LEAs who are about to implement, or will take part in, a process of staff appraisal.*

This is not a 'how to do it' book. The subject of staff appraisal is too complex and the context of individual schools and colleges is too varied to suggest that there is a 'right' way to design a staff appraisal system. It is for that reason that the book has theoretical and conceptual sections. These are to aid understanding and challenge existing ideas. It is for each reader to think through his or her own design of an appraisal system. However, this book contains much stimulating material and much accumulated experience to aid this process. There is also much that is practical in this book. The implementation steps in the action plan provide a framework to guide practitioners in thinking through these detailed steps and provide a range of decisions to be made at each stage and illustrate the range of possibilities which may be considered before arriving at a decision.

This book particularly draws on the experience of six individual schools and colleges in England and two LEAs which have introduced a form of staff appraisal and also on the experience of non-educational organisations (mainly in the UK). These sources have been selected in order to present *a managerial approach to appraisal at the institutional level.* Much writing on appraisal has treated it as an issue in assessment or staff development: as a process which checks on the quality of teaching in a rather independent way or as a process which is solely concerned with developing staff. Much American experience described in the first Suffolk study (Suffolk LEA 1985) is written from such an assessment perspective. Describing the results of an analysis of appraisal schemes in the USA in the late 1970s Wood and Pohland (1983) found that the practice of teacher evaluation largely provided

> assessment suitable as a basis for administrative/organisational decision-making in the areas of staffing and compensation instead of...efforts to improve teaching practices.

It is the contention of this book that industrial and other non-educational experience which see appraisal as part of the managerial process of the institution offers a model which is positive and developmental and actually *could* lead to improvements in the education of children and young people.

This model accepts the inherent conflict of a process which is both evaluative and developmental and also seeks to balance the needs of the individual with organisational needs, and sets out to minimise such conflict. A managerial approach to appraisal is required because appraisal looks at the objectives and performance of individual members of staff. How such objectives and performance contribute to the overall work of the institution is a *vital* concern to the management of any organisation. Further, any proposals for further training or development which arise from an appraisal process require resources, human or financial, to make them possible and deployment of resources is similarly a vital managerial concern. Finally appraisal provides an important opportunity for *two-way* communication between those who play a part in management and those who directly provide the service. However, let there be no misunderstanding, this is not to propose a particular *style of management.* Whilst all organisations have to be managed they do not have to be managed in the same way. A highly participative collegial approach emphasising leadership and team-work is one style of management. Further discussion of this theme is to be found in section 1.3 and in *Planning Your School's Strategy* (Fidler, Bowles and Hart, 1991). Other than advocating a managerial approach to staff appraisal within a school or college this book is not prescriptive and does not offer a blue print for an appraisal system. Quite the reverse, it seeks to illustrate a diversity of practice. However, on reading through the case studies and theoretical writings the reader will observe a number of common threads. These are brought together in the final section of the book.

In early sections of the book and elsewhere much use is made of the noun *organisation.* This is not used in a technical sense but rather because of its generality and consequent economy of writing. It can be taken to mean any group of people working together for a purpose. As such it covers a commercial firm, an industrial factory, the civil service, a school, college or LEA. A more detailed illustration of the concept is given by Paisey (1981).

Structure of the book

This book is somewhat more than an edited collection of individual contributions. It has substantial sections written by the editors which facilitate continuity by providing an analytical framework for other contributions; a consideration of staff management; and a concluding discussion and action plan. It is one of the first books to place appraisal explicitly within the context of the management of staff and to look at related issues such as job descriptions and organisational structure, managerial competences, handling poor performers, and performance related pay.

The book begins with a theoretical discussion of the rationale for appraisal in general terms and an exploration of the problems associated with the process in any organisation with some suggested solutions. The place of appraisal within staff management and its contribution to the management of staff are explained. A brief description of theories of motivation is given. Reference is made to the pervasive influence of the *management by objectives approach* leading to concentration on key result areas and target-setting. Goal theory provides the underlying principles of successful target-setting. Some particular difficulties associated with adapting a managerial approach to appraisal in schools and colleges are outlined and assessed. From this section a set of criteria are devised which an appraisal system should meet.

INTRODUCTION

The second section expands aspects of staff management and appraisal. Bob Cooper analyses aspects of staff management and stresses the need to adopt an appraisal scheme which is consistent with the culture of the school or college. John West-Burnham focuses on one of the components of staff management – staff development and proposes a strategy for staff development. This includes prioritising INSET and designing learning activities. Barry Mountford concludes this section with advice on implementing a major change such as appraisal within a school or college.

Section three contains the case studies. The overall structure of the appraisal process is explained in detail. The requirements of the Regulations are clearly differentiated from other recommended activities to make appraisal a success. The case studies cover two primary schools, two secondary schools, and two colleges. Further case studies cover LEA approaches to appraisal in schools and the appraisal of head teachers. The case studies cover institutions in Barnet (Ian Duckett), Berkshire (Keith Barnes), Cheshire (Mike VaughanEdwards and Kevin Quinlan), Cumbria (Iain Johnston) and Salford (Peter Delaney). Cumbria and Salford are the two pilot LEAs covered by Vanessa Champion and Dallas Hackett. Each group of case studies is preceded by an account from published sources of the staff appraisal developments in general in that particular sphere.

Component processes of staff appraisal are examined in section four. Brian Fidler explains the importance of organisational design and offers some parameters for examining the structure of schools and colleges. The final element in the organisational structure is the job description for each individual teacher and lecturer. Chris Kyriacou examines the problems of observing classroom teaching and offers guidelines for conducting a lesson appraisal. Different types of interviews are introduced by Bob Cooper who also lists different categories of questions which are used in appraisal interviews. Keith Diffey provides comprehensive guidance on successful appraisal interviewing. This covers the component parts of the interview and the skills required. Bob Cooper develops an approach to counselling which can be used in association with appraisal or for generally helping staff with problems. Finally, in this section, David Trethowan, who has pioneered target setting in schools, explains how to set targets.

Section five examines issues which impinge on appraisal. Bertie Everard explains approaches to managerial competencies and how these could be used in the appraisal process. Brian Fidler develops an earlier contribution on how to handle poor performers. This explains legal requirements and outlines a range of areas which need consideration in cases of poor performance – the job and its context, management and the individual. After examining the experience of a target setting approach to performance related pay (PRP) from published sources, David Cracknell describes his experience of operating PRP in an education department and gives a critical appraisal. David Turley describes the progress of Kensington and Chelsea towards PRP for head teachers and deputies.

The final section written by Brian Fidler and Bob Cooper gives a detailed overview of the whole process and a guide to successful staff appraisal before outlining an action plan to implement staff appraisal and providing a sequence of steps with the accompanying decisions which have to be made at each stage.

The book is intended to be self-contained although those who require further details and students on courses in education management will find a very full set of references which they may follow up.

We doubt that anyone will read this book from cover to cover sequentially. Rather we envisage readers will first dip into it according to their state of knowledge and attitude to appraisal. We suggest that those who know little about appraisal or are sceptical of the process should first read the case studies in section 3: they will find much that is reassuring and heartening. Also we think that readers will find much value in reading the case studies from sectors other than the one in which they teach.

Those who know more and wish to organise their thoughts might start at section one or section two.

Before moving to develop and implement an appraisal system all readers would be advised to read sections one and four before sections two, three, five and six.

Aims of Staff Appraisal

We reiterate three requirements for an appraisal system from *Staff Appraisal in Schools and Colleges:*

— it should carry credibility with the public as a check on the quality of work in schools and colleges;
— it should lead to improvements in the learning experiences of pupils and students;
— it should lead to greater job satisfaction of all those who work in schools and colleges.

We believe that these are difficult and professionally, very challenging aims but that no worthwhile appraisal system should ignore any of them. Any appraisal system should work progressively towards meeting all three more fully. These are summary aims within which we believe all other objectives can be subsumed.

We hope as a result of reading this book readers may be enabled to look at the concept of appraisal differently because of the insights they have acquired.

To begin to work towards the aims above it is important for all those who work in the education service to understand the appraisal process and its place within staff management so that they can play their part and benefit. This is just as true for those who are to be appraised as for those who are to do the appraising.

SECTION 1: CONCEPTS & THEORY

1.1 Concepts and theory in staff appraisal and staff management

Brian Fidler

Introduction

In the time that appraisal has been a feature of the educational scene it has changed from being viewed as an evaluative process, through being seen as a staff development exercise to being seen as an integral part of staff management. This book aims to develop the concept of staff management to more clearly locate staff appraisal within it.

What is quite striking, when looking at the theory of appraisal and its practice in well managed (but not all) industry, commerce and other public services, is that appraisal is positive and developmental. Many of the anticipated problems of applying appraisal to educational situations have also been experienced in other organisations and there is a great deal which can be learned from their experience which will enable us to avoid the same mistakes. Unless we study and learn from the experience of others we shall find ourselves with either a cosy system which achieves little and lacks public credibility or a system which is draconian in its application and similarly achieves little because of the hostile reaction it provokes. Almost all concepts of appraisal in other organisations can be taken into an educational context. One feature which may have no parallel in other organisations is any requirement to observe systematically the work performance of the appraisee. There appears to be no equivalent of observation of teaching performance.

This section describes the theory of appraisal and identifies inherent conflicts in the process. Section 1.2 briefly examines experience in other organisations whilst Section 1.3 looks at a number of problems associated with translating such experience to schools and colleges. Finally a checklist of essential features of an appraisal system is produced which acts as a summary of this section.

Terms

Staff appraisal is the term used in this book for the process by which an employee and his or her superordinate meet to discuss the performance of the employee. There is a huge variety of terms used – performance appraisal, performance review, staff review, staff reporting, and more especially school teacher appraisal – which have no accepted difference of meaning. Some writers from the USA and Australia confusingly use teacher evaluation to encompass teacher appraisal (Gitlin & Smyth, 1989). Staff development on the other hand as the name implies is wholly concerned with the increase of knowledge, skill or experience of staff without the evaluative connotation associated with appraisal.

Increasingly, however, staff appraisal has been concerned with staff development. Recently staff appraisal has concentrated on improving individual performance at work and so both terms have become closer.

Another related process is institutional evaluation or review. Inevitably school and college evaluation reflects on individual teachers' performance and in many schemes of institutional review there are self-appraisal or self-review documents for staff to complete. However, in this book the focus is upon staff appraisal as a managerial activity whereby a manager engages in an appraisal process with a subordinate for whose performance he or she is, in some sense, accountable.

Appraisal system

It is helpful to differentiate between appraisal as a process for any individual and the whole system of which this one appraisal is a part. The system comprises all the procedures involved in implementing the appraisal of individuals.

Accountability and development

Many writers prefer to see appraisal in education as either concerned with accountability or with development. Whilst this would make the process much simpler, it also makes the purposes which appraisal could serve much less worthwhile and consequently harder to justify its cost in terms of the corresponding benefit. As we shall see in non-educational organisations appraisal is concerned with both individual development and accountability or evaluation. It is precisely this combination which gives appraisal such central importance and makes it so difficult to accomplish.

The appraisal process is a combination of reviewing the past year's work (evaluation) and planning training or setting targets for the coming year (development).

In designing a particular appraisal system it is important to be clear about the extent to which it is intended to be evaluative and the extent to which it should lead to individual development. It may be useful conceptually to try to mark the position of a particular system on a display which has evaluation and development as axes (Figure 1.1.1).

An appraisal system could be placed anywhere between the axes depending on its particular balance between evaluation and development.

We shall later return to the fundamental contradiction inherent in using appraisal for both evaluative and developmental functions.

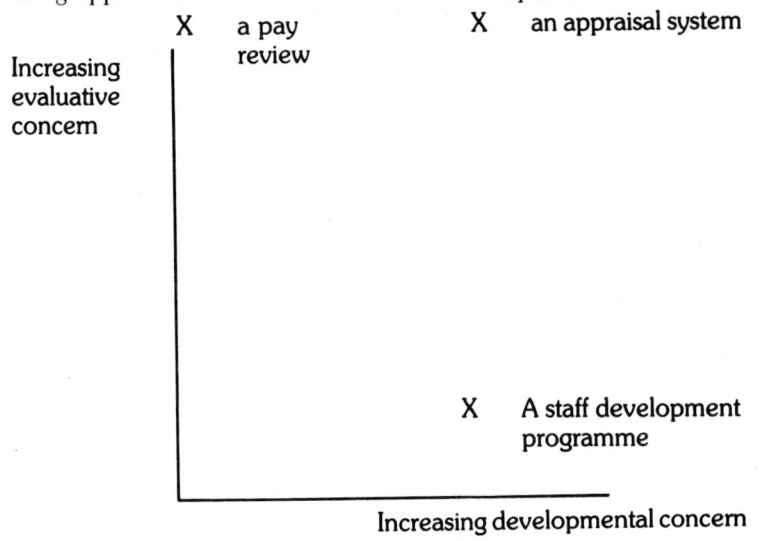

```
                    X   a pay            X   an appraisal system
Increasing              review
evaluative
concern




                                         X   A staff development
                                             programme

                                Increasing developmental concern
```

Figure 1.1.1 Display of evaluative and developmental contributions of appraisal

Appraisal theory

Appraisal of some kind has been used in organisations for a long time. In industrial and commercial concerns it was initially used in the 1920s to assess workers' rewards. Although the process became more sophisticated it was basically used as a performance control strategy in a rather mechanical way. Much effort was devoted to developing rating scales of personal qualities of workers.

After the second world war three different types of appraisal could be distinguished:

(a) reward review;
(b) performance review;
(c) review of potential for promotion.

As we shall see there may be inherent conflicts in these three types of activity and Randall et al (1984) advise

> organizations attempting to develop their staff appraisal and development procedures are strongly advised to keep the three activities of *performance, reward* and *potential review* not only separate in time but also in paper work, procedure and responsibility. (p 14)

The theory of appraisal really came of age with the advent of the Management by Objectives (MBO) movement in the 1960s.

Management by objectives (MBO)

Although the concept is generally attributed to Peter Drucker it was Douglas McGregor who allied it to performance appraisal (Strauss 1972). MBO is seen by many as a device for ensuring that employees in an organisation are all engaged on work which is consistent with the organisation's overall objectives as identified by the most senior personnel in the organisation. Others have seen MBO as emphasising employee participation, better communication and enhanced motivation through clearly identified goals and the achievement of results (Giegold 1978).

Schuster and Kindall (1974) have identified three structural elements to MBO:

1. Performance goals or targets initiated periodically by the employee;
2. Mutual agreement of a set of goals by the employee and his or her superior after discussion;
3. Periodic review by the employee and his or her superior of the match between goals and achievements.

These are the features of MBO which changed the nature of the appraisal process. The appraisal process is then concerned with the performance of employees as demonstrated by the extent to which they have achieved targets to which they were committed. Some appraisal systems use MBO explicitly whilst others concentrate on performance and may talk about targets and results without taking on all the features of an MBO approach. Clearly an appraisal inteview has a very clear rationale under MBO and so this approach has been very pervasive. The value of target setting has received increasing empirical support and theoretical development by Locke (1968) which has come to be known as Goal Theory.

Goal theory

Some hypotheses on the effects of goal setting on performance were proposed by Edwin Locke in 1968. These have been elaborated and tested over 20 years (Latham & Yukl, 1975; Locke et al, 1981; Tubbs, 1986).

Goals need to be made explicit but can be self-set, assigned or participatively set.

There are some terms which need to be defined in order to understand the theory. Whilst goal is self-explanatory as the object to be achieved or task to be performed to a given standard, it has two associated terms – commitment and acceptance.

Goal commitment is the degree of determination to reach a goal.

Goal acceptance is used to refer to the degree of commitment when the goal has been assigned by someone else.

Goal achievement is a function of three variables:

1. difficulty of the goal
2. ability of the goal seeker
3. goal commitment or acceptance.

Better performance will be defined as the achievement of more difficult goals and this is encouraged by:

1. Setting specific goals rather than unspecific or no goals (instructions to 'do your best' were less effective);
2. Setting hard goals providing they are accepted;
3. Providing feedback on performance and support

These three tenets of the theory are well supported as the next section shows but the evidence on two further propositions is more mixed. These relate to the effect of participation on goal setting and the effect of financial incentives on performance.

Participation It might be expected that participatively set goals would lead to better performance than ones assigned by someone else. The evidence on this is inconclusive but Locke et al (1981) suggest that the effect may be an indirect one. It may be that more difficult goals are set if they are set participatively with a supportive manager. A further effect might be that the goal becomes clearer if there is discussion about it.

In a later paper, Locke et al (1988) find that 'tell and sell' is as effective for performance as participation but that both these are more effective than 'tell'.

Monetary incentives Again the effect of monetary incentives on performance is not clear from the research carried out. Latham and Yukl (1975) found some evidence to suggest that large incentives could improve performance but that small incentives were no more effective than no incentives at all. More recent work (Wright, 1989) failed to identify improved performance resulting from a bonus incentive for achieving a goal but did detect higher goal commitment. However, there were weaknesses in the experimental design used.

Support for theory

All the work reported here was carried out in the USA. It has consisted of carefully-controlled laboratory experiments and field studies. The laboratory studies generally involved university undergraduates carrying out fairly trivial clerical tasks but the field studies reported results from a range of occupations many of them managerial in a range of organisations.

Latham and Yukl (1975) reviewed 27 studies and found them generally supportive of the three propositions. Locke et al (1981) reported support from studies undertaken between 1969 and 1980 and Tubbs (1986) in a meta-analysis of 87 studies found strong effects for the three propositions. The effects were weaker in the field studies than the laboratory experiments.

Whilst individually some of the studies may not inspire too much confidence in the theory in the real world, the sheer number of studies (up to 100) and the large degree of support (up to 90%) lend some weight to the assertion:

> Reviews of the literature have shown that goal setting theory is among the most scientifically valid and useful theories in organizational science
> Locke, Latham & Erez (1988) p.23

They go on to identify some of the determinants of goal commitment as:

> External influences (authority, peer influence and external rewards)
> Interactive influences (participation and competition)
>
> Internal factors (expectancy and internal rewards).

However, it should be accepted that the factors which cause the theory to be effective have only recently begun to be investigated.

One study is of particular interest for teachers – Latham, Mitchell and Dossett (1978) examined the effects of goal setting on highly qualified scientists and engineers engaged in research and development work. In this case higher performance was obtained from participatively set goals.

Implications for school management

Goal theory provides underpinning for target setting as a technique which can raise performance if the three basic propositions are followed. Participation in target setting will increase commitment and may help to clarify the nature of the target and aid its achievement.

Although the target should be specific and hard, it should be achievable by someone of the ability of the target seeker if they properly apply themselves. There is every reason to believe that success breeds success and that targets attained yield a satisfaction which encourages the pursuit of other targets. On the other hand, there is little reason to believe that repeated failure to reach targets is very motivating. As Latham and Locke (1979) p.132 remark:

> Like any other management tool, goal setting works only when combined with good managerial judgement.

Appraisal and management

Whether appraisal is on classical lines or part of MBO it is quite clear as Freemantle (1985) says in *Superboss*, that 'appraisal is an integral part of management, not a system external to it'. Beer (1986) also points out 'performance evaluation is an important element in the information and control system of most complex organisations'.

Appraisal has implications for the appraisee, the appraiser, central planning and control of the organisation and the outside world. It is an all embracing process. Since generally there is a concentration of attention on the appraisee and appraiser it is worthwhile stating the range of purposes which appraisal may serve for central planning and control of an organisation. Stewart and Stewart (1977) list the following:

(i) Manpower skills audit;
(ii) Manpower forecasting;
(iii) Assessment of employee potential:
(iv) Succession planning;
(v) Salary planning;
(vi) Training planning;
(vii) Equity between subordinates;
(viii) Downward transmission of company objectives;
(ix) Problem and grievance detection and handling.

Following the devolved personnel management functions accompanying LMS and LMC (Fidler and Bowles, 1989), appraisal can be expected to contribute information to a number of these areas for use in manpower planning and strategic planning.

For a public service organisation, demonstrating accountability to the outside world is also an important purpose of an appraisal system.

Staff management

Processes of staff management

The processes which comprise staff management are

Selection: selecting appropriate staff for particular posts and appointing new staff;

Induction: ensuring that new staff are introduced to and prepared for the new job in a systematic way;

Motivation: providing staff with enthusiasm and determination to achieve good results;

Control and direction: ensuring that staff know what they should be doing and monitoring progress;

Delegation: ensuring that staff are given increasing amounts of invigorating work for which they are accountable;

Appraisal: taking stock of the past and preparing for the future;

Training and development: diagnosing needs and ensuring delivery of training and providing training opportunities;

Coaching: working with and encouraging staff to acquire and perfect new skills;

Counselling: helping staff deal with work related problems in a sympathetic way;

Rewarding: ensuring that staff receive appropriate rewards for their efforts;

Discipline and grievance: dealing with staff who are not performing appropriately and handling any complaints; and

Debriefing of exiting staff: finding out from leaving staff why they are leaving and obtaining details of their former job.

There are other management processes which impinge on staff management such as leadership and the management of change but these are more major managerial processes than subprocesses of staff management.

Appraisal and staff management

The management of staff requires that staff fully contribute to the work of the organisation (Fidler, 1989). To do this they have to:
(a) be motivated;
(b) work on task; and
(c) be given help to improve their performance and develop new skills.

Appraisal directly or indirectly contributes to each of these processes.

Motivation Appraisal provides a formal opportunity to compliment the work of teachers both indirectly by taking an interest in their work but also directly by praising work which they have done well. They can be further motivated by being able to discuss their career plans and see how their current work fits into long-term aims.

Work on task It is possible for teachers to work very hard but to concentrate on things which are not highly valued by the school and to be unaware of the mismatch. Teachers are likely to have genuine problems of prioritising aspects of their work particularly in such a period of innovation overload as we are currently experiencing. They may have gradually taken on new tasks and have inadvertently begun to neglect essential aspects of the job (Trethowan 1987). Appraisal provides an opportunity to examine the teacher's job description to see how faithfully it reflects the reality of the situation and to amend it as necessary.

It should be emphasised, in case the above sounds very directive, that the manner in which the 'task' is agreed may vary from the highly collaborative and collegial to the highly autocratic and directive. But no matter how the task of the whole organisation is agreed it is the manager's job to see that it is achieved. Equally the way that the manager goes about this can also vary from the cooperative to the directive.

Performance improvement   This may be achieved by setting targets, by coaching, and by training courses. Appraisal provides the occasion to negotiate targets either to raise performance up to an acceptable level or to take on a new challenge. Coaching involves giving feedback and advice in a cooperative way to improve performance. Appraisal should lead to a programme of improvement of which one element for many teachers may be some form of in-service training.

Any deficit in performance is not only a problem for the teacher it is also a problem for the manager. Merely telling a teacher to improve is unlikely to be effective nor will it meet the requirements of employment legislation in dealing with unsatisfactory performance.

Professional development   Can be achieved by taking on new tasks or undertaking training courses in preparation for new tasks.

These processes are fundamental to staff management and appraisal makes an essential contribution to each one. Whilst an appraisal interview may be the one formal occasion each year when these issues are addressed it cannot be too strongly emphasised that staff management goes on all year long.

Capability equation

To ensure capable performance staff have to be recruited with appropriate general abilities and skills, they should then be prepared for the job by training, gain expertise by learning from their experience and finally be motivated to achieve results. Capable performers need to be delegated appropriate tasks in order to produce worthwhile results.

> **ABILITY + TRAINING + EXPERIENCE + MOTIVATION = CAPABLE PERFORMANCE**

Any missing aspect from this equation will be a potential cause of problems.

Motivation theory

Though motivation is clearly important in the management of staff, as indicated above, it is not an easy concept to specify and theories on it abound. Only two theories appear to have received notice in popular school management literature – Maslow's *Needs Hierarchy* and Hertzberg's *Motivation–Hygiene Theory*. Whilst these have an intuitive appeal in terms of their simplicity and universal applicability, they do not have wide empirical support nor are they currently regarded as worthy of further development. There are, however, more individualistic cognitive theories which are worthy of attention. Perhaps, the most significant advance is to stop seeking universal explanations of motivation and to concentrate on factors which appear to motivate individuals. This short section is intended to introduce other more individual and mostly cognitive theories of motivation as a source of ideas with which to analyse the motivation of individuals.

In seeking to define motivation Landy and Becker (1987) (p.5) point out:

> There is general agreement that motivated behavior consists of any or all of the following behavioral elements: initiation, persistence, intensity, and termination.

They suggest that the search for a single theory of motivation is misguided and that the present range of theories provide worthwhile explanations providing a theory is chosen which is appropriate for the particular facet of motivation which is of interest.

Thus when considering the motivation of individuals or groups, the first step is to identify which facet of motivation is the key to understanding the particular work behaviour – how people feel about work; what keeps them motivated and improves work performance; or how people choose the task and the degree of effort to expend from among a number of such possibilities. Having selected the facet the range of theories which are helpful are then indicated below.

Landy and Becker consider that the domain of suitability for each theory of motivation is as follows:

> Need and equity theory may be useful in exploring affective consequences of work;
> Reinforcement models and goal theory seem well suited to understanding specific work behaviours; and
> Expectancy theory is suited to the prediction of choice among alternatives

Theories of motivation

Need theories Those of Maslow and Hertzberg are covered elsewhere (Everard and Morris, 1990; Hoy and Miskel, 1991) and so will be considered only briefly here. Maslow proposed a hierarchy of need levels ranging from basic needs of hunger, thirst, sleep, sex etc, through needs of safety and security to three higher levels of need. These three higher levels move from social needs of friendship and association, through a need for esteem from others and self to the highest level of self-actualisation. This latter is the state where work and play are indistinguishable. When lower level needs have been satisfied then the next higher level need can act as a motivator. Landy and Becker are sceptical of universal hierarchies and suggest they may be individual, time bounded and context dependent.

Hertzberg's two factor theory assumes that there are a range of positive motivators such as achievement, recognition, responsibility, advancement and the work itself, and a range of possible demotivators called hygiene factors. Hygiene factors included interpersonal relations with peers or superiors, working conditions and salary. The hygiene factors had to be made satisfactory but further increasing them did not provide motivation. Reviewing the empirical evidence supporting the theory Miner (1980: p.102) concluded:

> It seems that motivation-hygiene theory lacks the support needed to confirm it, in spite of an extended period of testing and a great deal of research.

The presence of salary only as a hygiene factor has caused conventional wisdom to concentrate on non-monetary motivators but this is likely to be a seriously inadequate account of the power of money as a motivator as Latham and Locke (1979: p.120) rather wryly point out:

> Money is obviously the primary incentive, since without it few if any employees would come to work.

However, these are not the only need theories, others cover achievement, power and affiliation. To the achievement motivated 'achievement through their own efforts is intrinsically satisfying' (Miner, 1980: p.48). Power motivation has levels ranging from being attracted by those with power, through exerting personal power over others, to exerting power for some greater good. Affiliation motivation is based on socialised power. Individuals wish to get on with and be liked by others. This is thought to be an important motivation for those in jobs which require coordination and have to operate through personal relationships rather than by contractual authority.

Equity theory is concerned with the calculations individuals make about whether the rewards received from work are commensurate with the effort expended. The calculations proceed by comparison with some other individual and are based on perceptions of the rewards and effort. The rewards that individuals value have to be determined and cover all benefits and not only monetary rewards. A series of consequences are predicted for both positive and negative inequities.

Individuals have different degrees of tolerance of inequities (Miner, 1980). Equity theory appears to be useful to compensation specialists who deal with salary and other benefits for different jobs (Miner, 1980).

Reinforcement theories are developments into an organisational context of techniques of behaviour modification originally formulated by Skinner. Desired behaviour is rewarded (positive reinforcement) and reinforced. Unsatisfactory behaviour is punished (avoidance learning). There is some evidence that the techniques work for small discreet aspects of behaviour (Miner, 1980), however, the mechanisms are likely to have a cognitive component rather than working by conditioning (Landy & Becker, 1987).

Expectancy theory deals with choices about future intentions. It seems best able to deal with situations where individuals have time to weigh up the perceived costs and benefits of different courses of action. Anticipated future benefits appear to be particularly important in the reckoning. The theory appears particularly well suited to large discreet choices such as which job or which target to take on rather than small scale continuous choices such as how much effort to expend and how well to perform a particular task (Landy and Becker, 1987).

Valence–instrumentality–expectancy theory calculates motivational effort from the product of three terms (Hoy & Miskel, 1991). Valence represents the strength of desire a person has for a particular reward or benefit. Instrumentality represents the perceived probability that this benefit will result from a given level of achievement. Expectancy is the perceived probability that a certain level of effort will produce a given level of performance or achievement.

Thus by combination, the level of effort expended is influenced by the strength of desire for a particular reward but this is limited by the chances of success for this level of effort and the chances of the reward following successful achievement. In simple terms effort will be high if the reward is highly desired, the goal is achievable and the reward will follow goal achievement.

Individual orientation The major development in thinking on motivation has been away from universalistic theories of unconscious motivational forces towards a series of theories of particular aspects of motivation which are largely cognitive and which differ for different individuals. This makes generalisations difficult but increases the precision for individuals. Thus the appropriate emphasis should be on understanding the motivation of each individual and ensuring appropriate levels of benefit and reward which they value.

Performance appraisal

Goals of performance appraisal

In an excellent review article Beer (1986) has identified the main theoretical issues in performance appraisal.

For the manager (and the organisation)   In addition to providing data to the central planning and control function in the organisation, appraisal is of direct benefit to the manager. It is a 'major tool for changing individual behaviour' (Beer 1986). The goals cover both evaluation and development. Beer lists eight goals:

(a) Evaluation
   1. To give feedback to subordinates so they know where they stand.
   2. To develop valid data for pay and promotion decisions and to aid communication of these.
   3. To provide a means of warning subordinates about unsatisfactory performance.

(b) Development
   1. To counsel and coach subordinates so that they will improve their performance and develop future potential.
   2. To develop commitment to the organisation through discussion of career opportunities and career planning.
   3. To motivate subordinates through recognition of achievements and support.
   4. To strengthen supervisor-subordinate relations.
   5. To diagnose individual and organisational problems.

Categorising these goals as evaluation or development emphasises that some of them are in conflict. The appraisal relationship required for the evaluation goals will be inimical to the trusting open relationship required for development. It is important for appraisal systems to recognise this problem. Decisions on pay and promotability can be separated in time from more developmental activities whilst within the appraisal interview there may be a sequencing of activities which seeks to minimise the potential conflict.

For the individual employee   Individuals have a number of possible goals which they may achieve by taking part in appraisal. I have identified six major benefits:

1. To receive feedback on their performance and progress.
2. To discuss their present job and amend their job-description if changes are agreed.
3. To identify opportunities for professional personal development.
4. To identify training opportunities.
5. To discuss their aspirations and career plans.
6. To discuss problems in the organisation and their relationship with their manager.

When feedback is positive and is consistent with the employee's own self-image the inherent conflicts in the process are minimised, however, when the feedback is critical of poor performance a defensive reaction from an employee may set up barriers which inhibit acceptance of this feedback and prevent open discussion of how performance might be improved.

Beer (1986: p.289) identifies a potential conflict between the individual and the organisation when accountability and development are combined,

> The individual desires to confirm a positive self-image and to obtain organisational rewards of promotion or pay. The organisation wants individuals to be open to negative information about themselves so that they can improve their performance. As long as individuals see the appraisal process as having an important influence on their rewards (pay, recognition), their career (promotions and reputation), and their self-image they will be reluctant to engage in the kind of open dialogue required for valid evaluation and personal development.

Clearly this conflict is at its most acute when dealing with poor performers. Inevitably an appraisal system which covers all employees will throw up a small minority whose performance is below an acceptable standard. This is known to happen in all organisations and there is a great temptation to avoid the issue by both parties in the name of good relations. This is at best a palliative and at worst undermines the whole appraisal system and leads to no improvement for the individual. This is a problem to which we shall return. (p23 and Section 5.2).

Reducing the fundamental conflict

Beer identifies a number of measures which tend to lessen the fundamental conflict:

Separating evaluation and development   As far as possible these purposes should be separated. Any concern with pay or promotion should be removed from the main developmental appraisal process. Separating these purposes in time by six months is often suggested. A target setting approach to performance related pay may be an alternative to an evaluative approach to performance pay.

Choosing appropriate performance data Performance data has to be related to the job being done. A systematic approach to this (Stenning and Stenning 1984) requires:

1. A clear comprehensive and accurate job description;
2. A statement of the results expected of the job holder which are as objective and measurable as possible;
3. A clear description of the abilities, skills, knowledge and personal characteristics of effective job performers; and
4. Data systematically assembled over the review period.

A comprehensive approach would suggest that each element of a job description should have an associated standard of performance attached to it. However, this approach suffers from two major disadvantages. One is that job descriptions typically have a large number of individual tasks and each of these would require a standard of performance. The second problem is that a multielement job description provides no indication of the priority which should be attached to each individual element.

The MBO approach is to select a limited number of important parts of the job description and to designate these 'key result areas' (Morrisey 1976). These five to ten specific areas then have objectives or measurable results associated with them. In addition to these work objectives which ensure the efficient operation of the organisation there would be personal development objectives which were intended to ensure growth and development of the individual (in areas not incompatible with organisational objectives).

An alternative approach suggested by Odiorne (Morrisey 1983) where much of the work is on going and repetitive is to identify three levels of objectives. The basic level of *regular or routine objectives* assumes that there are already well established levels of performance for most of an individual's work activities. To deal with problems which have been identified in the routine work there would then be *problem solving objectives*. Finally there would be *innovative objectives* which represent a major change or development in the work of an individual which would benefit the organisation. The personal development objectives could involve both problem solving and innovation. This latter approach may be worthy of consideration in trying to appraise the work of teachers.

This introduces another potential conflict in the appraisal process – that between the needs and desires of the individual and those of the organisation. Where the individual is engaged in an appropriate job and the job has potential for development, this conflict should be minimised if, in addition to these areas where individual and organisational development are coincident, additional areas for the personal development of the employee are also given due weight.

The appraisal interview provides an opportunity to review periodically the job description and to amend it to ensure that it is a faithful record of the current job.

Clarity can be achieved and defensiveness minimised if feedback on performance refers to specific behaviours and actual incidents as exemplars of more general behaviour. This data, however, must be collected over a substantial period and not only refer to incidents in the preceding week or two otherwise it will lack credibility in the eyes of the appraisee.

On the other hand any problems should be discussed with the employee as they happen and not stored up only to be discussed at the appraisal interview. Supervision and coaching should be continuous as should any modification of targets and objectives arising from new circumstances. The appraisal interview should summarise and recap such events during the year not add new evidence.

Whilst an MBO approach focuses on accomplishments which are tangible it is less concerned with how they are achieved. There may have been organisational reasons which precluded success and are no reflection on the performance of the appraisee. It has been suggested that behavioural ratings on the way objectives were achieved should supplement the MBO performance data as these would be useful for development purposes.

Recognising individual differences in system designs   Beer suggests that not all employees should be appraised with the same frequency. Some, particularly upwardly mobile, may need more feedback on performance whilst those who are competent but have reached the peak of their capabilities should only be appraised every two or three years.

Upward appraisal   Allowing an employee to rate the performance of his or her manager can help to break down barriers and may give the manager useful feedback on how his or her performance is perceived. It can generate a dialogue and allow the manager to demonstrate the open non-defensive behaviour which it is hoped the employee may also show.

Using an appropriate interview style   Maier (1976) has characterised three interview styles as *Tell and Sell, Tell and Listen* and *Problem Solving*. These may be appropriate for different interview situations. In the *Tell and Sell* style the manager directs the interview and gains the acceptance of the appraisee to take steps to improve performance. The *Tell and Listen* style requires the manager to give authentic feedback but then to allow the appraisee to respond. Communication and understanding may be much improved. Changes in performance, however, depend upon a change of attitude following improved communication.

The *Problem Solving* style as the name implies requires both appraiser and appraisee jointly to acknowledge problems and to work on them together.

Beer suggests that a mixed mode interview moving from the *Problem Solving* style to the *Tell and Sell* or *Tell and Listen* may be appropriate for a variety of situations. This would permit open ended discussion of problems and possible solutions before moving to an agreed plan but allowing the manager to ensure that difficult issues are faced if they are not raised by the appraisee.

Other research evidence suggests that agreeing the content and process of the appraisal interview beforehand is worthwhile. Self-appraisal by the employee in preparation for the interview allows for a more equal discussion in the interview and provides an opportunity for the appraisee to prepare any problems which they wish to raise about the job, the organisation or their relationship with their manager. The interview should conclude with a concrete plan for performance improvement. Such a plan should encompass any training required and any new aspects of the job which are to provide development. Clearly it is vital that any training, job change or other resources which are agreed are actually provided. Cynicism can be expected fairly rapidly if commitments on one side are not met.

Management and poor performance

A point worth emphasising is that the appraisal interview is a unique formal occasion in the year when employee and manager sit down to discuss work performances. But there should be informal ongoing discussions particularly if improvement needs guiding and monitoring. The appraisal interview may need supplementing with a counselling interview either if intensive help is needed or a neutral exploration of issues is required. For cases of extreme and persistent underperformance then a separate disciplinary interview may be required.

Only a very brief discussion of poor performance is given here, a more comprehensive account of the causes and responses to poor performance are given in section 5.2.

Steinmetz (1985) has presented a useful analysis of reasons for unsatisfactory performance. These are characterised as:

1. Managerial or organisational shortcomings;
2. Individual personal shortcomings of the employee; and
3. Outside influences.

Cutting across these, however, is the fundamental attitude of the employee to the job. He presents a helpful summary table which demonstrates that many problems of poor performance involve managerial failures.

Reason for failure to perform	Whose problem	Remarks
Can't do	Management	1. Training 2. Provide resources 3. Remove obstacles
Won't do	Individual	Change Attitude
Doesn't know what he/she should be doing	Management	Improve communication

Table 1.2.1 The causes and correction of performance failure
Source: Adapted from Steinmetz (1985)

In his small scale study of mainly secondary schools in the UK, Everard (1986a) reported that:

> few schools reported no serious problems of inadequate staff performance and more worryingly the relatively few there are have an influence on the head's peace of mind and the school's reputation out of all proportion to their numbers.

Appraisal procedures will throw up evidence of poor performance. Some shortcomings in otherwise good performance can be tackled by setting targets which raise these particular aspects of performance to acceptable standards. More serious evidence of under performance might best be tackled by more intensive coaching and counselling outside normal appraisal procedures. The procedures developed by Montgomery (1985) may be helpful in improving teaching performance (see p.276). Only where such positive and developmental efforts are ineffective and no alternative solution can be found should separate disciplinary procedures be instigated.

Keeping efforts to improve poor performers separate from normal appraisal procedures will help prevent the impression being created that appraisal is concerned primarily with removing incompetent teachers. There is a real danger of this because the time spent on poor performers will be disproportionately greater than for other staff and could be seen, therefore, as the real thrust of the appraisal system. Whereas the real thrust should be the improvement of the performance of *all* staff. Staff who need such a greater degree of help to raise their fundamental competence should be provided with the professional support procedures common in most schools, colleges and LEAs.

Organisational culture

The final point is that the appraisal system must be consistent with the organisational culture. If the organisation is participative, dynamic and has a clear sense of direction then the appraisal system should reflect this by following a target setting, problem solving approach. If, however, the organisation is more authoritarian and hierarchical then the appraisal system should mirror this more evaluative approach. Mixed messages are more likely to be confusing than successful. As Long (1986: p.62) reported after studying 300 appraisal systems:

> 'ready made' performance review systems imported from other organizations rarely function satisfactorily. The failure is due in part to organizational cultural differences.

1.2 Experience of appraisal in non-educational organisations

Brian Fidler

Introduction

Fletcher and Williams (1985) in their book *Performance Appraisal and Career Development* describe the history of appraisal practice and give an 'Identikit picture' of a British appraisal system. They look at problems and issues encountered in operating appraisal systems and also try to foresee future developments.

A feature of appraisal systems is that they are constantly being changed and reviewed. Long (1986) found that one third of the systems in his survey had been in operation for three years or less. It is, therefore, somewhat difficult to describe adequately this moving picture. However, from two surveys by the Institute of Personnel Managers in 1977 and 1986 some trends are clear (Gill 1977; Long 1986).

Purpose of appraisal

In each sample of around 300 organisations over 80% had performance appraisal systems and very few had abandoned appraisal. By 1986 *most systems were primarily concerned with improving current performance rather than future potential.*
The main purposes of performance review schemes in the survey in

order of usage was to:

Review past performance	(98%)
Help improve current performance	(97%)
Assess training and development needs	(97%)
Set performance objectives	(81%)
Assist career planning decisions	(75%)
Assess future potential/promotability	(71%)

Although not directly using MBO almost two thirds of schemes used a results oriented approach to appraisal.

Appraisal document

Appraisal forms generally consisted of a combination of rating scales and open ended questions. Fletcher and Williams (1985) describe a typical appraisal form as having four sides. The first has biographical details of the job holder and a job description. The final page, which is not generally seen by the job holder, has an assessment of the job holder's promotability and long term potential. Whereas all previous sections are completed by the appraiser this page has a section for the manager's manager to comment. The middle two pages written by the manager lists the objectives which the appraisee has been concentrating on in the past year and comments on the extent to which these have been achieved. The manager outlines possible future improvements in performance and associated training and development needs. The manager gives an overall performance rating typically on a seven point scale from 'poor' to 'outstanding'.

There is a space at this point for the appraisee to sign the report and to add any comments which he or she wishes (knowing that these will be read by the manager's manager). However, Long reported that only half the organisations had a formal appeals mechanism.

Interview

Over 80% of organisations had an interview preparation form for appraisees. The interview was reported to be generally problem oriented with a joint problem solving style of operation rather than being evaluative and judgmental. Almost all organisations provided notes of guidance for appraisees and almost 80% provided appraisal interview training. The practice of combining reviews of performance and potential has declined in the later survey.

Main weaknesses reported

There were three main weaknesses reported by Long's survey respondents:

1. Unequal standards of assessment amongst different appraisers
2. Some lack of commitment to the process among line managers
3. Some lack of follow-up action on training and development plans.

There was growing recognition that a successful appraisal system has to attempt to meet the needs of individuals, line managers, and the organisation.

Some particular systems

Fletcher and Williams (1985) provide (anonymous) case studies of appraisal systems in a variety of organisations. The Civil Service have published a trainer's resource pack (1985) which both describes their system and prepares appraisers and appraisees to use the system. It contains a training manual, a video and an audio tape. This marks a major change of emphasis in the Civil Service appraisal system towards improvement of current performance and uses a results oriented approach. This is a major attempt by a non-profit making service organisation to use this approach.

The appraisal system at ICI Plant Protection Division is described in the proceedings of a BEMAS appraisal conference (Laycock 1987). The sequencing of appraisals is shown in Figure 1.2.1. Junior staff are appraised first. Their appraisal reports then form part of the appraisal of their manager by their 'grandparent' manager. This both provides a safeguard for junior staff in the sense that any adverse indications or comments on their relationship with their manager will be picked up as a problem by the 'grandparent' manager, and also ensures that the management of staff is a major focus in the appraisal of managers. This does mean, however, a rather wider circulation of appraisal reports.

This Division of ICI employs a large number of professional scientists engaged on research and development work. Although part of a commercial organisation this particular Division has the problem of professionals engaged in work where it is not easy to assess results, and particularly where some of them may be very long term. The Civil Service and this Division of ICI appear to offer closer parallels to the situation in educational organisations than most other industrial and commercial organisations.

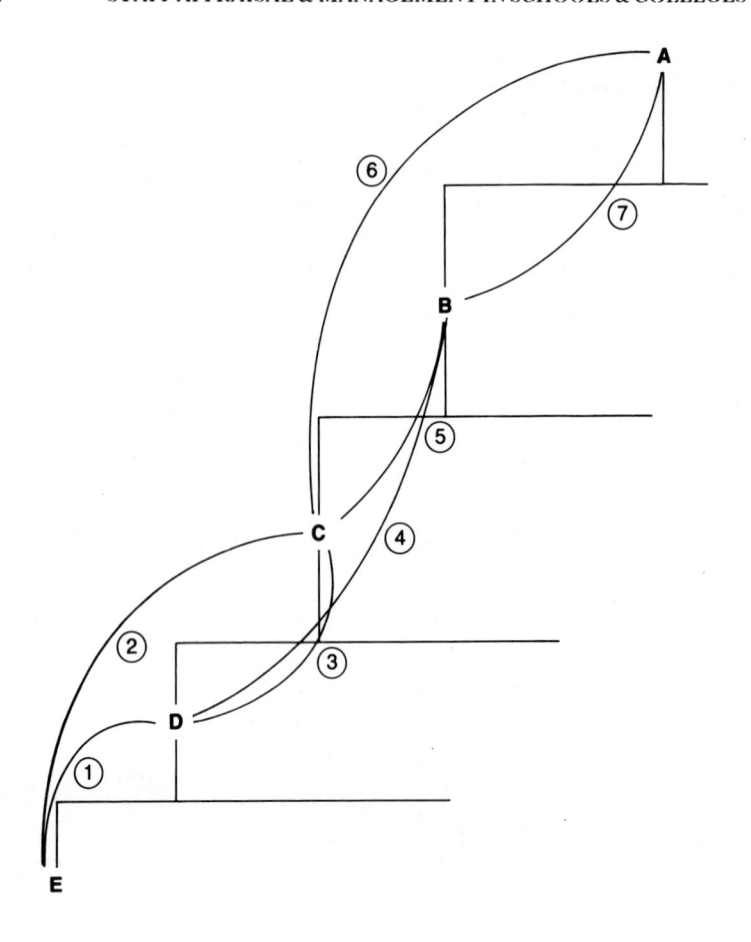

Figure 1.2.2 Sequence of staff reviews at ICI Plant Protection

Source: Laycock 1987.

Note: Manager D appraises employee E (1) and the appraisal report goes to grandparent manager C (2) before C appraises D (3). Thus the management of E by D forms part of D's appraisal and so on for other more senior managers.

Other appraisal experience is described by Everard (1986b) and Hayes (1984). Everard describes mainly experience at ICI, whilst Hayes chronicles the introduction of appraisal at Nicholas International. The Suffolk study (1985) describes some general industrial and commercial experience. Richardson (1987) writing from an industrial perspective examines the training and development policies of large multinational companies and considers their applicability to a 'mass public service profession' such as education.

In a recent article Whyte (1986) surveys some management literature on appraisal mainly between 1980 and 1984 to look for implications for teacher appraisal. The article interposes US and British non-educational appraisal practice and has a section which deals with possible gender bias in appraisal.

Reasons why appraisal systems fail

Having looked at why systems fail, Long (1986: p.69) cites inadequate preparation as the major reason and in particular insufficient:

Consultation with top management to clarify objectives

Consultation with line management to clarify their needs

Time allowed for induction and appraisal skills training

Consideration of the resources needed for refresher training for line managers, induction training for newly appointed managers; and most importantly

Resources to meet the individual training and development plans arising from the review discussions.

He concludes:

unless a performance appraisal system attempts to meet the needs of the individual, line management and the organization, it is likely to fail through lack of support.

On closer inspection of the literature (*see* Banner and Graber, 1985; Banks and Murphy, 1985; Bernardin and Klatt, 1985) and getting behind the article titles that the complaints are that the developments in the theory of appraisal systems are simply not finding their way into practice. Is it that the theoretical ideas are unknown or is it that newer developments are ignored? Bernardin and Klatt found from research in the USA that smaller companies were likely to be less satisfied with the operation of appraisal systems than larger ones. Authors offer advice on improving practice and also speculate on the reasons for the research–practice gap (Banks and Murphy, 1985). One conclusion is that some theoretical developments have been ignoring organisational constraints and have thus become more irrelevant to the day-to-day operation of organisations. However, much of the practice described appears to be ignoring fairly basic thinking on performance appraisal. One reason frequently cited is that appraisal satisfies a number of functions in an organisation and some of these conflict (Banner and Graber, 1985). This has been called the 'Christmas tree' effect. So many in the organisation can see potential benefits from an appraisal system that they merely add on their requirements to the system rather like decorating a Christmas tree. But the price of lack of clarity about the purpose of the system is that the resultant hybrid is satisfactory from no one's point of view (Banner and Graber, 1985). The greater satisfaction of larger organisations with their appraisal systems would also tend to give some support to the lack of knowledge explanation as larger organisations could be expected to have greater expertise at their disposal.

Long (1986: p.62) concludes:

> There is no such thing as the perfect performance review system. None are infallible, although some are more fallible than others.....The relative success or failure of performance review, as with any other organizational system, depends very much upon the attitudinal response it arouses.

1.3 Problems of appraisal in education

Brian Fidler

Introduction

When studying the theory of appraisal and its application in other organisations it is clear that there are substantial differences in the context and culture compared to publicly funded educational institutions. I have identified seven problem areas concerned with adapting this experience to schools and colleges and suggest some ways forward. Two particular issues arising which are further explored are the nature of 'line management' in education and the appraisal of heads of institution. Finally, I list the features of an appraisal scheme which seem to be most important from the foregoing theory and experience.

Problem areas

Management of professionals

The management of professionals poses a basic problem. Handy (1984) describes many professionals as independent operators and in this model management and appraisal are inappropriate. However, on more detailed analysis there are a number of issues to be pursued:

- What is a profession?
- Employed professionals; and

— Teachers as professionals.

What is a profession? The following six characteristics have been most frequently associated with a profession (Johnson, 1972):

1. Skill based on theoretical knowledge;
2. Provision of training and education;
3. Testing the competence of members;
4. Organisation as a professional group;
5. Adherence to a professional code of conduct; and
6. Altruistic service.

These have been drawn from what has in the past been seen as the 'true' professions and form an *ideal* type. This notion of an 'ideal' type is based upon an abstraction from professions of long-standing such as medicine and the law. The basis is atheoretical.

Since historically professions have been accorded high social status and have been granted rights of self-regulation rather than state intervention, there has been a noticeable increase in the number of occupations seeking professional status and from some quarters a more critical evaluation of the benefits to society of increasing professionalism. Although there is some debate about both the definition of a profession and the appropriateness of defining a profession in this way, it will suffice for the present purposes.

Employed professionals Whilst the archetypal professional is self-employed, increasingly professional workers are employed within other organisations which are generally structured on bureaucratic lines (*see* section 4.1). This changes the accountability mechanism operating on the professionals. In addition to legal and moral responsibilities which may apply to all workers, professional workers have a responsibility to follow an ethical code of conduct regulated by their fellow professionals and, in the case of self-employed professionals, there is a direct, if somewhat crude, form of check on the functioning of the professional in terms of being directly paid by the client.

In the case of employed professionals this direct financial relationship with a client is replaced by a contractual relationship with an employing organisation. The organisation undertakes to provide a service to the client and receives recompense whilst the organisation ensures that appropriate standards of professional service are provided by its contractual relationship with its employed professionals.

Teachers as professionals Thus teachers as employed professionals should undergo appraisal as one form of accountability for their service to the organisation's clients.

From the above list of criteria for a profession it is clear that the status of teachers as professionals is problematic. They meet some of the criteria in full in terms of training certification but not in terms of a professional code of conduct or self-regulation. The situation as regards the theoretical knowledge of pedagogy underpinning the teaching skill of the profession is also a difficulty. Darling-Hammond, Wise and Pease (1983: p.293) look at teaching as labour (i.e. supervised work), craft, art, and profession. They point out:

> The more variable or unpredictable one views the teaching environment as being, the more one is impelled towards a conception of teaching as a profession or art.

Teachers have a number of the attributes of a true profession. They carry out a task which cannot be narrowly defined, which calls for skill and judgement acquired through training and experience, and which calls for individual treatment for each client. But they are, in the main, publicly employed and accountable by their contract of employment to provide a reasonable level of service to their clients. Appraisal provides both a check on this and also support and encouragement to improve performance.

As organisations become more complex, co-ordination of some kind is required and for larger organisations some form of management is essential particularly in turbulent times. With the gradual acceptance of management in education a balance has to be struck between management approaches and professionalism. This is a situation met in some other spheres where appraisal is used.

Results unclear

When the purpose of the whole organisation is somewhat unclear then appraisal of the leader is particularly problematic and this is also true of others in the organisation. The problem of assessing institutional performance is in three parts:

- Defining organisational goals;
- Measuring goal achievement; and
- Comparing goal achievement in different organisations.

First there is a requirement to decide on the purposes or objectives of the institution. These are generally many and complex and may be viewed differently by outsiders.

The second requirement is to find ways of assessing how well those objectives have been met. Some may be assessed quantitatively but most can only be assessed qualitatively.

Thirdly the problem is how to make valid comparisons between institutions when the nature of the output in terms of educated students is crucially dependent on the level of ability and other characteristics of the students on entry and over which the school or college has little direct control. Even at the level of examination performance, comparisons between schools can be radically transformed when adjustments are made for the quality of the intake (Gray 1982). This is also the case when the results of an individual school are compared over time (Glogg and Fidler, 1990). Such adjustments can be done in a quantitative way for exam results. How much more difficult then to make such adjustments conceptually for those measures of output which can only be assessed qualitatively. For a discussion of recent research on school effectiveness *see* Reynolds (1985).

Finally when the success of the institution can be assessed there is a further problem associated with assessing the contribution of the leader to this success.

Institutions need to be clear about their purpose even if the purpose may be difficult to assess except in qualitative terms. A statement of objectives provides the yardstick against which to assess performance. All other organisations have a multiplicity of objectives and need internal performance measures. Many of these are difficult to assess. Commercial firms have other objectives in addition to overall profitability.

Rewards and performance related pay

Industrial and commercial organisations generally have rewards which they are able to bestow after assessing work performance. Thus financial and other benefits are connected with appraisal. The connection may not be direct – it may be staggered in time – but there is usually a relationship. There is little prospect in educational practice of directly rewarding good work in any financial sense. Sir Keith Joseph one of the most fervent disciples of relating payment and performance came to accept that merit pay or annual increments should not be related to annual appraisal procedures (DES 1986). Although such annual merit awards in education are unusual, data collected through appraisal could be reflected in references and promotion some time in the future. However, personal and professional recognition of achievement should not be underestimated in its motivating potential.

There is an approach to performance related pay which may be applicable to schools and colleges. This is the target setting approach (*see* section 5.3). The main features of this approach are:

1. Rewards are based on target achievement;
2. Targets are jointly negotiated;
3. Targets are as precise as possible;
4. Targets are challenging and worthwhile;
5. Targets cover only a small part of the total job;
6. Extra rewards are modest; and
7. Rewards are open to all who achieve targets.

This approach as part of a 'performance management' culture has been found to be effective in public service and other non-profit making organisations.

Difficulty of assessing teaching

Assessing the work of a teacher is particularly difficult. The most fundamental point is that from the school or college's point of view the emphasis should be on student learning rather than teaching *per se*. Again the problems are manyfold – it is difficult to:

1. Specify desired learning outcomes;
2. Measure desired learning outcomes;
3. Differentiate the extent of learning achieved;
4. Measure teaching; and
5. Find a clear relationship between learning and teaching.

Learning is multifaceted and so for most lessons it is difficult to specify the immediate outcomes of learning let alone the medium or long-term outcomes. The more long-term and ill defined outcomes are particularly difficult to assess. Both of which make it more difficult to measure the extent of learning between the initial state of knowledge and understanding of the student and the final state. Compounding all these difficulties is the problem of how to measure teaching and find the relationship between teaching and learning. If for a given learning outcome one had the above evidence to support a particular teaching performance one could assess the teacher's actual performance against this theoretical ideal. Darling-Hammond, Wise and Pease, (1983: p.299) review conceptual difficulties and the research evidence concluding:

> Research on the stability and generalizability of measures of teacher behaviors lend support to a context-specific view of teaching.

And as Stodolsky (1990) points out, if teaching is context dependent, obtaining reliable and valid evidence on which to assess it is problematic. Observing similar behaviours will increase reliability but at the expense of a valid assessment of teaching performance as a whole. As the likely sampling fraction for classroom observation is 1/2000 in a two year cycle, such problems are acute.

Given that, in the main, the research evidence required above does not exist, the base for assessing teaching performance has to be experience and received wisdom about what are good teaching practices. As a pragmatic solution this is quite acceptable but it is important to bear in mind that this is the basis which is being used and that there is no 'right' answer. Whilst different states in the US claim to have research support for their teacher assessment schedules, since they are all different it is difficult to place much credence in such assertions. Thus observation of teaching performance and discussion of it should be appropriately open minded rather than dogmatic and recognise the difference between convention and more valid judgements.

Setting standards

As Ray Sumner (1988) of NFER observed 'the utility of taking an ideal as the standard for judging performance seems highly questionable' yet that is what tends to happen when describing teaching performance. A counsel of perfection is not an adequate baseline for judgement. It is very easy to fall into a dichotomy by which standards are either judged from an ideal – 'a deficit model' or from a zero base – 'a bonus model'. The deficit model, which tends to be used for good performers, compares performance with an ideal and notes any discrepancies. Thus excellent performance is almost always unobtainable **solely as an artifact of the assessment model used.** Whereas the bonus model, which tends to be used for weak and poor performers, regards any signs of performance above a very meagre base as encouraging and noteworthy. Described in this way the inequity of the two models is transparent particularly when they tend to be associated with selective use of anecdotal and *ad hoc* evidence. The alternative is to seek to assess performance, both good and weak, relative to a common standard of competent performance.

If a realistic standard of competent performance on various aspects of the teacher's job can be agreed then the assessment of teaching performance might reduce to an overall acceptable/ unacceptable judgement. Remedial measures will be needed for those judged unacceptable whilst for the overwhelming majority who are judged acceptable there may be individual elements of performance which need raising in standard and which could be set as targets for the coming year. For the *acceptable* the dialogue between appraiser and appraisee would be a professional dialogue intended to stimulate reflection and new ideas. A danger of a checklist approach to assessing teaching performance as observed by Peaker (1986) after a visit to the US is that it tends to encourage 'safe' teaching, i.e. static and didactic teaching. Whilst measuring the work of teaching presents problems so does measuring the work performance of intermediate level personnel in other organisations and particularly those in service functions within the organisation.

Sumner (1988) has drawn up the following array showing possible teaching instruments for collecting data on teaching performance. Table 1.3.1 shows 18-22 ways in which information might be gained, assuming that student opinions are admissible.

INSTRUMENT

Assessor	Student Progr.	Exam.	Question-naire	Simul-ation	Observ-ation	Inter-view	Activity Schedule or Diary
Teacher	X	—	X	—	X	—	X
Peer	X	—	?	?	X	?	X
Superior	X	—	—	X	X	X	X
Assessor	X	X	—	X	X	X	—
Student	—	—	X	—	—	—	?

Table 1.3.1   Possible teaching instruments

No other organisation observes the work performance of its personnel in ways which resemble classroom observation.

Too many bosses

For head teachers and most teachers in secondary schools there is no direct superordinate. The head has a number of people and groups to whom he or she is accountable. Equally those in secondary schools with both subject and pastoral duties have at least two people to whom they are accountable. This more complicated form of organisation is usually referred to as a matrix structure (*see* section 4.1). The pastoral–academic matrix organisation of the secondary school does have counterparts in other organisations (Morrisey 1983) but generally there is a strong arm of the matrix which is close to line management and through which the major elements of appraisal proceed. Problems of co-ordination and communication between the two people to whom an individual is accountable have been noted. Schools will need to consider such problems and ensure that data on performance in other tasks is fed into a designated main appraisal chain.

A further problem associated with the complexity of the work done in schools and the degree to which it is compartmentalised is that most middle managers (HoDs, team leaders etc) have an incomplete view of the work of the whole school or college. Yet as part of their work appraising other teachers they will be required to assist those teachers in setting priorities which go beyond the direct sphere of knowledge of the appraiser. This will require a great deal of education and communication with middle managers.

Lack of time

Appraisal carried out properly in any organisation takes a lot of time. This poses acute problems in education where generally the time allowed for management is too small (Handy 1984). Other organisations accept the importance of appraisal and regard the time taken by the process as an effective use of time. In schools the two-yearly appraisal cycle reduces the time required overall. But the time requirement will fall unevenly. The greatest demands will be on middle managers who are both appraised and also appraise others. Past evidence is that such staff have little time in which to carry out their present management work.

Various estimates of the time required for appraisal have been made. The second Suffolk report (Suffolk LEA 1987) assumed that an appraiser would appraise only seven teachers and involve three periods of classroom observation for each of them. This would take 5.25 hours for each teacher. In addition there would be initial and ongoing time required for training in appraisal skills. There would also be a need for extra administrative and clerical staff too. The costs are assessed at £125 per teacher and £600–£1,100 per head teacher (at 1987 prices).

The assumption made by Government that little extra time is required for appraisal since a good deal of the work goes on already, ignores the substantial extra demands made by classroom observation which generally does not now go on and which has no analogue in other organisations from which to estimate the extra time required.

Lack of infrastructure in LEAs and institutions

Well managed organisations recognise that there are service functions which need to be provided to those carrying out the direct work of the organisation. Two of these directly link with appraisal – personnel and training. Personnel oversees the whole process of appraisal and co-ordinates such work across the organisation. It ensures that action is taken as a result of appraisal be this training, a job change, career progression, or whatever. Training looks at training needs across the organisations and either provides or purchases training to meet these needs.

LMS and LMC and some devolved INSET funds have begun the process of focusing attention on these processes at institutional level. However, the demands of appraisal will put intense expectations and pressure on these two functions. Appraisal will generate increased demands and raise expectations about training and development. It will be important both to provide speedy answers to requests for training and development and that the answers are not too often negative.

If managers are to be made more accountable for the performance and development of their staff, then they should also be responsible for a training and development budget from which they can prioritise the training and other needs of their staff. This suggests that fewer larger units within a school or college should be the basic managerial unit for managing staff otherwise the delegated sums for INSET are so small as to be inflexible in any one year. Units comprising 10-20 staff would provide a unit large enough for INSET fund flexibility whilst not being too large as to be impersonal. Within such a 'faculty' structure there should be further delegated staff management responsibilities.

There is a need for both personnel and training functions to be co-ordinated right across an LEA. This would provide a unit of ample size and scope for both these functions to be carried out effectively and efficiently. But this will pose new manpower needs for most LEAs at a time of devolution and change.

Appraisal and line managers

In other organisations line managers play a key role in the appraisal process because appraisal is an integral part of the management process not an unrelated activity. The term line manager refers to the 'line of authority' which passes from the chief executive officer (headteacher or principal) to those delegated positions in the organisational structure.

It is line managers who control and direct the activity of subordinates and are accountable for their performance. These activities go on throughout the year and an appraisal interview is the formal stage in the year for stocktaking these activities.

Staff should be appraised by their line manager because he or she:

1. Is accountable for their performance;
2. Has a wider view of organisational needs and possibilities;
3. Controls resources which may support and improve their performance;
4. Can facilitate a change of job both within and between sections of the organisation.

Although the term *line manager* may conjure up the vision of an authoritarian figure barking out orders the term also applies to a leader operating within a team in a participative, problem solving mode. The term here is used to identify the person who is accountable for the operation of a section of the organisation and who has human and other resources available to achieve results. It is a matter of style how the manager operates in order to achieve these results. In an organisation largely staffed by professionals the successful approach is more likely to involve leadership and teamwork than a bureaucratic authoritarian style.

However, from the point of view of accountability and control of resources the team leader has the attributes of a line manager and this is the term other organisations use. If this term jars then the reader should replace it with the term team leader when thinking about appraisal in education.

Line managers in education

In educational institutions the identification of a line manager has hardly been considered (*see* section 4.1). In a primary school it is clear that the head teacher occupies a position equivalent to a line manager from the point of view of a teacher within the school, although where there are team leaders they may exercise a middle management role. In a secondary school, on the other hand, the position is much less clear. Firstly, in a typical secondary school there are too many teachers for the head teacher to exercise a direct line management function. Secondly, there are at least two sets of middle managers in the pastoral–academic matrix structure as has already been remarked. The most stable grouping is the academic or subject grouping and so this is probably the most appropriate to identify with line management type functions. It may be that if heads of department are required to appraise staff within their department this will bring about a more managerial outlook from such middle managers. As line managers these middle managers are both appraised and also appraise others. The main thrust of the appraisal of this group should probably concentrate on their managerial function rather than their classroom performance since their key role is to manage their departments or pastoral teams and thereby contribute to the overall work of the school. However, their teaching performance should not be neglected. Appraisals should be carried out by this group of middle managers before they themselves are appraised since the appraised reports which they write provide information on their management performance. This is the sequencing of appraisals practised at ICI (See p.23).

Colleges with a matrix structure will similarly have to identify middle managers who are to carry the main appraisal function.

Heads of institution

Other organisations have most difficulty in appraising senior management. In the case or educational organisations difficulties are compounded by the fact that heads of institutions do not have an equivalent of a line manager. Legally they are accountable to their governing bodies and in employment terms they may be employed by a local authority which has other more senior positions within it – both line (education officers) and staff (inspectors/advisers).

Proposals to deal with this situation have ranged from introducing a line manager for heads into the educational system (Trethowan 1987), to allowing heads to appraise each other by peer group review, with many suggestions between these two extremes.

The requirements of providing public credibility, being part of the management process and enjoying the confidence of heads cannot all be met. The regulations require two appraisers (*SI 1511, 1991*) to be appointed by the LEA (for county schools) after consulting the governing body. One of these should be or have had experience as a head teacher of the appropriate phase of education in conditions similar to those current in the school. The *Circular (DES, 1991)* recommends that the other appraiser should be an LEA officer or adviser. It is recommended that if only one appraiser observes the head teacher teaching or performing other duties then this should be the person with headship experience. Head teachers should not be able to choose their appraisers but the Circular recommends that their appraiser should have no conflict of interest.

The governors and staff may be asked to provide information after consultation with the appraisee and a copy of the appraisal statement is to be made available to the chairperson of governors. In view of the substantial responsibilities given to governing bodies for the running of schools under the 1986 and 1988 *Education Acts*, their part in the appraisal of head teachers is clearly anomalous. They have the right to dismiss a head teacher but not to play a significant part in his or her appraisal.

Deputy head teachers may have two appraisers at the discretion of the appraising body (LEA for county schools) one of whom must be appointed by the head teacher according to the Regulations whereas the Circular states that both should be appointed by the headteacher who should be one of them.

Summary

Essential features of an appraisal system

It should be part of the managerial process.

It should be positive and developmental whilst still maintaining credibility as a check on quality.

It should ultimately improve the learning experiences of pupils and students.

It should be combined with some element of career development and progression.

It should formulate training needs and professional development opportunities.

It should provide a two-way dialogue by which the appraisee gives feedback on the manager's performance and is able to raise organisational problems.

It should have an infrastructure to provide the back-up to plan and deliver training and co-ordinate professional development through experience in other parts of the organisation.

SECTION 2: STAFF MANAGEMENT AND APPRAISAL

2.1 Staff management

Bob Cooper

Introduction

One of the main objectives of this book is to stress the fact that, if a staff appraisal system is to be successful, it must be fully integrated into the general management processes of the school. The appraisal system which is introduced must become an integral part of 'the way things are done around here', and not simply an appendage which has been put into place because the Government requires it, or the head thinks it might be a good idea. The appraisal of teachers' performance was made statutory in the *1986 Education Act (Section 49)* and the *Circular No. 12/91* was published finally in July 1991. In practice, individual schools and colleges will have flexibility in deciding the structure and the working processes of any scheme introduced, and will be responsible for the integration of the scheme into the overall life of the organisation.

All schools and colleges are unique institutions, made up of unique combinations of people, and set in a unique context. It is the responsibility of the management of the school or college to manage these unique circumstances in such a way as to maximise the effectiveness and the efficiency of the education which is provided for the children and young people entrusted to its care. The quality of that education is largely dependent on the quality of the teachers in the school, who have the main responsibility for delivering the curriculum. Our general contention is that a properly constituted appraisal system can help to enhance the quality of the education provided by the school or college, by improving the morale and the job satisfaction of the teachers. We would further contend that such a system ought to include within it the appraisal of the senior staff of the school, and the ancillary and support staff of the school, but the main thrust of this book is towards the introduction of a system of appraisal for teachers.

Appraisal and the general management of the school

The managers of any enterprise communicate their expectations of their staff in a whole range of ways. Clearly, expectations are communicated through personal actions and through the contacts made by senior managers with the rest of the staff, and through the culture and traditions of the organisation. When a person becomes a member of staff in a new school they quickly become aware of the different mores and value systems which underlie the behaviour which is expected of them. Expectations are also communicated through the way in which the organisation is designed. Lorsch (1977) maintains that:

> an organization's design is management's formal and explicit attempt(s) to indicate to organization members what is expected of them.

He is talking about commercial and industrial organisations, but the same holds true for schools and colleges. He goes on to suggest that the following elements are included:

1. *Organisation structure.* The way in which individual jobs are defined, and the relationships between them.
2. *Reward systems.* The rewards given by management in return for the individual's work. In the past, there has been relatively little scope for school or college managers to control additional monetary rewards, but this will become more important in the future.
3. *Selection criteria.* The way in which staff are selected, both initially and for internal promotion.
4. *Training.* The encouragement given to staff to improve knowledge and skills.
5. *Planning, measurement and evaluation schemes.* The pro-

cedures for establishing the goals of the organisation, the methods used to measure progress and the means by which feedback is provided about performance.

It is this latter element that many schools and colleges have tended to neglect in the past. There are some difficulties in establishing precise educational goals, it is true. It is often easier for commercial and industrial firms to identify and state clear objectives over a limited time scale. If an organisation is unclear about its objectives, it can lead to inconsistencies in the methods used, and to imprecision in the way in which progress is measured (Handy, 1985). If a school's sole objective is to obtain good examination results, and if this is clearly understood by all concerned, it will tend to lead to the employment of particular methods of teaching, particular selection criteria for staff and pupils, and encouragement and rewards given to staff to improve academic knowledge. The feedback about performance can be given in terms of the objectives, and can be stated in quantitative terms.

Most schools, however, have very much broader educational aims and objectives, and it is often much more difficult to state these in precise behavioural terms. This means that it is more important in these circumstances to have debate and agreement about the school's aims and objectives, and agreement needs to be obtained also about the methods to be used to achieve those ends. The school or college needs a strategic plan (Fidler, 1989; Fidler, Bowles and Hart, 1991). It follows from this that the feedback system devised by the organisation should be appropriate to its needs, and an appraisal system is essentially part of that feedback system. The way in which it is introduced, designed and operated will give messages to the staff about the management's expectations and the management's goals, whether or not these expectations are explicitly stated.

Management processes

Appraisal systems do not exist in isolation. They are an integral part of the way in which an organisation is managed. Any appraisal system which is set up in a school or college has an interface with other management processes and becomes part of the context within which management actions take place.

Within this context, the school manager is responsible for a variety of processes. Hunt (1986) suggests that there are nine essential processes with which the manager neds to be concerned:

1. Recruiting, selecting, inducting;

2. Goal setting and getting commitment;
3. Negotiating;
4. Training and coaching;
5. Motivating;
6. Appraising and performance review;
7. Rewarding;
8. Team building; and
9. Continuity, directing, linking past to future.

Appraisal can contribute directly or indirectly to all of these processes. It should provide data which will be of great value to the manager

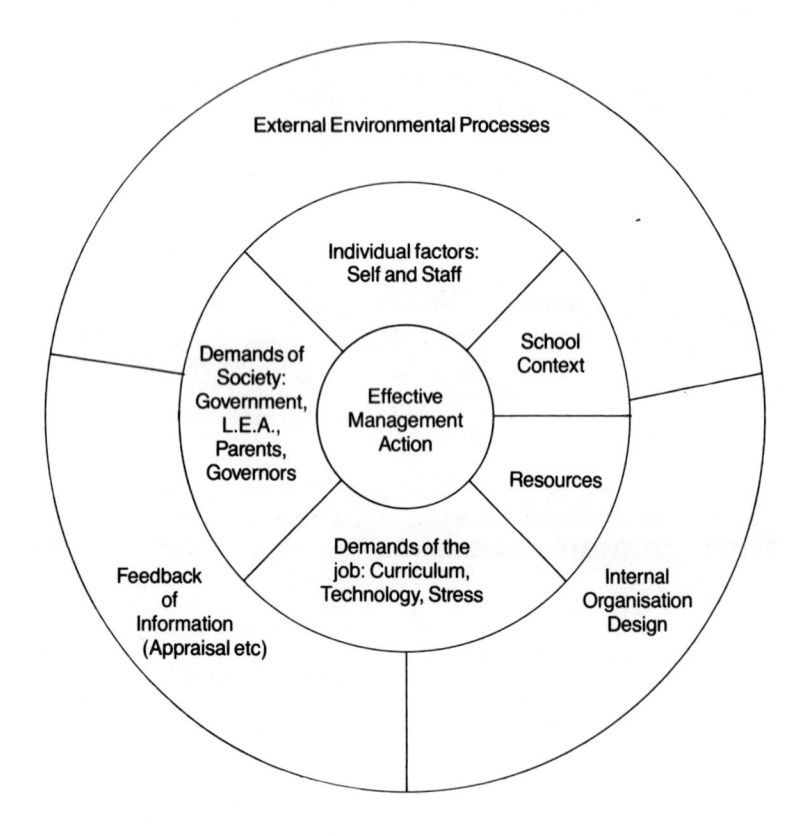

Figure 2.1.1 Context of management action within a school

in recruiting, selecting and inducting new staff. A major aim is to identify training and coaching needs. Motivating staff is an extremely important aspect of the manager's job. The appraisal process has been shown to be motivating by providing an opportunity to praise work which has been well done, by taking an interest in work and career plans, and by discussing ways in which the teacher's individual goals may be fitted to the collective organisational aims. Many teachers who have been through an appraisal process have found that it is rewarding in itself and that it has helped in team building and in linking present work with future development prospects.

Evaluative and developmental approaches to appraisal

It has been suggested earlier (Section 1,p.3) that staff appraisal systems can be thought of as a balance between evaluative and developmental goals. This matrix approach is clearer than the distinctions made by Barber and Klein (1983) and by Turner and Cliff (1988), who refer to formative and summative schemes, and by Wise et al (1984), who refer to bureaucratic and professional evaluation schemes. The emphasis in American schools has been towards the evaluative axis. Appraisal schemes there have been particularly concerned with the measurement of teacher competencies based upon classroom observation and the assessment of pupil performance (Soar et al, 1983; Wise et al, 1984). The most fully worked through schemes in Florida (1983) and in Georgia (1984) both appear to be of this kind, and both include very detailed observation schedules as part of what is essentially an evaluative process.

In this country, appraisal schemes and thinking about appraisal have been more influenced by industrial models which have emphasised the developmental aspects of the appraisal process. The *ACAS Working Group Report on Appraisal/Training* (ACAS 1986: p.2) defined appraisal as

> a continuous and systematic process intended to help individual teachers with their professional development and career planning, and to help ensure that the in-service training and deployment of teachers matches the complementary needs of individual teachers and their schools.

The whole report stresses the need for teachers to be fully involved in the processes of appraisal and the need to think of it in developmental terms. If this approach is adopted, it does not preclude classroom observation or a consideration of pupil performance, but it does mean that if the goals are different, the process is likely to be different. When a school or college is introducing an appraisal scheme, it should be clear about the main purpose and function of the scheme, which should fit in with the school's mission statement and overall development plan.

The emphasis in the LEA pilot studies which have taken place over the past three years has been upon a developmental rather than an evaluative approach (Bradley et al, 1989) *see* case studies in Section 3. All the reports have stressed the importance of consultation with the teachers all through the process, of establishing the right climate, and ensuring that the teachers feel that they have ownership of the scheme and will benefit from it. The teachers' associations have also stressed that appraisal should not be seen as a

> bolted-on extra, but should be embedded and integrated into the way schools, as dynamic institutions, develop their human resources
> (NDCSMT, 1989).

It has been unfortunate that at times ministerial statements have seemed to contradict this general trend and way of thinking. Sir Keith Joseph, at the North of England Conference in 1986, appeared to be advocating a strong evaluative line with the main purpose of appraisal seen as rooting out weak teachers. There were echoes of a similar approach in the statements made by Kenneth Clark at the Conference in 1991. The school manager cannot ignore factors such as this, because they are part of the external environment against which the internal affairs of the school or college have to be arranged.

Managerial approach to appraisal

A third approach to the problem may be termed the managerial approach. This addresses the tensions which inevitably exist between the evaluative and the developmental approaches described above, and between the needs of the individual and the needs of the organisation. It envisages these needs as part of the context within which the staff of the school needs to be managed *see* p.15.

The school manager is no different from any other manager in that he or she has a responsibility and a duty to uphold the quality of the work being performed within the organisation. This is not to deny that teachers themselves have a professional duty, but it is to acknowledge that those being managed are both evaluated and provided with opportunities for development.

The evaluative aspect of the manager's job is to identify those who are performing well, to acknowledge and reward their efforts both financially and with praise, and to help maintain and further develop a continuing high standard. Equally, it is a part of the manager's job to identify those who are not performing well, and to provide them with opportunities through which their performance might be improved. The educational standards of the school or college are not only the problem of the teacher; they should also be an integral part of the responsibility of the manager of the school. The appraisal interview may be the formal occasion when those issues are specifically considered, but it is an ongoing and intrinsic aspect of the management of staff.

The process of staff appraisal may be expressed as in Figure 2.1.2. Those who are appraised fall into two broad groups – those who are basically competent in their work and those who are less than competent. Those few who are less than competent should receive professional support procedures to help them raise their performance to a generally acceptable level. Those who are on the whole competent performers, the vast majority of teachers, can be further subdivided into 'good performers' whose performance sets a very high standard with no significant areas in need of improvement; and 'patchy performers' who are generally competent but who have one or more important area of their performance which is in need of improvement.

The 'patchy performers' need some specific targets to improve areas where they have important weaknesses but also other targets which provide them with new challenges and possibilities to develop new capabilities. The 'good performers' need targets wholly of the developmental kind.

This design is inevitably a generalisation. It is within a particular culture and a unique climate that all managerial decisions have to be taken. Because the culture and the climate of schools vary, the individual manager may have to decide which is the best appraisal system and what are the best means of introducing that system to any particular school. The case studies in this book describe systems in action, and it will be seen how the appraisal systems vary and relate to the culture of the school.

Culture of the school

School culture is made up of all the perceptions which staff and students have of the school. Included in this are the procedures, policies, structure, communications, relationships, rules – indeed, all of the systems which go to make up the perceived reality of the organisation. This reality is not necessarily the formal face of the school as represented in brochures or organisation charts. It is within this culture that all the members of the organisation act, on the basis of

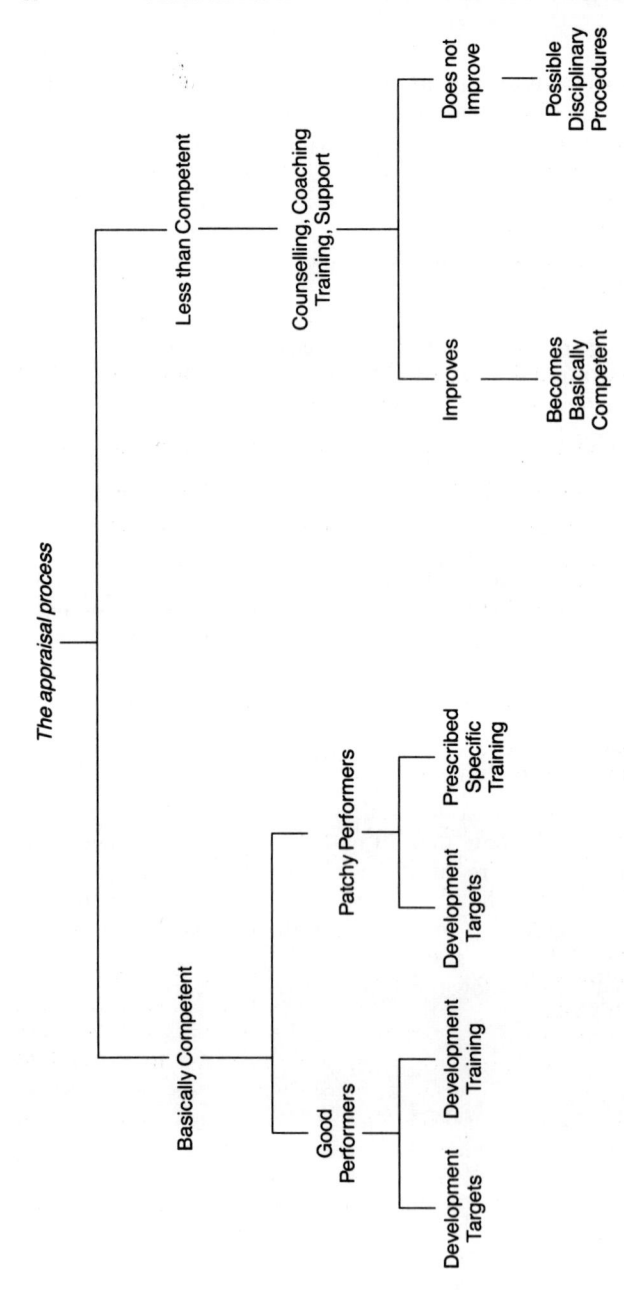

Figure 2.1.2 Appraisal process

their perceptions of reality, and it is within this culture that any appraisal scheme will have to operate. If the culture of the school is generally positive, if there is a sense of openness and a tradition of debate about professional issues, if there is a feeling of trust within the school, then it is likely that the introduction of an appraisal scheme will be seen as a chance to improve the opportunities for growth and development available within the institution. It is within such a culture that the reflective practitioner can be developed (Schon, 1983).

After an extensive survey of the available literature, Hopkins and Bollington (1989) conclude that an appropriate climate for appraisal will occur when the following conditions are met. They suggest that when preparing for appraisal a school must:

1. Reflect a high level of commitment from the policy making group.
2. Involve all interested parties in planning for appraisal.
3. Reflect the educational values of the LEA, area and school.
4. Be developmental, and explicitly linked to staff development.
5. Include a methodology for appraisal that is valid, soundly based, utilises a variety of appraisers and data-collection methods, but is not prescriptive.
6. Place a high priority on training, especially of appraisers.
7. Emphasise the active involvement of teachers, particularly in establishing the rhythm of the process and the setting of criteria.

If the culture of the school is not conducive, it will often not matter how much care and thought is put into the introduction of the appraisal scheme. If the general management of the school is inefficient; if job responsibilities are not clearly defined; if the authority structure is unclear or inconsistent; if there is widespread suspicion about the motives of senior management, then it will be difficult to convince staff that a systematic approach to development is going to make a great deal of difference to them. There will be a tendency in these circumstances to pay lip service to the new system, and individual teachers will attempt to use it for their own purposes.

The activity of teaching, like the process of managing, is an individual and personal thing. Both activities are about achieving results through other people, and about influencing others to act in particular ways. Successful teachers, like successful managers, can achieve good results using very different methods. This is the art of teaching and of managing. Of course this has to be done within clear statements of policy, and within the constraints of the school curriculum, but if an appraisal scheme is going to encourage individual growth and development, it must be within a culture where a certain amount of experimentation and innovation is acceptable, and diversity is encouraged.

Teachers grow and develop by doing; by trying something new; by reflecting upon the practice and then by evaluating. A number of LEAs have been introducing Teacher Profiles, which act as self-evaluation instruments and as records of the teacher's in-service activities and achievements (Cooper, 1991). The main purpose of the profiles is to encourage the teacher to reflect upon their own practice, and to provide opportunities to talk to a colleague who acts as a 'critical friend.' The process of encouraging teachers to talk together freely and openly about their own educational and management practices has been found to improve the climate of trust within the school (Day, 1989).

It is possible for the school or college to imply that it does not really care about its staff developing. The secondary school teacher who wants to introduce individual or small group methods of learning; the primary school curriculum leader who advocates a more active approach to the teaching of maths, can be 'told' in many subtle ways that 'that is not the way we do things here'. Real development and growth, whether individual or institutional, is difficult to sustain against such a background.

Leadership

The head teacher is of central importance to the school culture. Whether or not it is true in every individual case, most teachers believe that the head teacher plays a crucial role in determining their future. It follows from this that the management methods employed by the head teacher; the attitudes and values expressed; and the general management style, is likely to be observed and imitated (Weindling and Earley, 1986).

Most authorities who have written on the subject suggest that the quality of the leadership of an organisation is crucial to the success of that organisation (Blumberg and Greenfield, 1980; Adair, 1983). Certainly it is a view which has been endorsed by the DES (DES, 1986). There is, however, little agreement about the qualities required by the successful head teacher (Murgatroyd and Gray, 1982; Harling, 1984) and ideas about the importance of the school leader change over time (Brown et al, 1982). One of the factors which senior managers in schools have to take into account is that schools and colleges are predominantly staffed by professionals. Handy (1984) suggests that:

'schools are organisations of professionals who, in the manner of professionals, like to manage themselves.'

Schools are not unique organisations in this respect, but it does have implications for the educational manager inasmuch as one of the characteristics of professionals is that they seek a measure of control over their working environment. In the reality of school life, however, teachers are too concerned with their work at the chalk face to devote much of their time to the management problems of the school, and are content that most large-scale responsibilities should be exercised on their behalf.

Many head teachers in today's climate of changes which have been imposed upon them, accept the necessity of a generally organic rather than a mechanistic style of management (Handy, 1985; Everard, 1986a. Such a style allows for bargaining, negotiation and participation in the decision making processes, rather than the imposition of predetermined structures and designs from the top downwards. This style of management has also been referred to as a collegial model, and is supposedly based upon a structure such as exists at some universities, where the members have equal authority in the decision making processes. Many colleges and larger secondary schools have introduced an academic board which is a direct parallel of the university system.

Hall (1983) talks of three styles of leadership in the US which may be used to manage change successfully in schools. These he refers to as the Responder, the Manager, and the Initiator. The Responder places emphasis on allowing the teachers to take the lead. The Manager tends to accept the decisions which are made outside the school or college and sees the role of the head or principal as being one of implementing external requirements. The Initiators have (p.23)

> clear, decisive long range policies and goals that transcend but include implementation of current innovations.... [Initiators] reinterpret them [district programmes] to suit the needs of the school.

One of the problems for the school leader in adopting a collegial or participative style of management is that it does take time. In schools generally there is often little acknowledgement of the need to find time for management purposes. A great deal of management time in industry is taken up in meetings and thorough discussion of management problems. In the circumstances of a school, this is often impossible. It means that in order to allow an opportunity for teachers to participate, time has to be found at the end of the school day. In situations like the present, when schools are being required to change rapidly in a number of different ways, it is often difficult to allow the time necessary for teachers to be fully involved in the processes leading up to the change, and to adjust to the changes once they have been implemented. Routledge and Dennison (1990) suggest that:

if appraisal is to be successfully implemented, time must be procured for it (both for training and the processes) while its outcomes have to be prioritised alongside all the other activities of the school.

Introducing appraisal

The way in which a scheme for appraisal is introduced is often crucial to its success (Suffolk LEA, 1985). In most cases it will be the responsibility of the school or college leader to initiate the change, and to provide the impetus for its development. In the case of the eight schools included by Turner and Cliff (1985), they suggest that four main strategies were employed:

1. Set up a pilot scheme, evaluate it, then extend it to include all staff.
2. Set up a scheme on a voluntary basis and later make it compulsory.
3. Introduce the scheme in stages, adding further components as confidence grows.
4. Start as you mean to go on!

They also contend (p.50) that the introduction of the schemes tended

> to follow the usual patterns of management and communication in each institution and it may be that attempts to operate in untypical ways in order to set up a scheme are most likely to fail.

It may be that many schools will have limited room for manoeuvre, and will be required to introduce a particular scheme for all staff by a particular time. If this is the case, it will still need sensitive and skilful management by the head teacher and senior management team.

Teachers

It has been a central contention of this section that there should be clarity about the purposes and functions of an appraisal scheme, and that these should be discussed and agreed in general terms by the staff of a school or college before the scheme is introduced. If the purpose of the scheme is seen to be mainly evaluative, this needs to be stated and the methods by which the scheme can be initiated will follow from this. If the scheme is seen to be aimed essentially at assisting the continued growth and development of the teachers in the school, it again follows that the teachers should be involved in the setting up of the scheme and consulted about the structure and working arrangements (Skitt and Jennings, 1989).

Teachers themselves are likely to have very differing views on the subject. Some will be influenced by the attitude of their professional association and will accept the collective decision whatever it is. Some will oppose the proposal, either overtly or covertly, because of their own personal agendas. Others will be supportive, again because of their own optimistic life views. While being concerned with, and managing the structures and the social context within which the everyday life of the school takes place, the head teacher and the senior management team need to take account of the individual reactions of members of staff, and the effects of group dynamics within the staff as a whole (Everard and Morris, 1990).

In some schools there will be individuals or groups of staff who will be resentful of the introduction of any change. This may or may not have anything to do with the merits of appraisal or of a particular scheme as such. The origins of the opposition may be in things which have occurred in the past and are now transferred to things happening in the present. These may be important factors in the successful introduction of appraisal into the school.

In their study of teacher appraisal, Turner and Cliff (1988) found that from the earliest stages in the introduction of an appraisal scheme into the schools they studied, some teachers took a positive view while others were generally hostile. The teachers who adopted a positive view often saw it as formalising what was happening in an informal way already in the school, and considered that it would improve communications between staff at different levels in the hierarchy, and would provide a much better system of support. Those teachers who took a negative view tended to see any scheme as a threat to their autonomy, and a chance for senior staff to find fault and criticise. Yet others took a cynical view, seeing appraisal as a bandwagon or a superficial exercise. It was noted that many teachers' perceptions of appraisal changed as a consequence of experiencing it, and they saw it in practice as more valuable and as less threatening. They concluded (p.169) that their evidence suggested that:

> whilst perhaps a majority of teachers will be favourable to a national scheme of appraisal, or may become 'converts', a significant and potentially vociferous number are likely to remain implacably opposed to the idea.

Conclusion

Nuttall (1986) neatly summarises the points which he suggests may be learnt from research into the introduction of appraisal into schools. He suggests that:

1. Experience with institutional self-evaluation and constructive self-criticism is very helpful.
2. Effective schemes cannot serve evaluative and developmental purposes simultaneously.
3. A good scheme ensures that the results of appraisal are linked to appropriate action.
4. It is important to involve those to be appraised in the scheme from the outset and not to impose procedures upon them.
5. Teachers must retain some autonomy.
6. A shared understanding of criteria and process is essential.
7. Schemes employing more than one observer gain reliability and validity.
8. There is a value in using ipsative rating scales – indicating relative strengths and weaknesses, using more than one dimension.
9. There is a need for adequate training, particularly of the evaluators.

If teachers are to be encouraged to grow as individuals and to develop their professional skills, they need two things. Firstly, they need new challenges which are within the range of their own capabilities, and secondly, they need feedback, knowledge of results and information about how they are progressing. If the challenges are too easy or too difficult it will lead to demotivation, and growth will be minimal. If the feedback is not available on how well the teacher is progressing, growth will be random and unsystematic. A good appraisal scheme should provide the teacher with valid information which will allow for positive and constructive development.

2.2 Appraisal and staff development

John West-Burnham

Introduction

This chapter examines the relationship between appraisal and staff development indicating their interdependence and proposes a model for their effective integration. It identifies the prerequisites for successful management of staff development strategies and suggests approaches to manage the specific issues of prioritising outcomes, designing effective learning activities and evaluating the impact of appraisal.

Linking appraisal and staff development

Appraisal which is not linked to staff development is likely to be only partially effective. Equally to try and manage staff development without an appraisal process will produce random, partial and peripheral outcomes. Properly managed appraisal provides the focus for staff development. An appropriate training and development strategy ensures that the appraisal process actually leads to change and growth. At its simplest, appraisal provides the diagnostic and analytic component of a strategy for effective professional learning. At a more sophisticated level an integrated strategy provides a sophisticated mechanism for managing quality in schools, enhancing the performance of individual teachers and translating the rhetoric of school aims into practical activity.

There are numerous definitions of staff development. However, an analysis of even a few of them produces the following criteria for effectiveness:

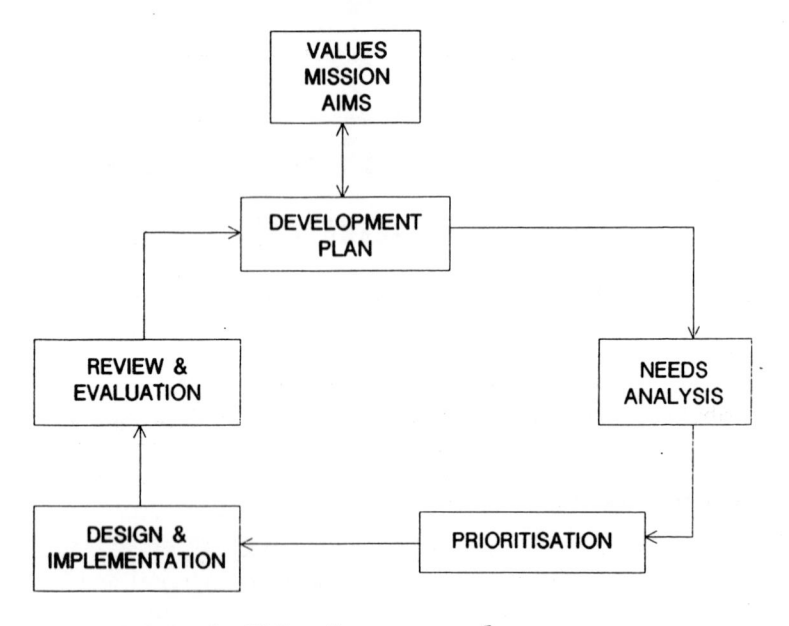

```
        VALUES
        MISSION
         AIMS
           ↕
      DEVELOPMENT
         PLAN
    ↗              ↘
REVIEW &           NEEDS
EVALUATION        ANALYSIS
    ↑               ↓
DESIGN &    ←   PRIORITISATION
IMPLEMENTATION
```

Figure 2.2.1   Staff development cycle

- Explicit relationship with institutional aims and development planning;
- Needs analysis process for the institution and the people who work in it;
- Outcomes of the needs analysis process have to be prioritised;
- Individual and organisational needs are reconciled;
- Needs are met through appropriate development activities; and
- The whole process is monitored and evaluated and managed so as to meet changing circumstances.

Combining these factors produces a simple model of the management of staff development (Figure 2.2.1).

This model has a number of significant features: it is dynamic, constantly building and improving. It is continuous, i.e., development is a fundamental organisational process and it is founded on the belief that organisations grow and improve by developing the individuals within them. Engaging in staff development is thus a professional responsibility and managing effective training and development an organisational necessity. Integrating appraisal and staff development creates the possibility of schools and colleges becoming learning

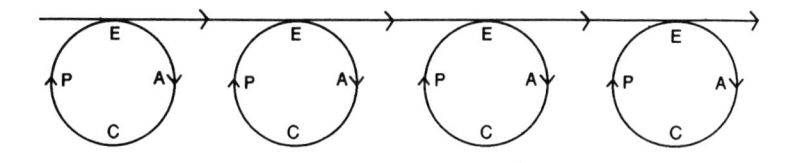

E = EXPERIENCING,   A = ANALYSING,   C = CLARIFYING,   P = PLANNING.

Figure 2.2.2 Development in the learning organisation

organisations for adults as well as children and students.

Drucker (1989), Handy (1990), and Lessem (1991) have all contributed to the evolution of the theory of a learning organisation. Translating their ideas into an educational context produces the following propositions to inform the management of professional learning and organisational change:

1. Organisations change and develop through the enhanced capacity of individuals;
2. Individuals come to terms with change through continuous development;
3. Such development is holistic, concentrating on knowledge, skills and qualities;
4. The organisation has clear and explicit values which refer to management processes as much as to outcomes;
5. Development integrates theory and practice in such a way as to inform action; and
6. There is a belief in the continuous improvement of the organisation, individuals, processes and outcomes.

Development, therefore, presupposes a dynamic critical awareness which is based on an analysis of the relationship between stated personal and institutional values and outcomes and existing practice. In this process appraisal provides the opportunity for review and analysis and staff development the means to implement change. The process is thus evolutionary, constantly adapting behaviour in order to meet changing circumstances. The traditional learning circle, therefore, has to be replaced by the notion of a continuous cyclical process.

One of the crucial features of this model is that it integrates the 'classroom and the staffroom', teachers are engaged in the same systematic and continuous learning process as their pupils/students. This has two important implications: it breaks the artificial distinction between pedagogy and andragogy and reinforces the moral commitment of schools and colleges to their employees as well as their clients. The learning and pastoral care of teachers is as significant an issue as that of pupils and students.

Managing appraisal linked to staff development

The practical issues in managing the relationship between appraisal and staff development may be largely derived from the nature and purposes of appraisal. The *ACAS Report* (1986) the *NSG Report* (DES 1989) and the *DES Regulations* (1991) produce the following features of the appraisal process:

- *Formative not summative* matched to criteria for development rather than being linked to pay or disciplinary procedures,

- *Developmental* related to an explicit staff development strategy with the appraisal process producing personal targets for growth,

- *Negotiated* based on shared perceptions recognising the significance of organisational goals and the need for personal growth,

- *Anticipatory* the process is concerned with the future rather than rendering account for the past,

- *Diagnostic* the process is analytical rather than judgemental.

APPRAISAL	⟶	GROWTH & DEVELOPMENT
PERFORMANCE RELATED PAY	⟶	REWARD
CAPABILITY	⟶	REMEDIAL ACTION
DISCIPLINE	⟶	SANCTIONS
DISMISSAL	⟶	ENDING OF EMPLOYMENT

Figure 2.2.3 Strategies for managing teacher performance

In order to reinforce this perspective it is necessary to place appraisal in the context of a range of personnel procedures. If the integrity of the appraisal process is to be maintained then the appropriate strategy has to be employed. It is not appropriate in this context to outline the components of each but rather to stress the existence of the full portfolio, emphasise the importance of maintaining the distinctiveness of each procedure and the importance of employing the relevant procedure for the desired outcome.

If appraisal is to serve the purposes outlined above then it is essential that it is firmly placed in the context of staff development and this relationship is best exemplified in the following diagram:

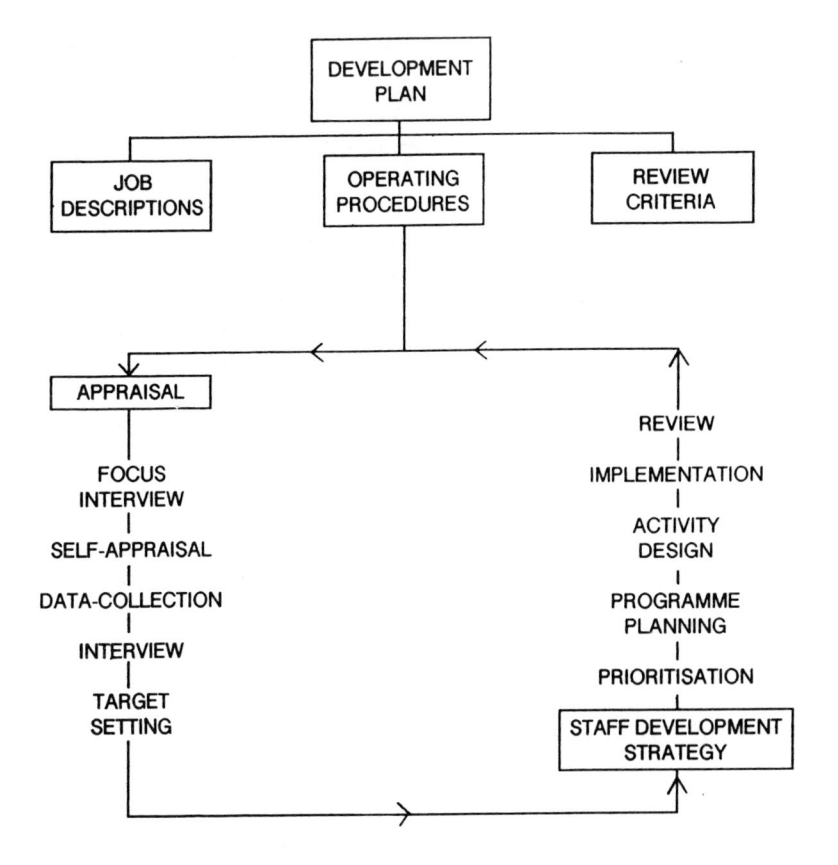

Figure 2.2.4 Model for appraisal linked staff development

Context of a staff development strategy

Staff development has to function within a clearly defined management context, it therefore requires a number of explicit guidelines in which to operate, i.e.

- A development plan
- Operating procedures
- Job descriptions
- Review criteria

Each of these components helps to define the outcomes which development activities are to address and provides information to the individual teacher as to the central elements of his or her job. The development plan sets out the strategy for the institution, provides clear priorities and translates the values and mission of the school or college into short and medium term objectives. Development planning therefore sets the agenda and provides the broad focus for the appraisal process.

Operating procedures will usually take the form of syllabuses and schemes of work, consultative and decision making processes, pastoral schemes and administrative systems. These components serve the dual purpose of providing quality criteria to review the operational affectiveness of teachers and establish a set of bench marks for training and development.

Job descriptions serve two primary functions, firstly relating individual activity to the overall management structure and translating the development plan into personal accountabilities and secondly providing the agenda for the individual appraisal process i.e., identifying what is to be appraised.

Review criteria are essential to prevent the appraisal process becoming self-indulgent and aimless or over critical. Their essential function is to create a common understanding and vocabulary so as to inform the analysis of existing practice and to generate the components of appropriate and effective development activities.

Staff development strategy

Once the context has been established, and it is important to stress the importance that all the above components be developed by, and relevant to the specific institution, then it is appropriate to formulate a

STAFF MANAGEMENT AND APPRAISAL

strategy for staff development. The key components of such a strategy are:

   Policy;
   Roles;
   Implementation; and
   Evaluation.

The staff development policy of a school or college needs to make explicit statements about the following issues:

Purpose:	Clear reference to the centrality of pupils' and students' learning, the place of the development and the professional responsibility to participate in the strategy;
Applicability:	Statement indicating that development applies to all adults employed in the school;
Management:	Indication of how the strategy will be managed, the key roles and the decision-making procedures;
Outcomes:	Identification of the range of appropriate development activities and the criteria to be used to inform the allocation of resources;
Needs Analysis:	Nature and management of the appraisal process should be described;
Specific Provision:	Clear reference to policies for managing the first year of teaching, induction of new staff, management development, and succession planning should be available; and
Record Keeping:	Statement as to what records will be kept, who will have access, and the purposes for which they will be used.

There are three issues relating to roles in the management of staff development:

   Responsibility of line managers;
   Functions of the co-ordinator; and
   Contribution of individual teachers.

If a line management approach to appraisal is adopted then the job description of middle and senior managers should not only refer to their responsibility to appraise but also to manage the training and development of the colleagues for whom they are responsible. This may require a significant shift in the role perception of senior and middle managers in extending the role to include responsibility for the learning of adults as well as the curriculum and resources.

The role of the staff development co-ordinator will vary according to the size of school or college. However, the designation of such a post, with appropriate seniority, is necessary to manage a complex process and to demonstrate unequivocal commitment to the development of staff. The components of such a role might include:

- Monitoring national and LEA policies on INSET and appraisal and advising on their application;
- Developing and maintaining a database of resources, training materials, providers and running a professional library;
- Monitoring the administration of development activities, the appraisal scheme and induction procedures;
- Publishing the staff development programme for the year, taking into account development plan priorities and aggregated appraisal targets;
- Ensuring training for those involved in the appraisal process;
- Providing advice and guidance to those managing school-based development activities;
- Managing the training and development budget; and
- Evaluating the effectiveness of INSET provision.

Managing the outcomes of the appraisal process

The central issue in the relationship between appraisal and staff development is that of implementation. If effectively managed, the appraisal process will generate individual targets for every teacher which are based on a systematic process of review, self-appraisal and negotiation which grow directly out of the teacher's own work. They will therefore have a very high degree of personal involvement and commitment. The credibility of appraisal will depend on the extent to which these targets are met through staff development activities. This raises two subordinate issues – the prioritising of the outcomes of appraisal and the design of learning activities.

Prioritising the staff development needs of staff has two components:

1. Reconciling individual and organisational needs; and,
2. Discriminating between the aggregated outcomes.

In one sense this problem is resolved if the development plan is sufficiently clear and specific and derived from a process of consultation and collaborative decision making. However, this would be to diminish the importance of developing the whole person and the individual's right to career enhancement. Appraisal must not raise false expectations and it should operate within clearly defined parameters. These should be defined in the staff development strategy and made clear in all appraisals.

One method of developing a model to structure this process is to operate a system which facilitates as objective an approach as possible. This requires a very clear correlation of values, aims, development plan priorities and the resources available. A whole school review process such as GRIDS might also contribute to this process. A process of consultation should then be used to identify the specific priorities, e.g., effective learning, development plan priorities and personal development. These factors are then interrelated in order to produce prioritisations which maximise the potential impact of time spent in training and development activities, i.e.,

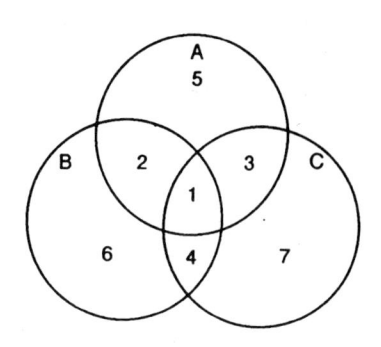

```
A       = EFFECTIVE LEARNING
B       = DEVELOPMENT PLAN PRIORITIES
C       = PERSONAL DEVELOPMENT.
1 - 7   = Priority to be accorded to targets.
```

Figure 2.2.5 Prioritising demands for INSET

Source: S. Williams, Weaverham School, Cheshire.

It would clearly be naïve to expect that there are courses available which could meet the complex range of demands implied by the first priority. However, this raises the crucial and central issue of designing learning activities. Such criteria provide the basis for negotiating with providers, planning the use of training days and informing personal development strategies. The design of activities will also inform the deployment of the INSET budget by facilitating objective budgeting. Equally significant is the potential of the appraisal process to identify knowledge and skills available in the school so that the developer is also developed.

Appraisal targets are derived from a detailed and systematic analysis of needs which generates a high level of personal commitment and high expectations that the activities will actually meet those needs. It is therefore essential that the design of learning activities addresses a range of issues which take into account motivation, effective learning and relevant methods. The design of professional learning activities, therefore, needs to respond to the following questions:

1. Are the outcomes of the activity expressed in terms of behaviour and the capacity to act?
2. Is the method of delivery designed to support implementation?
3. Are the methodologies employed appropriate to the participants in the activity?
4. Are the needs and perceptions of participants taken into account?
5. Is a problem solving, team based approach adopted whenever possible?
6. Are the resources available to ensure implementation, follow-up and review?

In order to ensure that, as far as possible, the above criteria are met, the following process might be applied to an appraisal target in order to turn it into a learning activity. See Figure 2.2.6.

Using this method, it is necessary to specify in as much detail as appropriate what the desired outcomes are and this in turn will inform the choice of method (e.g., action learning, seminar, course attendance, etc) and the choice of process (e.g., coaching, shadowing, role play, etc). Although mundane, the practical details do need to be specified in order to facilitate implementation and planning the staff development programme. Most important, however, is the need to negotiate and specify the criteria by which success will be established. The criteria serve two functions: firstly to establish the attainment of the target, and secondly to facilitate evaluation of staff development activities. These points can be demonstrated in the following example:

1. Appraisal Target:
2. What are the desired outcomes in terms of:

   Knowledge..............................
   Skills..
   Qualities..................................
3. What are the appropriate learning methods?

   ....
4. What are the appropriate learning processes?

   ....
5. Who will manage the activity?

   ....
6. When will it take place?
7. Where will it take place?
8. What are the criteria to indicate success?

   ....
   ....
   ....
9. Learning Activity

Figure 2.2.6 Designing learning activities

Appraisal target: To prepare for the implementation of appraisal by developing skills in appraisal interviewing.

Learning activity: To attend a county course on 'The Appraisal Interview' in October 1991, to understand the stages of the interview and to practise the skills of active listening, giving feedback, questioning and target setting so that you feel confident in interviewing colleagues, obtaining feedback from them and identifying future training needs.

Evaluation

Three levels of evaluation of staff development activities may be identified:

Monitoring   Ensuring that the activity actually takes place, checking costs and identifying organisational issues

Review   Checking on satisfaction with the activity, suitability of the provider appropriateness of design etc.

Evaluation   Establishing the extent to which the activity has directly contributed to the achievement of the specified learning outcomes through meeting the specified criteria.

Given that the primary purpose of appraisal is to enhance the capacity of teachers to manage the quality of children's learning then the primary purpose of evaluation must be to establish a correlation between the need, the activity and the outcome in terms of classroom and management practice.

Evaluation should, therefore, be seen as an integral component of the appraisal and development processes and needs to be managed according to the same principles, i.e., formative, developmental, negotiated, anticipatory and diagnostic. Whilst evaluation needs to render account and indicate satisfaction, its primary purpose should be to indicate the extent to which the appraisal and staff development processes have served the implementation of the development plan.

Conclusion

The evaluation of the LEA pilot schemes (Bradley et al, 1989) indicated that one of the most important outcomes of appraisal was an enhancement of INSET provision. Most notably through greater precision in the identification of needs, more exact targeting of provision and a greater awareness of the potential scope of INSET. Equally significant was the awareness of appraisal as a development activity in its own right. This latter point is crucial: appraisal has no validity in its own right, it is only significant as a process which enables and facilitates change and change is best implemented through professional learning.

2.3 Implementation of change

Barry Mountford

Introduction

Whether the introduction and implementation of an appraisal scheme is effective or not has little to do with appraisal. From what we have seen already, appraisal outcomes and process can deliver significant benefits to the school or college and its members – so the rationale is well founded in theory. The critical issue then is how the appraisal scheme is managed as an aspect of change – changing people, changing the organisation. Most people do not like change, largely perhaps because it involves 'loss, anxiety and struggle'. The comforts of routine and even ritual have to be abandoned. Yet there are learning opportunities in change. So many of us are involved in education and training for change yet we somehow fail to recognise its benefits when directly challenged ourselves.

Theory for change?

There is no shortage of material on how change in schools and colleges can be managed. My experience as a manager has been that the people I work with have not read the same books. Much of the theory assumes that organisational life is characterised by rationality in which a sound idea for change (appraisal?) is immediately recognised for its benefits eagerly anticipated and implemented in a coherent manner by a co-ordinated staff body.

There is a view in the theory that change in schools and colleges can be managed by brute sanity. The organisations I have worked in are characterised less by their sanity and rationality than by subversion, special interest groups, and idiosyncratic behaviour. There is a 'dark underworld' to the management of change which needs to be acknowledged and accommodated if something other than cosmetic changes are to occur. This sort of deep structure change will only happen if the people-related issues are pre-eminent in our thinking and strategy. Too many change ideas have foundered on structural change and policy documents: there is an assumption that these *are* the change. However, in terms of change, people are more significant than structures. Where does this leave the status of theory? Theory can be helpful in providing frameworks for understanding people (motivation theory for example) and schools and colleges (organisation theory). This help whilst useful is limited. Necessarily theory is general. It is about schools and/or colleges *in general.* Theory has to be general so that generalisations can be made which apply to all institutions – herein lies its strength and its weakness. The generalities of theory can help us to structure our thinking in say, introducing appraisal. The principal weakness of theory on change is that it is not about *our* school or college. The theory often does not reflect where we are in terms of policy, practice and people. Indeed it is unreasonable to expect theory to do this. The diversity of change situations is infinite often with idiosyncratic factors operating. Generalisations to cover such a spectrum of operation would be so general as to appear irrelevant perhaps even banal. This is to argue that theory can be useful but that this usefulness is limited.

Intuition and technique as aspects of managing change

The view developed on the limited value of theory in relation to managing change is supported by the reality of management in the school or college. Most day-to-day operational management in schools and colleges is done by people interacting in an intuitive manner. Often there is no time to refer or reflect on theory in order to consider options and the best course of action. A decision is called for, expected and often given without recourse to any aspect of formal theory. In short we make it up as we go along or as the theory (Lindblom) puts it we 'muddle through.' The intuitive component to management is also present in the process of managing change. These intuitive skills (often derived from experience of people and organisations) are essential but more effective if buttressed by technical and conceptual understanding and skills.

Managing change

To be an effective manager of change, and appraisal schemes involve significant amounts of change (to people, policy, structure and practice), we can see that three sorts of competence are called for:

Technical knowledge A detailed working knowledge of the change activity (appraisal in this case) is essential.

Conceptual understanding An understanding of the conceptual base and context of change generally is called for.

Human or interpersonal skills An ability to make things happen with the people we work with (rather than those we like) is critical.

In a team approach these understandings and skills need to be covered by the change team. Of the three aspects for bringing about change effectively, technical knowledge is perhaps the easiest to acquire.

Technical knowledge for change management

The manager of change needs to have knowledge, and extensive detailed knowledge at that, of the change he or she wishes to introduce, implement and maintain. A manager of change in some aspect of the curriculum would soon come unstuck if their knowledge base was inadequate. In the context of appraisal a minimum knowledge base would include:

(a)	Legislative framework	(SI 1551; DES, 1991);
(b)	Evaluation of the pilot schemes	(Bradley et al, 1989);
(c)	Outcomes and benefits of appraisal	school development INSET career development;
(d)	Positions on	Appraisal and pay, LMS, disciplines and views of local professional associations;

(e)	Appraisal process	Climate settings awareness raising start-up meeting initial review self-review classroom observation follow-up interview/review recording issues resource issues;
(f)	Appraisal	Head teacher/deputy Non-teaching staff Governor
(g)	Task analysis	what competences are to be assessed? how can these be agreed/defined? classroom, curriculum, management competences?
(h)	Classroom observation	acceptability objectivity confidentiality reliability and validity issues; and
(i)	Evaluation	benefits outcomes process.

Conceptual understanding for change management

Change managers also need to understand the change envisaged (appraisal in this instance) in a broader perspective of policy and practice. The context for change is critical in its management. A technical knowledge of appraisal is necessary but not sufficient to bring about change. The change activity has to be located somewhere and knowledge of the location of change and understanding the process of change are complementary aspects of conceptual understanding for effective change.

The process of managing change is heavily dependent on the location and context for change. We may be able to refer to some overall outline to guide the process of change e.g. technical knowledge base to appraisal (a–i above), but where we begin and how far or fast we can travel depends on contextual factors. These main contextual considerations include:

Necessity for change

If staff members are unconvinced of the necessity for change, they will not change. At best any change will be cosmetic. In the case of appraisal there is a legislative force driving it. More powerful however will be a shared understanding of the potential benefits – drawing on the technical knowledge argued for earlier. *Desirability* replaces *necessary* as the driving force for change. Appraisal is after all one of the few recent initiatives to be done for teachers rather than to them.

Change has a number of dimensions

The introduction of any change is not self-contained. Changing the curriculum, for example, also changes structures, resource allocation and people. There are system effects to any change. Appraisal will call for changes in people, professional/career development patterns, INSET profiles, teaching and learning strategies etc. These 'knock-on' effects need to be anticipated and planned for. This is part of the wider conceptual grasp of what change involves.

Location of change

All change has to be located somewhere and each location is uniquely significant for how the change process is managed. The climate of the organisation with respect to change is a significant part of the assessment for change process. In institutions with a weak record for innovation there is always the possibility of changing the climate to change by the introduction of change. However there is a double jeopardy here. You might fail on both counts creating a worse climate for change.

Expectation can determine success

In first introducing change into a recalcitrant organisation there is only one principle – it must work! The benefits of the change (however insignificant to outsiders) must flow to the staff concerned. Arranging for rubber buffers to classroom chairs was my first change in headship. This action reduced the noise level in classrooms much to the relief of staff. Successful actions of this sort create a climate of expectation that the next initiative will also succeed. More powerfully we seem to actively work to support the expected outcome. This is fine if you are 'one up or two up', but the theory also works in reverse. Get it wrong once or twice and you are creating a climate which sponsors negative outcomes. 'It didn't work last time and it won't work this time,' and they make sure that it doesn't! Expectation theory is acknowledged for children's classroom learning but is underrated in the management of change process.

Schools and colleges – the inertia problem

When you returned from a recent INSET activity were you greeted with 'have you enjoyed your break/holiday/rest?' This common reaction tells us several things about schools and colleges and the change process.

Much change activity in schools and colleges is generated by INSET provision and we often return to our institution fired with enthusiasm for bringing about change. Unfortunately there are re-entry problems.

Firstly, the organisation attempts to absorb us as we left not as we returned with new knowledge and skills. Whole staff and school based INSET can do much to resolve this problem.

Secondly, our attempts to bring about change are often frustrated by our inability to bring together the necessary ingredients for change. Time, senior manager involvement, resources, apathy, hostility, commitment to other activities and interests represent an organisational inertia which has to be overcome. An understanding of this helps us to sustain our efforts. A knowledge of how to tackle the inertia will help us to overcome it in order to bring about change. We each need to come to know the place we work in, in this and other respects, if we are to be effective managers of change. A knowledge of the centres of resistance as well as the locations of support can be critical in the management of change.

Policy for change and a change policy

Preferred change will not happen accidentally, it has to be planned and sustained. We have argued that an idea, however self-evidently good, is not enough for things to change. In addition to a good idea – appraisal being one of the best – there needs to be a change policy. Someone, somewhere needs to be in control of the change process. It needs to be thought through, managed, and evaluated if the 'good idea' for change is to be introduced, established, and maintained. In this context issues of timing, pace, and scale of change are significant and those with intimate and detailed knowledge of the location of change are best placed to make such judgements and policies.

Interpersonal skills for change management

We may have a full and detailed knowledge of appraisal and we may have a conceptual grasp of the wider issues, context, location, change process etc yet very little happens. Why is this?

We all know how to lay bricks yet not many of us can do it well or quickly. There is a logical difference between 'knowing how' and 'being able'. People who are unable to swim or ride a bicycle, 'know' how to do it. Managing change is about making it happen and moreover making it happen with the people you have rather than the people you would like to have. I remember tutoring an experienced head teacher over a two year part-time course in education management. At the end he came up to me and said, 'I've understood most of what has gone on and I can't wait to try it out in my next school.'

There are substantial and significant training issues in the area of interpersonal relations. If we do not have the technical knowledge or wider conceptual understanding to support change activity, we can acquire them through training and education.

In the area of interpersonal skills such uprating is not so easy. It seems to me that we either like people or we do not. If we do not like people we are better advised to seek employment in a people reduced environment.

Returning to the issue of training for enhancement of interpersonal skills. It seems clear that there must be limits to interpersonal skills, perhaps best expressed as thresholds. There are some people whose interpersonal skills are such that they are confident and competent in every conceivable social or professional setting. Such people are 'through the ceiling threshold' and require little or no further training. In such people we find a very high level of intuitive interpersonal ability. At the other extreme, there are some people whose interpersonal ability is of such a low order that communication is difficult to initiate and impossible to maintain. These are 'below the floor threshold' and no amount of quality interpersonal skills training will make any difference. Most of us are 'above the floor' but 'below the ceiling' and training can make a difference. Part of this improvement takes the form of self-analysis and audit of your personal skills by others as a way of establishing your personal skills profile. This will suggest components of interpersonal skills in need of training and improvement. Key areas for personal skills development for change managers include:

- Negotiating
- Pressure and support

- Empathy/listening/counselling
- Meetings
- Conflict/stress

Following the *Education Reform Act* of 1988 many schools and colleges are run as businesses. We need to remember that they are in the people business. Central to our 'business' is relating to, working with, and sponsoring people. This is as true for managers as it is for teachers and lecturers. If managers can sponsor the professional development and growth of the teaching staff, the teaching staff will be better placed to provide for growth in their students. In many schools and colleges this requirement for logical consistency is absent and the students get a better deal than the staff – to the detriment of the students. An effective appraisal scheme can do much to redress this imbalance by valuing and sponsoring the staff.

Returning to the issue of interpersonal skills for change management, it is widely recognised that the individual is the unit of change. Attitudes and beliefs must be tackled before behaviour changes *permanently*. This sort of change can take up to two or three years in industrial or commercial settings. There is no reason to believe that teachers can do it or will do it in less.

Change – even and perhaps especially appraisal – involves loss, anxiety and struggle. All too often this personal perspective on change is ignored by the change managers keen to get their system up and running before moving onto the next aspect of school improvement. All change requires more effort and we do ourselves no service by pretending otherwise. In this connection we will need to be sensitive in exercising pressure and support. For some encouragement will be sufficient to stimulate action and change. For others (and we know who they are) 'dynamite' rather than diplomacy might be called for. Being a manager of change is a high risk activity – particularly if you want to be liked. It is easy and rewarding to work with those who think as we do. The person who can work openly and closely with those who oppose his/her efforts has arrived as a manager of change. Working effectively and openly with the people we have is a key performance indicator – and these days this includes students, parents and governors as well as teaching and non-teaching staff. Thus a key challenge in managing change in schools and colleges is in the area of sponsoring 'ownership' of change ideas and policies across these diverse constituencies in order to promote organisational development in tune with changing times and circumstances.

Conclusion

We live in changing times and schools and colleges will never be the same again. The successful ones will be characterised by a clear sense of 'mission' based on a shared value system about what is educationally worthwhile as well as what is politically expedient, and appraisal is both of these.

The school or college manager of change has a pivotal role in this difficult but critical task. In addition to technical knowledge, conceptual understanding and high-level interpersonal skills he or she may also be in need of a little luck.

Finally, any school or college engaging in appraisal will need to ensure that three sets of questions are addressed:

- Do we have adequate technical knowledge about appraisal? Where does it reside?

- Do we have the necessary conceptual understanding with regard to the location of change and the process of change. Who has this?

- Do we have the necessary interpersonal skills in range and depth? Who has these?

There are training issues if these sets of questions cannot be satisfactorily answered. A team approach seems essential, not least because it is unlikely that the necessary knowledge, understandings and skills could reside in any single person.

SECTION 3: APPRAISAL EXPERIENCE

3.0 Overall structure of the appraisal process

Brian Fidler and Bob Cooper

Introduction

Legal requirements

For the appraisal of school teachers the legal requirements are laid down in *The Education (School Teacher Appraisal) Regulations 1991* (SI No. 1511, 1991) and further non-statutory guidance is given in Circular 12/91 *School Teacher Appraisal* (DES, 1991). The Statutory Instrument gives remarkably little detail of the appraisal process although it does give detail on who should appraise and when the cycle should start in varying cases of changes of job and how appeals should be operated. The regulations do give the aims of appraisal. These range from helping teachers develop and improve their career prospects to helping teachers having difficulties and improving the management of schools.

The statutory requirements for the appraisal of a school teacher comprise:

> Observation of teaching on two occasions in the first year of the two year cycle (para 9.(2)).
>
> Appraisal interview before the end of the first year to review the teacher's work, achievements and aspects needing development, identifying training and development needs and setting targets for action (para 10.(1)).
>
> Written appraisal statement prepared by the appraiser in consultation with the appraisee recording the main points of the interview and any conclusions reached (any targets for action are to be recorded separately within the statement) (para 10.(2)).
>
> Opportunity for the appraisee to add comments within 20 days and to complain about it formally within the same period (following a complaint, a review officer is to be appointed to review the appraisal with wide power to make changes to the statement or order a fresh appraisal) (paras 10.(3), 11.(1), 11.(2), 11.(6), 11.(7)).
>
> Appraisal review meeting before the end of the second year to review the statement and progress in meeting any targets and to set revised targets (para 12.(1)).
>
> Written note of the main points made by the appraiser and teacher and any conclusions reached (para 12.(2)).

Appraisers are to be chosen by the head teacher.

The Circular gives further guidance which is 'designed to encourage and achieve good practice in schools' but is not legally binding. This guidance includes:

> appraisal should be on the basis of an established job description (para 19)
>
> appraisal may include an initial meeting to plan and prepare for the appraisal (para 33)
>
> appraisal may include self-appraisal by the appraisee (para 34)
>
> appraisal may, after consultation with the appraisee, include the collection of data from sources other than classroom teaching (paras 37, 38)

Good practice

The Regulations prescribe the minimum which must be carried out and the Circular gives further guidance but study of appraisal as described in this book suggests that rather more is required to make staff appraisal really effective. The following is put forward, with reasons, for individual schools and LEAs to consider. Where appropriate reference is made to the Regulations and Circular advice.

Appraisal process

Although in much discussion appraisal is referred to as if it took place at a single point in time, in fact it is a series of sequential events which take place over two years for each cycle.
The main components are:

- Informal self-appraisal
- Initial planning meeting
- Self-appraisal
- Collection of evidence
- Classroom observation and feedback
- Interview
- Written statement
- Follow-up action
- Review meeting (following year)
- Next cycle

These processes are mainly sequential. The preferred sequence is given above but the collection of evidence, classroom observation and feedback, and formal self-appraisal could go on simultaneously or in any order.

When the system has been planned, discussed and agreed, who appraises whom should have been decided.

Informal self-appraisal

Both appraisee and appraiser need to prepare for the initial planning meeting since at that meeting decisions will be made about the particular focus of parts of the appraisal process. The appraisee needs to give particular thought to the classroom observation which is to be planned. What particular features of his or her teaching would it be valuable if someone else observed and gave systematic feedback? What aspects of the appraisee's general performance would he or she find feedback of value in terms of future career development? Are there particular difficulties in the job which they wish to bring to the attention of their appraiser and could further evidence on this be gathered which might make a solution more likely? In short the appraisee needs to take to the initial planning meeting ideas which will ensure that the appraisal process is of benefit to them.

The appraiser similarly needs to spend time reflecting on the appraisee and their job within the school or college to ensure that the appraisal process includes aspects of any performance in the job which are not being done to an acceptable standard and evidence which could open up opportunities for the future. Although these things should come up at the appraisal interview, the initial planning meeting is the opportunity to see that they are placed on the agenda and that any factual or other evidence which could throw light on the issues is collected in preparation for a successful appraisal interview.

Initial planning meeting

The purpose of the planning meeting is to plan the whole process for *the particular individual being appraised.* The process should not be conducted in a mechanical way as if the whole process operated like a conveyor belt. Either everyone can be treated the same or everyone can be treated equivalently. A bureaucratic approach would favour the former and a managerial approach would favour the latter. Thus the process should be tailored to the individual and particular features of them, their job and its context should be considered.

The meeting should cover three areas:

(a) Reassurance
(b) Special features
(c) Timescale

However much effort has been devoted to allaying the fears, suspicions and uncertainties of staff when the framework for the appraisal scheme was introduced and agreed, there will be for all staff to some degree a need for reassurance about the purpose and spirit in which the process will be conducted for them. The extent of reassurance needed must be carefully judged for each individual but it would be a mistake to underestimate the feeling of vulnerability of otherwise confident staff.

There will be the framework of the whole process for the school as an agenda to work through and agree a timescale but there should also be a consideration of special features. At almost every stage of the whole process there will be a need to identify features on which to concentrate special attention especially in the collection of evidence and classroom observation. These should be negotiated where there are differences of emphasis between appraiser and appraisee. The whole process needs to be productive for both parties and so within the bounds of reasonable time, no area which is important for either party should be neglected in the whole process.

Self-appraisal

Arguably the most valuable part of the appraisal process is for the appraisee to take time to stop and reflect about his or her work and the future. Some proforma which contains cues for reflection is generally very helpful in ensuring that all important areas are covered.

The framework introduced by Circular 12/91 has left self-appraisal as non-compulsory but encouraged. However, there is great merit in formally incorporating self-appraisal into the process and requiring a self-appraisal form to be completed as a document to form part of the agenda of the appraisal interview. This has a number of advantages particularly for the appraisees:

    they have prepared

    introduced evidence

    provided part of the agenda

    they should receive a considered response.

Appraisers are able to prepare for the interview knowing some of the thoughts of the appraisee. If there is any mismatch of expectations the appraiser has the opportunity to plan how to handle this in a skilful and effective way. Any suggestions which the appraisee makes about the future can be carefully considered before a response is made and any such response can then be more definite.

In many ways the formal self-appraisal helps to even up the relative positions of appraisee and appraiser and should make the whole process more productive.

Collection of evidence

Where the appraiser does not see the whole of the work of the appraisee, and this is endemic in a matrix structure, then there will be a need to collect some evidence on the performance of other important parts of the work of the appraisee. Some of this may be in documentary form but in addition it will almost certainly involve talking to other individuals. The particular appraisal scheme adopted in the school should contain the ground rules for the ethics of collecting such evidence but for each individual appraisee there will be a need to agree:

(a) from whom?
(b) in what form?
(c) about what?

Clearly in a matrix structure a principal contributor of evidence should be the other line manager of the individual. In secondary schools where the main appraisal chain is through subject departments, the appropriate pastoral leader should be one principal contributor of evidence.

Classroom observation and feedback

It should be remembered that any observation of teaching can only cover a tiny fraction of the teaching which a teacher does in a year. The sampling fraction is very small (about 1/2000) and thus its reliability and validity as a reflection of day-to-day teaching performance would be in some doubt even if the teaching observed were chosen to be representative. Anyone whose basic teaching competence is in doubt would require a much more intensive programme of classroom observation than could possibly be given to every member of staff. Thus classroom observation for the purposes of appraisal can only give a very rough and ready guide as to the teaching performance of the observed teacher. For, in addition to the problem of sampling there is the additional distortion of an observer in the classroom.

Probably the most valuable function of classroom observation is to give feedback to the teacher on aspects of his or her teaching which they would find particularly helpful. There may also be areas where the appraiser considers that feedback would be instructive to the teacher. There should, thus, be agreement about what aspects of teaching should receive attention and the sort of evidence which would be worth the considerable amount of time and effort required to gather it.

The evidence should be systematically collected and not be a series of summary judgements. At the feedback session shortly after the observation has been completed the evidence should be presented so that there is common ground before proceeding to make comments and inferences.

There needs to be agreement on classroom visits which covers:

to what groups?

when?

to see what?

for what purpose?

Circular 12/91 states that 'teachers should normally be observed teaching for a total of at least one hour, spread over two or more occasions' (Para 36). Where there are any serious doubts about aspects of teaching performance much more time will be required to collect evidence on which to build a secure improvement plan.

It should be remembered that although for the personal appraisal of teachers, teaching is the main focus of attention, it is pupil learning that is the ultimate aim of the school. Appropriate evidence, direct and indirect, of this should also be given due weight after making any allowance for the particular context of the teaching. Clearly, whilst it would not be right to hold the teacher solely accountable for their pupils' learning, equally the teacher should not be isolated from these effects. This needs very sensitive and realistic handling.

It is recommended that the feedback of the results of the observation of teaching should be discussed within two working days.

For those whose principal task in the school is not teaching, observation or other means of collecting evidence on the performance of their main activities should be used in place of or additional to classroom observation.

Interview

Agenda   The interview needs an agenda of some kind. There is a great deal of material to be covered. Either a few days before the meeting a provisional agenda needs to be prepared by the appraiser and circulated to the appraisee and briefly amended at the start of the interview or a fair amount of time needs to be spent at the start of the meeting negotiating an agenda. The second course of action is more difficult to accomplish successfully since it runs between two dilemmas. On the one hand there is the risk of being too rushed and either things being forgotten or of the appraisee receiving the impression that the agenda is all the appraiser's. Whilst on the other hand there is the risk of the discussion of the agenda slipping into an unstructured discussion of substantive issues which takes valuable time and makes further structured discussion of the same or related issues later rather repetitive.

If the formal self-appraisal document has been completed by the appraisee beforehand and the appraiser has had time to study this then a provisional agenda emerges and any features which need to be major features of the agenda will have been signalled.

General discussion Some specific areas which should be covered in the appraisal interview follow but the interview would lose its value if it only mechanically went through those issues. It must be a spontaneous dialogue on important issues for appraisee and appraiser. These include important developments in the past year; what areas of work give the appraisee satisfaction; praise from the appraiser for work genuinely well done and effort expended.

For the appraisee it provides a formal opportunity for them to be listened to. He or she is the centre of attention for a considerable period of time. He or she has the opportunity to make their point of view heard and to ask questions.

For the appraiser it provides an opportunity to reinforce school priorities and to examine perceptions of important events and developments for the school or college.

Check job description The appraisal interview provides the opportunity to check whether there have been changes to the job that the appraisee is doing or a change of emphasis which has not yet been recorded on his or her job description.

Checking through the job description can also be a useful way of checking perceptions of the relative importance of various elements on the job description.

Targets One of the outcomes of the interview which is recorded in the report should be a small number of targets which are

> Challenging but achievable;
>
> As precise as possible; and
>
> Worthwhile to the organisation and the individual

Questions to ask to help identify and firm up on targets:

1. How will you know when it is achieved?
2. How will you know you have done it well enough?
3. What is the challenging component (e.g. time, quality, innovative, uncertainty)?
4. What help and resources are needed from others in order to achieve it?
5. How can the manager help?
6. When should it be completed?
7. What are the potential sources of failure?
8. Are there any milestones or subtargets along the way?

The targets are in addition to the normal ongoing more routine work thus they should be few in number – probably not more than five at most. They may be:

Remedial	bringing an aspect of the job back to an acceptable level of performance;
Developmental	developing an aspect of the job;
Problem solving	finding a way of overcoming some problem aspect of the job; and
Personal developmental	identifying some temporary task which contributes to personal development but which may not be part of the enduring job description

Targets can be expected to change regularly. Many will be completed in one year.

Training and development Some areas for development should emerge from the appraisal process. They may be developments to the task from which the appraisee learns and develops or they may be personal developments largely unrelated to the main job. Such developments will need some degree of planning in consultation with the appraiser or other person.

Where this involves a modification of a part of the job of the appraisee others may be involved.

To prepare for a new task or to improve the performance of an existing task, training may be required. If the training is by an external course or if other resources are involved, these costs have to be obtained. It is highly likely that more training needs will emerge from the appraisal process than can be funded so mechanisms to prioritise the funding of training will need to operate in conjunction with the appraisal process. Any decisions from this prioritisation process have to be communicated to the appraisee and appropriate modifications to the appraisal plans and report have to be made. Thus a swift decision is required on each request before the appraisal of all individuals is completed. If decisions are to be made at the whole school level, sophisticated arrangements are needed to consider each case taking account of the recommendation of the appraiser.

In a large school or college where there are sizeable numbers of staff in a subunit, a more flexible arrangement may be to delegate reasonable sums for training purposes to the head of the subunit so that decisions can be made quicker and with a greater degree of knowledge of all the circumstances. This should also facilitate the anticipation and communication of priorities by appraisers to appraisees so that unrealistic expectations are not built up during the appraisal process.

Job changes One possibility which may arise from appraisal is the need for an individual to widen their experience by undertaking either additional tasks or replacement tasks. This can contribute to their development if it is a planned learning opportunity and aid their career development.

For those who have done the same job for some time a change of parts of the job may prove stimulating if the need for a change is suggested by the appraisee or at least is approved by the appraisee.

Career plans The appraisal interview provides an opportunity for the appraisee to explore their career plans and to receive feedback from their appraiser on its realism. Some appraisees may need encouraging to be more ambitious in their career planning and others may have to be told that little further career progress is possible in this school in promotion terms.

The appraisal process also offers the opportunity to facilitate the career plans of individuals by allowing the planning of development opportunities which are particularly appropriate for their chosen career path or to explore a number of options in order to help decide on the right one.

Organisational changes The appraisal interview provides a formal opportunity to raise organisational blockages or other organisational constraints which make the teacher's job harder or less rewarding.

Even if no immediate changes are possible this provides a valuable intelligence gathering opportunity for the manager. It may be when the interviews are completed that clear trends have emerged which in the medium term it may be possible to move towards a solution or at least an amelioration.

Statement

The appraisal statement provides an enduring record of a long and wide ranging discussion. It has to provide the continuity to the next appraisal interview in two years' time. Thus important points of agreement for action by both parties should be recorded.

The record is written by the appraiser from notes taken at the time but the record has to be approved by the appraisee who may record any points of disagreement if they so wish within 20 working days of the appearance of the statement (DES, 1991).

The review meeting in the following year will amend the statement if there have been changes to targets or other action points in the intervening period.

A separate record of targets and training needs is required because both have a wider circulation than the essentially confidential report. The chair of governors has a right to view the targets of staff (DES, 1991) and the staff development coordinator or other person responsible for INSET needs to know of training and development needs.

Follow-up

At the appraisal interview and in the report there will be references to plans and targets. These may involve:

Attendance at training courses;

Coaching;

Work shadowing;

Change of job;

Extra resources;

Developments to the job; and

Personal development.

Some of these may involve negotiation and sanction of others or the deployment of resources from limited funds. In which case, at the time of writing the report they may be provisional or even speculative. At the earliest opportunity any such tentative plans should be confirmed or altered so that as soon as possible feasible and reasonably precise plans can be agreed.

All parties should play their part in helping to realise the plans. What has been agreed by the school and manager should be delivered to facilitate the efforts of the appraisee. There should be brief but regular follow-up to discuss the achievement of progress on the plans. If any major event occurs which throws the achievement of the plans or targets into doubt, the plans should be renegotiated at the earliest opportunity rather than wait until the review meeting in the following year to rather limply discover that no progress had been made due to circumstances outside the appraisee's control.

Review meeting

The review meeting during the early stages of the following year is the formal opportunity to review progress on the plans and targets.

Any agreed changes to the plans and targets made at the appraisal interview should be recorded in the appraisal statement. The fact that the review meeting has taken place and its date should be recorded on the statement.

Next cycle

Having completed one two yearly cycle much valuable experience will have been gained with which to begin the next cycle. And in addition there will be progress to review on the plans and targets which were set at the first appraisal interview. This is the pattern for the future – it is the first cycle which is the unusual one when there are no plans to review at the first appraisal interview and a whole range of pent up issues which have never been discussed before.

3.1 Experience from pilot schemes of staff appraisal in schools

Brian Fidler

Introduction

Six English LEAs received funding from the DES between 1987 and 1989 to pilot schemes of schoolteacher appraisal. The LEAs were Croydon, Cumbria, Newcastle, Salford, Somerset and Suffolk. The schemes were evaluated by a team from the Cambridge Institute of Education (Bradley et al, 1989). This section largely draws on that experience although other LEAs and individual schools have continued to operate or introduce pilot schemes of appraisal and thus there is wider experience on which to draw. There follows first hand accounts of appraisal in two primary schools from Ian Johnston of Cumbria and Peter Delaney of Salford in sections 3.2.1 and 3.2.2, and two secondary schools from Keith Barnes of Berkshire and Mike Vaughan-Edwards of Cheshire in sections 3.3.1 and 3.3.2.

The following are the areas from which there is evaluation data:
- Training
- Preparation and data gathering
- Classroom observation
- Appraisal interview and target setting
- Appraisal and school development

Training

Training of two types was found to be needed – awareness raising and skills for two groups – appraisers and appraisees.

There is a further need to deal at some length with scheme design for any school adopting and tailoring an appraisal scheme to meet its needs, rather than taking on an off-the-peg LEA scheme. This would go far beyond anything which could be described as 'awareness raising'. When the scheme is designed it then needs commitment from all who have to operate it. INSET days provide an excellent opportunity for the whole school teaching staff to spend considerable time dealing with these issues.

Courses which bring together staff from different schools and from different levels were thought to be valuable.

Where appropriate management training has already been provided, a number of concepts and skills involved in staff management cover many of the appraisal skills. The training should not all be 'front-end loaded', i.e. some top-up training should take place after practice has been attempted.

Preparation and data gathering

As a preparation for appraisal, whole school review can be used to generate data relating to quite a lot of the school's operations. In addition to providing some 'neutral' data this can also focus attention on appraisal as a way of improving the education of children rather than being solely about staff and their performance.

An initial planning meeting of about half an hour for each appraisee was found to be very important at the start of the appraisal cycle. Self-appraisal was found to be very important and for many work was needed to encourage them to be more positive and less self-critical, although not surprisingly, the pilot schemes found varying levels of honesty displayed by appraisees.

Two stage documentation was found to be helpful. The first stage was a very private process by which the appraisee considered their own work in confidence and as a second stage, documentation was completed by the appraisee as a contribution to the appraisal interview.

Further informed opinion was found to be useful (Bradley et al, p.16) (including observation and self-appraisal) but the problems were found to be:

1. Time taken;
2. Some individuals are over-used;
3. Confidentiality/ethical/honesty problems in giving feedback on another

(these problems were especially the case for heads and others with a management role)

Classroom observation

The pilot schemes regarded classroom observation as 'an essential component of the appraisal process' (p.19).

All the schemes used a 'clinical supervision' cycle:
   Preparation;
   Observation; and
   Feed back.

There was initial apprehension before observation and a general unease about the criteria for effective teaching and the making of judgements. Generally it was the appraiser who observed in the classroom. Feedback was given within 48 hours but was sometimes in two tranches – immediate and considered. The very high costs in terms of teacher time were noted and at least one LEA suggested that classroom observation need not occur each year. However, many participants considered that the observation was very valuable for both appraiser and appraisee.

The pilot schemes provided some preparation for classroom observation skills. These and observation practice were better at illustrating the complexity of trying to appraise teaching validly than at developing skills.

The pattern of observation tended to be a first observation which was general and more accountability based whilst the emphasis for remaining ones was more specific and focused. It could be negotiated and was more developmental.

Despite training which emphasised the need to collect data which was descriptive, there was some evidence of notes recording judgements rather than facts, thus for some appraisers a great deal of carefully supervised preparation will be necessary to ensure that their appraisees are enabled to develop.

The evaluation concluded 'careful preparation and immediate feedback are essential to the success of classroom observation' (Bradley et al: p.22).

Appraisal interview and target setting

The evaluation report (p.27) stated:
> The interview discussion was seen by the majority as the most rewarding part of the appraisal experience

It built closer relationships between appraiser and appraisee and improved communication in school.

A number of methods were used in the pilot schemes to set the agenda for the appraisal interview but what was quite clear (p.26) was that it is

> vital that appraiser and appraisee are both aware of the agenda that is being followed and have prepared carefully for the interview

The skills needed for a successful interview (listening, problem solving approach and appropriate questioning technique) and the factors likely to lead to a successful interview (preparation, clear agenda, adequate time, good skills, giving it high priority and no interruptions) were very predictable. It was found better for an appraiser to conduct only one interview in any one day.

The previous relationship between appraiser and appraisee was found to condition the appraisal interview. This was less of a problem in some pilot schemes where there was an element of participation in the choice of appraiser by appraisees. In a managerial approach as laid down in the Circular, the appraiser should normally be someone with 'management responsibility' for the teacher. Thus any difficulties in the relationship between appraiser and appraisee should be worked through not only for the appraisal process but for the on-going managerial relationship.

Writing the agreed statement should be done immediately and proved trickier than expected. The appraiser generally took notes during the appraisal interview and wrote the report as soon as possible after the interview. One possibility was to pass back a draft of the report to the appraisee and to negotiate the final content.

Appraisal documents should have a clearly stated confidentiality. A separate more public INSET or resource requirement document could be made available to collate staff development needs.

Targets were long and short term covering classroom strategies, school performance and career development.

Appraisal and school development

As the evaluation report (p.31) noted:

> Teacher appraisal, headteacher appraisal, whole school review, school development plans, curriculum planning and INSET planning are all related and might beneficially be linked in a coherent and coordinated strategy in order to achieve maximum impact

One pilot LEA got schools to do a GRIDS (McMahon et al, 1984) whole school review before appraisal as one way of bringing school needs to the fore. This worked better in primary schools than secondary. The support of the head for the process was found to be crucial in both. Appraisal could focus on issues identified in school review.

3.2 Appraisal in primary schools

3.2.1 A tool for performance and professional development at St Edmunds RC School, Salford

Peter Delaney

Introduction

Appraisal will become a working reality for every teacher in England and Wales during 1991–95. The publishing of the National Steering Group Report, *School Teacher Appraisal: A National Framework* (DES, 1989) was the beginning of a period of further appraisal innovation at St Edmunds School. A fully operational appraisal scheme had been established in 1983 and had functioned quite effectively until industrial action brought it to a halt in 1987 (Delaney, 1988).

The staff and I decided to reintroduce and redesign the scheme and incorporate the main features of the National Framework, taking into account the experience of the six pilot LEAs who contributed to the National Steering Group Report. In the face of the rapidly changing world and the increasing demands on schools in the 1990s it is becoming even more important that individual and school development should be a more controlled process focused to achieve what is best for children in our school and supporting our aims and objectives. Our focus on individual growth and institutional development will make our appraisal process an integral part of our school development plan.

The National Steering Group Report recommended an agreed National Framework for supportive and developmental appraisal. We recognised that setting up an appraisal scheme is an integral part of school management at a time when much attention is being paid to management issues. One clear reason is the demand which arises from the wide range of reforms introduced by the 1986 and 1988 *Education Acts*.

It is worth reiterating that school management has not changed as a result of the reforms. The essentials remain the same. Managing is about people and how to work together to achieve certain goals. Having those goals redefined does not make dealing with people any harder or easier. Once we begin to work with and through others by delegation and dialogue to achieve mutually agreed aims, then appraisal is part of the process. The capacity to communicate, to delegate, to influence and encourage, to motivate and value, is the very essence of managing appraisal.

The evidence from the six LEA pilots indicates that this essence lies in relationships – in feedback from one human being to another. Our appraisal scheme must be based on trust and provide for the continuous professional development of the staff. The experience of the pilots has demonstrated with overwhelming forcefulness something that seems almost too self evident to be worth stating. Giving time and attention to people gives high dividends.

Many in management positions bring out the cliché from time to time that people are our most valuable resource. Yet do we always acknowledge this in what we do? People often slip down a school's agenda pushed out by deadlines, systems and paper. We felt that appraisal gives people priority and provides a new dimension to staff development approaches.

There is a history of in-service training largely being offered on an à la carte menu from which teachers made their selection. Our view is that appraisal can lead to a development plan and a negotiated training contract between teachers and schools. We hope that this situation will bring fresh insight into the meaning of professional development. Too often in the past this has been interpreted as preparation for promotion to a new post. While it may be appropriate at certain times to focus on this aspect of career development it is immensely stimulating and rewarding to work on the continuing enhancement of skills needed in the current job.

School description

St Edmunds RC Primary School is a Group 2 primary school in Salford LEA. It is situated in an outer suburb of the city which was formerly a division of the Lancashire LEA. It is a one form entry school comprising a nursery unit, three infant and four junior classes. We have eight full-time teachers, one nursery nurse and myself. Areas covered by curriculum specialists include:

- Science;
- Maths;
- Computer technology;
- Reading and language development;
- Humanities;
- Music; and
- Parental liaison.

The school is organised in normal age bands. Of the 230 on roll, two thirds live in a well established council estate and one third in private housing inside the parish boundaries. There are strong links between the school and the local community. Many of the parents were educated at the school and show great loyalty and support to all aspects of our provision. We have a well established PTA.

Since the 1970s we have had a stable staff with the opportunities that offers for school cohesion and the development of shared perspectives. A high level of in-service activity and school based debate and dialogue has characterised the school.

Introducing the scheme

We adopted the pilot strategy of appointing an appraisal co-ordinator as a 'change agent' as the formal appraisal structure was introduced into our school. The stages in the introduction were as follows:

1. Creating a favourable climate

The staff reached agreement on these key concepts:

- Appraisal is not a device for detecting and removing incompetent staff. Procedures already exist for doing this. True developmental appraisal starts from the premise of teacher acceptance.
- The teacher in our school is central to the process. Appraisal is not done to them. The appraiser and appraisee are professional partners in a structured review of the appraisee's work. The aim

is to acknowledge our teacher's successes and achievements to identify areas for individual development and to agree a pattern and a method for improving work with inbuilt time to review targets.

- Appropriate relationships should exist in our school, i.e. those conducive to trust and confidence in our appraisal process to those conducting it and their credibility.
- An appreciation that our senior management team accepts staff development as a major function inside the school development plan and will therefore link appraisal and needs identification with support and positive action to follow.
- Appraisal must reflect the usual development and growth initiatives at both personal and organisational levels.

2. *Preliminaries to introduction*

- We have clear aims/guidelines for curriculum management and organisation.
- Staff job descriptions for 'core' and 'foundation' subjects are negotiated and published.
- Our administrative systems are able to facilitate the collection, organisation, use and recording of data which is produced by the appraisal process, e.g. staff profiles, updated job descriptions, classroom observation prompt lists, summary reports, appraisal interview agendas, self appraisal documents etc.
- Our school has a clearly stated, agreed and shared perception of the nature of effective teaching and classroom organisation.
- The senior management team is fully committed to the process and procedures of appraisal.
- We agree that improvement in performance can only be achieved if the appraisal is able to raise areas of concern and possible aspects to improve. Our experience at St Edmunds indicates that unless a teacher is told about the less good things, and constructively criticised when it is warranted, performance appraisal is less than effective.
- Visiting and working alongside colleagues in their classrooms must be accepted practice in our school. Classroom observation will extend and structure the shared analysis and examination of classroom provision.

3. Planning the programme

Familiarisation An 'appraisal co-ordinator' was chosen by the staff. A training programme was devised and carried out, so this teacher could become a 'catalyst' in the staff familiarisation process. Over a two week period she became aware of the purpose and procedure of appraisal embodied in the National Framework. Her training programme was school and LEA based. She quickly became equipped to speak from a point of authority and confidence and was able to answer colleagues' questions and reassure doubts. Her acceptance of the underlying values and objectives of the National Framework and its potential for professional development assisted her in putting across a positive image and allaying genuine anxieties.

Dissemination and discussion Over a period of four weeks the appraisal co-ordinator set up a series of staff meetings, informal discussions, a 'training day' and input from LEA Appraisal Development Officers. These activities led to the setting up of a 'School Development Group' to share in the next stage of designing the scheme devising an implementation strategy and creating a sense of ownership of the process. The 'School Development Group' reflected the different levels of experience and seniority in the school, i.e. a broad spectrum of experience. The school co-ordinator chaired the group and produced the documentation of the final programme. The main task of the 'Group' was to draw up documentation about the nature and purpose of appraisal and to facilitate debate, analysis and examination of the components of the National Framework. At the end of the four week period the 'Group' had produced:

Job descriptions for all staff including the headteacher;

Staff professional development career profiles;

Agreed policy for effective classroom teaching and classroom observation;

Self-appraisal forms to assist appraisal interview preparation;

Agendas and topics for the appraisal interview.

4. Implementing the programme: essential elements

Job description We agreed that job descriptions should be drawn up before any data was gathered on the teachers' performance. There was general agreement that this description of the main tasks and responsibilities of a job needs to be agreed rather than imposed and is to be seen as a means of clarifying staff roles and responsibilities and can provide criteria for reviewing the work of individual teachers. We regarded the document as a working agreement between head teacher and teacher rather than a contractual device. Conditions of service provide the latter. We felt that when appraisal leads to the identification of new skills and expertise or underutilised skills, this in turn would lead to a modification of the job description.

Initial meeting This is between the head teacher and the teacher at the start of each appraisal cycle and is crucial to the rest of the process. This meeting is the occasion for establishing or confirming sound rapport between the appraiser and teacher; setting a context in which the negotiation of the appraisal agenda is seen to be important; and clarifying for both parties what will happen and when. We also agreed the format and use of documentation for self-appraisal, the arrangements for classroom observation and the methods other than classroom observation by which data for the appraisal should be collected, i.e. discussions with colleagues etc. An appraisal interview preparation agenda and logistics were also clarified and agreed.

We found that time committed to the initial meeting should not be skimped if the teacher is to feel confident and clear about the process: clear shared sense of purpose is essential. The time and care we took at this initial meeting led to the smooth running of the rest of the programme. Brief and hurried initial meetings could be followed by a mismatch of expectations and perceptions as the appraisal gained momentum.

Teaching observation and support This is a process whereby the staff are supported and assisted by an experienced colleague in a combination of self-appraisal, classroom observation and objective setting. It was agreed that my deputy or myself would conduct the actual observation in the classroom.

To prepare for this aspect of appraisal, schools need to encourage an open climate of collaborative work in which visiting colleagues' classrooms becomes a regular activity for all teachers. If classroom observation takes place only once during the annual appraisal it is bound to be intimidating for many staff. The staff at my school appreciated the opportunity to share the complexities and uncertainties of classroom activities.

It marked the beginning of a sharing of experience and openness of approach and a move away from competition and closeted individualism.

The components of a scheme were:

(a) Development of a teaching policy which will help to form the shared basis for observation. Our teaching policy reflected recent research into teaching effectiveness and the practical knowledge of teaching in the school.

(b) Actual process and procedures. We adopted the LEA pilot position on classroom observation procedures. All advocated a three phase cycle:

Planning,

Observation of Teaching, and

Feedback Discussion.

Planning meeting This meeting is to make sure the purpose is clearly understood; to decide how the observation will be conducted; and what the observer will look for; to clarify when and how data in the classroom will be gathered and recorded; and to agree how feedback will be provided and how long the teacher will be observed. The teacher and observer also review carefully curriculum projections, schemes of work, and general class teaching priorities. A convenient and suitable time for the visit is selected.

Observation of teaching It was made clear that the observation should be seen as one key part in the process of gathering information about the teacher's classroom practice as a prelude to the appraisal interview. It is crucial that observers have a clear understanding of the context in which the observed lesson is given and its aims and purposes. I was fully briefed by the teacher prior to the visit with special attention being paid to the focus of the observation. We adopted the practice of balancing general and specific observations, i.e. a general observation for the first observation as a means of identifying areas for specific focus for subsequent observations.

Feedback discussion The staff and I felt that we should have a meeting or feedback session as soon as possible after the observation, i.e. certainly within 48 hours. The main objectives for this meeting were to jointly analyse and interpret the observation information, to prepare targets for the modification or improvement of classroom effectiveness and to give the teacher scope for informed self-analysis. Solutions agreed by the teacher and myself became the focus for the teacher's self-initiated development plan. We also drew up a negotiated and agreed summary report which was further discussed at the subsequent appraisal interview.

In the early stages the staff looked forward to observation with some anxiety but generally found it a stimulating rather than daunting experience.

Appraisal interview The extended discussion between the teacher and myself is an essential component of appraisal and requires a great deal of planning. Objectives are to review the teacher's work, identify success areas which could be developed, identify training or development needs, and agree targets for further action.

Arrangements for the interview at St Edmunds ensured that it took place in comfortable surroundings with no interruptions. With an agenda for discussion agreed in advance, the teacher felt he or she was able to talk about their work in a supportive atmosphere and a mutually convenient time was chosen with at least one hour set aside for the meeting.

The interviews covered the following points:

> Review of the teacher's job description.
>
> Review of the work done, successes and constraints and areas for development.
>
> Discussion of a plan for development in agreed areas.
>
> Discussion of INSET and professional development needs and career development if appropriate.
>
> Agreement on the points to be included in the summary statement.

The staff and I considered the interviews successful only when both parties were well informed and well prepared, the topics to be discussed were agreed in advance, discussion concentrated on the areas on which information gathering had focused, and the interview was free from interruption.

The staff felt that the interview discussion was the most rewarding part of the appraisal experience but it was dependent upon the quality of relationship between appraiser and appraisee.

Summary record We followed the pilot practice of drawing up a summary record after the interview. This record is a summary of the interview discussion and includes objectives or targets for the appraiser and appraisee. We found the majority of actions involve future tasks and responsibilities to be carried out by the teacher and supported by the head and school.

I found it advisable to write the summary record immediately after the interview. I as appraiser found it useful to paraphrase and agree each action with the teacher as we went along. To maintain momentum and impact I handed the draft summary record back to the teacher as soon as possible, which allowed them time to read through and negotiate the content if required.

My experience indicates that, in the main the teachers and I were able to negotiate amicably the summary record and the majority of disagreements were of a minor nature, e.g. wording, incorrect dates etc.

Summary and conclusions

Our appraisal scheme has been operational in its present form for one school year. We owe a great deal to the work of the pilot LEAs whose research and endeavours will be reflected in the National Appraisal Framework which will be obligatory in all LEAs from 1991.

Can our experience at St Edmunds help other schools to introduce formal appraisal schemes? We feel that the following conditions are essential for successful introduction:

1. Vigorous and whole-hearted support of head teacher and senior staff.
2. Recognition that appraisal is not just an evaluation of the teacher's performance but part of a feedback loop which helps to indicate whether the whole system is working. Appraisal should be developmental for the school as well as for the teacher.
3. Appraisal must be socially acceptable. Staff must be willing to use it and regard it as a vehicle for support and encouragement.
4. Process and procedures should be administratively convenient and should be tailored for application in individual schools. It should be regarded as a regular process of development rather than as a threatening ordeal.
5. Appraisal should fit into the managerial style and overall culture of the school and must not limit that degree of professional independence which is so important to teachers.
6. Above all, there must be a climate of trust, because judgements and feeling about each other must be shared freely, openly and honestly. Schools must recognise this fact and in the early stages should not expect interactions of a nature and quality which usually only occur in special relationships. Patience, mutual trust, and respect are required in full measure.

3.2.2 Pilot appraisal scheme at Arnside National School, Cumbria

Iain Johnston

Introduction

The case study concerns a medium sized rural primary school with a staff of eight teachers. The teachers work collaboratively and participate actively in decision making and in a variety of INSET activities. This case study is intended to give a picture of a school which saw involvement in teacher appraisal as an opportunity for enhancing its development work for the school as a whole and for the teachers as individuals. The text is written by the head with extracts from the diaries of two members of staff.

Preparing for appraisal

Appraisal is more than simply classroom observation or the appraisal conference. Indeed to have the impact which is wished, both for the individual teacher and the school, appraisal has to be embedded into the rhythm of the school's day to day activities. Among the preparatory activities are the establishment or enhancement of a positive climate, and the involvement of the staff in making decisions about school development.

Towards the end of 1986 the school was already actively concerned with an organised pattern of whole school development and individual counselling towards professional development and career planning. The staff had begun to explore various published guides to assist the school audit. They had taken a provisional look at GRIDS (McMahon et al, 1984) to concentrate thoughts and direct them towards a positive approach. Straight away this stimulated staff discussion in a most constructive manner and members were encouraged to talk freely about their strengths and doubts and to consider areas of responsibility they would wish to assume under the soon to arrive 'Conditions of Service'.

It was at this stage that the school became involved in the LEA's pilot for a national scheme of teacher appraisal.

Extract from Sue's diary, 5th March, 1987:

> Staff Meeting – Iain brought up the subject of appraisal and asked how we would feel about being involved as part of the first group in the national pilot. The staff were very positive. I felt that if appraisal were going to be introduced into education along with increased accountability, it would be beneficial to be involved from the beginning.

This extract from Barbara's diary illustrates the dangers of a negative school climate:

> I have to admit I felt terribly defensive at any suggestion of appraisal. I once worked in a school where the head teacher allowed undercurrents of rumour, stress, and criticism among his staff. The thought of that head conducting an appraisal was soul destroying. My new job at this school, however, is much more satisfying, although informal after lunch discussions in the staff room about 'appraisal' did little to comfort me. This head, for whom I have a lot of respect, did make the point that the whole aim of appraisal was to raise the standard of teaching and we all agreed that we would be happy to take part in the pilot.

Barbara and Sue agreed that:

> The school has a very special ethos of positive enthusiasm and communication and the teachers genuinely work together supporting and caring for each other. This would be a distinct advantage in appraisal.

Training

Training began in March 1987 and involved all members of staff in two-day residential sessions to consider the needs of an appraisal scheme and the bases for its development. Also included were interview and personal interaction skills, awareness raising and self-review techniques for all delegates. The whole process was developed by the teachers involved and included patterns of good practice and full discussion of the potentially contentious issues, all the time producing a supportive, non-threatening process. The training sessions were exciting and promoted enthusiastic responses from even the most apprehensive of teachers.

Barbara:

Things began to move very fast. In groups we attended the conferences. I was open-minded, enthusiastic but nervous. After about two hours of the first day, it seemed that everyone was talking from different standpoints. The course leaders seemed to know about appraisal, what it involved, etc. but they weren't telling us. Instead we were busy doing things on experiential lines, breaking the ice, getting to know each other and about our schools and jobs. I thought the main event was passing me by. Then we did an exercise which made us think hard about our jobs, about teaching and about children. We had a time limit and I was working with a partner I hadn't known previously. As the atmosphere lightened we chatted more easily. I had to write down my aims for education, how I saw my job at school, how things could be improved. Suddenly it was a relief to move away from the demands of four and five year olds and to have the opportunity to talk about new research, recent movements, basic philosophies and our own personal attitudes in education. It was good too to hear about the problems and strengths of other schools. Later I realised that I had been asking the wrong questions about appraisal. I had been expecting a package to be imposed, instead we were approaching the whole process from the ethos that appraisal should be about self-analysis, self-exploration and communicating with others.

We watched videos of teachers at work as though we were appraisers and we tried to work out a basis for teaching analysis. We seemed to pose a lot of questions but came up with no definite answers. One thing emerged, however, that appraisal is a two way process and that appraisee and appraiser must meet beforehand in an atmosphere of mutual trust, confidence and communication to negotiate groundrules.

Sue:

We took part in role playing sessions in which we were in turn appraiser, appraisee, and observer. We realised the tremendous potential of the situation – a chance to make our own professional views known and to justify our beliefs and practices. This part of the training gave a clear understanding to the trainees that being an appraiser was a far more difficult task than being an appraisee. Assertiveness became a password and it became clear that teachers need to be absolutely sure of what they want to say and be prepared to say it.

The training for appraisal left some of the members feeling enthusiastic, empowered to cope, and with a boosted self-esteem. Older, more experienced teachers expressed regret that appraisal had not been around fifteen years ago believing that it would have helped them in their professional development.

Whole school review

Our approach to appraisal as part of whole school development requires some form of school review and self-evaluation. This strategy fulfils three purposes:

1. Provision of a context for appraisal – it is far less threatening to individual teachers if the school has been 'appraised' first. They can then set their own individual appraisal within that framework.
2. Improvement of communication between teachers to reach a common understanding of the implications of change upon available resources.
3. Linking school review to teacher appraisal results in a much more powerful strategy for school improvement.

We viewed appraisal as a developmental rather than an accountability exercise so if the teacher is appraised within the context of the school, then school improvement will result. Again we used GRIDS but in the light of previous experience, we altered the questionnaire slightly and changed the grading from a three point to a ten point scale. This gave a more precise indication of areas for review and the measure of priority given to these concerns. The use of a scheme like GRIDS or IMTEC (Dalin and Rust, 1983), although not perfect for our needs, is better than isolated self-review as the questions which are posed may not be the most obvious and they help to concentrate thought on a wider spectrum of issues. Over a period of two weeks the package was introduced, completed and the results collated.

The collated results revealed several minor, easily rectifiable, but nevertheless important issues, some concerning lack of communication. Liaison between primary and secondary was highlighted as an area of concern. Actually this school works very closely with its 'partner' secondary school but the liaison has been mainly between teachers of upper juniors and first year tutors. The teachers who had expressed their concern were involved with younger children and had never been included in the arrangements. A 'training day' visit by all members of staff to the secondary school whilst it was in session immediately began to correct that issue.

Concerns of the teaching staff, not unnaturally, centred on the curriculum but rather than simply identifying subjects, the process had given the opportunity finely to tune the specific areas for review. In maths a review was needed to fill in the holes and improve the scope of the published scheme which was the basis of work in the school. In English the identified need was for a more adequate and standardised system of record keeping to ensure development. Two working parties were set up with myself (maths) and the deputy (English) as equal members of the teams. It proved to be an invaluable exercise in staff involvement, giving the opportunity in school time to work together and to contribute equally to the formulation of new codes of practice and the confirmation of curriculum statements. Because of their involvement, teachers became more aware of other teachers' strengths and also the problems faced by their colleagues even within the primary phase. The identification of areas of strength as well as weakness within the school assists in the ordering or priorities for individual teacher development as well as highlighting the implications for whole school in-service training. The reports and findings were presented to the full staff for discussion. Care had to be exercised at this stage not to raise hopes which could not be fulfilled within the resources of the school. Merely because an area has been identified for development does not necessarily mean that it can be dealt with immediately nor that funds or expertise will be readily available. Awareness of the danger of raising false expectations is an important feature of appraisal management.

Managing appraisal

The management of the process must ensure that appraisal is:

Planned with identified goals and objectives and realistic resourcing,

Organised so that individuals and groups are clear about their roles and the expectation placed upon them,

Monitored so that plans and organisations can be adapted and modified in the light of accumulated experience,

Able to offer appropriate stimulus/incentives for teachers to want to become meaningfully involved, and

Developmental creating opportunities for teachers to build and grow through direct experience.

Some of the diary notes made during our first experience illustrate these points.

With all members of the staff involved, discussions continued at the school maintaining a high degree of consensus over the way forward. It was established that my deputy and I would each appraise three members of staff and the whole process would begin with my appraising the deputy.

Sue:

> There was some concern at school over who was going to be appraised by whom. After the training I felt the matter of appraiser was not so crucial, as we had been shown how to conduct the interview as a dialogue.

Barbara:

> Iain said he wished to do some of the appraisals, of course, but he also wanted our recently appointed deputy to do some too. Sue, Gill and I said that we didn't mind being appraised by Nick. We agreed on dates for our appraisals. I chose my particular week avoiding any chance of PMT.

The arrangements for each appraisal were made individually between appraisee and appraiser. They followed a pattern which was open to individual negotiation. The procedure began with an initial meeting during which agreement was negotiated over a suitable timetable, the establishment of groundrules and priorities for the classroom observation, time for 'instant feed-back', the date, time and venue of the conference and the identification of areas for discussion.

Classroom observation

This was accorded a prime place in our appraisal process but it was by no means the only way to gather information for appraisal. The ACAS Report (1986) said that classroom observation should 'reflect the balance between the teaching load and other responsibilities outside the classroom'.

At the initial meeting it is important to agree what the appraiser should do when present in the teaching area. Various options are open, from one extreme: a formal (non-participant) observation session, where the appraiser sits unobtrusively within the teaching area perhaps taking notes or referring to a checklist of areas of focus drawn up by the appraisee and appraiser before the session; or at the other extreme: the wholehearted involvement of the appraiser in the teaching during the session(s) (participant observation). In our experience the arrangements always approached the latter to a greater or lesser degree.

In this school co-operative teaching takes place all the time. This is both a product of the design of the building and the management style in which staff contributions to whole school development are given equal value. Even before the appraisal project there was already a positive and constructive attitude to working as a team and sharing each other's strengths and enthusiasms. Despite this collaborative and caring climate within the school, and the appraisal training for all participants, there was still a degree of nervousness amongst the appraisees as the time for their observation sessions came closer.

The length of the observation is negotiable but usually involves two sessions (say the equivalent of half a day in all). It is followed by a short feedback session when both appraiser and appraisee can comment on instant impressions or point out the peculiarities of that session. Care must be taken not to make too much of this chat and pre-empt the full discussion which is to follow. As an appraiser I find the observation sessions to be very rewarding experiences, quite different from the frequent occasions when I work alongside my colleagues. During an appraisal there is a sharpened focus and the expectation of fruitful discussion. Areas of focus chosen by the appraisees as the focus for the task observation ranged through relationships, dealing with emergencies, development of individual learning programmes, record keeping, displays, lesson planning, topic work and integration, in fact almost the whole scene of activities engaged upon by a class teacher.

Sue:
> I spent the previous evening worrying about whether I had been wise in choosing the deputy as my appraiser, as our philosophy and teaching styles are so different. I mentioned this to Nick and we managed to arrange a short meeting. I felt this was very important and it is essential that provision is made for such meetings to discuss fears as they arise before they get out of hand.

Barbara:
> (23 Oct.) I spent a day planning the next few weeks' work running up to Christmas. My appraisal was to be the next week. Nick and I had planned a programme of discussions beginning on Monday, but we had already talked about what would happen in the classroom during the task observation. I was anxious to make him understand that my day would be totally 'normal', planned as usual, that nothing extra or special would take place just for the sake of appraisal.
> (2nd Nov.) Last minute nervousness. So far I had been very positive, reassuring myself that appraisal is a good idea if it takes place in an atmosphere of good communication. Nick and I were due to meet at 2.30 today to discuss the basis for classroom observation. He arrived and was apprehensive too. We agreed that he should come to my classroom at 8.45 as I opened the doors for the children and parents, and stay until lunchtime. He should sit unobtrusively during his observation. I asked him not to initiate any discussions or exploration with my class, but if the children approached him he should respond positively.
> (3rd Nov.) Nick arrived just as I was opening the doors for the parents. He was visibly apprehensive and I fell into a reassurance role. Then he disappeared from my consciousness as I became involved with the children. At the end of the morning we were to have a 10 minute immediate feedback session. As the children left for lunch the room became terrifyingly quiet and I was so nervous, wondering what he would say. However, he seemed very happy with all he had seen during the morning....relief, exhilaration! I was on a high. But then I began to wonder....surely there must have been something wrong. Surely some improvement could be made. These misgivings began to preoccupy me and this post-analysis paranoia increased when the head came to ask me how I was feeling. 'Nick is pleased,' he said, 'and I'm sure you'll have a good conference tomorrow. I think there'll be

plenty to talk about.' BANG! HELP! There was something wrong – and he had discussed it with the head. So much for confidentiality. My reaction was one of self-defence. Iain quickly saw that I was hurt and angry and we had a good half hour's calming down session. I was concerned that Nick had gone to the head with criticisms. I realised that the head is officially in charge of my appraisal and must know how things had gone. 'But we must talk it all out together,' I protested.

My anger, though understandable, was completely unfounded. Nick had not discussed anything behind my back. Nothing had been said beyond, 'How was it?' 'Fine, great, looking forward to tomorrow.' In my state of heightened sensitivity I had misinterpreted the head's words. A lesson for the future – watch out for those emotions. We're all vulnerable.

Barbara emphasised the importance of the appraiser's knowing the context and aims of the lesson. She also valued the instant feedback. She has since had the experience of classroom observation from the appraiser's point of view and her experiences have been an invaluable source of professional development.

Appraisal conference

The conference is the hub of the appraisal process. The information gathering preparation activities and task analysis can, we have seen, serve as opportunities for development in themselves. Nevertheless they can only be considered truly successful if they inform a productive appraisal conference. That is the opportunity for reflection on previous work with the aim of agreeing plans for the future. It is potentially a sensitive occasion, dealing as it does with matters at the heart of a teacher's career and job. It is also an occasion which can trigger further professional development and growth.

The conferences took place within a day or so of the task analysis. The venue and times were again chosen by the appraisees. In each case the agenda was agreed beforehand so that both appraisee and appraiser could prepare the areas for discussion. The outline agenda included:

> *Classroom observation* The first part of the discussion. A two way conversation with constructive and critical comment from both parties. It is a useful time when teachers can justify their actions and can bounce ideas off a professional colleague.
>
> *Current year* The agenda continues with a reflective view of the appraisee's last year, looking firstly at the good things, celebrating the success and analysing the factors which led to it. The same process can then be applied to less successful or disappoint-

ing events and the consideration of ways of effecting improvement in those areas. Somehow we are more aware of our failings but as a result of training and awareness raising, colleagues are now more confident in identifying success. This is an important element of the process.

Improvements The next consideration is, 'How can things be improved and who can help?' This gives the appraisee an opportunity to identify areas for development and nominate facilitators, e.g. head or deputy, colleagues or self, or outside agencies and trainers.

Professional development Here the teacher is asked to look at his/her career aspirations and identify areas in the self-evaluation or in the school's review which might benefit from in-service training.

Aims and targets From the discussions so far the appraisee may well be able to highlight some key targets which he or she will aim to achieve within an agreed timescale. This is a matter for negotiation between appraisee and appraiser but it is important to identify targets which are achievable both within the capabilities of the teacher and the constraints of available finance, resources and expertise.

Job specification As a result of this conference a more clear picture will emerge of the appraisee's strengths and weaknesses and from this a job specification with agreed areas of responsibility can be set out. This will be a compromise between the interests, enthusiasms and expertise with the identified needs of the school.

Summary The conference takes up to half-a-day and as soon as possible afterwards the appraiser produces a written summary of the conversation. Once this has been agreed with the appraisee, both parties add their signatures and the copy becomes the property of the appraisee. No part of the document should be used without the appraisee's consent. Confidentiality and trust are cornerstones of the process and there must exist no sense of threat.

Barbara:

We were to meet for three hours. The morning was both productive and enjoyable. We talked about classroom organisation, relationships with parents and children, control and discipline – in fact everything to do with my job as a teacher. Nick asked a lot of questions and I felt glad to be able to talk about the theory behind my work, my recent reading, problems, disappointments and my successes. We also talked about my career prospects and after coffee he went over the notes he had made so that he could begin typing up my appraisal statement the same afternoon.

The following day:

> I read my newly finished appraisal statement today and felt it was fair, to the point and well written. I was happy to read the nice things, and this boost of confidence lasted for days. I have the only copy of the statement. Next year we will go over the statement and review it. I feel very positive about the process. Teachers should not be worried about it if it is approached professionally and without prejudice. A great deal depends upon relationships and good communication.

Sue's diary for the same week included:

> Barbara was very positive about her appraisal and I felt the school heaved a sigh of relief as the first one had been completed.

Sue's feelings on the day of her conference:

> I was amazed how nervous I felt. Nick sent me for a walk round the garden to calm down. The interview went well but I would have preferred more input from the appraiser rather than concentrating on my own thoughts and ideas and I think I should have been more positive about my abilities. It does concern me that those less vocal members of the profession might have a less satisfactory appraisal because, in this model, emphasis is placed upon the ability to review yourself.

The final statement includes a section on targets and in our process in cases where the head was not the appraiser this section was completed with him later.

Follow-up

The theme of this case study is that appraisal is a valuable means of promoting professional development of teachers and their schools. We have taken the view that this development can occur in each phase of the process – during the preparation and initial training, during the task analysis, the conference and in the follow-up. Much of this development appears to arise in part from the way appraisal can prompt reflection and self-awareness. It also appears to arise from the potential within the process for clarifying aims and priorities and bringing about a sharper definition of responsibilities. Furthermore school and individual development is enhanced through more collaboration and better communication.

Whilst much development is possible, and indeed probable, in the early stages, a vital opportunity is lost if care is not taken over the follow-up. This involves the setting of realistic targets with appropriate resources and support and monitoring progress towards them. At this school, interim meetings were held for all staff after a year to see what progress was being made and to evaluate the process.

Sue: (The following term):

> I had mentioned in my appraisal that I wouldn't mind having a student again and today I found that this would be possible.

Barbara:

> As the new term approached I read my appraisal statement again and realised that some of the areas identified as targets had already begun to resolve themselves. Did the appraisal highlight these or would I have focused on them and sorted them out anyway? As I went on reading I began to identify other areas for my concern – self-appraisal if you like.

In retrospect, one of the factors which took the teeth out of the process was the inability of the school to offer solutions to some of the identified needs as funding was not at that time in the hands of the appraiser. Although both parties might agree on the need and even a possible route to solution, the funding would have to be sought by bid from a central pool. This situation has now changed with the GRIST, ESG, and GEST allocations and we are more able to identify needs with the confidence that the school can list the needs in a priority order and fund them. With the financial tools to offer help and support, the term professional development does really mean something and more definite plans can be made and more precise dates given for meeting identified needs. Since the first round more thought has been given to the identification of the areas for consideration during the conference. The process might well follow the pattern for headteacher appraisal where each party selects an area for debate. In this way popular and unpopular areas can be approached with the same confidence.

Reflections

Although this case study only refers to one cycle of appraisal the process has become very much part of the school's culture and is looked forward to as an opportunity for growth and development. Despite the individuality of the experiences outlined in the case study there are some general issues that lead to the success of the process.

1. The importance of raising awareness and creating a positive climate within the school.
2. School self-evaluation can provide a strategy for implementing appraisal as well as a means of linking it to school development.

3. Whole staff participation in considering the school development plan can be a lead in to the appraisal process or be a product of it.
4. The importance of training for all participants in both awareness raising and skill development.
5. The emphasis that the appraisal process is positive, supportive and non-threatening.
6. The importance of mutual respect between appraisee and appraiser.
7. The initial meeting is vital for setting the tone as well as the agenda for the process.
8. Self-appraisal and reflection are cornerstones of the process.
9. Teaching/Task analysis is a sensitive area and the criteria need to be explicit and agreed.
10. The conference agenda needs to be set and agreed in advance by both parties.
11. The summary should be completed as soon as possible after the conference.
12. Adequate follow-up and resources are needed.
13. The importance of recognising the dangers of raising expectations too highly thereby damaging the status of the process.
14. The realisation that appraisal is an on-going process that leads to more open-ness and communication within the school.

Two things are clear from this case study. The first is that appraisal does not exist in isolation, and that its long term impact seems likely to depend upon how far it is integrated with other strategies for review and development. The second is that any change is a process of individual growth that involves a degree of anxiety and uncertainty. Support in the form of a healthy school ethos, advice on the skills involved, and positive reinforcement, is needed if growth for the individual and the school is to occur. Above all the purpose of teacher appraisal is to improve the opportunities for children's learning in the classroom.

3.3 Appraisal in Secondary Schools

3.3.1 First steps in appraisal at Emmbrook School, Berkshire

Keith Barnes

Introduction

The attempt to initiate work on appraisal emerged as one of several ideas connected with planning for change which occurred during a fertile period of development at the Emmbrook School, Wokingham, Berkshire during 1986-88. The school, which had opened in 1965, had enjoyed a period of successful development under its first headteacher who retired in 1983. In a period of educational stability, the school had prospered and gained a large measure of support from the local community. It had, however, been somewhat unambitious in its development, and retained some features which looked distinctly 'old fashioned' to those who arrived from other comprehensive schools which had responded more rapidly to changing times and circumstances. The present head, in conjunction with his senior staff, planned a massive programme of educational changes, both in response to external demands, and to the increasing demands for innovation and forward movement demanded by a relatively large number of new staff he had to appoint during his first two years in post.

The school grew to a maximum size of about 1200, before the falling birth rate began to influence the intake numbers, and it recruited a sixth form of just over 200, the majority of whom studied for A-levels. Pupils continue to be drawn predominantly from an area of detached private dwellings, but the school also attracts pupils originating from more modest circumstances. The Special Needs Unit is a valuable and important feature of the school, and deservedly draws considerable acclaim from both the community and LEA advisory staff. Until the recession of 1990–91, employment prospects for young people in the immediate area were bouyant, and parental employment was typically in electronics or related service industries, often at managerial level. A small, though significant number of parents ran small businesses of their own.

Academic success in the school remains high, with a continuing large proportion of successful A-level candidates entering higher education at all levels, including Oxbridge. The changes made in the school were planned to find a point of balance between those staff who had remained in the school and those who were appointed by the new head. Staff who largely espoused 'traditional' approaches to the curriculum and school organisation, needed to be dovetailed along an interface with those whose arrival in the school, and earlier experiences had been more 'progressive'. In management terms, the problem was to preserve the best of traditional practice and to blend it with innovation so that there was no sacrifice of standards or quality. This was not easy but the school's point of equilibrium has moved markedly towards a climate more favourably suited to accommodating change.

Initiation

During the period of fertile planning for change, a number of projects were initiated which called heavily upon the voluntary participation of those most interested in bringing it about, or sustaining or managing it. Thus the impetus and conditions of support for innovation were drawn from wide support across the school. A number of developments already undertaken in other local schools were rapidly brought about, and these touched off ideas for yet further exploration. Some of the longer serving members of staff were drawn in, and a real feel for progress was soon evident. The aims of the school, for example, came under close scrutiny, as did the programme for personal and social education. Changes were made to the reporting system, and this finally emerged into a fullscale profiling movement. Changes in the ways that INSET was managed and organised encouraged staff to consider ways in which they could acquire new teaching skills and disseminate to colleagues some of their own expertise.

An early attempt to stimulate interest in appraisal faltered when it was realised that job descriptions, other than for some senior staff, had not been adequately developed on paper. Subsequent changes took place to the academic structure of the school – a response to the vibrant participation of keen individuals in planning for the future. This included forward planning for the National Curriculum. Progress with job descriptions was soon effected within the newly created faculty structures, and was encouraged by the need to generate new specifications for staff whose roles altered, and for those who were being appointed to replace a significant number of staff who were retiring at the ends of their teaching service.

Development

With the previous difficulty of job descriptions overcome, a group of interested staff started meeting regularly to reconsider the issues associated with introducing an appraisal scheme. This group was drawn widely from across the school, from standard grade to senior teachers, and included three heads of faculty who viewed appraisal positively. Anxious not to have to 're-invent the wheel' the group collected for study copies of the appraisal schemes from five other schools where these had been recently developed. Access was also gained to a number of industrial or commercial schemes, most important of which were probably those of Waitrose, and the Civil Service. These schemes were examined critically over a period of several months, and were set against Berkshire's own guidelines for school appraisal systems. It soon became clear that:

(a) Judgemental or 'control model' schemes used in some industrial settings offered no basis at all for us to use as a model;

(b) Some industrial schemes had important elements of personnel development and growth reflected in their designs;

(c) School schemes had exclusively used the development model, but were improvable in a number of ways; and

(d) Criteria for appraisal established by the LEA were well within an area represented by the encouragement of self-motivation, negotiated target-setting and professional development.

Whilst the design of a scheme on paper, building upon what had already been seen, was not considered to be a difficult task, the working group identified the real problem areas to be:

(a) Establishing how staff might be trained in applying the appraisal system, once the design had been completed;

(b) Retaining the interest and support of the rest of the staff, on whose behalf the group was undertaking its work; and

(c) Replacing theoretical discussions about how the scheme might work in practice with modifications brought about as a result of practical experience.

Several strands of development occurred within the school, which, when taken together, helped to resolve these difficulties. Of these the most important influence was that brought about by the school's links with Waitrose. Links with this company were attributable to, and sustained by, the presence on the Governing Body of an experienced personnel manager whose knowledge and skills have proved to be most valuable on numerous occasions. Through this link, the group was able to gain access to the training manager responsible for appraisal training for the company's managerial operatives. Copies of the training materials were generously made available, and the group was able to borrow the training video, used as part of the residential training offered to Waitrose staff.

Although the school had developed some expertise in running in-house training, based upon its earlier involvement with TRIST and its need to utilise staff INSET days, it lacked confidence in its ability to do much on its own about appraisal training. The possession of training materials for appraisal – generally before they became available in educational literature – was therefore a considerable advantage. It represented a way for the group to self-instruct its way along, whilst matching this to the scheme which by now was beginning to emerge on paper.

With so much activity now taking place, it became necessary to plan with greater care. This required more time. Meetings of the group, which were originally held after school were now held within INSET time, with staff released from some lessons. This target was specified in the School Development Plan. In practice, the plan is the subject of negotiation between many staff in the school, and always emerges as a compromise between often opposing perceptions of staff at different levels. In this way, appraisal was kept prominent as a global target worthy of the school's continuing attention, although much of the detailed discussion about what was happening was restricted to group members. Nevertheless there were several opportunities for informing other staff of what was happening, either through reports given at staff meetings or via presentations given to other staff groups.

Appraisal trial

Useful progress was made in areas (a) and (b) mentioned above, and the group seriously turned its attention to (c). With so much support running in favour of what was being achieved, a limited but structured appraisal trial was readily agreed. Volunteers for the trial were drawn principally from the working group, but two staff outside this group were easily persuaded to opt in to balance the trial. It was decided to include staff at the most senior level so that when statutory appraisal is formally in place, such staff will have benefited from earlier involvements and thus be better placed to carry out their responsibilities.

The scheme involved the following pairings:

(a) Head teacher ....appraising Senior teacher
(b) Deputy head (1) ......appraising Head of faculty
(c) Deputy head (2) ......appraising Year head
(d) Head of faculty........appraising Head of subject
(e) Head of subject........appraising Main grade teacher

These pairings represented as nearly as possible the model of line manager appraising a subordinate. Since the position of systems manager in the school represented a somewhat anomalous position in this respect (the systems manager was a member of the working group), it was agreed that she should not be included in the initial trial.

In order to prepare all participants for the trial, together with other members of the working group who were not participating directly, a self-training session was held using materials whose origins derived from ideas included in the Waitrose package. The most useful part of the package proved to be the model for the appraisal conference between the appraiser and appraisee which was set forth in the training video. It seemed to be a case of 'showing the teachers how to do it so that they could get on with it themselves'.

Opportunities were provided for simulation or role play – so that staff could practice the skills of active listening, and of asking open ended questions. An animated discussion followed, in which it was finally decided that the advantages of the trial would easily outweigh the disadvantages of the participants not, perhaps, being fully prepared.

In establishing the formal basis for the trial, which under LEA rules for school development plans, could not be permitted to be other than 'preparation for appraisal', the group agreed the following:

(a) Stages of the appraisal were identified as:
Completion of the self-appraisal document;
Setting the agenda for the appraisal conference;
Appraisal conference itself;
Negotiation and compilation of an agenda report;
Specification of future targets;
Identification of possible INSET directions; and
Follow-up interview, if necessary.

(b) Boundary conditions upon the trial were set as:
No contractual obligation on either party
'Play it for real' basis
Voluntary participation – but with an expectation that career enhancement discussions would be viable
Confidentiality between appraiser and appraisee
Ownership of appraisal documentation by appraisee – with copy lodged with headteacher
Non-use of appraisal records for any professional reason – unless with consent of appraisee.

Each member of staff involved within the pairings was free to make the necessary arrangements for preliminary discussions, and agenda setting, prior to agreeing a date and time for the appraisal conference. Acting within their specific management areas, and within their own role specifications, appraisers were asked to take to the agenda setting meeting those issues which they thought to be properly their concerns as line managers, and to set these against the issues brought by the appraisees. In this way it was expected that the appraisal conference would not only project the developmental interests of the appraisees, but might also reflect the evaluation of performance required by the appraisers, and ultimately by their own managers. The participation of staff in appraisal conferences was covered from the resources identified in the School Development Plan, with an uninterrupted period of at least two hours set aside. The summary of interview discussion was planned to take place outside these limits, and in most cases was undertaken at home.

Self-appraisal document

The self-appraisal form produced for the appraisal trial was modelled extensively on documents of a similar style in use in schools elsewhere.

Before use, it was examined by the staffing committee of the Governing Body, to whom a presentation on appraisal was made. As a result, a number of suggestions were incorporated in the design, so that there was a sense in which the governors had themselves some ownership of the scheme.

The document was broken down into five sections, with an inbuilt checklist to guide respondents into thinking fully about how they performed within each of the specified areas. For example, under section B: *leadership*, the prompt read:

> You could indicate changes in direction, policy modifications or other self-directed initiatives in which you have been involved.

The areas specified were:

A. Job specification

Principal responsibilities	main tasks
Teaching commitment	main planning tasks
Pastoral involvement	significant features

B. Team membership and management

Co-operation and teamwork	tasks undertaken
Management skills	achievement
Leadership	directions established

C. Review of past year

Targets achieved	targets not achieved
Satisfactions	disappointments
Developments	obstructions
Suggestions for sustaining	suggestions for avoiding
Growth and development	disappointments and overcoming obstructions

D. The future

Further training needs

Further experience needs

Potential for growth

Potential for carrying additional responsibility

Career aspirations

E. Target setting

Targets

Action plan   resources ....   timescale ....   strategy

Attainment criteria

Progress note

Trial in practice

Although the interviews with staff were confidential to those who had participated, an important set of observations grew from the subsequent discussions held separately both with the appraisers and the appraisees. Amongst the appraisees, the experience of completing the self-appraisal document had been salutary. They reported that they had not, for some considerable time, sat down to examine what they had been doing, or consider how well they had been doing it. This produced a comfortable feeling, they suggested, as they began to think about their achievements. For most of the time they were caught up in the hectic swirl of school life, with little spare capacity for thinking about themselves or what they were achieving. The knowledge that they were expected to confront negative aspects of their performance had come as a relief. There was, they reported, feeling of well being that certain anxieties had been aired within the security and confidentiality of the appraisal conference.

The interviews were reported to be, without exception, positive and rewarding experiences. Typical reactions were:

> How pleasant it was to sit down and talk to someone who really listens.
>
> I've never sat down to talk to someone about what I do before!
>
> Just to take time out to think about what I do is therapeutic.
>
> I'm glad that I got ..... off my chest!

Considerable optimism surrounded the setting of targets, which, taken as a whole ranged from 'improving the organisation of my subject teaching' to 'the promotion of opportunities for INSET for colleagues working within my faculty.'

Appraisees were given every reason to believe that, within the inevitable constraints operating, resourcing would be offered to help bring about the achievement of the targets. In some instances, it was not so much financial resources that were needed, as opportunities arising through other means. Was the INSET co-ordinator, for example, able to negotiate, within existing non-contact time, some work shadowing of a senior colleague? Or would a head of faculty be prepared to release responsibility for overseeing a particular set of tasks?

Within the group of appraisers it was agreed that the appraisal discussions had not been that easy to conduct. It had certainly helped to create the right atmosphere, with unplugged telephones, chairs disposed in mutual juxtaposition, coffee on hand, and other freedoms from interruption. The adoption of a reflective questioning, eager listening style had been harder to achieve, but this success was claimed, to a greater or less extent, by all the appraisers. In one case, a tape recorder had been used to record part of the appraisal discussion so that transcribed materials might later be used in future training.

Typical comments were:

> It was difficult not to butt in ....
>
> After a while, I found I was summarising what she said ..
>
> I needed to concentrate hard because I couldn't take notes ....
>
> The experience was a lot different to the usual quick chat as you walk to your next lesson.

A common difficulty experienced by all the appraisers concerned the style of writing to be used when completing the section headed 'summary of interview discussion'. Little attention had been given to this matter in the self-instruction preparation. It was easy to fall into the trap of imagining that a confidential reference was being put together – with all its possibilities for evaluative judgements. A very different style was called for – one which personalised the discussion, yet objectively summarised into wider perspectives, individual points of view put forward by the appraisees. Without breaching any of the confidential discussions that had taken place, the appraisers shared their thoughts on the form of comments, with each agreeing to aim for a common style.

Although time had been allocated for the discussions, it was envisaged from the start of the trial that the writing up would probably need to be completed at home. When all the appraisers and appraisees met to share their experiences of the trial, an estimate was made of the average time which had been devoted to all the stages of the trial. This average approached 8 hours per individual (about 1.6 days, estimated in teaching periods). No doubt this average reflects partly on the fact that all tasks were being faced for the first time – perhaps in time the processes can be speeded up. Nevertheless there was a strong feeling that adequate resourcing must be available if appraisal experiences are to be as positive as they were in the trial. Whether the Secretary of State for Education is able to achieve this remains to be seen.

Subsequent developments

The experiences of the trial were reported to the whole staff during a staff training day, as part of a programme organised to raise staff awareness to the issues of appraisal. The presentation was headed by a speaker from the Industrial Society who skilfully set appraisal in the kind of positive framework to which staff were able to relate. These messages were reinforced significantly by two speakers who had taken part in the trial – an appraiser and an appraisee.

During the latter stages of the day, attention turned to classroom observation, a component of appraisal which had been omitted from the trial. Staff reaction was much more positive than had been imagined, and the appraisers expressed the view that they doubted whether their appraisal outcomes or targets would have been changed if this component had been added.

Currently, the group is considering how to normalise visits of staff between classrooms when teaching is in progress in an effort to condition them to accept observation, initially on a voluntary basis. This is helped by the presence of students on teaching practice, and newly qualified teachers, all of whom are visited in their classrooms.

A concerted effort has been made by the head and INSET co-ordinator to do as much as possible to encourage the realisation of targets set during appraisal. This has been regarded as a high priority focus, especially important in helping to shape staff views of appraisal being a positive, developmental process, albeit with accountability elements.

A significant further stage of development was to take the results of the appraisal trial back to the working group in order to address the following tasks, which are currently being pursued to:

(a) Improve the structure and design of the present self-appraisal document, in the light of experience of its use;

(b) Take into account more fully the evaluative aspects of appraisal in respect of performance according to role-specification;

(c) Sketch a model for line-management across the pastoral or academic divisions in the school;

(d) Formalise the role of 'teacher as tutor' within the process;

(e) Outline a strategy of introducing classroom observations in as unobtrusive a way as possible;

The senior staff believe that the trial appraisal was so successful, and had been received so well by the staff as a whole, that they have recommended that the school opts into Berkshire's appraisal training scheme at the earliest possible moment. This implies that statutory appraisal of some staff will be undertaken almost as early as it is possible for this to happen. The crucial participation of year heads and faculty heads not included in the trial is regarded as critical in establishing the credibility and authority of future involvement.

Conclusion

The appraisal trial represented a valuable experiment for those in the school seriously contemplating how appraisal might be introduced, and proved to be a worthwhile and rewarding experience for those who participated. The stimulus for the work grew from staff participation at all levels in the management of change. This had been carefully planned by the management group to blend innovation with existing good practice. The speed of change was a key factor – most staff were taken along at a pace which proved not to be too uncomfortable. There was a feeling that practical work on appraisal would not represent undue pressures on participants: indeed, the experience, staff thought, might prove to be beneficial. In the event, the work undertaken proved to be useful in ensuring that unforeseen difficulties were countenanced not merely through discussion, but also through experience.

In all, the appraisal trial proved to be an experiment well worth conducting. The conditions and time were right. The outcomes were positive, and the staff reactions were characterised by a cheerful acceptance that appraisal can work, under the right circumstances. It is fervently hoped that statutory appraisal will be resourced sufficiently well to sustain this notion. It could do much to uplift sagging morale across a hardworking but besieged set of teachers.

3.3.2 Developmental approach to appraisal at Birchwood Community High School, Cheshire

Mike VaughanEdwards

Introduction: the school

Birchwood is the creation of the Warrington New Town Development Corporation. It consists of three residential 'villages' and a number of business sites to the north east of Warrington. The villages include a wide range of housing types from high density local authority housing to expensive private developments. Generally Birchwood is a pleasant place, filled with greenery and open spaces. It clearly benefited from being among the last wave of new towns and it is easy to see that here the planners got it less wrong than in many early new towns.

The first wave of occupants were promised that plans included a secondary school for the area. However, as the demographic downturn progressed it became clear that in Warrington as a whole there was no need for a new secondary school so plans were scrapped. A highly successful local campaign eventually succeeded in persuading the County Council that Birchwood must have its own school. Birchwood Community High School opened in September 1985 with a tangible level of local support and goodwill, 190 pupils and a young and enthusiastic staff of 14. The school had been built to current DES regulations for an anticipated roll of 750 pupils – the initial ratios of pupils to rooms, equipment and teachers were luxurious.

This was the time of continuing industrial action and low morale throughout the educational world. To be at Birchwood was like being on an island of optimism and excitement in the midst of a sea of gloom. In these circumstances those of us on the staff should indeed have been shot if we could not create an example of the best educational practice.

The school's roll has now passed the anticipated 750 and a three phase building programme has begun to cater for our anticipated growth to about 900 pupils. As pupil numbers have risen the ratios of pupils to teachers and equipment has come into line with other schools. We still benefit from comparatively new equipment but suffer from the miserly size of teaching areas.

Initiation: introducing appraisal at Birchwood

When Birchwood opened, the idea of appraisal had been put firmly on the agenda by the Secretary of State, Sir Keith Joseph. The statutory framework allowing the government to introduce regulations requiring the LEAs to introduce appraisal schemes was contained in the 1986 *Education No.2 Act* which became law during the school's first year. In the climate of the time it was perceived as being intended as a way of weeding out poor teachers and was linked with the notion of merit pay. It was certainly regarded as part of the general 'bash the teachers' attitude of the government. Many teachers were still hostile to the idea of being appraised, which had not been presented as something that could work to their advantage. On the contrary they saw it is something threatening which would be done to them by those who held significant power over them.

However, it seemed at the time that schools would inevitably be required to introduce appraisal sooner or later and the head decided that sooner would be better than later.

There were a number of reasons behind this decision. Firstly, the staff was young and enthusiastic without the normal quota of staffroom cynics and those who might try to block such developments – the introduction could be expected to be less painful than might otherwise be the case. Secondly, if appraisal were established straight away at Birchwood, applicants for any subsequent jobs at the school would have to accept that it was part of the school culture, as was being a no-smoking school, and this would avoid a more difficult introduction when the staff had become, as it inevitably would, more like a typical school staff. Thirdly, and most importantly, he did see it as a positive discipline which would work for teachers rather than against them, enhancing their professional satisfaction and the quality of teaching available to the pupils.

At a staff meeting early in the school's year the head made it very clear that we would operate a scheme of appraisal, but that the form it should take would be the subject of consultation with the whole staff. He also made it clear that he would be appraised and that teaching staff would be involved in this. The staff was small enough to make separate working parties unnecessary so further discussion took place both informally and at staff meetings. The staff were quick to see the positive possibilities of appraisal and several read the influential report by Suffolk LEA, *Those Having Torches*, which was published that year. The main summary of its findings began:

> The cornerstone of appraisal schemes is the belief that teachers wish to improve their performance in order to enhance the education of their pupils. Following from this is the assumption that appraisal systems should have a positive orientation: that its purpose should be to develop teachers professionally rather than to 'get at' them. This developmental process should be characterised by negotiation and agreement about priorities and targets.

It also painted a more positive picture of practice in industry. It included a survey of practice in thirty firms and distinguished between newer 'active' schemes and older 'passive' schemes. This was part of a significant move away from autocratic management approaches, towards open processes which incorporated self-appraisal.

> A significant number believe the open and participatory aspect of their scheme makes the largest single contribution to its success.

The report concluded that effective appraisal in industry is positive, constructive, honest, and non-threatening.

Implementation

First interviews

The form and content of our appraisal interviews were closely based on the recommendations of *Those Having Torches*. An interview checklist was agreed to provide a comprehensive prompt list from which staff could indicate areas they wished to discuss. Many staff used this checklist for a crude self-assessment scoring 0–10 for each point, but without any particular criteria. Before each interview the head had an informal discussion with the interviewee. In most cases he also made informal visits to lessons. The interview took place in a location chosen by the interviewee, though this was usually the head's office as there are very few other appropriate rooms in the school. In most cases the interview was recorded and the recording was available for the interviewee to take away and listen to and come back on. The head then wrote a summary of the interview including training needs and targets for the forthcoming year. This summary was amended until both parties were happy with it and then signed by both.

A middle ranking teacher on a Scale 2 was given the job of co-ordinator of the professional development interview. By the end of the summer term in 1986 all teaching staff had experienced their first interview and he had debriefed each interviewee in order to consider further developments. This feedback indicated that the interview itself had provided a variety of experiences. Below are some of the comments made by staff.

> The climate of openness and honesty was very good ... a professionally conducted interview.

> Everyone needs to know how they are doing; the interview was helpful, much to do with the head teacher who was very relaxed.

> It was fine as it stands, but the second round of interviews are more crucial and difficult. The interview does not yet reflect a normal school.

> It was more pleasant than anticipated, you were made to feel important and wanted.

> The interview was not long enough, time constraints spoiled it to a certain extent.

> Interruptions broke up the flow of the interview.

> Why did the interviewer sit on the other side of the table? ... would have preferred the low informal chairs.

> It was a structured interview rather than formal.

> The exercise did not reflect the importance given to it, due to the postponements of the interview. It had to fit in rather than take precedence over other activities.

> Not enough reference to the checklist form.

> How does the information get back to a head of department, for example, a member of department requests a responsibility, while reflecting the confidentiality of the interview?

It was clear from this feedback that the interviews had, by and large, got off to a good start. Certain developments were made to answer some of the criticisms. The head realised that his basic style and approach to the interviews were widely appreciated but that he had to give them higher priority in terms of not allowing interruptions and postponements. He began to make greater use of his red 'engaged' light to make this possible.

Another development was to allow staff more freedom to set the agenda. In the initial round of interviews the checklist formed the agenda. Later on staff were given the freedom to use the checklist in any way they wanted, or to not use it at all.

Meeting the training targets

The targets and training needs as identified in the initial interview with the head were recorded as part of the agreed confidential appraisal record. By the end of the first year it was clear that this arrangement would not do. If the school were to attempt to meet the appraisee's needs then the information needed to be shared. Accordingly it was decided that the targets and training needs would be recorded on a separate sheet which would be passed on to the school's INSET Co-ordinator.

The school has a programme of weekly INSET sessions and these are planned to try and meet the needs of the school and of the staff. Over the years we have developed a pattern of including in each term's programme, sessions which relate to personal development, such as ones on assertiveness and public speaking, to management skills such as team management and timetabling, and to aspects of classroom practice. In this way we have covered a lot of ground and the sessions are in general highly valued. We also use the training needs identification to pinpoint who to send on particular LEA courses.

Classroom observation

From the start of the school the head made it his business to make many informal visits to classrooms and this gave him much information about the atmosphere and effectiveness of a range of lessons. This clearly contributes to informal appraisal. However, at Birchwood the emphasis has always been on staff development rather than appraisal. The interview component of the scheme focuses on targets and training needs for the future rather than quantifying performance in the past. Thus it was felt that any formal programme of lesson observation should have staff development as its main purpose.

A pilot study in classroom observation was launched in early 1987. Volunteer pairs of teachers were to observe each other's lessons. Whenever possible this would be in non-teaching time but a limited amount of supply teacher time was also available to free observers from their normal teaching. A range of recording formats was suggested but observation records would be confidential to the volunteer pairs. Most of the staff who took part found it an interesting and useful experience but the pilot scheme was not taken any further. This was largely because of time constraints – the volunteer pairs simply did not have enough non-teaching time for more than one-off observations. Supply teacher time was used for some of the pairs but it would have cost far too much to pay for cover for similar opportunities for the whole staff.

Head's appraisal

The first appraisal interview for the head was conducted by a panel chaired by a deputy head and including two other staff members, a governor (who was also the head of a local primary school) and the school's adviser. Obviously the head was under more pressure than the rest of the staff as he was facing a panel of five. It was felt that certain areas, such as staffing, could not and need not be discussed with subordinates. These were the subject of a supplementary interview carried out by the adviser. Other than the very few 'no go' areas the head was prepared to discuss any aspect of his job. The confidentiality of the head's interview could be relayed to other staff to satisfy them that the process had been gone through correctly. As with most of the first round interviews, the head's first interview was a very relaxed affair and, as we all thought fairly highly of each other, was inevitably rather cosy. However, it was felt that the mere fact that it happened and started a pattern was important. In each subsequent year there was a different panel of staff but the co-ordinator attended as an observer in the interests of continuity so that he could advise panel members on procedure. The fact that the head's interview is an exercise in upwards appraisal is unusual.

Development

Mid-year interviews

After the first year the cycle of interviews has continued to follow the same broad pattern. As the number of staff has increased to over 40 the interviews are now spread over a longer period but everyone is still seen by the head about every fourteen months. In addition every member of staff now has a mid-year review with one of the deputy heads. This is intended to be a discussion of progress towards the agreed targets and training needs, and offers the opportunity to amend or add to either of these. The deputy has access to the record of agreed targets and training needs but not to the confidential record of the interview with the head. Interviewees have the choice of which deputy to see, introducing an element of choice which is often absent from appraisal schemes.

Occasionally deputies found that the targets which had been set, and which formed the agenda for the interview, were so vague as to be unhelpful. For instance it is easier to discuss progress towards a target of:

To establish a junior gym club with a regular programme of training;

than:

To develop relations with the staff.

The second was clearly the tip of an iceburg with a submerged subtext. Although deputies always knew the general context of such targets they sometimes did not know the precise terms in which the target had been discussed in the confidential interview with the head. Such problems were few and far between, however, and both interviewer and interviewee generally found the targets clear and useful.

So far the co-ordinator has had little difficulty in ensuring a broadly equal workload for each of the deputies. In general staff like the idea of developing 'friends at court' and the deputies find the interviews useful in keeping abreast of what staff are doing.

Changes in the interview pattern

As the school has grown the need to hold an interview with each member of staff has generated an ever larger role for the head. Several times we have been poised to develop the system and then decided to wait because the national picture seemed to be constantly shifting. It was clear for a number of years, though, that an eventual national system of appraisal would involve middle managers and that we would need to move away from the head appraising everyone. We have held several rounds of consultation to discuss such moves.

One major factor against change has been that the staff like things as they are. They like direct access to the head because it is clearly linked to what many of them see as the key payoffs of appraisal. Most obviously, those applying for other jobs know their references will be largely based on their agreed appraisal statement and will thus give a fuller and fairer picture of their work than is sometimes the case when staff have less access to the head. Most staff, whether references are important to them or not, value the fact that the interview with the head, and the associated observation, means that their work is known and valued by the head. This obviously depends on an atmosphere of trust in which staff are confident that their strengths will be recognised and the less impressive aspects of their performance will neither be attacked as failings nor unhelpfully ignored, but will be discussed as development needs.

Birchwood's first head left at the end of the school's fourth year and was succeeded by one of his deputies, who had been the original INSET co-ordinator. She also had the confidence of the staff and interviews with her continued to be as valued as those with the previous head.

Another factor which made staff mistrustful of change was the idea that the heads of department, as line managers, should conduct the appraisal interviews. Levels of confidence here were inevitably more varied and some staff were less than enthusiastic.

Alternative compromise solutions were considered by the senior management team. The favoured one retained a biennial interview for all staff with the head which would concentrate on career issues. An annual appraisal with the appropriate line manager would concentrate on classroom performance. We were concerned to balance several elements: the access to the head; a degree of choice of interviewer, as in the Mid-Year Reviews; and the need to bring heads of department into the system increasing their role in staff development.

In practice because the national picture changed regularly and the attitude of the professional associations blew warm and cool in response we have not yet implemented any changes. Now that the picture is at last clear, following the Secretary of State's decision to go ahead with a compulsory national scheme, we have identified the development of our system as a key management task for the forthcoming school year.

Future developments in INSET

Just as the pattern of appraisal interview is now ripe for development so the way in which we use INSET to meet the training needs identified during appraisal must be regularly evaluated.

Like most schools we feel that we have had far too many staff out of school in the last few years for INSET and moderation activities related to the introduction of the National Curriculum. As we try to cut this down we must think again about how our in-house programme can meet training needs. Sometimes an INSET topic will span two or three weeks but in general they tend to be one-off hour and a half sessions. This has had the benefit of allowing us to cover a very wide range of topics but also means that they are rarely dealt with in depth. One possible development for the future is the creation of small study groups which would commit themselves to using a series of INSET sessions to pursue particular themes. The school's INSET budget could fund the necessary resources, including visits and visitors. It may be possible to link such study groups with action research into topics of interest to the school and to academic accreditation now being offered by a number of Colleges of Higher Education for this sort of work.

Classroom observation

At the moment the head sees lessons by all staff both before their appraisal interview and on other occasions as appropriate. However, as we place the emphasis on professional development aspect of appraisal we wish to promote other kinds of classroom observation as well. An article by Erault (1986) summed up a useful distinction:

> In so far as an appraisal interview is leading to an agreed statement about performance great care must be taken to collect sufficient evidence. We can probably assume that classroom observation will be undertaken before the interview by one or more senior teachers. In contrast, where a development interview system operates any classroom observation will be undertaken after the interview, with a developmental rather than evidential purpose; and it will probably be carried out by a less senior, and therefore less expensive, person.

With this in mind we are currently developing a new classroom observation programme. The idea is that the limited amount of resources, including supply cover, should be used intensively with a small number of teachers, say a single department, rather than spread thinly across a larger number. Currently we are asking participants to set themselves targets related to classroom performance. Pairs then act as observers for each other and use feedback from the observation to help them meet the targets. It is too early to comment on the effectiveness of this procedure but there has been no shortage of staff volunteers.

In parallel to this we have investigated the use of pupil evaluation of learning tasks, which inevitably includes an element of pupil evaluation of teachers. This might seem rather threatening to some staff but is no different to the widespread use of student satisfaction returns which are increasingly common practice in some areas of higher education. A questionnaire has been used by some staff with their own classes to evaluate a unit they have just taught. As such it is an extra tool for the teacher's self-evaluation.

Special features

Birchwood's appraisal system is the product of its history. It is an accepted part of the way the school runs, is valued highly by the staff, and must be regarded as successful. A key factor in this success is the skill of the head teacher in conducting the interviews. She communicates warmth and appreciation of the staff but is not afraid to the tell the truth when it is less than pleasant. In moving to a system which involves middle managers in conducting the interviews we shall hope to give them the confidence and the skill to balance support and frankness in the same productive way.

The initial appointment of a fairly junior member of staff as co-ordinator for the Professional Development Interviews was another key factor in the success of the system. It contributed a sense of staff room ownership of the scheme. The co-ordinator has in fact now risen through the ranks to be a deputy himself and we are considering moving the responsibility back to a junior member of staff for that reason.

INSET, professional development, and appraisal have always been considered as different facts of the same thing. The co-ordinator for the Professional Development Interview has always also been the assistant INSET co-ordinator and the two have worked as a pair. In terms of the graph in Section 1, showing the balance between evaluation and development, the Birchwood system has always seen its evaluative concerns as being subordinate to its developmental concerns because its prime aim is to help staff deliver the best possible teaching to the pupils of the school.

Conclusion

In the year ahead we shall have to modify the system we have evolved to come into line with the national regulations. In doing so we shall work hard to maintain the sense of staff ownership and genuine dialogue which we believe have made our system a success.

3.4 Appraisal of head teachers

3.4.0 Experience from pilot schemes of the appraisal of head teachers

Brian Fidler

Introduction

The appraisal of head teachers proves to be the most difficult area to deal with both conceptually and in practice. Head teachers do not have the equivalent of a line manager and so the managerial model breaks down. The options are either not to appraise head teachers by formal means or to devise *ad hoc* schemes which combine evaluation and development and thus provide some comparability with the appraisal of other teachers. Some experience of the appraisal of head teachers has come from the six LEA pilot schemes (Ganes, 1989; Bradley et al, 1989) and two brief first hand accounts from Vanessa Champion of Cumbria and Dallas Hackett of Salford follow in sections 3.4.1 and 3.4.2.

The pilot LEAs employed a variety of schemes to appraise head teachers (Bradley et al, 1989). Circular 12/91 requires that head teachers be appraised by two people and recommends that these be selected by the CEO for county and voluntary schools and the governing body of a grant maintained school.

One of the appraisers should have experience of headship of the appropriate phase and the other should normally be an officer or adviser for an LEA school. Both appraisers should be present at the initial planning meeting and at the appraisal interview.

Observation of teaching or other duties can be carried out by one or both of the appraisers but it is recommended that if only one is used he or she should have had experience as a head teacher. Head teachers are not to be able to choose their appraiser but conflicts of interest or other mismatches should be avoided.

Appraisers

Some of the LEA pilot schemes were broadly similar to this. Where more than one person carried out an appraisal it was found that some attention had to be given to clarifying the respective function and involvement of each. In particular, the identification of a 'key appraiser' helped.

Appraisers with head teacher experience were either serving heads carrying this task out as an additional task or were seconded heads. The choice of officer or adviser was clear if there was someone with a close knowledge and relationship with the school and head teacher.

The selection of appraising heads calls for personal characteristics and modes of operating which are appropriate for this particularly sensitive task. These are needed in addition to impressive experience. As the evaluation report states,

> The evidence so far suggests that simply deploying those heads who are acknowledged as good practitioners will not suffice – training and a thorough understanding of the process are important
>
> (Bradley at al, 1989; p. 41).

From the point of view of the appraising head teachers the task of appraising another head teacher was found to be 'one of the most valuable professional development activities they have experienced' (p. 40).

Training

Training was regarded as vital. This should focus on head teacher appraisal and should combine training and the development of approaches to the appraisal of head teachers.

Data gathering

Since one or both appraisers may be unfamiliar with the school and head teacher, a great deal of data had to be obtained. Some of this was supplied by the head teacher and some was supplied by others within and outside the school. The range of providers of data was negotiated. Classroom observation was found inappropriate for most head teachers and task observation, though it helped to illustrate the context of the job, yielded little useful data.

Data provided by others within and outside the school was clearly very important but posed particular problems. Obtaining data about the head of the institution from such people was a novel experience and posed problems of divided loyalites. The pilot studies showed a need for clear guidance on procedures and ethics of such data collection.

The ACAS guidelines, on which the pilot schemes were based, made no mention of the role of the governing body. Consequently the pilot schemes offer little evidence on the involvement of governors either as sources of evidence or, in the case of chair of governors, taking a major role in the whole process. The Circular suggests that governors are an appropriate source of evidence in the appraisal of head teachers and requires that a copy of the whole appraisal statement on the headteacher should be made available to the chair of governors. The governors are also required to ensure that the head teacher is operating appraisal procedures for other staff in accordance with the prescribed regulations.

Appraisal interview and follow-up

The interview was generally limited to a particular range of issues from among the whole work of a head teacher which had been negotiated. Even with this limitation the interview lasted for over three hours. Head teachers generally welcomed such feedback on their performance from knowledgeable appraisers. Many heads found the whole process had the effect of causing them to think critically about their job and to increase the importance of planning school activities.

The key appraiser wrote a report based on notes taken during the interview. This contained targets and other developmental activities. However, there was no clear mechanism for monitoring progress on these since the appraisers did not necessarily have an ongoing relationship with the head or school. A further problem was how public any such targets should be.

Resourcing

The Circular recommends that serving heads should appraise no more than three head teachers at any one time. This begins to recognise the enormous time demands on senior personnel which the appraisal of head teachers makes.

3.4.1 Cumbria's experience: 'Not out of the woods': Dilemmas in the statutory appraisal of head teachers

Vanessa Champion

Introduction

A good system of appraisal will be one which is seen to operate equitably, on identical principles (albeit with sensitive variations in practice) across the whole of an education service. That all appraisers should also be appraisees not only reinforces the credibility of the system in the eyes of participants, it also demonstrates the notion of appraisal as an entitlement for all and acknowledges the centrality of staff development in the development of the service.

The appraisal of the head teacher therefore will be central to the development of appraisal within the school. Many head teachers and LEAs have recognised this and there has been no shortage of experimental work in head teacher appraisal both within and outside the national pilot scheme – often to the considerable benefit of those involved.

Unfortunately, much of this initial work took place in an educational context and climate which is already historical. The accelerating pace of the Education Reform Act has swept aside old orders, relationships and assumptions. Local Management of Schools and the modified role of the LEA mean that there are changes in accountabilities, managerial relationships and financial arrangements and hence a whole new agenda of critical issues which will need addressing in implementing the statutory appraisal of head teachers. Progress will be hampered by the fact that LEAs are no longer the stable structures they were and the likely future shape and role of the organisations are far from clear.

Three issues

Three particular concerns for Cumbria at the moment are:

Who appraises head teachers?

The Statutory Regulations and Guidance between them clearly anticipate that the appraisers of a head teacher are likely to be an officer of the LEA and another head teacher with recent and relevant experience in the same phase. There has been a case put for the appraisal of head teachers solely by head teachers but the involvement of the LEA officer upholds a basic principle operating in school teacher appraisal i.e. that there should be some element of managerial involvement in an individual's appraisal.

Questions lie not so much with the principle as with the practicalities of operating that principle within the current (and future) context. For example, even as I write, there is much speculation about the role of the LEA inspection or advisory service within the new dispensation. Ministers speak speculatively about a greater emphasis on a rigorous and independent inspectorial function and already there are many LEAs in which the changed nomenclature hints at the revision of role which is taking place. (Advisers have become Advisor/Inspectors, then Inspector/Advisors and subsequently Inspectors.) This has often been accompanied by a changed function, and in many areas traditional 'patch' responsiblities have disappeared and the relationship with schools is being redefined. In some cases the central team has diminished in number quite considerable.

Many would argue that the inspectorial role does not sit comfortably alongside the supportive, developmental role required of the appraiser. Others would suggest that the relationship is not significantly different from that of head and teacher appraisee and it is possible to accommodate both. But there are other concerns attached to this developing situation. One is simply that of having enough personnel to do the job. In Cumbria, in order to comply with legal requirements, 200 head teacher appraisals will need to take place each year. With the current size of the inspectorate, this means that every inspector will have to appraise eight head teachers and be involved in the follow-up review of a further eight head teachers every year thus adding considerably to the workload of a team which is already stretched. Financial constraints within LEAs mean that, for many, expansion of the team to take account of this requirement is not an option. It may be that the wider involvement of other LEA officers will become a necessity – and that decision has implications in terms of training needs.

A second concern is that the intimate relationships which many inspectors had with individual schools are less likely to exist in future. It is possible that the appraiser of a head teacher will have had little previous contact with the school. Although there may be advantages to this, the drawback is that more time will be required for the inspector to gain a picture of the school which is sufficiently detailed to support the head's appraisal. Suddenly the exercise becomes rather more expensive.

Nor is the involvement of peer head teachers without its difficulties. Some questions which come immediately to mind are:

(i) Will all head teachers in an LEA automatically be available as appraisers? Should there be any 'qualifying limit' in terms of length of time in post? What of head teachers who are struggling? If there is going to be any form of selection, then who will make that selection and on what criteria?

(ii) If there is to be some element of choice in the selection of the peer appraiser then how will selection arrangements protect those heads who are seen as 'desirable' appraisers? What will be the reaction of governors to the possible involvement of their head teacher in the appraisal of up to three colleagues – and the inevitable time away from school that will require?

(iii) How will arrangements for selection of peer appraisers take into account the necessary concerns regarding catchment rivalry and competition. And if the appraiser head is to come from further afield, has the LEA fully comprehended the travel or time costs that will be incurred and made decisions about how these will be paid and by whom? (This is a particular concern perhaps for large, rural areas where schools can be widely scattered.)

How big an exercise is the appraisal of a head teacher?

Statutory regulations state a minimum model for the appraisal of a head teacher. LEAs are left to decide the extent to which they wish to enlarge on this. In the Cumbrian pilot the appraisal of a head teacher consisted of initial meeting, preliminary visit, task observations and **three** conference (interview) sessions. For many of the head teachers concerned it was seen to be one of the most important and rewarding experiences of their professional lives.

Such a luxurious model is clearly not an option given the current financial constraints for LEAs, but the question remains as to the optimum size of the head teacher appraisal process. How possible is it to encompass the extent and range of the job within the space of a single interview every two years? Local heads who were involved in the pilot scheme have suggested that anything as brief as this will barely glance at the surface of the head's work and is in danger of being shallow and of little worth. Where the appraisers are unfamiliar with the school and the appraiser, the situation will be exacerbated. Experience suggests that, particularly where appraisers are neither highly skilled nor fully informed, far too much precious time is consumed in giving information and overcoming misconceptions with too little remaining for the central task.

Even a minimum model of head teacher appraisal will take significant resource. LEAs will wish to be assured that such an investment is to have a high yield in terms of future benefits but there is a real danger that the potential quality of the head teacher appraisal process could be sadly diminished by the paucity of resource, or disinclination, or lack of understanding within LEAs when it comes to making critical decisions about enhancing the process.

Head teacher appraisal and head teacher assessment

The discretionary powers of governors in relation to the pay of teachers and head teachers have brought a new set of tensions. There are already a number of head teachers who have approached governors with a view to obtaining enhanced salaries. Governors, many of whom are bewildered and unprepared for becoming involved in this critical decision, are casting around for ways in which to assess the merits of the claim and, most understandably, have fallen eagerly upon the appraisal statement as precisely the document needed.

It is not easy to explain to concerned governors the reasons why the appraisal statement is neither appropriate nor available for this purpose, without incurring considerable perplexity and maybe some anger. The source of the difficulties lies in the different understandings and experiences of appraisal which exist within such a group of people. Where governors have experience of appraisal it may well be of a crude accountability model rather than one which has professional development as its purpose. Helping them to come to an understanding of the differences in principles and practice takes time and thoughtful planning or presentation – another item for the already overburdened agenda of governor training.

Thus, LEAs not only have a significant task in terms of educating governors about appraisal, they will also need to be quite clear about what kind of guidance or instruments they will be giving to governing bodies who are seeking help in matters of salary enhancements.

Conclusion

As LEAs and appraisal steering groups go about the task of implementing statutory appraisal they will have a series of critical decisions to make about the size and shape of the appraisal process they are implementing. Although many of these issues will ultimately be mediated by the schools, in matters of head teacher appraisal, the LEA will have a continuing responsibility for co-ordination and implementation. In these straitened times the minimal model will seem like an attractive option.

The question that must be asked is 'At what point does the cheapest option become an expensive mistake?' The answer is 'Where the appraisal of head teachers becomes a shallow or meaningless exercise without worthwhile outcomes for those involved'.

Experience of head teacher appraisal in Cumbria has consistently emphasised the potential of the process for enhancing the professional practice of the head teacher. Many appraisees have spoken warmly of the opportunities it gave for serious and critical reflection, for supporting innovation and development and for reducing the isolation of the job. Many appraisers have remarked that involvement in the appraisal of another head teacher has been a most significant staff development activity in itself and has often caused the appraisers to reflect upon and refine their own thinking in the selected areas of focus.

In making decisions about the future for head teacher appraisal, it will be important to bear in mind that, where head teachers have experienced appraisal as a worthwhile, purposeful and supportive process for themselves, they are more likely to make it so for the teachers in their schools.

3.4.2 Salford's experience 1987–91

Dallas Hackett

Introduction

The value of appraisal, according to one recently appointed head participating in pilot appraisal work in Salford, lay in giving her the opportunity to 'sit down at length and talk in depth' about her performance – for the first time. It gave her confidence in prioritising her tasks and clarified her direction as a new head teacher.

Ironically, we had intended to exclude 'new' heads from such demanding pilot work, but this response was typical of nearly sixty heads, at various stages of headship, who were appraised between 1987 and 1991.

Readers are referred to chapter 3.6.2 on teacher appraisal in Salford for details of the LEA's early work in appraisal, the principles underpinning pilot work and the arrangements for organising, conducting and monitoring it. Support for professional development was fundamental to head teacher as to teacher appraisal and the intention was to evolve through consultation and trial an approach and materials which would genuinely support head teachers in their increasingly demanding role.

Starting out: a learning experience

Prepilot work in head teacher appraisal in Salford included an adviser or head teacher partnership, working out an appraisal procedure. There had also been substantial raising of awareness and appraisal skills training for all secondary heads, advisers and about half the primary heads.

In addition, a training programme was run, involving seven pairs of head teachers analysing each others' performance, with the help of a consultant. We learned much from this about training for appraisal, information collection, task observation and appraisal interviewing, and sorted out at least some of the teething problems. The programme also gave us a nucleus of heads experienced in appraisal, some of whom later became appraisers and trainers.

By the start of pilot work, we had produced, through consultation, the first draft of an appraisal scheme. We also had a generic job description for head teachers, evolved by a representative task group and fundamental to all key aspects of the process – establishing a focus and criteria for the appraisal; determining relevant information to be sought; furnishing an agenda for the interview; and influencing the targets set and support needed.

The heads of our twelve pilot schools (see chapter 3.6.2) automatically became appraisees, supplemented by nine volunteers from all phases. The heads opted for one of four models:

1. Two head teachers were partnered and conducted simultaneous appraisals;
2. Two head teachers were paired – one appraising the other;
3. An adviser appraised a head teacher; or
4. An adviser and a head teacher appraised another head teacher.

Great care was taken in the pairing and there were no difficulties with this or with the choice of models.

Meanwhile, the LEA's major role in head teacher appraisal was defined. These were

Responsibilities in evolving a framework;

A training programme;

Documentation; and

Supporting materials.

The LEA consulted, provided supporting personnel, monitored and evaluated work done and sought to respond to the outcomes of appraisal.

This early work culminated in a six day training programme for appraisees and appraisers jointly. It was in-house and crossphase and, apart from informational and skill building sessions, concentrated on small group work to produce materials and procedures for self-appraisal, information collection and processing, task observation and documentation for the process.

The draft scheme was thus fleshed out and we all benefited from the learning experience.

Outcomes of the pilot work

Work was monitored through regular meetings following training and implementation. Outcomes were discussed at steering group meetings and publicised in newsletters.

Pilot work gave us a process, procedure, documentation and growing expertise. It also gave us an insight into the time and money costs of appraisal, the organisational implications for the LEA and the benefits to be gained. *'Head teacher Appraisal – A Handbook'* was published and used as the training manual in later work.

Our preferred model involved a peer head teacher and an LEA adviser as appraisers. This capitalised on the breadth of experience available; aided continuity; strengthened links with the LEA's mechanism for professional development; and shared the work load. This last was so considerable that it resulted in the use of seconded head teachers as appraisers in work in 1990–91.

Head teacher appraisal was seen as biennial, with interim support and review in year two, the process spread over seven to eight weeks and immediately following training.

Appraisal work 1990–91

Lessons learned from pilot work were applied in the appraisal of 24 volunteer primary head teachers.

Two primary heads were seconded for two terms (with release for follow-up during the rest of the cycle) to appraise the 24. Their role and that of the advisers assisting, was carefully defined in training.

Since the appraisal process used is now inherent in the national framework, I propose only to highlight particular aspects of the process or training which LEAs starting appraisal might wish to consider.

Process

Aspects include:
1. The biggest single factor in success is 'quality' appraisers. They **must** be experienced and professionally credible. They must inspire trust and confidence. They need good interpersonal skills and technical skills in processing information as well as negotiating and reporting outcomes. There is much behind the scenes work and organisation and much 'homework' to do.

2. The second most important factor is preparation. Appraisers need to spend much time in familiarising themselves with the school and its operation. Appraisees need to furnish information, brief staff and governors, and keep them informed throughout. The initial meeting should be thoroughly 'scripted' and prepared.
3. An appraisee can only derive maximum benefit by being proactive – in giving access, furnishing information, devoting time, prioritising the exercise, and adopting a receptive stance. Being appraised is not a passive experience. The appraisee determines the quality of his or her self-appraisal and thus of the interview, and the success of the process, by his or her response to feedback and in the formulation of targets.
4. There is a need for supportive materials and documentation. A job description is vital. People need help with self-appraisal and information collection should be documented. We documented the appraisal timetable; the information–collection agreement and instruments for it; self-appraisal; the job description; the summary statement; targets set; and the timetable for follow-up work.
5. Information collection is potentially the most threatening part of the appraisal process. We laid down consultation questions and used a standard questionnaire for teaching staff to complete. We also introduced **a feedback session (rather as in classroom observation) a week prior to the interview proper,** and would recommend this. It gives due importance to the large amount of information which might be collected and gives the appraisee the opportunity to digest this before the interview and before setting targets.
6. Task observation was seen as desirable but difficult for operational and time reasons and there is still work to be done in developing this.
7. Target setting presents difficulties. It is hard for head teachers to stop short of setting institutional targets to revolutionise the school within six months! Nor were targets always related to the outcomes of the process. To enable targets to be properly addressed rather than tagged onto the end of a three hour interview, we used **a separate target setting meeting** a week after the interview proper. This worked quite well but there is still a need for more training in setting appraisal targets.

Training

Appraisees and appraisers had a three day training programme, half of it shared and all of it in-house. Implementation followed immediately and indeed training time was used to start off trials on the process proper. The sessions were as follows:

Induction – half a day This was concerned with addressing anxieties, establishing principles and making initial arrangements.

Process – one day This aimed to familiarise all participants with the process, procedure, instruments and documentation.

Skills for appraisee participation in appraisal – one and a half days This gave training in self-appraisal; receiving feedback; the appraisal interview; and target setting.

Skills for appraiser management of appraisal – one and a half days This offered training in information collection; processing and feedback; interviewing; writing the summary statement; and supporting the outcomes of appraisal.

The training was seen as valuable in its own right and certainly gave people confidence in handling the appraisal process and maximising the benefits from it.

Conclusion

It is true to say that **all** our heads benefited from appraisal. They brought much to it themselves, had 'quality' appraisers and considerable support through the LEA scheme and training programme.

There are obvious difficulties – in finding time in schools and the LEA to do justice to appraisal: in ensuring the quality of appraisers; in finding time to train properly; in meeting targets and supporting needs; in organising a complex system centrally; and in maintaining impetus and quality for all head teachers over a long period.

The fact remains that appraisal is too valuable a lifeline to fail and must be prioritised despite difficulties. The 'new' head teacher will still need support in her last appraisal before retirement.

3.5 Appraisal in further education colleges

3.5.0 Experience from pilot schemes of appraisal in further education colleges

Brian Fidler

Introduction

In 1989–90 six LEAs ran pilot appraisal schemes for FE with funding through ESG involving seven colleges. General principles for the pilot schemes were drawn up by the National Joint Committee (NJC) Working Party. The experience was monitored and evaluated by a team from NFER (Lee, 1991).

One of the colleges was a small agricultural college and the other six were of varying size and organisational structure. Four of the colleges had a faculty structure. Within three of these colleges there were schools or divisions within the faculties and a modified matrix structure. The fourth had Boards of Study. The remaining three colleges had departmental structures.

The pilot colleges were in varying states of readiness. Two had formal annual staff reviews. Only three colleges included all teaching staff in the scheme.

This section reviews this experience and Ian Duckett writes a first hand account of one of the pilot appraisal colleges, Barnet, in section 3.5.1 and Kevin Quinlan presents Cheshire's CEMP scheme in section 3.5.2.

Appraisal procedures

There was some variation among the schemes but the main elements of the procedures were the following (Lee, 1991: p. 20):

Preparation	initial meeting
	self appraisal
(negotiation of job description)	
Teaching/task observaton	classroom teaching
	managerial tasks
	administrative tasks
Review meeting	data collection
	discussion
	agreed actions
	written records
Agreed action follow up	professional development activities arranged
	internal adjustments discussed and/or implemented

Thus the procedures were similar to those already being piloted in schools but there was more attempt to observe non-classroom activities than was the case in schools.

In the main appraisers were line managers but in some cases there was choice, there were also logistical problems over numbers and peer appraisal was tried in some cases.

Observation of teaching

In some colleges there was concern that the observer of teaching should have been teacher trained on the basis that appraisees would have more confidence in such people. One college had the following checklist from its previous experience of observation:

Preparation and planning;

Presentation and performance;

Relationship with students;

Records and record keeping;

General standards of work;

Approach to syllabus;

Lesson plan;

Knowledge of course; and

Knowledge of students.

Observation in some cases made appraisers more aware of current conditions in classrooms and the need for support. Classroom observation received mixed views as to its usefulness. Classroom observation takes a great deal of time – two options are to split observation from the rest of the interview but passing the results forward or making it optional. Regular less formal visits to classrooms provided there was feedback as soon as possible offered another alternative.

Observation of non-teaching tasks

Some non-teaching tasks observed included:

Interviewing prospective students;

Arranging work placements;

Keeping records;

Co-ordinating a course team; and

Chairing a meeting.

The value of observing non-teaching tasks was somewhat questionable and very variable. A greater degree of selectivity in choosing what was studied was suggested as a possibility for the future. Other data and documentation was also examined.

Appraisal meeting

Not all schemes made a link between classroom or task observation and the remainder of the appraisal process. Although most staff found the appraisal meeting 'reasonably useful' there was a group who were dissatisfied with the whole or parts of the process and the institution in which they worked. Following the appraisal meeting a report with agreed targets was written with a portion on staff development which was more public. By conducting the individual appraisals in the context of departmental and college reviews it was intended that development priorities would emerge for the institution which could inform the prioritisation of individual INSET needs since resources would not stretch to meeting all needs.

Some schemes had a later formal review meeting to check on progress on targets and staff development.

Staff development

Some mechanisms were set up to co-ordinate staff development needs e.g. HoDs or deputy HoDs or staff development officers. In some cases the senior management team made decisions.

> If the colleges sell the idea of appraisal to staff as a means of identifying needs and developing staff, then it is essential that the managerial and financial commitment is not only encapsulated in college policy, but that its implementation is visible and recognised
>
> (Lee, 1991: p.45)

There was particular concern about the ability to deliver staff development if the appraiser was not the line manager of the appraisee.

Relationship or other college structures

Most colleges had or were in the process of introducing course review procedures but departmental reviews were much rarer. Although there were college development plans in place there was a feeling that these had little impact on individuals or their appraisal.

> In order to benefit individuals and the institution and thereby enhance the quality of service provided, the links between individual appraisal and corporate review need to be firmly established
>
> (Lee: p.77)

Appraisal of senior management

In only two cases was there any appraisal of the principal even though all staff were intended to be appraised. In one case the chair of governors and the principal of another college undertook the appraisal. Providing training for such people was a problem as was the case in some colleges where the chair of governors declined to appraise the principal.

Implementation

It was recommended that any appraisal scheme needs to be approved by the staff. Staff need to feel a sense of ownership. It was also suggested that a steering committee of various interest groups should be set up and that there should be monitoring and evaluation procedures for the process. The view of staff was that the process should be voluntary.

Preparation for appraisal

A general awareness raising session should have a member of SMT and NATFHE present to answer questions and give credibility. Where there were no job descriptions it was thought important to discuss and agree responsibilities before appraisal.

It was recommended that there should be some training to introduce general principles where there was no familiarity with individual review and to outline the specific scheme followed by more detailed training for appraisers and appraisees.

In the interests of promoting equal opportunities, it was recommended that

> The opportunity for assertiveness training should also be provided for all staff. (Lee: p.82)

Further recommendations

The relationship between appraiser and appraisee and the ability of the appraiser to conduct the appraisal were regarded as the keys to success. There appeared to be a fair amount of cynicism that any changes would be brought about by appraisal. The role of the HoD or equivalent in co-ordinating the results of individual appraisals and corporate and departmental policies is vital[1].

Some recommendations (Lee: p.81) regarding appraisers are:

> Appraisees must have some choice over who their appraiser is, and must be able to choose freely from the alternatives.

> For the observation of teaching, appraisers should preferably, be teacher trained, but at the very least, should have received appropriate training as part of the appraisal scheme.

> Line managers have many advantages as appraisers, because of their power to enact changes and their access to resources, but peer appraisers can be equally effective if appropriate structures are available to support them in this role.

3.5.1 Staff appraisal at Barnet College

Ian Duckett

Barnet College

Barnet College, a college with 1,500 full-time and 12,000 part-time students, is located in north London and is part of the two college authority, the London Borough of Barnet. Of the college's 180 full-time lecturing staff, 143 underwent the pilot appraisal scheme which ran from April 1989 to March 1990.

Barnet scheme

Following the 1988 Agreement between the National Association of Teachers in Further and Higher Education (NATFHE) and the employers, general principles were worked out and agreed by a National Joint Council (NJC) Working Party for the Pilot Appraisal Schemes in Maintained Further and Higher Education (NJC, 1988)[2].

At Barnet, the principal submitted a proposal, which at this point he had discussed with NATFHE branch officers and which later formed the starting point for the working party and became incorporated into the *Notes for Guidance* (Barnet College, 1989). When the NJC selected the Barnet Scheme as one of the six pilots it was the beginning of the college's involvement.

Further involvement stemmed from a number of lengthy discussions and a detailed consultation process. The NATFHE branch were involved throughout and debates and votes took place on three occasions, prior to the introduction of the scheme. It agreed to the establishment of a working party and elected four members, three with a long standing involvement in staff development, with the branch secretary, to serve on the working party. The *Notes for Guidance* were also supported by the branch in February 1989, and provision was made for regular reports at committee and branch level. The gestation period from February 1989 to September 1989 when the scheme proper began is generally agreed as having been useful. No college wishing to implement an appraisal scheme should overlook NATFHE, without whose support the scheme at Barnet would almost certainly have floundered.

That is also why Barnet branch of NATFHE has pushed for a return to the Annual Review process that was in operation prior to the pilot pending the recommendations of the NJC and the principal has announced the end, for the time being at least, of appraisal; this being done, however, it is likely that in the light of the appraisal process and in possession of the *Notes for Guidance* that future reviews will be coloured by the appraisal experience[3].

Designing the scheme

Background

Once the Pilot Appraisal Scheme Working Party set about its task there were a number of parameters that it had to bear in mind. Those parameters were used throughout the period of the working party's existence as a kind of checklist and series of reference points. The first concern had to be with the NJC guidelines. Second, there was a commitment throughout to the scheme to conform to NATFHE's views on appraisal at both national and branch level. Third, the scheme had to be practicable: time, financial implications, and the skills that appraisers and appraisees would require to participate in the scheme need to be taken into account.

In retrospect it is possible to identify three phases of the appraisal scheme.

1. Producing the terms of the pilot;
2. Development of the terms into a working scheme (the *Notes for Guidance*); and
3. Preparing to implement the scheme.

What follows is a brief history of the design process, beginning with before the working party was even conceived of, as outlined below.

Decision to participate

Phase One was the most intense of the three phases. The initial decision to bid to be part of the National Pilot was made by the principal, who kept NATFHE officers and the staff as a whole informed. Throughout the design process reference was made to staff development interests and the requirements of college management. At this point the staff were concerned with both the benefits to the college and the positive impact it hoped to have on the national pilots. NATFHE participated in the process throughout by criticising and making objections both in a broad sense and in detail.

Design

Phase Two began with a recognition that the terms of the pilot which had been selected along with five other schemes up and down the country by the NJC to form the national pilot provided only the bare bones of the scheme. The terms of the pilot merely pointed members of the working party in a particular direction: at this point there was no indication as to how to get there.

The Barnet Scheme was the first of the pilot schemes off the mark. It was recognised that to leave the development until the start date of 1st April 1989 would be courting disaster. There was a further recognition that detailed guidelines would need the approval of the NATFHE branch in advance of the start date. Recognising the importance of acceptance by the whole staff the working party had to take a chance on the fleshed out scheme being rejected before the pilot had even begun.

From December 1988 until February 1989 the working party set about its task of taking the draft scheme and providing notes to explain and support and in some cases alter the processes that were to be included in the scheme. After its initial meetings, it was agreed that total immersion would be the most effective way forward and that in addition to weekly business meetings the group would meet on three full days, having prepared individually or in groups, papers, which after discussion, would form part of the final text. It is worth dwelling a while on the subjects of the papers which were initially submitted so that they can be compared to the final document.

In all some 28 papers were considered (Barnet College Pilot Appraisal Scheme Working Papers, 1989). There were varying degrees of discussion around the issues and in February there was full agreement on most of these issues with votes being taken on two before a final decision was made. The process of refinement is one which cannot be overlooked. Without this attention to detail at the working party meetings and discussion elsewhere a scheme that the vast majority of staff were happy to work with could not have been possible to provide.

Particular areas of difficulty were, first, the general encouragement to participate. There were justifiable concerns about appraisal and these had to be balanced with the enthusiasm of others. Second, although the annual review process had involved appraisal type interviews, the content and organisation of the appraisal interview provoked a good deal of discussion both in the working party and elsewhere, most significantly on the relationship between individual appraisal and team appraisal. The transfer of information from one to the other was considered to have serious implications for confidentiality. Third, evaluation of teaching contributions. Classroom observation was never a prescribed part of the annual review process and had not been a significant activity. Discussion was centred on the importance of the evaluation of teaching as an effective process, what methods were appropriate and how appraisal could tackle the problems.

Acceptance

Once the *Notes for Guidance* were approved Phase Three began. The working party had laid great emphasis on the training programme which was to consist of training for participation, training for appraisers and appraisees, training in recording the process and training to enable the delivery of outcomes. (Barnet College, 1989)

Appraisal in theory

Most significantly the job of the working party was to ensure that the pilot scheme would not only enable lessons to be learned nationally, but would be acceptable to colleagues, and hopefully have value to individuals and to the college as a whole.

The *Notes for Guidance* inform the operation of the pilot scheme in a sensitive and supportive way. All colleagues had a copy. It was believed they provided information and reassurance. It was hoped they would also give all of us – whatever our responsibilities in the process – confidence to participate fully in the operation of the pilot scheme.

By participation in the pilot appraisal scheme the college exerted a positive influence on the final national appraisal scheme[4].

The approach at Barnet College is to locate appraisal within a staff development framework which is recognised as a vital part of a lecturer's job. Any appraisal scheme must be implemented in the light of clearly established educational principles and college policy statements, in Barnet's case particularly Antiracist/Multicultural and the Sex Equality policies.

Teachers in the college needed to be convinced that appraisal is a legitimate part of a continuous process for the improvement and extension of their professional skills. In order to achieve this view the professional development of teachers was to be central in the appraisal process. It should certainly feature prominently in informal discussions between heads or line managers and teachers, as well as in any more formal appraisal interview or written report.

The introduction of formal appraisal will put extra demands on senior staff of all levels. Their ability to observe lessons; chair meetings on appraisal issues; write reports; and conduct what should be sensitive and positive interviews may mean the difference between success and failure of the college pilot scheme. If they are to perform their appraisal function effectively, this will require recognition and adequate allocation of time.

Any members of staff involved in the role of appraiser had to be positively supported as they developed and extended their expertise. 'Positive support' includes adequate staff development, and that means sufficient funding for the extensive training programme required.

The potential goodwill of staff towards the pilot scheme could have been destroyed if appraisers were inadequately prepared. Similarly, appraisees must play their part in preparing for the process. The Barnet scheme sought to reflect that: flexibility should be a major part of the scheme; individuals have different needs; it must be seen to be fair and just; everyone must understand what is being appraised and the process by which it is being appraised; all criteria sought to be objective.

The pilot scheme operated within the objectives of the college staff development policy formulated in 1981 and progressively implemented since that date. It would thus be placed within a set of well established institutional arrangements. More importantly, the scheme operated in an environment which encouraged supportive staff development within an open and participative management structure.

The college's Four Year Development Plan provided the institutional framework for the pilot scheme. It was intended that these arrangements should reflect that the quality of the service is just as much a function of institutional priorities and commitment as it is the contribution and achievements of individuals and teams. The main provisions of the scheme were:

1. To cover all teaching staff within the college;
2. To build upon the college's existing voluntary annual review process, which is part of its established staff development policy.

All colleagues will have an opportunity for appraisal during the autumn term with their managers. The scheme details the arrangements for appraisal and, throughout, the emphasis is on appraisal as a process. This process will include evaluation of teaching contribution, will emphasise that the process must involve a dialogue and will culminate in a negotiated agreed record to include outcomes and action;

3. To make arrangements for the appraisal of senior staff, including the principal, in line with existing arrangements for annual review;
4. To provide explicit guidelines for the evaluation of teaching contribution, giving particular weight to the centrality of this evaluation, while stressing its sensitivity and hence the need for thorough preparation.
5. The preparation of a profile of training and development needs within all areas of the college's work. At present the faculty profiles derive from the annual review process. A similar practice will apply during the appraisal pilot;
6. Thorough training for all participants. Members of the senior management team have been trained to undertake annual review. It is recognised that the pilot appraisal requires further training for appraisers and appraisees. Much of that should be joint training.
7. An appeals procedure has been included. No written records will be retained beyond the duration of the pilot without the appraisee's written agreement.

(Barnet College, 1989)

Appendices to the *Notes for Guidance* amplified the main provisions of the scheme. The training period for the appraisal pilot was specified, for example, together with the phasing of the appraisal process itself. Guidelines are provided for the appraisal interview: where problems and difficulties about working practice exist they should be addressed directly by the appraiser or appraisee, with the emphasis on ways of resolving such problems. It was noted that the appraisal process does not form a part of any agreed disciplinary machinery.

The primary roles which senior staff undertake were spelled out in order to distinguish their tasks within the work of the college. The main agents for senior staff appraisal were identified and it is recognised that a variety of appraisers may be desirable.

The activities relevant to evaluation of teaching contribution were identified, as were associated factors. Teaching observation is clearly one mechanism for appraisal that the emphasis should be on the process and skills used to meet particular teaching objectives; that is the planning, organisation, methods of presentation and the staff/ student interaction that takes place.

The perception that teams are more than groups of individuals has been recognised by providing staff development in this area. The need for teams to evaluate or appraise themselves on a regular basis is clearly desirable. The working party identified two areas where appraisal could be effective: appraisal of the way in which a team works; and appraisal of the effectiveness of the work that the team does. It has also been suggested that the conclusions of team appraisal might be included in an individual's appraisal meeting.

The scheme made provision for staff development needs to be identified via faculty profiles produced by heads following appraisal sessions in conjunction with needs identified by Boards of Studies and Course Teams.

An extensive training programme for the pilot scheme was arranged for the summer term. Workshops were held on training for teaching observation; supporting and assisting the appraisal process; understanding the pilot scheme; participating in appraisal; and managing outcomes of appraisal.

The working party felt that the monitoring of the scheme was an essential component of it. This was to form the basis of an evaluation at the end of the pilot scheme. It was agreed that the monitoring group should comprise representatives of college management and NATFHE and meet as required, but at least every four weeks.

Provision for colleagues to have recourse to the appeals procedure was built into the scheme where:

1. There is significant and enduring failure in effective communication or lack of constructive criticism or loss of trust between the parties.

2. When the appraisee thinks the appraiser's judgement of the situation is unreasonable, unfair, or simply wrong;

3. When the appraiser attempts to establish what the appraisee believes are unfair or unrealistic targets/goals or performance expectations for the next academic year.

(Barnet College, 1989).

After the scheme was made public, a branch meeting again supported the implementation of the scheme. The approach to the pilot appraisal scheme, and to staff development as a whole has over many years been one where NATFHE and college management have sought to work together. Moreover, the college's experience in staff development has been sustained because a range of colleagues within the college have had responsibilities in this area. In consequence the college has built up a network of support, interest and expertise, which will be vital to the introduction of appraisal schemes (Duckett and Skitt, 1989).

The *Notes for Guidance* constituted, in the words of one member of the working party, 'a network of fail-safes' which were neither inflexible nor exclusive. Team appraisal, for example, could be included; teaching observation 'may' form a part of the process; there was an appeals procedure if required.

Appraisal in practice

The *Notes* state very clearly the reasons for Barnet College's participation in the national pilot: 'By participating in the Pilot Appraisal Scheme we hope to exert a positive influence in the final outcome.' This remained the intention throughout.

Throughout the pilot, appraisal was located within a staff development framework, implemented in the light of established educational principles and with reference to college policy statements, especially antiracist/multicultural and sex equality policies. On the whole the experiences of those who participated in the pilot accepted that these principles were applied. There were however a few notable exceptions (Duckett, 1990).

The scheme also sought to 'limit the potential damage to the profession... by current movements in education'. Certainly at Barnet the consensus seems to be that appraisal was not, in the pilot at least as damaging or threatening as many feared it might be. Without constant reference to staff development and the college's experience of staff development in the wider sense, however, the outcome may have been much different (Duckett, 1991). Similarly, whether the Barnet Scheme represents a model for future schemes or not, is not yet known. It is certainly worth pointing out at this stage that the model would not be appropriate for colleges without an already fairly highly developed staff development policy. For Barnet it may well have worked; other colleges, although they may wish to use the Barnet scheme as a starting point, will need individually tailored schemes to meet their own needs as recognition of the importance of the design of the scheme and the refining of the process in Barnet's experience should demonstrate.

'Teachers will need to be convinced that appraisal is a legitimate part of the continuous process for the improvement and extension of their professional skills' the *Notes* proclaim. At Barnet College, members of staff, largely because of the support of the NATFHE Branch, gave the scheme the benefit of the doubt on the basis that it was a pilot.

One of the major factors that has influenced this view is the additional demands that have been placed on senior staff. The workload that appraisal entailed was phenomenal. Ultimately the ability of line managers to observe lessons, chair meetings on appraisal issues, make appraisal records and reports to inform a full institutional appraisal, the need for which has now been agreed by union and management, played a large part in the debates surrounding the desirability of a review/appraisal scheme beyond the pilot. Equally, it is their conduct in terms of sensitive handling and a positive approach that made the difference between the success and failure of the scheme in individual cases and, consequently, the scheme as a whole.

The *Notes for Guidance* drew attention to the need for the goodwill of staff if the scheme is to be a success. 'Nothing', the working party noted, 'will destroy the potential goodwill of staff towards the pilot scheme as the perception that there are inadequately prepared appraisers.' In practice, this was clearly the case. Those heads of faculty who were sensitive, able and well prepared were the ones who were perceived by appraisees as being responsible for effective appraisals.

The *Thinking Behind the Scheme* and *Making it Work* sections of the *Notes* stressed the importance of fairness, simplicity, objectivity and flexibility. Again, appraisees who were positive about the operation of the scheme felt that those four criteria had been operated.

In terms of the operation of the scheme the *Notes for Guidance* were perceived as having been generally useful. The timing and phasing of arrangements followed the outline plan. The setting up and managing of the appraisal interview went, in most cases, according to plan, although line managers made arrangements that varied slightly.

In most cases the appraisal interview itself seems to have followed the pattern of:

(a) An agenda setting pre-appraisal interview;

(b) Classroom observation;

(c) Feedback on the classroom observation;

(d) Fuller appraisal interview; and

(e) Meeting to agree the record.

It should be noted that in several cases, teaching contribution was not appraised, especially where it was seen not to form a significant part of a lecturer's duties. Most appraisees saw appraisal as a process, rather than a product, as was hoped by the working party and it was in most cases used as an opportunity to take stock and reflect on practice.

A great deal of attention was paid to the appraisal of senior staff. The principal's appraisal was only partial, that being the case not because of any reluctance on his part, but because a request made to the Chair of the Governing Body was not taken up. Instead senior management team (SMT) members adopted a two way approach to appraisal when being appraised by the principal. The rest of the SMT were appraised in much the same way as other appraisees, though of course with special emphasis on their role as managers.

Inevitably the evaluation of teaching contribution was the focus of most comments even though the working party had recognised that 'teaching contribution is more complex than those activities which take place in the classroom'. The activities which support teaching and learning: preparation, curriculum development, course design, marking, moderating, profiling, record keeping, tutoring, report writing etc, were emphasised in most appraisals.

The inclusion of the word 'may' in a sentence about teaching observation forming part of an individual's appraisal was a major item for discussion at working party meetings and was in the end accepted on the grounds that appraisal could only be effective if both it and components of it were voluntary[5]. Some of those who opted out of appraisal seem to have done so because of the perceived expected inclusion of classroom observation, but not a significant number.

Team appraisal was the least effective element of the scheme. Only one faculty paid serious attention to the role of teams as a vehicle for appraisal. In other faculties a handful of individuals asked for team appraisal. The *Notes for Guidance* draw attention to 'the need for teams to evaluate or appraise the team performance on a regular scheduled basis' and the college has, over recent years played an active part in team building exercises. While the absence of team appraisal from the formal appraisal process was bemoaned by some members of staff, it ought to be pointed out that many teams do appraise the way they work and the effectiveness of that work at end of year team reviews and have done so over a number of years.

Some individuals felt positive about the scheme because they got something tangible in terms of staff development out of their participation. Others felt that appraisal added nothing in this area and that seniority and favouritism was operative in the doling out of course and conference attendances in much the same way that it always had been. Appraisal on one hand was perceived as an integral part of staff development; others felt that the money could have been better spent on other aspects of staff development (Duckett, 1991).

The training programme was carried out according to the working party's identification of needs and some sessions were repeated during the Autumn term, with a general session for new staff in the spring term. Additionally, up to the end of March, three conferences have been held under the auspices of the INSET Board of Studies that drew on Barnet College's experience as a pilot scheme college.

3.5.2 Professional and management development in Cheshire

Kevin Quinlan

Introduction

The Cheshire Education Management Programme (CEMP) did not set out to become an appraisal system and it is not perceived in Cheshire to be one. Its purpose – to improve the performance of the organisation – is however the same, and like all appraisal systems it has a personal review at the heart of the system. CEMP shares many characteristics of those appraisal systems that lean heavily to the developmental model.

The development of CEMP started in 1985 with a management challenge: how to make management development integral with organisational development; how to make it relevant to the needs of the individual and the organisation; how to bring planning, coherence and progression to the process; and how to make it affordable.

CEMP has been operating over the past four years in Cheshire's seven further education colleges, the adult education service and the prison education service. In 1990 seven secondary schools and a sixth form college introduced CEMP as a pilot, and a further seventeen secondary and special schools plan to adopt the system in the next phase of extension in 1991. Over a four year period the number of Cheshire staff on CEMP has increased from 39 in the pilot to around 500. This expansion has been achieved within existing training budgets. CEMP delegates include senior school and college managers, lecturers and teachers with management responsibilities or potential, librarians and administrative staff.

The CEMP system has been adopted or adapted by LEAs and individual colleges outside Cheshire – in Northern Ireland, Scotland, Wales and England.

Initiation

Needs analysis

The development of CEMP started in 1985–86 with a major needs investigation, supported by the Further Education Unit (FEU) and the Training Agency, to propose a specification for an organisation based management development programme. The investigation involved over 100 education managers in Cheshire and elsewhere, officers and advisers, national validating bodies, universities and polytechnics, The Staff College (then the Further Education Staff College), and private sector employers.

Some of the conclusions were:

> Existing education management training provision was widely held to be too academic, insufficiently related to current education practice, inflexible, outmoded in learning and assessment techniques, and too expensive both in cost and time.

> Relatively few managers received systematic training or work-based support in their management and leadership roles. They felt unsure in their current managerial roles, and unprepared for higher managerial roles, and unprepared for higher managerial responsibility. Most thought their organisations did not fully recognise their ability, achievements or potential.

> Training opportunities were available but access to them was based on the 'hands-up' principle – that is, they were voluntary, unrelated to organisational needs, and with little if any follow-up by the organisation.

> Substantial demand existed for management development: from experienced managers who felt they needed continuing development; from inexperienced and potential managers who wanted a more open, systematic approach to management preparation and development; and from senior managers who wanted a process of management development that worked for the organisation's purpose.

Specification

During 1986–87 a specification was devised for a new system of management development. It was agreed that such a system should:

> Replace ad-hocery with planning;

> Work within the organisation's management structure – no bolt-on systems;

Satisfy the unique needs of each individual within the context of the organisation's purpose;

Provide systematic professional support, not just training;

Emphasise the practice rather than theory of management;

Ensure recognition of achievement *within* the organisation; and

Make management development available to all managers, career long.

Management development should be integral with organisational development

The specification was turned into a process and system during 1986–87 and piloted in 1987–88 in Cheshire's seven further education colleges and the adult education service. Following the pilot, CEMP was adopted by all participating organisations. Over the following two years the process and management instruments were refined.

What is CEMP?

It is a framework and process for organisation and management development. At the heart of the process is a personal review between delegates to the programme and their line or reporting manager. System and rigour is provided through firm management of the process, clarity of organisational purpose, and CEMP instruments.

The purpose of CEMP is, like all staff development and appraisal systems, to bring sustained management commitment to people and to maximise their contribution to organisational performance. In summary, CEMP seeks to:

Support the organisation by	Working within existing management structures
	Emphasising organisational purpose
	Placing management learning in the context of organisational need
Respect the individual by	Recognising that each individual has unique needs
	Providing career-long support
	Encouraging personal responsibility for professional development

Enhance the line manager role by	Systematic personal reviewing
	Linking job performance with personal development
	Providing work-based coaching
Improve planning by	Systematic individual needs identification
	Planned and progressive learning opportunities
	Monitoring and evaluation
Achieve value for money by	Recognising the value of work-based learning
	Targeting learning opportunities to need
	Increasing learning opportunities within budget

CEMP Process

The process is shown in Figure 3.5.2.1, and the elements are described below.

Induction

The induction is designed to introduce delegates and managers to the CEMP philosophy, processes, and roles and responsibilities. Delegates and managers are trained in the skills of one-to-one reviewing, and in a technique for identifying learning needs and translating them into workbased learning.

Preparation

Before each review, delegates take stock of their professional and management skill, knowledge and experience and consider how they wish to develop to meet the development needs of the organisation as well as themselves. This information is passed to the manager before the review. Thorough preparation is of the highest importance. The quality of the preparation directly affects the quality of the personal review itself.

APPRAISAL EXPERIENCE

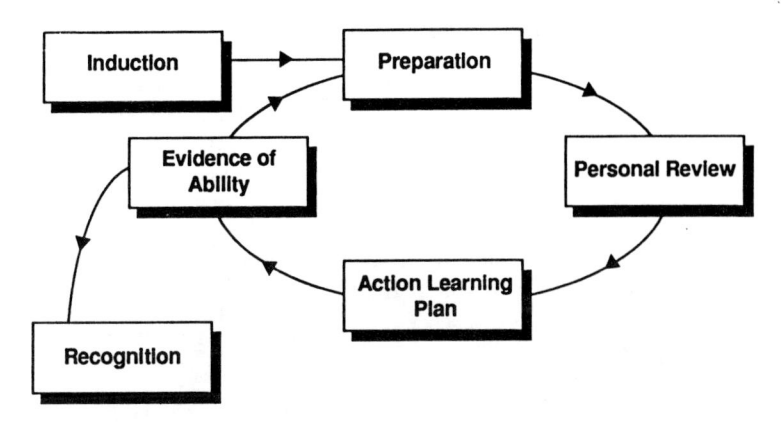

Figure 3.5.2.1 CEMP process

(Diagram showing cyclical process: Induction → Preparation → Personal Review → Action Learning Plan → Evidence of Ability → Recognition)

Personal review

The review provides the opportunity, context and time for special attention to be given to each delegate, and for feedback on performance, achievements, ideas and potential.

Delegates have a special role in the system because personal development must ultimately be the individual's responsibility. The delegates' role in the review is to prepare a proposal, gain agreement and implement the agreement.

The manager's role is to help ensure that learning plans are appropriate for the individual, satisfy the developmental needs of the organisation, and are adequately supported and resourced. Without commitment and support from the manager the review process will not work.

Action learning plan

The action learning plan is a 'learning contract'. It is a record of the agreed learning opportunities, methods of learning, support arrangements, criteria for achievement, and target dates. Enough information is needed to ensure clarity of purpose and provide the basis for evaluation of learning outcomes. The manager, through agreeing the plan, has accepted responsibility for supporting the learning activities and ensuring that appropriate resources are provided. The CEMP recording system is used to record the action learning plan.

Evidence of achievement

As a delegate's action learning plans develop, a variety of evidence is generated to illustrate growing management ability – skills, knowledge and experience. Some achievements will be tangible: some will have involved processes and achievement through other people that require observation and judgement from third parties. The evidence, when put together, becomes a management portfolio of evidence of achievement. The CEMP recording system is used to summarise the evidence of achievement to inform subsequent reviews.

Recognition

For most staff, for most of their career, recognition of achievement and potential is more important within their organisation than recognition provided by validating bodies. This is equally true for the organisation. The CEMP recording system provides a source of information for organisations on the development of their managers and teachers.

Colleges and schools will wish to support a minority of their managers in gaining a nationally recognised qualification in management. Two CNAA endorsed Manchester Polytechnic qualifications have been developed to support the CEMP process – a Certificate in Management and Diploma in Management – with progression to the Polytechnic's masters degree in management by action learning. Learning opportunities are negotiated through the personal review and competence is demonstrated at the workplace. There is no requirement for candidates to attend the Polytechnic. Having gained a qualification delegates continue in CEMP to ensure continuing professional development.

Structuring the process

A system must be flexible if it is to work at the level of the individual in a wide range of organisations. If it is to be effective it also needs structure. Within CEMP the structure comes from the way the system is managed within the organisation, the organisation's development plan, Cheshire Management Abilities Profile, and the CEMP Recording System.

Organisation development plan

The purpose of management development is to improve the performance of the organisation through enhanced performance of the individual.

CEMP provides the framework and processes for individual needs identification. The development plan should provide the context within which personal development takes place. The clearer the organisation's plan and development objectives, the easier it is to integrate the individual's learning opportunities.

Cheshire Management Abilities Profile – (MAP)

It is as important to be clear about the management abilities required of staff as to be clear about organisational objectives.

The Cheshire MAP comprises a range of ability descriptors. The first version of the MAP was tested during the pilot and subsequently refined in consultation with the Further Education Staff College. Relatively minor changes had to be made for use in secondary schools. The MAP is currently under revision in the light of recent national work, notably by the Management Charter Initiative.

The Cheshire MAP helps by:

Providing a common management vocabulary;

Widening perspectives on management;

Opening up and helping to structure the Review discussion; and

Providing the basis for recognition of achievement.

The MAP is also a management instrument that can be used for:
Skills audit;
Role analysis;
Planning and targeting learning opportunities;
Monitoring and evaluation;
Job and task descriptions; and
Staff appraisal.

CEMP recording system

The recording system is simple in design and open in format. Its purpose is to support the review process by encouraging delegates and their managers to prepare thoroughly, provide a record of agreed learning plans, and to record evidence of achievement.

It provides the means of opening up the process to management scrutiny to ensure quality and recognition of achievement.

Evaluation: some issues

Evaluation has been a feature of CEMP over the six years of design, piloting, implementation and refinement. This has been carried out within organisations by the CEMP co-ordinators; by regular county-wide focus groups of participants considering issues like the Cheshire MAP, workbased learning, recording evidence of achievement, training for review, and the county programme of seminars and workshops; a full scale evaluation review of CEMP in FE in 1991 by LEA advisers and officers; and an evaluation of CEMP– Secondary by staff of the Education Management Centre North West and University of Manchester Institute of Science and Technology. Some of the issues are discussed below.

Who are the managers?

In colleges and schools, management competence and leadership qualities are needed throughout the organisation. In the context of CEMP in Cheshire, managers are defined not only by grade but by the tasks they perform and the scope and potential of their managerial responsibility. A manager is one who has responsibility for the performance of other staff, for learners, and the curriculum. The challenge for the organisation is to provide within budget systematic, career-long professional support for all its managers, as in the wider context it must do for all staff.

Workbased management learning

Workbased learning works. Most managers learn to manage through experience, and indeed most teachers learn to teach that way. Cost effective learning opportunities abound in, and near, the work-place. They include:

    Supported management tasks;

    Workbased projects and assignments;

    Job rotation;

    Job change;

    Group tasks, learning sets and learning friendships;

    Shadowing;

    Informed discussion;

Workbased coaching;

Short term secondments; and

Guided self-learning

The challenge is to ensure that work-based learning is systematic and progressive, relevant to the individual and the organisation, appropriately supported, and that evidence of achievement and potential is recognised and acted on.

Who reviews?

CEMP is organisation based. Its primary purpose is to improve organisational performance. It follows that a review process should be built on the line (or reporting) management relationships where responsibility for performance is already placed.

This has a number of significant advantages. Line managers who undertake personal reviews are encouraged to become more 'people centred'. Communication between colleagues can improve dramatically, delegation is likely to increase, action learning plans are more likely to reflect organisational needs and be adequately resourced. Most importantly, the link is recognised between job performance and personal development.

There is an important place for 'mentors' and 'learning friends' in management and professional development, notably in support of workbased learning. Experience suggests, however, that when mentors are used for reviewing there is a marked tendency towards weak organisational commitment.

Manager as coach

The successful manager in CEMP needs to be adept in the role of 'coach', which is a management role more widely recognised in Germany and Japan than in the UK, and in industry more than in education. This is ironic since education managers are almost invariably qualified and experienced teachers. The role of coach (in Japan called 'teacher') involves the ability to delegate; to devise workbased learning opportunities (and recognise the difference between learning opportunities and 'task dumping'); provide on-the-job support; give systematic feedback on performance, and recognise achievement and potential.

Issue of Time

The CEMP process makes systematic what many would regard as the responsibility of all managers – to give support and feedback to staff to ensure they function to their highest potential; and of all staff at all levels – to seek developmental opportunities to maintain and enhance their personal effectiveness.

Personal reviews are conceptually, and in practice, at the heart of the process and evaluation has demonstrated the high value that delegates and their managers place on them. They are time consuming, and rightly so because the time taken is a measure of the need.

In Cheshire the guideline is that reviews should take place on three occasions in the year. This recognises that personal and organisational development cannot be an annual (let alone a biennial) event. It recognises that over time the difference between 'informal' feedback and 'formal' reviews becomes blurred, but also that it remains important for personal reviews to be regular, scheduled and recorded.

Managing the process

CEMP is an organisation based system and must therefore be managed within the participating school or college.

In Cheshire, CEMP is a partnership between the education authority, schools and colleges, and participants to the programme.

The education authority has been given by the colleges and schools responsibility for development, co-ordination, certification, and for providing an induction programme and a county programme of seminars and workshops. College principals and head teachers are responsible for managing the system within their organisations. This means ensuring the link is made between management development and the organisation's development plan, and for devising a management system to ensure CEMP is effectively organised and monitored for quality.

Delegates and their managers share a responsibility for ensuring the personal review works for the organisation's purpose and meets the needs of the individual.

Evaluation has demonstrated the obvious – that the quality of CEMP is dependent on the quality of management of the process within the organisation. Participants understand the system and hold it in high esteem.

Development

One test of CEMP in Cheshire is whether the partner organisations accept it. All the colleges and the adult education service have remained with the system and expanded it within their organisations. The number of participants in FE increased from 39 in the 1987 to 250 in 1991. The colleges and the LEA are forming a consortium to ensure that CEMP continues as a partnership enterprise beyond 1993 and incorporation.

A second test is whether CEMP can be transferred beyond Further Education. In Cheshire 24 secondary schools are adopting CEMP-Secondary in 1991 and a planned extension will take place from 1992. Discussions are underway to bring CEMP into County Hall. The system has been adopted by LEAs and colleges outside Cheshire.

A third test is whether the CEMP system has sufficient internal logic for it to be developed for other purposes. The following three developments suggest it is capable of adapting to the government's requirements for appraisal; uniting an organisation's provision for initial training, continuing professional development and management development; and extending its application into the private sector.

Whole organisation professional development system.

In three of Cheshire's FE colleges, a sixth form college and a secondary school, CEMP is being further developed to become a professional development management system for the whole organisation. This means bringing management development, professional development and appraisal into a coherent management system.

The CEMP personal review process remains the key to achieving a coherent system. The Cheshire MAP will be extended to include descriptors of classroom practice and the CEMP Recording System may need slight modification.

Initial teacher training

CEMP has been adapted to provide an initial teacher training programme that is organisation based, coherent, experiential and accessible. The personal review remains at the heart of the process. The programme is validated by Crewe and Alsager College and endorsed by CNAA. Progression into CEMP following certification will be automatic as staff wish to extend their professional competence.

CEMP into industry

CEMP has been adapted to support management development in the private sector. Cheshire FE colleges will provide CEMP styled programmes for corporate clients and, in association with a Cheshire TEC (Training and Enterprise Council), to small and medium firms. The programmes provide Manchester Polytechnic qualifications and have MCI (Management Charter Initiative) endorsement.

Concluding comment

Leadership and good management are needed together with the urgent implementation of the appraisal system: gains are demonstrated in review and fears eradicated.

CASE STUDIES

Case study one: sixth form college

David Henderson, Principal, Priestley College

Priestley College has had a staff development programme in operation for the past three years. We have always seen that the development programme would be the first important stage towards the introduction of an appraisal policy. Indeed we see appraisal as being merely the more structured and focused dialogue relating to staff development.

Our development programme had, however, been fairly unstructured and I was looking for a method by which a more systematic approach could be taken. I was delighted, therefore, to be shown the CEMP material which I saw that the competencies (The Cheshire Management Abilities Profile) were exactly the analysis I needed. In order to test the process we spent a year with myself as 'manager' in review with delegates from various levels and backgrounds – some were teachers on 'E' and 'C' allowances and one was the college registrar.

The scheme will be extended next year to include more managers and an additional six or so delegates. When the CEMP process develops a competency profile for classroom interaction, we will have the ideal instrument for our future needs.

Case study two: further education

Christine Tyler, Head of Staff Development and Janet Mather, Staff Development Assistant

Halton College has a needs-led staff development programme. The CEMP personal reviews provide the opportunity for identifying individual needs in a systematic way. Our managers take part in in-house events, and gain the wider perspective from the LEA's programme of Further Learning Opportunities.

A common problem for managers in FE is that they feel unprepared for new roles. CEMP helps managers gain the necessary knowledge and, because the system emphasises competence in management with opportunities to practice and develop management skills. Many delegates have experienced a rapid growth in confidence as a result of mixing with colleagues from other colleges. There is an excitement created through frank exchange of views.

At Halton College we have harnessed the energy generated by the Authoritywide CEMP process and absorbed it into the college. Examples of successful CEMP workbased learning opportunities include the development of a computerised crosscollege timetabling system, a secondment to the LEA to develop records of achievement which has led to the implementation of a college system, and participation in a successful college Total Quality movement. It is this balance between the individual 'wants' of the CEMP delegate and the college's needs expressed through the development plan, that makes CEMP significant in the college. For this the CEMP personal review is crucial.

In the review delegates are encouraged to perceive learning opportunities as part of their working life. Instead of inventing 'projects' to satisfy areas of the Cheshire MAP, the delegates recognise the potential of departmental or college priority development objectives as vehicles for their personal learning.

Our next step is to evaluate the impact that CEMP has had on the college, before extending the system throughout the organisation. We need to ensure a coherent framework to help us all meet our institutional objectives. Because the review is such an essential part of CEMP, the role of the line manager is vital in shaping Halton College's human resource development.

3.6 LEA appraisal schemes

3.6.0 Experience of piloting staff appraisal in LEAs

Brian Fidler

Introduction

The evaluation report of the pilot schemes looked at how the six LEAs tackled the implementation of appraisal (Bradley et al, 1989). Individual accounts of appraisal in the pilot LEAs come from Croydon (Willis, 1989), Cumbria (Buckler, 1989) and Newcastle Upon Tyne (Payne, 1989) with Vanessa Champion's and Dallas Hackett's first hand accounts.

Organisation

The LEAs appointed an appraisal co-ordinator and it was found beneficial if the person had had experience at a senior level in school. A widely representative consultative or steering committee was found worthwhile. These made some impact on the schemes but also ensured a suitable climate for appraisal.

As appraisal is connected with so much other managerial work in schools, LEAs found it important to ensure liaison between appraisal and others in the LEA.

The level of support which the pilot schemes provided to schools is unlikely to be provided when appraisal is extended.

Those at LEA level involved in appraisal included officers, advisers and inspectors. They were involved in preparing for appraisal, appraising headteachers and for managing appraisal. Awareness raising and training was found to be necessary for this group. For inspectors there was a potential conflict between undertaking appraisal of senior school staff and their normal work as an inspector.

Scheme design

The evaluation of the pilot schemes drew attention (Bradley et al: p.45) to the tension between uniformity of approach and tailoring to particular institutions

> At times we have noted a tension between some LEAs' wishes for a common approach and the desire of schools to adopt schemes to suit their own circumstances

Wide involvement in the design of the LEA scheme was found valuable. Awareness raising courses with a mixed clientele were found beneficial. Whole school review was also found useful in setting an appropriate climate for appraisal.

Documentation

LEAs documentation can have a significant effect but it is good if this can be modified by an individual school. LEA documents typically cover:

- Publicity/awareness;
- Proformas;
- Advice on carrying out the process; and
- Less on implementation and management.

The language used in documents was important in conveying a positive approach to appraisal. This could also ensure awareness of the relationship of appraisal to policies such as equal opportunities.

Implementation

There are many benefits from a phased implementation – allowing some schools to volunteer. It is important that there are reported positive experiences from the first schools to carry out appraisal. There must be a sense of ownership of the scheme at school level. One way of linking the school work with LEA developments which was found successful was for appraisal working parties at school to link with the LEA co-ordinator in designing and implementing a school scheme.

Monitoring and evaluation of the working of appraisal in schools has been worthwhile in the pilot LEAs. There are a number of ways in which this has been done – external evaluators, a schoolbased evaluator, LEA appraisal co-ordinator, and a trainer associated with the school.

Records and confidentiality

Strict attempts to ensure confidentiality of appraisal records between appraiser and appraisee leads to difficulties in facilitating INSET, career development and school development.

> A crucial balance must be struck between making appraisal information more widely available than has typically happened in the pilot study and providing enough confidentiality to guarantee frank discussion
> (Bradley et al: p.47)

Bradley et al (1989; p. 47) from the pilot schemes put forward the following points that are associated with successful appraisal:

- There is clarity over who has responsibility for each task at the follow-up stage;
- Targets are tied to the provision of necessary support and monitoring;
- There is a clear time-scale;
- There are clear procedures for putting needs forward from the school to the LEA.

3.6.1 Cumbria's experience

Vanessa Champion

Introduction

Say 'Cumbria' to many and they will conjure up visions of lakes, fells, sheep and rain. They are perhaps less likely to picture the industrial or urban parts of the county – particularly those on the West coast – a number of which have multiple problems deriving from the demise of traditional industries and their distance from main transport routes.

Romantic views also prevail when the conversation turns to the subject of living and working in the county. Of course, it is a splendid place to be; but as with all large rural areas, difficulties of sheer size, of geography and communication must consistently be reckoned with. The increased centralisation of administration in Carlisle requires especially effective communication and linking if those who are over one hundred miles away (by road) are not to feel neglected or excluded.

The nature of the educational provision in the county is also a reflection of its geography. Distances are such that small schools, serving local communities have been the obvious choice when set against the considerable journey children would otherwise have to make to school. Thus, of the county's 360 primary schools, over 100 have three teachers or less: of the secondary schools, 13 have fewer than 500 on roll and 7 have 300 or less. Many of these schools have suffered falling rolls in recent years as a result of the changing nature of the population. High housing costs in 'desirable' areas have compelled young families to seek cheaper housing and more job opportunities in urban areas. There are presently villages in the Lake District National Park in which almost 33% of the houses are second homes.

Throughout the pilot, a consistent challenge was to evolve an approach to appraisal which was as compatible with the structure and organisation of a two teacher primary school as with a large secondary or special or nursery school.

Initiation: Shared ownership – shared understandings

One of the myths pervading rural counties such as Cumbria, which are geographically peripheral and distant from 'the centre' is that they are backwaters of quaint historical practice, far removed from the momentum of the outside world. Moreover, the natives are so inclined to collude in perpetuating this belief (it is very good for the tourist trade), that they begin to believe it and it is not until county initiatives meet head-on with developments elsewhere that the considerable progress of the local work is perceived – often to the surprise of the participants.

Thus it was only when Cumbria was invited by the DES in 1986 to become one of the six authorities to pilot appraisal schemes that the extent of developments within the county was fully appreciated. For involvement in the pilot scheme, far from being the beginning of appraisal activity in Cumbria was, in one sense, a culmination of two years hard work during which many of the foundations of the subsequent scheme were established but could not develop without funding. Involvement in the national pilot study provided precisely the support that was needed to take the scheme forward in a purposeful way.

Work in the LEA before the 1986 pilot had arisen in response to the DES white paper on *Teaching Quality* which was published in 1983. A working party was set up to examine 'the need for schools' self-evaluation, staff development and appraisal'. The working party is notable for the respresentative nature of its membership which included elected members from both major political groups on the county council, representatives of the recognised teachers' associations, officers and advisers from the LEA, and local head teachers. Without doubt, an important strength of this group lay in its diversity.

The preliminary work was to gather information. Examples of good practice were sought from elsewhere. Subsequently and most usefully, modest pilot schemes were initiated in local schools which focused specifically on what were to become the two complementary strands of the Cumbrian approach:

(a) Participative whole school review; and

(b) Individual career reviews.

However, in order to progress this dual approach, the working party had to give attention to a number of critical questions about the direction and purpose of the evolving scheme. These included:

— What is the most suitable instrument for school review, given the

diverse nature of Cumbrian schools, and the particular position of the small primary?
- What place, if any, has assessment in career review procedures?
- What levels of confidentiality will best support either of the two areas?
- What kinds of information are needed to support the career review process and how might this be collected?
- Is there a place for the observation of a teacher at work?

and finally, but most importantly,
- How may these two strands of school review and appraisal be brought together most effectively?

It was through the process of answering these questions that the philosophy and principles of the Cumbrian scheme were being developed and agreed. Indeed, with hindsight it is clear that a great strength of the scheme is that the early foundations were secured as a result of the debate within the working party. That this group representing as it did a cross-section of expertise, interest and accountabilities in the LEA, could come together to confront issues, discuss principles and through this to develop shared meanings was undoubtedly central to the acceptance and support the scheme received throughout the county.

Implementation

The decision to adopt the GRIDS (McMahon et al, 1984) approach to school review and development was a significant one for this was the catalyst which could bring together the two strands of institutional review and individual appraisal. Moreover, it could help to ensure that the rhetoric of shared ownership could become a reality for schools.

GRIDS is a 'democratic' approach whereby all staff are involved in reviewing and establishing the priorities for school development. As such it both sets the climate and gives an excellent context for the appraisal of individual teachers for where teachers have been involved in developing the priorities for the school, they have a framework within which they can set their own professional development targets and understand the resource implications of each.

The mutual interdependence of the school review and teacher appraisal was explained as follows in the Cumbrian submission for an Educational Support Grant (1985):

Central to this development is the recognition that individual staff appraisal and development must operate in tandem with whole school self-evaluation. This emphasis is confirmed by the following points:

- Both have an impact on student learning;
- The quality of teaching and the learning experience is influenced by both the effectiveness of the individual teacher and the quality of the school's curriculum and organisation;
- Individual staff appraisal identifies needs for whole school development: whole school self-evaluation identifies needs which may be fulfilled by individual teachers' roles which in turn facilitate their professional development.

Indeed, this submission to the DES was perhaps a seminal document in the development of the scheme and it clearly illustrates the degree to which the working party had, by then, established many of the basic principles on which future developments were to be based. The following extracts give some of the flavour of it. On individual teacher appraisal:

> The principal purpose of the scheme is to assist staff in developing to their full professional effectiveness and career prospects. If this can be done successfully, then benefit should accrue to the individual members of staff, to the school and its pupils, and to the education service generally.

and,

> It is anticipated that the [appraisal] procedure should be:
> (i) Universal, i.e. it is hoped that everyone will take part.
> (ii) Structured, i.e. the framework and basis of discussion should be common to all.
> (iii) Open, i.e. a copy of the agreed statement will be given to the individual teacher.
>
> (Cumbria Submission to the DES, 1985)

This submission had been completed by October 1985 but it was not until December 1986 that the requisite funding became available and policy could be put into practice.

However, although this was cause for optimism locally, nationally the picture was rather less encouraging as teachers' associations and the government came into conflict over pay and conditions. For those associated with the pilot this was the first of what were to become increasingly common experiences in ensuing years as policy changes, disputes, media coverage and conflict at national levels produced fallout on local developments.

Nevertheless, it was just such events which served to emphasise the value of the structure which was at the heart of the scheme i.e. the working party. The considerable involvement of the teachers' associations on the working party and in developing local policy was accompanied by a corresponding commitment to it so that, despite problems outside the county, there was unanimous agreement that the work should go ahead. This positive support was to remain throughout some very difficult times over the next three years and is a substantive reason why Cumbria, unlike some other pilot LEAs was able to continue a high level of work.

Recognising that changes in the nature of the activity required a different pattern of management, the working party decided that operations should be the joint responsibility of a steering group (which included teacher association representatives, the chief adviser, an LEA officer and an independent chair) and a project director, who was seconded from the senior management team of a county secondary school. The wisdom of this arrangement is considered retrospectively by the chair of the steering group:

> The administration of the Cumbrian project may seem on the face of it to be unnecessarily large and unwieldy, involving progressive delegation from a working party of some 25 members to a steering group responsible for the implementation of the scheme with, in turn, delegation to the project director for day-to-day planning and organisation, as well as the input and development of ideas. While it is true that communications have sometimes proved difficult, (especially in a county as large as Cumbria) this arrangement ensured continuation of the wide, thorough and exhaustive consultation which has been a feature of the work in Cumbria since 1984 and which has, we believe, contributed in great measure to the success of the project.
>
> (Cumbria County Council, 1989)

It should be noted that both groups still exist and continue to supply an invaluable consultative forum as appraisal becomes statutory.

Pilot group

The identification and training of schools and teachers to be involved in the pilot scheme was the next stage. Initially, 30 schools were involved, in three groups of 10. Some features of this process are worth mentioning.

    (i)   The sample was to provide a representative cross-section of Cumbrian schools in terms of size, sector, urban/rural. Each group of ten schools was to reflect that sample.

    (ii)   All schools were to run a participative school review.

(iii) The chance to become involved was open to all county schools, though a prerequisite for involvement was that all staff had been consulted with and the participation jointly agreed by all. All teachers should be volunteers.
(iv) Training would be provided for school review co-ordinators, appraisers **and** appraisees.
(v) Awareness raising for head teachers in the form of Contracting Conferences.

Items (iii) (iv) and (v) were significant in helping to transfer a sense of ownership to the participants.

Other aspects of the developing scheme were to promote that process.

Training for all

In addition to enhancing the status and effectiveness of the event, training for all meant that appraisees in particular developed notions of appraisal as a shared process in which they too had real responsibility. The training was grounded in an active learning approach whereby participants were encouraged to develop shared meanings through shared experiences. For both appraisees and appraisers, the chance to 'sample' the other role through an experience of the process gave important insights into the dynamic of the relationship.

'No secrets'

In order to augment the notion of review/appraisal as a professional partnership and not the stronghold of managers, it was ensured that all those involved had access to the same information, documentation and support throughout the process.

Clear strategies for feedback and evaluation

Furthermore it was made clear to participants that, whilst there was an agreed framework within which to work, much of the responsibility for developing the details of the scheme was now vested in them as the practitioners. Through feedback and evaluation (local and national) their experiences, responses and thoughts were to inform, not only subsequent developments for future schools but, in all likelihood the eventual national scheme.

Involvement of teachers in the developing design

These were exciting times in the life of the project as teachers, charged with such responsibilities, embraced the challenge of putting theory into practice. And whilst some of the critical areas were predictable in advance (e.g. the observation of teaching, developing job descriptions), many others were to emerge which required hard thinking and careful development (e.g. the vocabulary of the scheme, equality of opportunity, credibility and the selection of appraisers, confidentiality of the statement vs. the 'need to know' in relation to INSET provision, the difficulties of skilful target setting and many more.)

Development

Although the progress of the scheme had a considerable internal momentum this was frequently enhanced (and occasionally checked) by events and developments elsewhere. Contact with the other pilot LEAs was fostered by the work of the National Development Centre, Bristol, whose job it was to co-ordinate the national pilot. The conferences which were run for participating LEAs provided a useful forum within which the emerging issues could be explored and experiences shared. NDC conferences often triggered fresh thought and action within the county. Similarly, national evaluation reports drew attention to concerns as well as strengths.

Thus it was that, having bid successfully for extension funding, the steering group could focus on some of the distinctive areas which had emanated from the, by now, considerable experience in the LEA.

For example, although much attention had been given to the *process* of appraisal, many questions remained about the outcomes, e.g. How successfully could professional development targets be provided for within current INSET arrangements? What were the resource implications for these? To what extent could the review and appraisal process be said to affect the quality of pupils' learning experiences?

And just as the experience of appraisal begged questions in schools about aspects of the management and development planning, so also the investigation of outcomes asked questions about the effectiveness of LEA structures, especially those related to the provision of INSET. An abiding memory from this period in the life of the project is of growing comprehension about the way in which a developed appraisal scheme infiltrates, affects and enhances so many facets of school and LEA life.

Special features of the Cumbrian scheme
Any selection of special features should be regarded by readers with some caution for it is a product of the inevitable subjectivity of the author and the educational climate which prevails when the selection is made. Emphasis in the Cumbrian scheme on establishing school review and development planning as a necessary complement to individual appraisal has proved most significant through the increasing importance of strategic planning and resource management in schools.

The school development plan is now a central document. It must address issues of developmental priorities and resourcing and decisions have to be made on the basis of best possible information. An established review and appraisal cycle can provide just this and many pilot schools remarked upon the relative ease with which development planning was accomplished in this situation. Moreover, where teachers felt they had been involved in setting priorities for school development, they were able to make informed decisions about their individual professional development targets within the wider picture.

The second special feature of the Cumbria scheme – the Teacher Appraisal Working Party – hardly needs further mention for it has appeared as a refrain throughout this text. Suffice to say that the particular contribution of this unique group was a central factor in the successful development of the scheme.

Conclusion
Of course, the development of appraisal in Cumbria has not all been plain sailing. There have been uncomfortable times, difficult situations – especially when the volatile state of the larger world of education affected the working lives and morale of local teachers. On occasions, developments occurred only after individuals or institutions had undergone uncomfortable experiences. At one stage, the perceived exclusiveness of the appraisal 'club' had to be encountered and dealt with.

But within all this two themes have remained constant with the:
- Premise that appraisal is a positive and supportive process which has as its central purpose the professional development of teachers;
- Belief that a sustained involvement of teachers in the development of the scheme is essential.

The challenge of the next few years will be to preserve these principles in the more hostile environment of statutory appraisal.

3.6.2 Salford experience

Dallas Hackett

Introduction

Teacher anxiety about the introduction of appraisal hinged on the interpretation of what Sir Keith Joseph, in a speech to the North of England Conference, 1985, called 'the management of the teaching force'. Sir Keith was anxious to deny any punitive intention and to stress his concern with:

> the whole range of positive advantages that would flow from applying to the teacher force standards of management that have become common elsewhere.

The work of the six education authorities involved in the national School Teacher Appraisal Pilot Study did much to convince teachers that to be better 'managed' could be to their advantage, provided the approach was supportive and positive. Appraisal pilot work in Salford, 1987–90, and its subsequent development, 1990–91, has emphasised 'support for professional development' as its cornerstone, and all work done has been geared to school ownership and development of appraisal, within this LEA approach and the national framework.

City of Salford is a small metropolitan authority with about 2000 teachers in approximately twenty secondary schools and sixth form colleges, and one hundred primary establishments. Pilot work involved seven primary schools, two secondary schools, a sixth form college and two special schools. About 170 teachers and 21 headteachers were appraised during pilot work. Since the pilot, a further 24 headteachers have been appraised and other schools have introduced appraisal or are developing some of its elements (job descriptions, classroom observation, staff development interviews).

An LEA commitment to developmental appraisal followed naturally from the work done in the Authority's schools from 1982 onwards on school self-evaluation, and the obvious links between sectional/

institutional review and development and the emphasis in appraisal on *personal* review and development. In addition, an appraisal scheme for officers and advisers already existed, as did an effective mechanism for LEA in-service support for the needs identified by schools. The climate therefore encouraged Salford's participation in national pilot work on teacher and head teacher appraisal.

Initiation

Mechanics

I was one of three head teachers, reflecting primary and secondary phases, appointed and inducted as professional development officers, working within the advisory section. In addition to working jointly to articulate the principles and evolve the model and procedure for appraisal in Salford, we each researched specialist areas and prepared training materials and drafts for consultation. We worked closely with officers and advisers and with a steering group of these, teacher association representatives, and representatives from the voluntary aided sector. The group produced agreed schemes for teacher and head teacher appraisal as the basis for pilot work.

Principles

Appraisal was firmly defined as support for professional development – a belief that teachers are able to do their job better if they:

> Know and agree what is expected of them;
>
> Receive feedback on their work from respected professionals;
>
> Are able to raise concerns and constraints with colleagues who have managerial or organisational responsibility for them;
>
> Receive support and guidance to achieve agreed objectives; and
>
> Have their contribution recognised and experience job satisfaction, a sense of achievement, and the opportunity for career progression.

Institutions were seen to benefit through:

> Clarification of objectives;
>
> Determination of priorities;
>
> Identification of strengths/weaknesses;
>
> Consideration of appropriate support;
>
> Planned staff development;
>
> Utilisation of talent; and
>
> Better planning and evaluation mechanisms
>
> (Salford LEA, 1988)

LEA's role

The draft national framework laid down the purposes of appraisal and a framework for the process. Within that, the authority identified a key role in:

> Controlling resources for appraisal and for appraisal training;
>
> Applying procedures within the national framework to all teachers to whom the regulations apply;
>
> Maintaining consultation/steering groups;
>
> Preparing materials on appraisal for schools, including guidance on the criteria for appraisal;
>
> Liaising between schools;
>
> Utilising the conclusions from the appraisal process to inform the LEA's programme for professional development and training;
>
> Operating the appeals/complaints procedure when required;
>
> Including appraisal within the scope of its monitoring and evaluation procedures;
>
> Managing and conducting the appraisal of headteachers.
>
> (Paper on the LEA's Management of Appraisal – Salford LEA, 1988)

LEA's approach

In an uncertain climate, it was seen as essential to address anxieties (and to go anywhere and meet anybody to do this); to emphasise school ownership of the appraisal process; and involve school and teacher associations in evolving both the process and documentation for it.

Approach in practice

Task groups looked at aspects of teacher and head teacher appraisal and at appraisal in the voluntary aided sector. Pilot schools were asked to nominate co-ordinators (not the head teacher) who were given a week's training in the principles and purposes of appraisal, elements in the process and the management of appraisal in a school. They were asked to establish a school planning group for appraisal. All training was delivered by the team of professional development officers and, where possible, was school based. We saw keeping people informed as a priority and prepared a booklet: *An Introduction to Appraisal* which was sent to all the authority's teachers. Regular newsletters were sent to all schools, describing the progress of pilot work. We visited thirty schools to describe proposed pilot work and contributed to management courses at all levels.

Safeguards and ground rules, relating to access to appraisal information; the use of such information in compiling references; appeals and incapability procedures were agreed within the steering group. These were incorporated into draft teacher and head teacher appraisal schemes which were then used in training and in pilot work.

Implementation

Readiness of schools

We felt that if appraisal were to be of practical benefit to schools and teachers, it should be appropriate to their stage of development.

Some schools were well prepared to introduce appraisal. They had sectional and institutional aims and objectives, clear curricular guidelines and a shared understanding of what constituted effective teaching and learning. They already had negotiated and published job descriptions; they carried out classroom visiting; had a programme of support for staff development needs; and mechanisms for reviewing individual and school progress.

Other schools, whilst not so far advanced, had established an appropriate climate for the introduction of appraisal. They featured consultative decision making; a supportive atmosphere and collegial working practice; open communications and some elements at least of self-evaluation and of staff development. These schools too could make a start on appraisal at another level.

Schools whose climate would not facilitate pilot work were not involved. In national implementation of appraisal, *all* schools would need to ensure that current management practice was favourable to the introduction of appraisal.

Preparation and training

We made at least two awareness raising visits to schools to outline the principles and practicalities of their involvement. Each nominated a school appraisal co-ordinator whose job it was, after training, to liaise with the school's management and with us, to lead the school planning group and to detail the school's appraisal training needs.

After awareness raising, the whole school staff had two days' training in the rationale for developmental appraisal, the appraisal process and procedures, and the documentation. Appraisers had an additional one and a half days, focusing on information gathering and the appraisal interview, and 'support teachers' (conducting classroom observation) had an additional day's training on observational techniques. (*See* Teaching Analysis and Support. The training programme was very successful. It emphasised:

> Whole school, customised training;
>
> In-house training, delivered by the professional development officers; and
>
> Continuity between training and implementation.

Introduction of appraisal

From then on, we encouraged schools to chart their own course, with LEA support. We gave the school co-ordinator and planning group one to two days' consultancy time in evolving their scheme. The planning group was responsible for:

> Identifying appraisers and support teachers (classroom observers);
>
> Matching appraisees with these;
>
> Scheduling observation and the programme as a whole within an agreed timescale;
>
> Managing cover for classroom visiting;
>
> Internal documentation;

Storage and retrieval arrangements for summary statements; and

Ensuring that outcome information informed the school development plan and staff development arrangements.

Other LEA support

In addition to preparation, training and support for the school planning group, we offered other support to the school. We did much research on effective classroom practice and encouraged schools to use this in agreeing a teaching and learning policy. This was to furnish the criteria for classroom visiting. We also provided sample documentation, proformas and self-appraisal prompts for schools to use. We made half termly visits to interview involved staff; to consult the log of appraisal activity kept by the co-ordinator; and to focus, through questionnaires and interviews on current elements of the process – the results all being card indexed. Termly meetings were held with co-ordinators and head teachers. All training events were evaluated and summative evaluation meetings were held at the end of the pilot. The Cambridge Institute of Education, official evaluators of the national pilot project, provided reports on ongoing progress and a summative report: (Bradley et al, 1989).

Development

Evaluation at school and LEA level, together with that provided by the Cambridge Institute of Education, endorsed the approach to appraisal in Salford. Particular strengths were seen to be:

Lengthy preparation and climate setting;

Thorough consultation with LEA officers and with the teacher association representatives;

Availability of detailed documentation:

- *Preparing the Ground*
- *The Teacher Appraisal Process*
- *Observation in the Classroom*
- *The Appraisal Interview*
- *Teaching Analysis and Support* and of supporting materials and proformas;

Personal support given to schools;

Dissemination of information at all stages;

Value of the school co-ordinator and planning group;

Emphasis on support for professional development;

Value of up-to-date and negotiated job descriptions;

Emphasis on the initial review meeting in ensuring a smooth appraisal process;

Heightening of collegiality, morale and job satisfaction;

Benefit of time set aside to recognise and discuss teachers' work; and

Help in prioritising individual and school needs and targets.

Difficulties experienced related to:

Disruption caused by the process in general and by classroom visiting in particular;

Lack of time to carry out the process as meticulously as schools would like;

Need for cover for classroom visiting and the interview;

Clerical time to process summary statements;

Teacher feelings of inadequacy in conducting teaching analysis and support (classroom observation);

Inadequate criteria for appraising the managerial and pastoral responsibilities of middle and senior management staff;

Unsuitability of some appraisers and support teachers;

Skills needed for effective self-appraisal;

Resourcing the meeting of teachers' development needs as identified by the appraisal process;

Anomaly inherent in operating a line management appraisal model in schools where flattened management structures and collegial practice were often the norm.

Overall, the process stood up admirably to pilot testing and few changes to the process and procedure have had to be made. However, it is possible that the proposed timescale for full implementation and the central funding available will limit the training which an LEA can directly provide. Schools will need to ensure that all their teachers have access to direct or 'cascade' training.

The following publications incorporate pilot philosophy, practice and experience and include documentation used in the process. They are in current use in training for and implementing appraisal in

Salford: *Appraisal and You* and *Appraisal and the School.*

Special features

Some have already been referred to, notably the emphasis on a model of appraisal offering support for professional development and the need for school ownership of the way it handles appraisal.

Teaching analysis and support

Classroom visiting has been much referred to in this section. In Salford, we developed a specific view of this as a process whereby a teacher is supported and assisted in an analysis of his/her classroom work by an experienced and respected colleague. We called this process 'teaching analysis and support' as being more descriptive of the activity than 'classroom observation'. We called the observers 'support teachers' since that was their function, and encouraged them to agree with the appraisees criteria for the teaching analysis, derived from an agreed school policy on teaching and learning. We felt that a 'critical friend' as opposed to a 'line management' approach to observation had more potential for sustained development, through encouraging self-evaluation and collegial target setting. Though the national framework requires appraisers to be those with some management responsibility for the appraisee, the use of peers in the observation process helps to mitigate the effect of 'top-down' appraisal. The approach has proved successful where appropriate support teachers are used, where an open climate pertains, and where time is given to this activity. Of all the elements in Salford's teacher appraisal programme, this attracts most external attention and is fully described in: *Appraisal and the School.* There are considerable spin-offs in the ensuing discussions on methodology and the formulation of a school policy for effective teaching and learning.

Whole school evaluation

Long standing work on school evaluation in Salford has ensured that appraisal is seen as related to whole school evaluation but as a different process with different purposes, procedures and reporting outcomes. Appraisal relates to the individual as sectional or school evaluation relates to groups. Individual, sectional and whole school reviews therefore contribute to and complement each other. A balance must be maintained between the needs of the individual and those of the school, and between the priorities identified during appraisal and school self-evaluation. Priorities identified by whole school review should form objectives for individual teachers in appraisal target setting. Appraisal outcomes of individual teachers should influence school planning and development.

Links with INSET provision

If appraisal is to deliver developmental outcomes for individuals and their schools, needs identified by the process must be communicated to school (and, where appropriate, LEA) mechanisms for addressing these needs. Salford has long delegated funds to schools for **institutional** development. This should help schools to address individual needs identified through appraisal when these relate to institutional needs. The following approach could be followed.

1. The school, and groups/phases within the school, should identify and prioritise their needs by means of whole school evaluation or review. These needs will have to take account of national, LEA, and school contexts and constraints.
2. Each school should have a staff development co-ordinator (who could usefully also be the appraisal co-ordinator) with responsibility for:

    Co-ordination of staff development and appraisal; and

    Liaison with the LEA, using the agreed procedures.
3. Needs identified and prioritised should be known to all staff.
4. Although these collective needs will form part of the future development activities of teachers, there should also be recognition of the professional and career development needs of individuals.
5. There should be some follow-up once needs have been agreed i.e. there should be some resultant change, for example in teaching, responsibilities, targets in the curriculum or school organisation.
6. To supplement school activity, there may be need to draw on an ongoing LEA inservice programme, addressing needs relating to national initiatives, management training, major local initiatives or supporting individual school developments.
7. Both school and LEA should monitor the appraisal/INSET interface and should evaluate both the procedures and the outcomes.

Conclusions

Salford is now beginning the phased implementation of appraisal for all its teachers and head teachers, in accordance with the national framework and timescale.

Because the education authority was involved in national pilot work, Salford has many advantages – full commitment from the LEA, a propitious climate, and LEA and school awareness of how appraisal must dovetail with other aspects of school and LEA management. We have substantial experience in schools, a training programme and trainers to deliver it, a fully documented scheme and considerable expertise among officers and advisers.

LEAs not so advanced will find the timescale demanding and expertise in short supply. The 'stop–go' situation, since the final pilot report was presented to the Secretary of State in summer 1989 has had the effect of destroying continuity, dispersing expertise, diminishing impetus and increasing anxiety and suspicion.

The introduction of appraisal presents many problems for institutions related to – attitude, the management of a major innovation, the logistical demands of appraisal and to the fact that this, like all management processes, is subject to human error and inadequacy. But the benefits of appraisal, for individuals, schools and the LEA are considerable and are catalogued in the Cambridge Institute of Education Evaluation Report (Bradley et al, 1989). Because appraisal is being introduced into a still uncertain climate, it behoves LEAs and schools to get it right – the penalties of getting it wrong are significant.

Climate setting, awareness raising and training are vital precursors. LEAs must be able to offer leadership, schemes, sample documentation, and support. School management teams who give appraisal a low priority and fail to capitalise on its outcomes will, at best, lose the benefits of a process which has major spin-offs for the health of the school: at worst, they will ferment frustration and discontent.

In some ways, this might be seen as a bad time to introduce appraisal: the available funding is inadequate, the ongoing workload is oppressive; and morale is low. For these very reasons, appraisal should be given a high priority – it is a potential miracle worker. Some Salford schools are now well into their second cycle having absorbed and institutionalised the process and cannot imagine how they ever managed without it.

SECTION 4: PROCESSES OF APPRAISAL

4.1 Job descriptions and organisational structure

Brian Fidler

Introduction

In any undertaking employing more than one person some form of organisational structure is required. Each person needs to know their own task within the organisation and that of others with whom they come into contact. *In toto* the individual tasks have to accomplish the mission of the organisation. In any but the most mechanistic organisation there have to be ways of co-ordinating the activities of different individuals and dealing with unusual events. Thus all organisations including schools and colleges have some form of organisational structure both formal and informal and more or less explicit.

Similar organisations may have different organisational structures. The organisational structure depends both on the function of the organisation, its size and on its particular culture and history. The structure provides continuity and predictability both for those inside and outside an organisation. Thus it cannot be changed too frequently without creating confusion and uncertainty but on the other hand periodically the structure should be evaluated to assess whether it is assisting the organisation to achieve its aims to a sufficient degree. New tasks tend to be 'tacked on' to existing structures e.g. TVEI, recording pupil achievement, public relations etc. However, there comes a point when a reappraisal is worthwhile to determine whether a major revision to the organisational structure would help the school or college function more effectively.

All organisational structures are compromises. There are various competing design parameters and it is a matter of judgement which structure is better than another. The acid test is how the structure works in practice after people have had time to become accustomed to it.

This chapter provides some background principles and concepts for organisational design before reviewing the design context for schools and colleges in the 1990s. The final element of the organisational structure is the individual job description for each employee. This needs to be written in a form which is helpful to the employee in knowing what is expected of him or her and forms the starting point for appraising staff.

Concepts

The long term future of an organisation such as a school or college involves a consideration of strategy (Fidler, 1989; Fidler, Bowles and Hart, 1991). Having carried out a strategic analysis of the present situation and chosen a strategy for the future, an important element in putting the strategy into practice is to revise the design of the structure of the organisation.

The basic structure allocates people and resources to the tasks which have to be done and provides mechanism for co-ordinating their work (Child, 1984). It consists of organisation charts, job descriptions and the constitution of policy making, advisory and other groups. It is literally the 'organisational backbone'. It provides basic working rules.

In any complex organisation one major problem is how to arrange the tasks and how to allocate individuals to the tasks. A related problem is how to continuously co-ordinate their work in a dynamic working environment. The extent of co-ordination and individual decision making can be reduced by creating policies which cover much routine decision making (e.g. school rules) and enunciate the principles which underpin further individual decision making (e.g. equal opportunities). The structure defines the decision making machinery rather than the policies and decisions which are created.

Policy making and executive action

It is convenient to divide policy making from the managerial process of carrying out policy but the two are clearly interconnected. For a school or college the governing body provides the strategic policy making and the head or principal carries out these policies. Within the school if there are other policy making groups then the organisational structure should make this clear and the interrelationships with other policy making groups and with executive functions.

Policy making groups should be clearly differentiated from advisory groups, fact finding groups, or other working parties. The composition and powers of such groups should be given in the organisational structure.

The other major element of the basic structure is the hierarchy of responsibilities and tasks of the organisation. Who is accountable to whom and for what should be made clear. The tasks and responsibilities which have been allocated by the organisational structure can only be amended by the powers that approved and legitimated the basic structure. This is in contrast to other responsibilities which have been delegated and which can be taken back by the delegator.

Organisational types

The study of organisational structures involves the consideration of three factors (Osborn, Hunt and Jauch, 1980):

(a) *Specialisation* the extent to which individuals specialise and carry out only one part of the work of the organisation;

(b) *Formalisation* the extent to which coordination and control is formalised; and

(c) *Centralisation* the extent to which power and authority are dispersed throughout the organisation;

The most widespread form of organisational structure is some form of bureaucracy.

Bureaucracy Max Weber enumerated the following characteristics of a bureaucracy (Hoy and Miskel, 1991):

(a) Division of labour and specialisation

(b) Impersonal orientation

(c) Hierarchy of authority

PROCESSES OF APPRAISAL

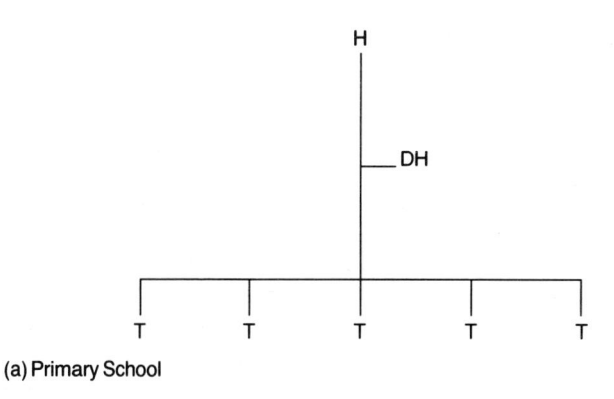

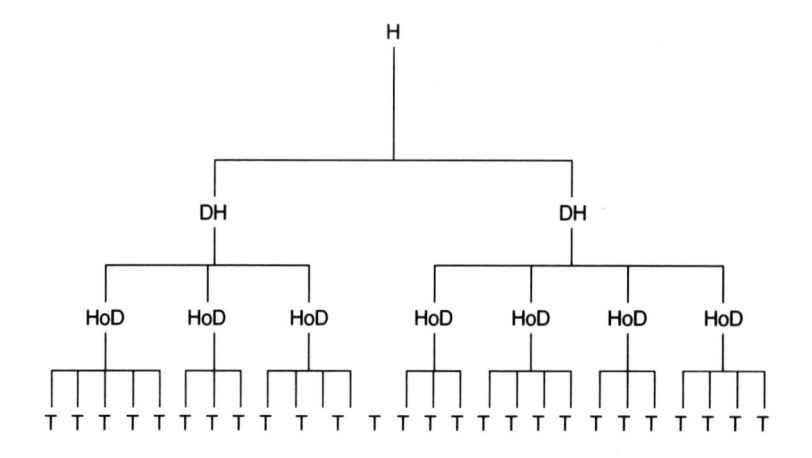

(a) Primary School

(b) Secondary School

Note: H = Headteacher; DH = Deputy Head Teacher; HoD = Head of Department; T = Teacher

Figure 4.1.1 Organisation chart for a simple hierarchy

(d) Rules and regulations
(e) Career structure

These are the features of a theoretical or ideal bureaucratic structure. Such a structure can be shown to operate with a high degree of efficiency. A great many organisational structures including most schools show some evidence of each of these characteristics though they are unlikely to be followed in pure form even in the formal organisation. Whilst organisations have a formal structure they also have modes of working not covered by the formal procedures and this is the informal organisation, e.g. individuals reciprocating favours not sanctioned by the formal rules. These are sources of both formal and informal power.

The concept of hierarchy is an important one and like bureaucracy as a whole can easily be satirised. Hierarchy means that each office holder in the organisation is accountable to a superior and the authority of superiors is based on position or level in the hierarchy (see figure 4.1.1). Appointment to a position in the hierarchy should be on the basis of merit. If there are many levels in the hierarchy relative to its size this is described as tall. Those with fewer levels are described as flat hierarchies (Child, 1984). Organisations with up to about 100 employees typically have four levels in the hierarchy – chief executive, HoDs, supervisors, and workers.

An alternative form of organisation which has been frequently proposed for professional workers is a collegial structure. Collegial authority is a form of organisational democracy by which there is no legitimate basis for differential access to organisational control and thus all equally participate in decision making. For groups of self-employed professionals carrying out their professional work together this may be the most appropriate form of organisational control structure. However, large numbers of professional workers are employed by organisations generally working on bureaucratic principles.

Professional Orientation	Bureaucratic Orientation
Technical expertise	Technical expertise
Objective perspective	Objective perspective
Impersonal and impartial approach	Impersonal and impartial approach
Service to clients	Service to clients
Major Sources of Conflict	
Colleague-oriented reference group	Hierarchical orientation
Autonomy in decision making	Disciplined compliance
Self-imposed standards of control	Subordinated to the organisation

Table 4.1.1 Basic characteristics of professional and bureaucratic orientations: similarities and differences
Source: W.K. Hoy & C.G. Miskel (1991) *Educational Administration: Theory, Research & Practice* (4th ed) McGraw Hill, New York (p.144)

Although bureaucracy and professionalism have much in common as the table shows, there are also potential sources for conflict. One of these is the expected internal/external orientation of members of the organisation. The reference group for members of a bureaucracy is those next higher in the hierarchy whilst for professionals it is their colleagues internally and their professional peer group outside the organisation. Thus professionals can be expected to have divided loyalties. For example, a maths teacher may belong to a professional association and a mathematical association which may pull him or her in different directions from the school. The other area of potential conflict is in the area of personal autonomy in professional tasks. In reviewing studies of accountants, engineers and scientists in commercial organisations where the conflicts might be expected to be most severe, Child (1982) found that although there were work dissatisfactions, the expected conflicts were not severe for those who expected to make career progress within the organisation.

In organisations which are largely professionally staffed an accommodating technique which may be used is to appoint senior professionals to managerial positions within the organisation – the professional-as-administrator (Hughes, 1985 p.282).

> The appointment of professional persons as heads of professionally staffed organisations has mainly been advocated, not in terms of their contribution to task achievement but on the grounds that such persons are well placed to have the confidence, and to elicit the cooperation, of professional staff.

Although it is fashionable to decry bureaucratic structures as being inflexible and unresponsive to change, the alternatives offered so far do not seem convincing and in the view of Jacques (1990 p.133) do not adequately address the basic issue of accountability. Research over many years has convinced him that bureaucratic structures contain the essential ingredients of success and that many of the alleged failings of bureaucracy merely reflect poorly designed hierarchies.

> We need to stop casting about fruitlessly for organisational Holy Grails and settle down to the hard work of putting our managerial hierarchies in order.

He suggests three principles to guide the creation of layers in the hierarchy

1. manager must not only be accountable for the work of the subordinates but for adding value to their unaided efforts
2. manager must sustain a group of subordinates capable of doing the work
3. group must be given direction which they will enthusiastically follow.

In short 'every manager is accountable for work and leadership' (p.130).

In his studies he has found that the timespan of the work carried out by the jobholder is an important indicator of difference in the job which may signify a different position in the hierarchy. He argues that many hierarchies are disfunctional particularly where a difference in salary level has been used to create a new layer of management. He shows examples of organisations where many more differences in salary level are required than levels in the hierarchy.

Rowbotton and Billis (1987) identify seven levels of differentiated work from operator (level one) to chief executive of a conglomerate (level seven). On these levels, a teacher would be at level two (having to make individual judgements); a head of department at level three; a head teacher at level four; an education officer at level five; and a chief education officer at level six.

They classify authority relationships in seven categories

1.	*line managerial*	managing staff to achieve results
2.	*supervisory*	help and supervision of staff to carry out *tasks set by a manager*
3.	*coordinating*	planning, monitoring progress to devise ways of achieving *agreed objectives*
4.	*monitoring*	checking on progress, reporting and *advising* on appropriate action
5.	*collateral*	mutual dependence; on the same hierarchical level
6.	*service*	responding to the expressed needs of another
7.	*prescribing*	prescribing tasks to be achieved and checking on results but *without any right to manage the process* to carry out the task

These provide a greater precision in setting up and communicating work relationships. Whilst there should be a separation of hierarchical levels between line managers and only one line manager on each level having a responsibility for any employee, there may be other relationships of a more limited nature on the same level.

They suggest representing the relationships on an organisational chart to highlight important differences, e.g. line management relationships in continuous lines, and monitoring and co-ordinating relationships in dotted lines.

Professional bureaucracy

Whilst a hierarchy may be the basis for the most appropriate form of organisational structure for a large school or college some allowance must be made for the professional dimensions of the work carried out. The highly educated workforce has expertise, both individually and collectively, which is vital for the successful operation of the school or college. It is appropriate, therefore, to recognise that teachers have claims no less strong than other highly educated and skilled employees to participate to some extent in whole school educational decision making. Mintzberg (1983) has coined the term 'professional bureaucracy' for a structure which is basically hierarchical but has professional workers in managerial positions and a participative mode of operation.

Mintzberg identifies five component groups of any organisation. The main work being carried out by three groups arranged hierarchically – operating core, middle line of managers, strategic apex. There are two groups who assist – technostructure and support staff. The five parts of an organisation are shown in figure 4.1.2

Strategic apex comprises those who lead the whole organisation and those who directly assist them, e.g. head and deputies. This group is responsible for ensuring that the organisation delivers the product or service to clients and satisfies those who control the organisation or have power over it.

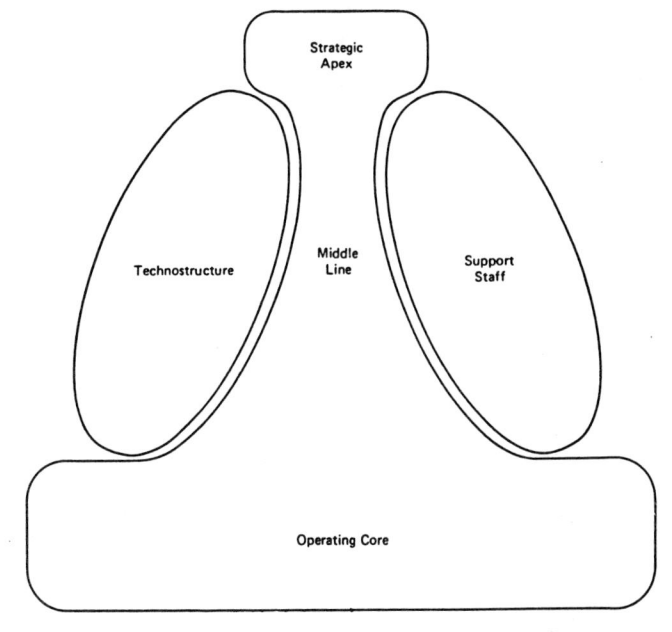

Figure 4.1.2 Mintzberg's five basic parts of an organisation

Source: H. Mintzberg (1983) *Structure in Fives: Designing Effective Organisations*, Englewood Cliffs, N.J., Prentice-Hall (p.11)

Middle line comprises middle and senior managers who directly control the work of the operating core, e.g. HoDs.

Operating core This group of workers actually make a product or deliver a direct service to clients, e.g. teachers. They form the largest group.

Technostructure These are analysts removed from the main work flow. They may plan work, change it, evaluate it or train people to do it. e.g., staff development co-ordinator.

Support staff These provide indirect support. Rather than advice they provide a service, e.g., canteen, resources technician, finance officer, caretaker.

In different types of organisation the five groups have different prominence. In the case of the professional bureaucracy it is the operating core (of teachers) which is the mainstay of the school or college. Typically the middle line are not very numerous as the professionals achieve co-ordination by having similar training and skills rather than having to be supervised. Similarly there is little technostructure as the professionals initiate change themselves. Generally there is a well developed support staff. Their function is to serve the operating core who in turn provide the basic service of the organisation to its clients. As Mintzberg (1979); p.360) observes:

> 'What frequently emerges in the Professional Bureaucracy are parallel administrative hierarchies, one democratic and bottom up for the professionals, and a second machine bureaucratic and top down for the support staff' (p.360).

The point at which the two hierarchies meet is of some interest since implicitly this identifies the relative levels of the two hierarchies if only by default – a chief administrative officer reporting to the head teacher is a different structure to one in which the CAO reports to a deputy head teacher.

Whilst both hierarchies are usually separated, there may be a need to bring them together in a functional unit e.g. science staff and laboratory technicians. Either both hierarchies meet at the head of science, or co-ordination is achieved in the unit by co-ordinating the two hierarchies through a matrix structure (*see* later).

Small organisations such as a small primary school can operate with a much simpler structure than a professional bureaucracy. The head teacher can supervise and co-ordinate the work of other teachers directly. Clearly there comes a point in terms of size of school when such centralisation of communication and decision making becomes dysfunctional because the head teacher becomes overloaded and causes a log jam in decision making. Further, a lack of delegated authority prevents others from taking responsibility and gaining managerial experience.

Span of control The number of subordinates that a superior is responsible for is called the span of control (the term control is misleading since it is really face-to-face interaction which is the limiting factor). How large a span of control can be and still be effective depends on a number of factors. The principle factor is the degree of complexity of the work being done. Where the work is complex and the work of individuals is interrelated then the span of control should be low, particularly where the superior has other tasks in addition to supervision. Since managers in schools traditionally supervise staff in addition to teaching, spans of control should be correspondingly smaller.

Unity of command One of the most basic of principles of any control and management structure is that of 'unity of command'. Whilst this has a rather military sound to it, it refers to any system of accountability and responsibility of an executive function. The principle is that any employee should be accountable to only one superior. This ensures that the employee does not receive conflicting instructions and that one superior has an overview of the entire work of each employee – there are no ambiguous areas. A corollary of this is that one person is ultimately in charge of any area of work. Again this gives unambiguous and clear lines of accountability. Indeed the term 'line manager' comes from just this source.

Line manager There is much confusion over the term line manager. This is not to be confused with the distinction betweeen line and staff relationships. A commonly used distinction is between line personnel who accomplish the direct work of the organisation and staff personnel who assist line personnel. Thus in a school the teachers would be the equivalent of line personnel and such others as cleaners, staff development co-ordinator, chief finance officer would be staff personnel.

However, the term line manager in the sense of appraisal relationships refers to the 'line of authority' which passes from the chief executive officer (head teacher) to those delegated positions in the organisational structure. This is referred to as the *scalar principle*.

> The more clear the line of authority from the top manager in an enterprise to every subordinate position, the more effective will be the responsible decision making and the organization communication system
>
> (Koontz and O'Donnell, 1978; p.285).

Thus there is the irony that staff personnel have their line manager i.e. their direct reporting relationship.

Matrix structures

Complex work Clearly these principles are ideals even in very formal organisations. In practice when much work is carried out in teams and work is interdisciplinary or otherwise multifunctional the principle begins to break down. There are two ways of tackling this situation:
- (a) Rely on informal 'mutual adjustment', or
- (b) Modify the formal structure.

(a) Mutual adjustment is a term used by Mintzberg (1983) to describe the simple process of co-ordination by which individuals meet and discuss any problem and solve it together as a joint decision. The weakness of such a mechanism is that:

1. No one person is responsible for taking an initiative to solve a problem;
2. No one person is responsible for a solution; and
3. If joint agreement is not possible others higher up in the hierarchy have to notice and become involved.

Such a co-ordination mechanism is much used in organisations with a very simple structure where there are few formal responsibilities allocated and also paradoxically in organisations where the work is complex, unpredictable, and pioneering. This is because no more

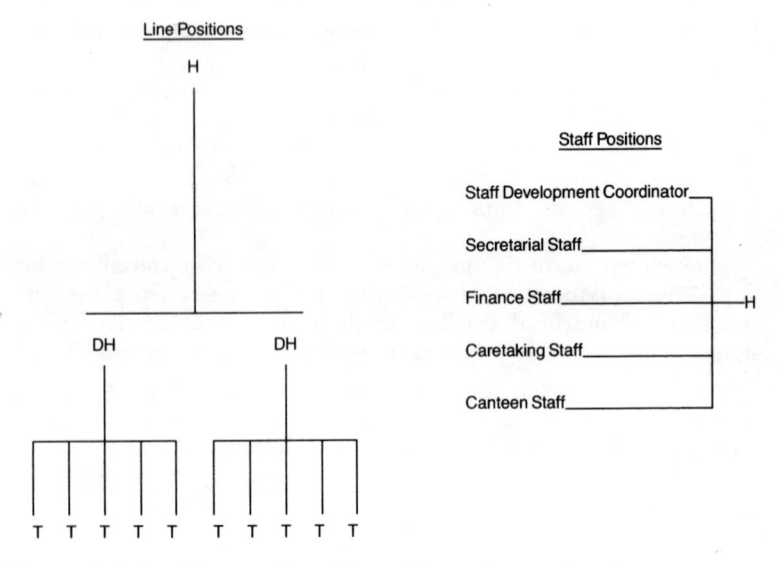

Figure 4.1.3 Line and staff positions in a school

formal structure can be designed to give flexible responses to unforeseeable problems. Thus there are honourable precedents for relying on mutual adjustment when other alternatives have been considered but found wanting. Mutual adjustment is extremely effective between co-operative people of goodwill but can be chaotic otherwise. Also it can be very time consuming and inefficient for dealing with routine and predictable problems.

(b) Modification of the formal structure A variety of modifications of the formal structure of increasing complexity can be made. The most straightforward is to make sure that teams have a clear and designated team leader who is responsible for the success of the team. Any group with an executive function needs an executive leader, however participative the mode of operation.

In most cases overlapping responsibilities prevent any obvious modification of the single line structure which works better because of the nature of the work. It is the work of individuals which cannot be neatly pigeonholed which is the root cause of the problem. For short term projects a task group, working party or other group can be brought into existence. If this arrangement is formalised then it is called a matrix structure. Some writers have reserved the term matrix only to cover the dual accountability involved in such temporary groups, however, the prevalence of this mode of working over long periods has meant that it is possible to envisage a permanent structure involving dual accountability and this is generally known as a matrix although Sayles (1976) has identified five types of dual accountability.

Matrix When the operating core is too large to be run as one unit it is necessary to divide it into subunits of a manageable size. In relatively simple organisations where individual employees perform one function then this subdivision can be accomplished fairly readily. However, when the employees contribute in a flexible way to a number of the subtasks of the organisation then any attempt to divide into subunits meets with problems. As Sayles (1976; p.2) states:

> Every organization faces two problems: first, how to specialise (creating a division of labour); and second, how to integrate the specialised parts to create a whole product or service.

In response to this dilemma he believes that many organisations have adopted some form of matrix structure but often without using the name.

An organisational structure in which large numbers of employees are in dual authority relationships can be represented in a two-dimensional matrix. Typically this represents the case of teachers in an FE college who are based in divisions of subject specialists but who contribute to multidisciplinary courses managed by a course leader. The course leader is responsible for the overall service to students – course structure, curriculum, provision of teaching, assessment arrangements – and for recruiting and counselling students. The head of the division is responsible for a particular subject area, its teaching, and the provision and development of the teaching expertise.

Child (1984) identifies three matrix control structures

1. *equal*   the two arms of the matrix are   equally dominant
2. *'co-ordination'*   functional is dominant
3. *'secondment'*   project is dominant for the life of the project

It is essential in each case to try to identify, where there is doubt, which of the two 'bosses' is responsible for which aspects of staff management. Failure to do so results in confusion, overlapping supervision, and omission of important functions. The amount of detailed specification will be greatest in case (1).

A formal matrix structure offers flexibility and adaptability to change. It has open lines of communication and a more diffuse managerial accountability giving greater responsibility to individual workers.

However, there is evidence of conflict, lack of accountability, many meetings and paperwork particularly where the nature of the dual accountability has not been fully appreciated and allowed for:

> The matrix structure attempts to formalize an already existing conflict between functional and product programme criteria
>
> (Child, 1984: p.102)

Matrix structures were explicitly introduced into industries producing contributions to space exploration in the US so that a programme manager could be identified to liaise with the client sponsor and oversee the particular development.

Organisational design

This is a combination of a rational and a political process:

> Structure itself often becomes victim to politics, and indeed it will not be allowed to operate effectively if it does not reflect political forces within the organization.
>
> (Child, 1984; p.15/16)

Such political forces include both the intrinsic importance of the section or interest group and also the personal importance of key individuals.

PROCESSES OF APPRAISAL 211

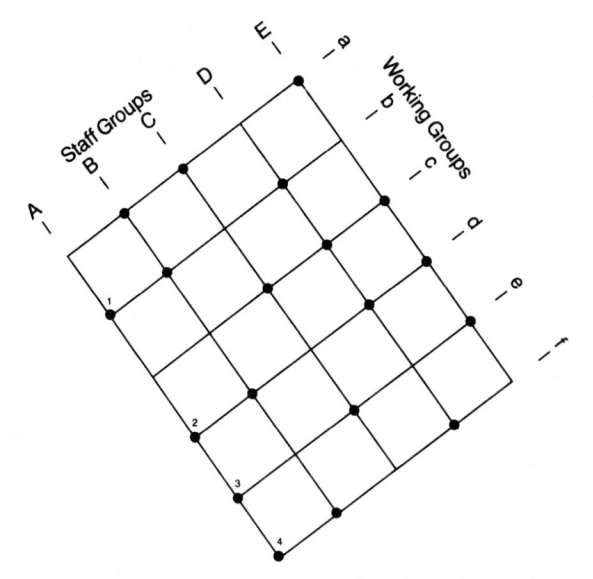

Figure 4.1.4 Simple matrix organisational structure

Note: Staff are grouped by their specialism into departments A to E. Staff from departments contribute to inter-disciplinary working groups a to f. For example, staff member 1 from department A contributes to working group b. The leaders of the working groups may be in departments or not and the HoDs may be in working groups depending on their other commitments.

In schools and colleges both HoDs would be in working groups and leaders of working groups would be in departments. If each member of staff were to contribute to more than one working group, a multi-dimensional matrix would be required to show the multiple relationships and responsibilities.

Functional managers will have their authority weakened. Particularly when dealing with outsiders it may appear that no one has power to make decisions. The principle of unity of command has been sacrificed in order to achieve greater horizontal communication.

In designing organisations it is not necessarily jobs which are the basic building blocks but tasks:

> ...it becomes more sensible to select the group and its task as the unit for design than individual jobs within the group.
>
> (Child, 1984; p.24)

The basic design problem is then how to assemble these tasks into units of reasonable size and to relate these units together both horizontally and vertically.

Horizontal structures

Units can be grouped horizontally in a number of ways, for example by:
- (a) Worker specialisation;
- (b) Product or service;
- (c) Geographical area; and
- (d) Function

In the case of a school or college (a) would group teaching staff by their teaching subject; (b) would group them by the class, year group or course on which they taught; and (c) would group them by the site on which they did their teaching in the case of a split site institution; (d) would group teaching and non-teaching staff separately and subdivide the non-teaching staff by their function – finance, personnel, caretaking, cleaning etc. Each of these groupings has some advantages and some disadvantages. Not all are mutually incompatible. Most schools would divide by (d) but then (a) and (b) are mutually incompatible for permanent groupings if the same staff teach more than one year group of course. The only way in which (a) and (b) can be used simultaneously is if a matrix structure is used.

Vertical structures

The vertical structure is concerned with:
- (a) Co-ordination and control of horizontal units;
- (b) Increasing strategic considerations at higher levels – long term, whole organisation and boundary crossing; and
- (c) Increasing organisational management and less direct contribution to client service at higher levels.

> The first step in any systematic design or redesign approach to this area is to bring out clearly which of any existing or proposed posts really are to be main line-management ones. The second is to define the exact authority, if any, to be exercised by all others in the status chain.
>
> (Rowbottom & Billis, 1987; p.17)

Structural context of schools and colleges

Although in many pronouncements from politicians and others schools have been likened to small businesses this is quite misleading. Whilst schools and colleges may be relatively small organisations, there the parallel ends. Schools are not free to decide what business they are in. That is already decided – their function is to educate young people of a certain age and they receive funding only to do that. Thus they are much more akin to local subsidiaries of a national organisation. Their most basic aim, many operating rules and funding are decided at central and local government level. Within these constraints the 1988 *Education Reform Act* has given individual institutions greater freedom to operate. This greater freedom has brought additional functions to most schools and the organisational structure needs to take account of these.

Whilst schools and colleges are educational organisations and have the education of young people as their principal concern, they also have to discharge administrative functions both to continue to exist and to prosper in the future as all other organisations do, for example, employing teachers and maintaining premises. Thus the organisational structure has to include not only educational activities but also general administrative and managerial activities. In the past some of these activities could be assumed to be the function of the LEA.

Thus the activities of an educational institution may be categorised as:

1. Providing educational services;
2. Organisational administration and maintenance e.g. personnel, finance, premises and plant maintenance; and
3. Planning future strategy e.g. strategic planning, marketing.

Some of these functions may be undertaken by specially appointed employees or others whose jobs can be redesigned to take on all or part of these functions but most will be further additions to the work of a number of the teaching staff.

Either as an adjunct to the marketing function or in addition to it there is a greater expectation that schools will be much more client oriented in their dealings with parents and students. Thus there is a requirement for a more 'user friendly' mode of operation than has been customary in many schools. What may be called parental liaison is an additional function which ERA has implicitly required of schools.

In many matrix structures the product manager is the pivotal point of contact with clients to co-ordinate communications to and from clients and between appropriate personnel in the organisation. Such a concept could be applied to schools with perhaps year heads in secondary schools and class teachers in primary schools being explicitly empowered to take on such a function. However, in adopting such a structure it should be recognised that the internal structure of schools would have to be responsive to the needs identified by such contacts with clients via such 'product managers'. The function is not only to communicate with the outside world but to be able to get things done on behalf of outsiders – this is somewhat more than communication or co-ordination.

Equally within the school there may be a need for a 'product manager' to deal with the needs of the individual student – to ensure that each receives a well balanced, high quality programme for example. A year head in a secondary school could carry out such a function or a new post of key stage manager (or subkeystage manager) could be created. Both of these proposals would, in most schools, augment both in quantity and prestige the post of year head. This could lead to a clearer career structure in terms of moving through a departmental leadership post into such a post before deputy headship and then headship.

Organisational design in schools and colleges

1. Identify functions to be discharged
2. Examine major areas for major sub-divisions
3. Decide how major areas are to be led and managed
4. Decide on the line management and other relationships between key posts. Line managers should manage staff and budgets to achieve objectives.

In figure 4.1.5 are some possible organisation charts for primary and secondary schools. It may be instructive to envisage the differences in working relationships and accountabilities of the different designs. All will have advantages and disadvantages in general terms. For particular institutions, the micropolitical dimension and the strengths of existing personnel will be equally important determinants of an appropriate organisational structure.

Job descriptions

Having devised an organisational structure the final element is to create job descriptions for all staff. For existing staff these need to be negotiated initially and then periodically renegotiated as part of the appraisal process. There is a good deal of misunderstanding about job descriptions.

PROCESSES OF APPRAISAL 215

(a) Primary School

Note: These represent a range of organisational structures with different reporting relationships and hierarchical levels.

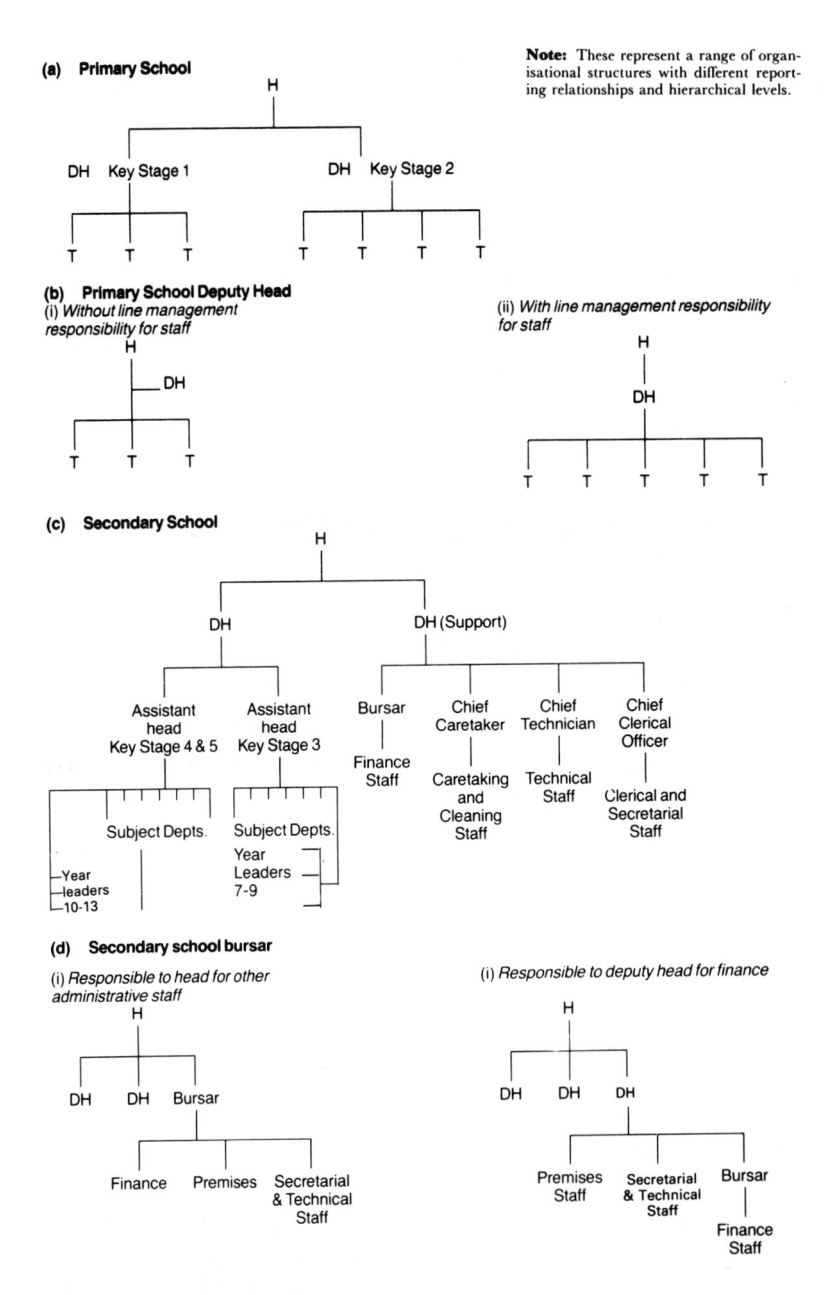

(b) Primary School Deputy Head
(i) *Without line management responsibility for staff*

(ii) *With line management responsibility for staff*

(c) Secondary School

(d) Secondary school bursar
(i) *Responsible to head for other administrative staff*

(i) *Responsible to deputy head for finance*

Figure 4.1.5 Possible organisation charts for primary and secondary schools

The objective of a job description is to record the facts about the job content. These should include the job title, reporting relationships upward and downward, the overall purpose of the job, a short description of the main activities, arranged in 'key result areas' (Ungerson, 1983; p.1).

It should not be an extensive catalogue of all the minute tasks which are included within the job for this does not allow the job holder to see 'the wood for the trees' nor to appreciate the relative importance of various aspects of the job.

Most jobs in school will be a combination of:

(a) Teaching;
(b) Pastoral work; and
(c) Management.

For different jobs the relative importance and relative amount of time spent on each of these three facets will be different.

Some tasks will be ongoing, some will be short-term developmental, and some will be rotating. Associated with these tasks will be a small number of targets requiring specific achievements over a fixed period of time.

The targets may be:

Remedial	bringing an aspect of the job back to an acceptable level of performance
Developmental	developing an aspect of the job
Problem solving	finding a way of overcoming some problem aspect of the job
Personal developmental	identifying some temporary task which contributes to personal development but which may not be part of the enduring job description.

The targets can be expected to change regularly. Many will be completed in one year.

Features of a job description

The job description should have the following sections (given in bold on the left) (Fidler, Bowles and Hart, 1991). The explanatory statements are given in italics on the right. See Figure 4.1.6.

PROCESSES OF APPRAISAL 217

Job Title:	This should be a short description of the job covering its teaching and managerial aspects e.g. Class teacher and mathematics co-ordinator (Primary) Maths teacher and deputy head of year nine (Secondary)
Responsible to	This should give the immediate line manager(s) of the post. This should normally be their appraiser e.g. Headteacher (Primary) Head of Mathematics (for maths teaching) and Head of Year Nine (for pastoral work) (Secondary)
Responsible for:	This should cover any teaching or non-teaching staff for which the post is responsible
Purpose:	This will outline the teaching duties and any more specific managerial tasks of the post, e.g. (Primary) – To carry out the duties of a class teacher as set out in paras 33-36 (inclusive) of the School Teachers' Pay and Conditions Document – To co-ordinate mathematics throughout the school (Secondary) – To carry out the duties of a mathematics teacher as set out in paras 33-36 (inclusive) of the School Teachers' Pay and Conditions Document – To assist the Head of Year Nine
Key Result Areas:	This forms the major part of the job description. These areas (not exceeding 10 in number) represent the coherent areas of activity which comprise the job. Each will be broken down into a number of more specific objectives. These will cover the teaching aspects of the job and also any managerial elements. For any namagerial elements there should be some indication of the precise managerial component of each task e.g. Leadership, Co-ordination, Liaison, Organisation, Training.
Targets:	Any specific objectives which are set for some fixed period should be recorded alongside the associated continuing objective part of the job (except for any personal development targets which are not part of the continuing job)

Figure 4.1.6   Job description

4.2 Observation of classroom teaching

Chris Kyriacou

Introduction

The appraisal of classroom teaching based on direct classroom observation ('classroom appraisal') is seen to be an essential component of teacher appraisal as outlined by the DES (1989, 1991). However, few teachers have had any experience of appraising a colleague's teaching. Indeed, in the majority of teacher appraisal schemes that have been introduced in schools over the last ten years, the scheme focused on an appraisal interview without any direct classroom observation involved (Turner and Clift, 1988). As such, the LEA pilot teacher appraisal schemes have provided a wealth of useful information concerning classroom appraisal (Bollington et al, 1990; Bradley et al, 1989) to add to the somewhat mixed picture of classroom appraisal that had been reported beforehand (Bunnell, 1987; Fidler and Cooper, 1988; HMI, 1989; Suffolk LEA, 1985, 1987; Turner and Clift, 1988; Wragg, 1987).

Purpose of classroom appraisal

In order to design a teacher appraisal scheme and monitor its success, one needs to be clear about its aims and purpose. This is equally true regarding the scheme as a whole and its constituent elements, in this case classroom appraisal. Five main purposes have been widely advocated for classroom appraisal:

1. To enable an appraiser to encourage, support and assist the appraisee to think about their current and future classroom practice.

2. To provide an opportunity for the appraiser and appraisee to share ideas about classroom practice.
3. To enable the appraiser to offer advice, guidance and support concerning any particular concerns, problems or shortcomings that could usefully be addressed.
4. To enable the appraiser to act as an extra pair of eyes to provide the appraisee with some useful data about specific aspects of the lesson.
5. To enable the appraiser to make a judgement and evaluation about the quality of the appraisee's teaching.

Looking at these five purposes, purposes one to four are generally considered to be aspects of a formative assessment aimed at stimulating self-appraisal and promoting the appraisee's professional development. The fifth purpose, in contrast, is considered to constitute a summative assessment, which could link the appraisal with enhanced promotion opportunities and salary for the 'best' classroom performers, and dismissal for 'weak' classroom performers who cannot be brought up to a satisfactory standard (Clarke, 1991).

Unfortunately, this tension between the formative and summative purposes is not easy to resolve. For example, an appraisee is much more likely to identify problems that deserve attention and to invite the appraiser to observe a lesson where this is evident if the purpose of the classroom appraisal is exclusively formative. If the appraisal also includes a summative assessment, an appraisee may well prefer to highlight their strengths and successes, and thus choose a lesson with only limited, if any, suitability as a stimulus for constructive dialogue about future development.

Role of appraiser and appraisee

The roles of the appraiser and appraisee are primarily to act together to ensure that the purposes of the scheme operate successfully, and that the appraisee gets as much benefit as possible from the process involved. Most schemes to date have focused on a professional development model, where the appraiser acts as a consultant to the appraisee, to assist the appraisee to review and explore current practice. In such schemes, it is essential that the appraiser does not see their role as telling a colleague what they are doing wrong and how they should be doing it right! Rather, the appraiser and appraisee are intended to share ideas. The discussion that takes place is one between equals, working in collaboration.

In schemes where to some degree summative assessment is involved, the role of the appraiser requires a great deal of sensitivity and impeccable fairness. The skills involved in giving useful and constructive feedback with appropriate sensitivity is the single most important area where appropriate INSET training is required to increase the likelihood that a classroom appraisal can be conducted successfully. Done badly, the consequences could be damaging for both the relationship between the two colleagues and for the appraisee's feelings of motivation and goodwill towards their work in the school.

Choosing the appraiser

In most schemes, the appraisee has been able to choose their appraiser, although often this choice has been restricted in some way to a list of colleagues who have agreed to act as appraisers. This list usually comprises senior members of staff in the school. The DES certainly favours a hierarchical, line management, approach rather than the diverse practice that has occurred to date, which has included appraisers and appraisees having equal status, and in some cases, even a 'bottom-up', (rather than a 'top-down') model being adopted.

Studies of recent practice indicate that it is very important that the appraiser enjoys the trust and confidence of the appraisee, and has credibility with the appraisee as someone who can give useful and valid feedback. This has meant that, with very few exceptions, the appraiser is a colleague within the school, who therefore knows the school, the appraisee, the pupils, and the learning context well. Outsiders are generally felt to be unsuitable as classroom appraisers.

What to look for during classroom appraisal

There is no definitive outline of what constitutes good classroom practice (Kyriacou, 1986) or a definitive list of the particular skills or qualities that need to be monitored when conducting classroom appraisals (Kyriacou, 1991). Nevertheless, there is a fair degree of consensus about such matters. The HMI, in their various reports (e.g. HMI, 1985, 1987a, 1987b, 1988a, 1988b, 1990) however, have been very influential in outlining what they see as constituting good classroom practice, and much of what they advocate has been echoed in the guidance produced by the National Curriculum Council to support the teaching of the National Curriculum (e.g. NCC, 1989a, 1989b, 1990).

For example, the HMI (1990) have characterised good lessons in secondary schools as being evidenced by:

(a) Active participation by pupils;

(b) High teacher expectations;

(c) Tasks well matched to learning needs;

(d) Work perceived by pupils to be relevant and challenging; and

(e) Good use of discussion and investigation

Reports by the HMI, DES and NCC, both in general terms about teaching and learning in schools, and in more specific terms about particular subjects, topic areas and age groups, can be seen to constitute the type of classroom practice that schools need to be achieving or moving towards. This implies, to some extent, that the appraiser and appraisee are familiar with, or can become familiar with, such an agenda, and that they accept and adhere to this agenda in planning and conducting the classroom appraisal.

Again, whilst there is no definitive list of classroom teaching skills, in broad terms, the following aspects are fairly typical (*see* Kyriacou, 1991, for a detailed elaboration of these):

Planning and preparation;

Lesson presentation;

Lesson management;

Classroom climate;

Discipline;

Assessing pupils' progress; and

Evaluation and reflection

Such lists have been widely used as an *aide mémoire* to guide the appraiser during classroom observation, and to provide subheadings to be used in subsequent lesson appraisal reports. As noted earlier, however, what is looked for, and how, will very much depend on the purpose of the classroom appraisal, and whether any particular aspects of the appraisee's teaching or the lesson have been agreed as being the focus of attention. Where particular aspects are to be explored, the approach to classroom observation will clearly become more exclusive. Thus, for example, a focus on questioning skills or techniques, may lead to the appraiser using some type of observation schedule which categorises different types of questions and related interactions, or using other types of data collection methods, such as videotaping.

Conducting a lesson appraisal

The first stage of any appraisal scheme should involve self-appraisal, and an opportunity for the appraisee to identify any aspect of their classroom practice that might usefully be focused on. A discussion between the appraiser and appraisee can then lead to a decision about which lessons might usefully be observed and whether any particular aspects might be highlighted, and how the observation should be carried out.

Most lesson appraisals involve the appraiser sitting passively at the back of the classroom making notes, with occasional forays around the classroom to more closely observe individual pupils' progress, and from time to time helping a pupil who appears to be in difficulty as a means of getting a better feel of the learning taking place. In some cases, albeit only a few, the appraiser has actively shared the teaching with the appraisee. By and large, however, studies indicate that being a passive observer with only very occasional, if any, departure from the back of the room, seems to be the most successful approach, as this enables the appraiser to concentrate exclusively on the teacher's performance and related aspects of the lesson.

After the lesson, feedback should be given as quickly as possible. Such feedback should initially take the form of exploring how the appraisee felt the lesson went, and any issues they wish to raise. Gradually, the appraiser can then introduce their observations and comments, as a means of stimulating such self-appraisal, sharing ideas, and highlighting aspects that might usefully be discussed.

Documenting lesson appraisals

After the appraisal interview has been conducted, a final record of the appraisal is produced, which will include a section on classroom teaching, either as a general subheading or broken down into its key components (e.g. plannng, presentation, management, discipline, etc.). Completion of this aspect of the final record will be based on the original notes made by the appraiser during the lesson observed, and the appraiser's notes of the discussion which occurred after the lesson, and the further discussion which took place during the appraisal interview. Once the final record has been drawn up, such notes are usually destroyed. However, in some schemes, a separate lesson appraisal is written after each lesson, and these are then included in the final documentation (see figure 4.2.1 for an example of a lesson appraisal report).

A number of important issues concerning such records have implications for what is finally produced and kept. Clearly, one important aspect of such records is that they are confidential. This normally means that the appraisee keeps a copy and that another copy is kept by the head teacher. In some schemes the head teacher was not given a copy, but in a nationally agreed scheme this is likely to be the case. There is still much discussion concerning who else might be given a copy. For example, the chair of the governing body of the school and an LEA adviser, might be given a copy. The wider the circulation, the more likely it is that the appraisee will be sensitive to any critical comments being recorded in the final document.

Another important issue is the use to which the final record is put. Again, if there are summative purposes involved, such as promotion, pay and dismissal, this will also increase sentitivity to critical comments. A third important issue is that the final record should be fair, and agreed to be fair by both the appraiser and appraisee. This means that the sources of evidence used should be based on explicit procedures, such as direct observation, and, with the permission of the appraisee, discussion with other colleagues or even other forms of data collection (for example, in a few schemes use has been made of feedback from pupils). Uncorroborated hearsay or contentious interpretation of ill conducted observation will justifiably be regarded as unacceptable by the appraisee.

As a result of such issues, records of appraisal have often tended to be more positive, or perhaps one should say diplomatic, than is strictly warranted if the record was to be as valid as possible. This naturally reflects a reluctance to record on paper anything that might be regarded as contentious or unfair. In many cases, the feedback discussion after a lesson and the subsequent appraisal discussion has been frank, honest and fair, but both appraiser and appraisee have then colluded, in part perhaps unconsciously, to produce a written record which, in terms of any critical comments, may be somewhat watered down. This may appear to be evident in the report shown in figure 4.2.1.

Target setting

A feature of the final record will be the inclusion of any targets for professional development regarding classroom teaching agreed by the appraiser and appraisee. This might outline changes in practice (e.g.

LESSON APPRAISAL

Name Mrs R. Barton　　　　　　　　　　　　Date 15/5/90
Subject Mathematics　　　Class taught 7(R)　　Period 3 & 4

PLANNING AND PREPARATION
1. Clarity and appropriateness of objectives.
2. Selection of materials and equipment, and of learning activities.

COMMUNICATION
3. Quality of voice and speech.
4. Clarity and intelligibility of language.
5. Use of non-verbal cues.

MANAGEMENT OF LEARNING
6. Organisation of pupils (individuals, group, class).
7. Organisation of aids and materials.
8. Lesson introduction, gaining and maintaining attention.
9. Sequencing of activities, pace of lesson, flexibility of presentation.
10. Skill in asking and adapting questions to pupils and in handling questions and responses from pupils.
11. Attention to safety (where applicable).
12. Achievement of objectives.
13. Lesson closure.
14. Pupils' interest, involvement and enjoyment.

RELATIONSHIPS
15. Skill in maintaining control.
16. Teacher-pupil rapport (individual and group).
17. Sympathy with the awareness of pupils' needs and difficulties.

APPRAISER'S COMMENTS
This lesson was basically sound and well presented, although I did wonder whether my presence may have had a deadening effect on the pupils' natural liveliness and enthusiasm (a point which you confirmed to me in our discussion after the lesson).

Judging the lesson as I saw it, I felt the pupils were getting a clear introduction into the topic, but I did wonder somewhat whether they were being a bit too passive (some of our first year groups seem to take a while to find their feet and confidence in making contributions).

I liked the way you tried to get some discussion going on the meaning of commutative.

Obviously one cannot generalise too much from one lesson, but I wondered what opportunities you set up for pupils to communicate with each other concerning mathematical ideas, as advocated by the HMI (although in discussion afterwards you did say that you set up some problem solving tasks based on small group teaching about one a month for each class in years 7 to 9).

When I inspected the pupils' books, I found marking had been conscientious and thorough and the work presented was generally neat. I noticed that John Riley had been given more advanced work (his parents had recently complained that he was gifted in maths but was not being stretched by our lessons, so it is clear that appropriate action has now been taken).

Overall, a good solid performance.　　　　　　　Signed *Arnold Morrison*
　　　　　　　　　　　　　　　　　　　　　　　　　　　　(Deputy Head)
　　　　　　　　　　　　　　　　　　　　　　　　　　　　16/5/90

Figure 4.2.1　Mrs Barton's lesson appraisal report

use of more investigative approaches; adopting a different teaching scheme; trying a different method of grouping pupils) or INSET activities (e.g. attendance at an appropriate course; joint planning of certain lessons with a colleague; provision of teacher support guides and materials). Such targets should be realistic, and take account of resource implications. It is probably unwise to suggest that clearly overworked colleagues attend several short courses during their evenings, or to rashly propose a reduced timetable that is just not possible.

The targets should be reviewed after an appropriate period of time to check that they are still appropriate, to monitor whether the necessary support occurred and was adequate, and to discuss the extent to which progress towards meeting these targets is being made.

CASE STUDY

> The following case study is designed to highlight the key issues involved in classroom appraisal, and will serve to illustrate that from some of these issues, there is no easy answer as to what should constitute good practice. This case study concerns the appraisal of Mrs Rosemary Barton.
>
> ### The School
>
> The school is an 11–18 comprehensive school serving a largely rural population. There are 980 pupils on roll, reflecting the full range of ability. The school is fairly popular with parents, and is generally considered to be successful.
>
> ### Mrs Rosemary Barton
>
> Mrs Barton is 46 years old. She has been at the school for 22 years, and has been head of the mathematics department for the last ten. Her style of teaching is fairly traditional, viz. largely based on exposition, demonstrating and explaining examples with the whole class, using questions to probe understanding, and then supervising practice. Pupils generally progress well under her guidance. She has found it difficult to adapt her approach to meet the demands of GCSE and National Curriculum Mathematics, but feels she has developed reasonably

well, and does now include specific lessons designed to incorporate different learning activities. Her main problem is that she tends to be rather aloof, which largely explains why she has found it difficult to develop the more personal style needed to facilitate investigative work and mathematical discussion.

Mr Arnold Morrison

Mr Morrison is 40 years old. He has been at the school for nine years, and has been deputy head for the last three. He teaches history and is well used to and comfortable with teaching based on using a variety of learning activities, particularly those based on small group discussion. He sees his main task in appraising Mrs Barton as encouraging her to think about her teaching with a view to further developing her approach. However, he does not want to 'push this hard', seeing himself as a facilitator rather than an inspector. Mrs Barton chose Mr Morrison to act as her appraiser from a list of four possible appraisers (the head, two deputy heads and the head of the science department).

Initial meeting

At this meeting, Mr Morrison explored whether Mrs Barton felt there was any particular aspect of her teaching he could usefully pay special attention to. Despite various probes, Mrs Barton declined to identify any specific aspects, and as such they agreed that the observation should be a general one. Mr Morrison took particular care to make this meeting relaxed, and to emphasise that the main purpose of the lesson observation was to help her to think about her current and future classroom practice. Nevertheless, Mrs Barton appeared tense and defensive. They agreed that a Year 7 class should be observed with a view to linking this with the introduction of Key Stage 3 Mathematics.

Lesson observation

In the appraisal scheme agreed at this school the staff have drawn up a lesson appraisal report form, which comprises an aide mémoire at the top (*see* figure 4.2.1 p.224). Each appraisee is to receive a written report after a post-lesson feedback session and before the appraisal interview. As such, the report can incorporate points made in the post-lesson feedback session.

Mr Morrison sits at the back of the classroom, and is introduced to the class by Mrs Barton as 'coming to look at the mathematics we're doing'. The lesson is a double period, lasting one hour and ten minutes. The class is mixed ability. The lesson takes place at the start of the summer term. At the end of the term the pupils will take a test, and are then allocated into sets for Year 8. The lesson is based on the principle of commutativity (viz. exploring whether the order of carrying out addition, subtraction, multiplication and division affects the answer; e.g. 4+6 gives the same answer as 6+4, but 4−6 does not give the same answer as 6−4).

The lesson, possibly because of Mr Morrison's presence or a slight nervousness on Mrs Barton's part, seems to have made the pupils less responsive than he expected. Even allowing for this, however, the lesson seems to be somewhat over directed by the teacher. The initial teacher–pupil exchanges are rather slow and laboured. Even when Mrs Barton tries to get some discussion going with the whole class about the meaning of commutativity, the pupils appear to display a mixture of nervousness, patience and boredom. Nevertheless, the lesson is clearly well controlled and ordered, well structured, and the key objectives of the lesson are accomplished. When Mr Morrison circulated around whilst the pupils were working on an exercise, most appeared to be working well, and those in difficulty received swift help from Mrs Barton.

Post-lesson feedback

Mr Morrison's honest feeling about the lesson was that useful learning had occurred, but that it was rather dull. He feels a livelier manner on Mrs Barton's part, a more positive rapport with the pupils, and a greater variety of activities to get discussion going, would have helped. Despite these feelings, he knows his role is to facilitate her thinking rather than to tell her how to teach.

He thus greets her at the end by saying 'Thank you very much, I found that very interesting'. Once they reach the departmental office, he asks her how *she felt* the lesson went. Her view was that the lesson was basically fine, but that a few particular pupils, whom she names, need to work harder and to be more attentive. After a few probes to get her to elaborate her thoughts on aspects of the lesson, he floats the idea of generating more discussion, both teacher–pupil and pupil–pupil, and gives examples from his own practice in teaching history. He is careful to adopt a tone of sharing views rather than hint at being judgemental. She is nevertheless, rather defensive, and says that whilst she plans certain lessons specifically with such discussion in mind, she finds adopting her 'usual' approach for most lessons seems to be a good balance of practice. Mr Morrison makes a mental note that this is a key aspect of her teaching they must usefully pick up again at the appraisal interview. He feels he has done enough for the time being to note his issue with her.

Writing the lesson report

Mr Morrison feels his report needs to be fair but also diplomatic. As this report is to be included in the final appraisal documentation, he feels it is essential to ensure he commits nothing to paper that is unjustified or based on flimsy evidence, or on hearsay he has picked up over the years. Nevertheles, he does feel it is important that some reference is made to the over directedness and lack of variety and interaction during the lesson. A careful reading of the report (figure 4.2.1 p.224) illustrates Mr Morrison's attempt to reconcile such concerns in a diplomatic way and to give credit where he felt credit was due.

Issues raised by the case study

Every appraisal is unique in its particular combination of appraiser, appraisee, the school, the class, the lesson, the scheme adopted. Practice to date indicates that there are five key issues that need to be addressed, and these are reflected in this case study:

> *Who sets the agenda?* Whilst most schemes are aimed at encouraging the appraisee to think about their own classroom practice, and as such set their own agenda, the vast majority of appraisees tend to expect the appraiser to take the lead, and often, to be evaluative. This can be particularly tricky for appraisers who are not subject or age range specialists in the area they are appraising. In setting up a scheme, appraisees need to be helped in how best to establish their own agenda. Even so, to the extent that the classroom appraisal has a summative purpose, part of the agenda will also come from a consensus notion of what constitutes good classroom practice.
>
> *Is the classroom appraisal fair?* Appraisees are naturally concerned that the lesson or lessons observed, together with any other evidence collected, can be used to give a fair appraisal. It is worth pointing out, that this is also just as common and great a concern for the appraiser. Whilst what is deemed 'fair' may not always be agreed, this should not be a problem as long as the appraiser and appraisee show goodwill and sensitivity towards each other's position.
>
> *Is feedback given with appropriate skill?* Feedback should be helpful and fair. Giving feedback that helps a colleague to think about and improve their practice, and does not

discourage and lead to resentment, demands social skills, in part not unlike counselling skills.

What can and should be committed to paper? Appraisees are very sensitive to critical comments they feel are unfair and/or are unsupported by evidence. This may easily lead an appraiser to water down their written report in order to err on the side of safety. Nevertheless, the written report does need to be a fair appraisal and sufficiently full to enable a subsequent follow-up review or appraisal to be informed by the earlier record. Nevertheless, problems over who will be reading the final record and the use this record will be put to, will clearly have a major influence on what is formally recorded.

What targets can usefully be set? Setting targets relating to classroom practice should be tailored to the professional development needs of the appraisee. They should be clear, reasonable and achievable. A pitfall to avoid however, is to set targets simply for the sake of it, that actually lack any real relevance or worthwhileness for the appraisee. As such, the appraisee's *real needs* should be identified, if and when appropriate, as the basis of target setting.

Conclusions

It will be evident from what has been discussed in this chapter that classroom appraisal involves a number of difficult issues that need to be addressed successfully if the appraisal is to be effective, and have benefit for all those concerned.

Studies of schemes already in operation have fortunately clarified the nature of the key issues, and indicated ways in which good practice can develop. Nevertheless, the most important aspect of any classroom appraisal is a climate of trust and goodwill between the appraiser and appraisee to work in cooperation in their effort to extract the potential benefits that appraisal can offer. Classroom appraisal needs to be seen as an opportunity, not a threat; and as something worthwhile, and not as a chore. With a positive climate for the classroom appraisal established, together with appropriate time, resourcing and appraisal skills development, classroom appraisal can make a real and worthwhile impact on developing classroom practice in schools.

4.3 Interviewing

4.3.0 Introduction to interviewing

Bob Cooper

Interviews

The word 'interview', according to the Oxford Shorter English Dictionary, comes from the French verb *s'entrevener*, which means 'to see each other.' An interview is further defined as 'a meeting of persons face to face especially for the purpose of a conference on some point.' This implies that there should be some kind of dialogue between the two parties, and that there should be an attempt at least to both convey information and to understand the messages being transmitted. Interviews are usually conducted in a variety of formal situations and have a distinct and specific purpose. This purpose will determine both the format and the process of the interview.

Types of interview

Interviews are commonly used for such purposes as selection, discipline, grievance and counselling, as well as the one being considered in this volume – appraisal. Managers need to make use of interviews to gather and to give out information on a personal basis. It is part of the process of rational decision making, especially on matters concerning staff employment.

No two interviews are exactly the same, but it is possible to identify a number of general considerations which need to be taken into account, and a number of skills which are common to all interviews. Cowling & Mailer (1987) suggest that the following list of guidelines need to be observed in all good interviews:–

1. Clarify the aims and objectives of the interview.
2. Collect and study the necessary information and paperwork before the interview.
3. Inform the interviewee in a manner appropriate to the occasion.
4. Plan the sequence of the interview.
5. Prepare the layout of the room.
6. Ensure there are no interruptions.
7. Open the interview in a friendly and controlled manner.
8. Ask open ended questions which require more than a 'yes' or 'no' answer.
9. Do not express personal judgements.
10. Monitor continually in the discussion.
11. Encourage interviewees to extend useful statements.
12. Do not make promises you cannot fulfil.
13. Listen with interest.
14. Observe non-verbal behaviour.
15. Avoid personal bias and prejudice.
16. Beware of the halo effect.
17. Make notes in an open manner.
18. Probe and follow up points made by the interviewee.
19. Ensure a satisfactory hearing.
20. Conclude the interview with firmness, tact and courtesy.
21. Allow time for recollection – making notes, etc.

These general guidelines are appropriate for all types of interview. In certain circumstances, of course, there will be more emphasis on some of the points than upon others. In a selection interview, for example, you may wish to open the interview in a very friendly manner whereas if the interview is largely concerned with discipline, you may wish to be rather more controlled in your approach.

An interview is a social situation and as such demands a display of social skills. All managers need to consider these skills because their job is to achieve particular objectives through other people. Management is very much about influencing, involving and motivating others, and this demands a high level of social skill. These skills are displayed particularly in formal and informal interview situations. All successful managers have these skills, but all managers can enhance their skills by training. In all the reports which have been written about the introduction of appraisal into schools the importance of training has been stressed. It does no harm to reiterate these comments once again.

Phases of an interview

Sidney, Brown and Argyle (1973) in their seminal book *Skills with People* suggest that interviews fall into four general phases which they label WASP – Welcome, Acquiring Information, Supplying Information and Parting. Each phase is important, and each phase demands certain skills.

1. *Welcome* It is important to establish the right relationship of trust from the beginning of the interview. This is particularly important for appraisal interviewing, because so many interviewees will come to their first such interview with a great deal of apprehension. The interviewer should attempt to convey interest and sympathy by both verbal and non-verbal signals.

2. *Acquiring Information* In all interviews an attempt should be made to establish an accepting atmosphere, within which the interviewee can feel secure enough to express their real thoughts and feelings. The interviewer should try, both through the things that are said and also by general posture and demeanour, to indicate a serious and attentive interest in what the interviewee has to say. Different skills will be required to deal with different kinds of people. With those who are rather shy and nervous it is usually appropriate to show special friendliness and informality. With those who are or who appear to be over-confident, it may be advisable to be rather more brisk and formal.

3. *Supplying information* It has already been intimated that all interviews are a dialogue. The appraisal interview is an opportunity for the middle manager to play an important management role. In order to do this successfully, however, it will be necessary for the middle manager to have knowledge and understanding of the defined institutional needs and of the resources available to meet those needs. If an appraisal interview is going to be successful, it must meet the needs of both the institution and of the individual. If a head of department is conducting an appraisal interview, he or she needs to be able to reconcile the needs of the one with the other. This requires both specific knowledge of the school's requirements, the resources available to fulfil those requirements, and also a good knowledge of alternative forms of

training and opportunities through which individual teachers may be encouraged to develop their expertise.

4. *Parting* The close of any interview is important. The interviewee should leave with the feeling that the experience has been worthwhile. In general there should be a summary of some kind, which should recapitulate the agreements which have been reached during the course of the interview. The action to be taken by both parties should be reviewed. There should be some kind of written statement about the discussion and the resulting decisions. In many cases this is best agreed by both parties at the time, though in some cases the written statement may have to be composed and agreed at a later date.

At different points in an interview, the interviewer will find themselves using a variety of social skills – persuading, motivating, clarifying, summarising, problem solving, listing, counselling. On many occasions it will be necessary to make use of questions. This in itself is a skill which may be enhanced by training and reflection. In general it is better to make use of open ended questions rather than closed questions, because one of the aims of any interviewer is to encourage a proper dialogue, and in most interview situations, the interviewer is in the dominant power position.

Types of questions

A number of different types of questions may be identified and evaluated:

1. *Closed questions* these are questions which can be answered 'yes' or 'no' or very briefly, e.g. 'Did you come by train?'

   There is little scope for the respondent to influence the reply.

2. *Command questions* these are a form of closed question. They are usually couched in a particular tone of voice, e.g. 'Why did you place the child in detention?'

   They limit the respondent's scope by requiring an explanation

3. *Open questions* these allow the interviewee to respond in the way that seems most appropriate to them, e.g. 'What is your view of the new maths scheme?'

   They help to establish two-way communication by inviting the respondent to decide the matters they wish to bring into the conversation. It encourages trust and suggests that the interviewer is prepared and willing to listen.

4. *Probe questions* these are questions which seek particular information or elucidation of some matter which is being discussed, e.g. 'Why do you think that?'

   They are generally open ended and show interest and concern on the part of the interviewer, although some probe questions may appear to be command questions because of the tone of voice used.

5. *Understanding questions* these questions test the interviewer's cognitive understanding of the respondent's previous statements, e.g. 'So it is the SATs which are worrying you most?'

   Such questions are invaluable for clarifying understanding of a complex situation for both people. They also demonstrate active listening.

6. *Reflective questions* these questions test the interviewer's affective understanding of the respondent's situation, e.g. 'You feel discouraged?'.

   These questions examine the feelings of the interviewee and are essential in order to appreciate the interviewee's perceptions of the situation. They also demonstrate active listening.

7. *Supporting questions* these questions offer help and support to the interviewee, e.g. 'How can I help?'.

   In dealing with a problem, such questions demonstrate a joint problem solving approach to the problem.

8. *Leading questions* these are an invitation to agree and permit only one answer if an argument is to be avoided, e.g. 'In view of the child's ability don't you think that GCSE is out of the question?'

   These should be avoided as far as possible, because they do not encourage a genuine dialogue.

9. *Rhetorical questions* these are questions to which the answer is self-evident and no reply is necessary, e.g. 'A formal appraisal scheme wouldn't suit us would it?'

   Again, these are to be discouraged because they do not help dialogue.

10. *Multiple questions* these combine two or more questions in one. Providing an answer involves unravelling the separate questions, e.g. 'Do you teach hockey in both summer and winter?'

    There is often a temptation to use multiple questions if you are a member of a panel at a selection interview. They can be very confusing to the interviewee and should be avoided wherever possible.

11. *Taboo questions* these are questions not permitted by equal opportunity or other legislation or embarrassing quesitons, e.g. 'Do you stay at home to look after the children when they are ill?'

    There are certain matters about which it is common courtesy not to ask questions at any interview. Matters which impinge upon personal privacy have no place in any kind of formal interview.

Conclusion

When preparing for any interview, a manager should be very clear about the purpose of the interview and the objectives to be achieved. Once these are clear, it is then possible to plan the general structure and strategies to be adopted. Planning and preparation are important for interviews, as they are for any other management activity. At the same time, room must be allowed for the unexpected. It has been stressed on a number of occasions that this is a social activity, involving two people. Although the manager may plan a general strategy for the interview, part of the skill of the successful interviewer is to be flexible enough to respond to an opportunity, and to have enough empathy to know when the chosen strategy is not working. The dialogue needs to be moved forward in the interests of the development of the interviewee and for the benefit of the organisation which he or she represents.

4.3.1 Effective teacher appraisal interviews

Keith Diffey

Introduction

The assumption that anyone can sit down for a chat with a teacher about his or her job, avoid the pitfalls and make it a purposeful and worthwhile event, is mistaken. If there were a simple procedure to apply in order to conduct an effective appraisal interview, the whole activity would be a manipulative operation rather than a complex human skill. Many staff in schools are very experienced in the skills of interviewing – with pupils and parents. However, the wholesale application of generic interviewing techniques is inappropriate:

> The appraisal interview is not like any other interview the manager is likely to have to conduct. It is private, usually, and the parties may be bound in confidence not to reveal what went on. It does not – should not – have the flavour of evaluation, which selection interviews, and dismissal interviews, often have.
>
> Stewart and Stewart (1977)

This chapter is divided into four parts of sequentially narrowing focus. The first deals with some *preconditions* which provide the appropriate context for successful appraisal interviewing. The second part describes the effective behavioural *characteristics* of appraisal interview participants. Thirdly, I will outline the specific process *skills* which participants will need. A final section will address some of the key *issues* in the identification of good practice. Given that the responsibility for conducting the interview lies with appraisers, it will become apparent that much of the advice is directed towards them.

Preconditions

Climate setting

The National Steering Group Report (DES, 1989), concluded that there is a need to take positive steps to establish a favourable climate for appraisal, including:

> Commitment from the LEA;
>
> Wide consultation on the LEA scheme;
>
> Implementing appraisal in an atmosphere of mutual trust and respect; and
>
> Associating appraisal with the implementation of the National Curriculum and the preparation of school development plans.

Part of setting the right climate is the realisation that appraisal takes place within an organisational context. If an effective appraisal interview is more likely to take place in a climate of trust and respect, the appraiser must cultivate this atmosphere throughout the whole year – it cannot be conjured up for one occasion.

> The appraisal interview is not something that is simply plugged in at a certain time. To be effective, the appraisal interview must be viewed as a continuation of professional and personal relationships between the teacher and evaluator.
>
> Haefele (1981)

One fundamental aspect of climate setting is that the concept of appraisee 'ownership' must be established. The importance of participation in decision making in the development of a teacher appraisal scheme is now widely accepted.

Recognition of the dimensions of appraisal interviews

Affective An appraisal encounter is often charged with emotion. Appraisees may be apprehensive and wary, the tension of appraisers may be interpreted as coldness, and a downward emotional spiral may develop. It is an essential precondition that participants are aware of the fact that the appraisal interview involves not only verbal and non-verbal communication of facts and ideas, but of attitudes and feelings as well.

Functional A recognition from participants that they are acting out 'roles' and that the interview requires a performance in line with expectations has an overarching significance.

Relational The nature of the relationships between appraiser and appraisee is of crucial importance. Interaction is most effective when the appraisee feels acknowledged as a person; that his or her behaviours are accepted; and that he or she has been listened to and understood.

Planning and follow-up

There is a great deal of work to be done before the interview takes place. The appraiser should review all records and gather all the facts about past performance and future developments. Classroom observation will be a major aspect of this preparation. Both participants must understand how the appraisal system operates and have undergone training.

Clearly the appraiser must have considerable knowledge about the job done by the appraisee. One frequently expressed complaint from appraisees is that appraisers simply do not know enough about the work they do, perhaps because they have not taken the trouble to find out, or, as Stewart and Stewart (1977) and Randell (1974) both suggest, because they lack the confidence to tackle discussion of a job description which is not their own.

> They appear to think that they are expected to be omniscient and perhaps to know more about their subordinates' jobs than the subordinates themselves. This may be a reason why many managers are not as effective as they should be at appraisal interviewing.
>
> Randell (1974)

Planning also entails taking care to get the environment for the interview right – a private place, office perhaps, without interruptions or telephone calls, and plenty of time to complete the interview. Proformas need to be completed well in advance and the appraisee given adequate notice of the meeting.

One of the most frequently expressed criticisms of appraisal systems is that little is done to follow up issues raised during the interview. Clearly, appraisers must write up any reports carefully, honestly and in consultation with the appraisee. Commitments to action must be honoured by both participants.

Characteristics

Research carried out by the author, (Diffey, 1991), has revealed that effective appraiser characteristics include an ability to make the appraisee feel at ease and promote responses. Appraisers should encourage self-reflection in a non-threatening way and give positive emotional support. Probing and reflective questioning can be used to good effect. They should control the interview with a loose rein. Effective appraisee behaviour emphasises a willingness to self-appraise frankly and openly, reciprocate the warmth shown by the appraiser, and avoid tension.

Other research evidence provides a highly complementary set of characteristics.

Buzzotta and Lefton (1979), describe four interview 'types' based upon two dimensions of interaction: dominance–submission and hostility–warmth. Their 'ideal', (termed 'Q4'), type has the following characteristics:

1. It is candid and aims to produce real insight into how the appraisee works.
2. It is balanced – dealing with both strengths and weaknesses.
3. It aims at appraisee self-awareness.
4. It is a joint activity.
5. It seeks commitment and ownership from the appraisee.
6. It is flexible and aims to tailor discussion to the needs of the individual.
7. It results in a detailed plan for appraisee improvement.

Drawing upon the work of Solem (1960), and others, Burke and Wilcox (1969), describe four characteristics of effective performance review and development interviews:

1. *High levels of appraisee talking* Solem (1960) found that when superiors do less talking, there was greater mutual understanding and a more positive response from both participants to the interview.
2. *Helpful and constructive attitude on the part of the appraiser* Solem (1960), found that when the appraiser used positive motivation, (listening, recognising good performance, taking the attitude of helper), this was associated with more effective interview outcomes.
3. *Focus on solving the problems which hamper current job*

performance of the appraisee, with the assistance of the appraiser.
4. *Mutual setting of specific goals for the appraisee* as opposed to no discussion or reference only to general goals, was found to result in twice as much performance improvement. The National Steering Group Report (DES, 1989), states that the setting of professional targets for future action is an important part of the appraisal interview.

Miles (1971) asserts that effective group behaviour results from the appraiser:

1. *Exercising leadership.*
2. *Paying attention to both getting the job done and maintaining emotional stability* This is analogous to management styles which distinguish 'task orientation' and 'person orientation'; and also to the functional roles of 'Group Task' and 'Group Building and Maintenance' (Benne and Sheats, 1948).
3. *Using process skills* such as: sensing or noticing; diagnosing or understanding; and taking action or doing something to help.

The results of a study by Nemeroff and Wexley (1979), demonstrate the necessity for appraisers to adopt a constructive attitude, the behavioural components of which are identified as: being friendly, ending the interview on a positive note, and praising. They found that supportive appraiser behaviour is related to the appraisee's satisfaction with the interview and interviewer, and his or her motivation to improve.

The Suffolk LEA (1987) study identifies the good appraiser as someone who:

1. Asks more questions, especially when looking for proposals and solutions that come from the appraisee.
2. Summarises more often.
3. Tests understanding of what has been said and agreed more often.
4. Is less likely to give information about his or her views and opinions, yet more likely to give information about his inner feelings.

Skills

A meeting of appraisers in one school identified three types of interviewee:

1. *Keen* – often new staff;
2. *Accepting* – often middle ranking staff and/or established in post; and
3. *Going through the motions* – some well established, stable staff.

The last category presents some difficulty for the appraisal interviewer.

Appraisees who are: over talkative, impatient, dogmatic, destructive, indifferent unco-operative or inattentive, for example, require appraisers with a very high level of interpersonal skills, and many other qualities besides. Dealing with difficult topics such as criticism of other members of staff needs tact, impartiality, and objectivity.

Under more 'typical' conditions the appraisal interviewer is dealing with an individual who may feel vulnerable, and in consequence hides or exaggerates his or her performance rather than discuss it openly and honestly. As already mentioned, this emphasises the need for the appraiser to create and maintain a relationship of confidence. The appraiser's reputation for discretion and fair mindedness precedes him or her. Even when these preconditions are satisfied they will not make the person a competent interviewer – he or she needs skills as well as integrity.

Twenty years ago the theoretical content of a course on interviewing typically consisted of a list of some 10 or 15 tips on interviewing. This 'maxims' approach would be based upon generalised personal experience of what makes an interview go well. As references to other sources have shown, knowledge is accumulating on the relationship between interviewer behaviour and interviewee response. The purpose of this section is to itemise the key process skills which must be employed to ensure the success of an appraisal interview.

1. **Establishing rapport**

Obviously at the beginning of the interview it is necessary to put the appraisee at ease and establish rapport. Whilst informality is important, one should treat the appraisal interview as a professional occasion. As far as the appraisee is concerned, lack of appreciation of the importance of showing that one has a sense of occasion can devalue the event. An air of enforced joviality and false good humour on the appraiser's part may increase rather than decrease apprehension.

2. **Exercising control**

Research evidence (Diffey, 1991) has shown that it is the appraiser who takes responsibility for managing the interview. This is widely regarded as perfectly appropriate:

> It is the interviewer's responsibility to give shape to the interview.
>
> Beveridge (1975)

However, there is a delicate balance between controlling and dominating, and the appraiser must adapt his or her behaviour to suit the situation. The chief variations in control are to be found in:

1. Relative amount of talking done by each participant.
2. Tempo of the interview.
3. Degree of freedom allowed to the appraisee.
4. Degree to which digressions are allowed.
5. Exercising 'focus' skill.

The focus skill helps the appraiser decide which of five potential areas of organisational problems merit attention, and thereby achieve the best results. The five focus areas are: *'person'*, *'problem'*, *'other'*, *'context'*, and *'self'*. A situation where an appraisee comes to complain about the appraisal process provides an example:

1. *Person* focus concentrates upon the appraisee. The person's first name, or the pronoun, 'you', can help the appraiser.

   'John, you sound frustrated about this appraisal business.'

2. *Problem* focus deals with the issue at hand while trying to get more information about it.

   'John, could you tell me exactly what the problem with the appraisal procedure is?'

3. *Other* focus highlights another person.

   'How do your colleagues feel about the system?'

4. With a *context* focus we are concerned with how the problem relates to the entire organisational system.

   'John, do you realise that all teachers are using the same procedures?'

5. In a *self* focus, attention is concentrated upon the appraiser.

   'John, I'd like to know if I said, or did anything in this appraisal process to upset you so much?'

3. **Attending skills**

The most important aspect is to listen *actively*, not passively, using techniques which include:

1. Appropriate 'body language' – for example leaning forward slightly with the upper half of the body.
2. Maintaining eye contact.
3. Speaking with a warm, natural voice.
4. Using encouragers – head nods, 'yes's' and 'Uh-huh's'.
5. Keeping to the topic under discussion.

Attending properly indicates to the other that you are attempting to grasp his or her facts and feelings. Listening attentively enables the participant to notice and explore the significant remark and the significant omission. Even silence needs interpreting. The skilled listener distinguishes between those that are 'awkward' – someone can not decide what to ask next; and 'pregnant' – the appraisee puzzles over how to answer an unexpected question. The former type of silence needs breaking, the latter should not be interrupted.

4. Allowing for moods, values, 'halo effect', and attribution

The emotional state or mood of a participant may have a profound effect on his or her ability to perceive the other's responses. Haefele (1981), draws attention to the need to be aware of one's biases:

> To evaluate teachers and to conduct effective appraisal interviews, it is vitally important that evaluators understand how their values affect their judgements of teaching competence.

Being impressed with or disliking one particular attribute of a person may influence our judgement about other attributes or facts about him or her – thus the 'halo effect'. Furthermore, as in many other contexts, in an appraisal interview we make judgements on the basis of the information available, which is itself derived from our own knowledge and beliefs about human nature. As Cave (1985), observes:

> The value of interviewing in arriving at judgements about people is controversial, mainly because, in our present state of knowledge anyone can inject his prejudice or his views into the debate without being proved wrong.

Some research work by Fletcher (1984), has focused on the appraiser's 'causal attributions' – the way in which he or she tends to explain good or bad performance (*see* section 5.3.0). In explaining one's own poor performance we make reference to situational and circumstantial factors, ('external' attribution). When explaining other people's behaviour, we have a tendency to see it brought about by the characteristics of the person rather than the situation, ('internal' attribution). Sometimes called the 'fundamental attribution error', this is something for appraisal participants to be aware of.

5. *Questioning*

As the major tool of the interviewer, much of the skills of the appraiser lies in the use of carefully phrased questions. The good interviewer will ask the kind of questions which enable the interviewee to talk freely and openly. The use of 'open' rather than 'closed' questions; and the avoidance of 'multiple' and 'leading' questions, are part of questioning skill (see section 4.3.0 p.232). Appraisers should utilise 'probing', 'reflective', and 'supporting' questions as appropriate.

6. *Feedback*

There is an expectation from appraisees that the appraisal interview is an opportunity to receive feedback about performance. In using feedback skilfully, the appraiser can open up communication channels for appraisee response.

The first component of feedback is that it should involve clear and concrete data, rather than vague, imprecise statements. Secondly, feedback should employ a non-judgemental attitude. Value laden statements especially negative ones, can be infectious, and invite a reciprocal emotional response. Thirdly, although an appraisal interview deals with performance over time, more can be gained by examining more recent problems than by dredging up long past incidents. Choosing the present over the past is a much more powerful tool for change.

Distant past feedback:	'Your departmental budget has been overspent for the past three years!'
Recent past feedback:	'In reviewing the departmental budget allocations last week, I found that yours was overspent as usual.'
Present tense feedback:	'John, we need to talk about your departmental budget. How can I help you become more effective in budget management?'

Finally, feedback should deal with correctable items over which the appraisee has some control. It may be of little good to ask a somewhat shy, but otherwise very effective teacher in the department, 'Why don't you spend more time with the gang, and become more a part of the group?'

7. **Reflection**

There are two aspects of reflection which promote effective appraisal interviewing. The first is the paraphrase – a concise restatement of the essence of what the appraisee has said. The emphasis is more upon the cognitive realm of fact than the affective realm of emotion. Effective paraphrasing clarifies for the appraiser, and indicates to the appraisee that you, 'understand', and it therefore encourages him or her to go on.

The second aspect is concerned with the reflection of 'feeling', and relates to the affective emotions of the appraisee. This skill is particularly germane to the appraisal interview where pride and fear, trust and suspicion, openness and defensiveness, are easily engendered. To recognise and reflect emotions can free communication and establish a close rapport and stronger relationship between participants – that fundamental, yet so elusive, prerequisite for effective human interaction.

Reflective responses can be 'confirming' or 'disconfirming'. Confirming responses acknowledge the other, agree about content, are supportive, and express positive feelings. Conversely, a disconfirming response is one that is irrelevant, tangential, impersonal, incongruent, or simply an inaccurate interpretation of the other's expression of emotion. For example:

Appraisee:	'I'd much rather work on my own'.
Appraiser:	'You feel you don't get along with other people'.
Appraisee:	'I don't feel any such thing!'

Skills of interaction

An awareness of the transactional nature of dyadic communication is fundamental to effective appraisal interviewing. Alteration of one person's behaviour produces changes in the other. Therefore, the best way to become more interactively skilled, and thus improve one's performance as an appraiser or appraisee, is to change one's own behaviour. Interactive skills are the skills used in face-to-face encounters to arrange our behaviour so that it is in step with our objectives. In so far as the other person's judgements about us stem from their observations of our behaviour, it is clear that behaviour matters very much. Amongst several other factors, the behaviour of participants, notably that of the appraiser, is one of the crucial items that helps to determine success in the interview. The following hypothetical encounter in an appraisal interview illustrates the thesis:

Appraiser   'Ben, you've had a difficult year. I must admit that there are several other teachers in the department who, like you, have found it difficult to teach the less able.'

Some empathy for Ben's situation is expressed but the implication of the 'person' and 'other' foci is that the perceived problem is partly Ben's fault: he may react negatively.

Ben   I feel I have been treated unfairly! I have four bottom set classes and I have to pack up and move rooms at least once each day! By the time I reach the classroom, the pupils are running amok. It takes 15 minutes to calm them down. Nobody has offered any assistance – I don't think the problem is all my fault.'

Through misinterpreting previous information, the appraiser has made an 'internal' attribution error. He should be prepared to modify his perception in the light of this new information and use it in a constructive way:

Appraiser   In other words, Ben, you feel that you've been placed in a very difficult teaching situation. I can understand your reaction. You've mentioned a major factor I seem to have overlooked.'

The appraiser has listened, paraphrased, reflected empathically, altered the focus to 'self', and changed his original judgement.

Ben is more likely to view this kind of interview as worthwhile, and feel that the appraiser is concerned about the problem and wishes to help. Ben can now begin to react constructively to the problem because an important objective of the appraisal interview is to determine what can be done to improve teaching performance, the appraiser might offer assistance.

Appraiser   Ben, you have been unintentionally placed in a difficult teaching situation. However, what do you think we can do to help with this problem?

The appraiser not only accepts substantial responsibility for Ben's unsatisfactory performance with the less able classes, but also indicates that a cooperatively developed plan might alleviate this problem. For example, the appraiser agrees to meet two of Ben's classes as they enter the classroom and a more experienced teacher volunteers to cover the other two groups until Ben arrives. Ben is committed to this plan because he had a personal stake in its creation. The key to a satisfactory outcome is the *change* in the behaviour of the appraiser.

There is a vital bond between objectives and behaviour. One of the indications of an interactively skilled person is that they frequently declare their objectives, openly and explicitly. Behaviour needs to be in step with objectives and should be consciously organised and controlled to achieve this. Behaviour shaping is a 'natural' process anyway – by making it a conscious one we harness the behaviour shaping processes more efficiently.

The essence of interacting, when there are objectives to be achieved in face-to-face encounters such as appraisal interviews, is to use your own behaviour to influence that of the other. As was seen in the example above, changes in the behaviour of the appraiser will allow the appraisee freedom to change, thereby opening the way to relationship improvement. Indeed, appraisers *want* to change appraisee behaviour – in the classroom perhaps – by working out a behaviour plan together with them. This is exactly what appraisal interviews are supposed to do.

Appraiser style – some unresolved issues

In any attempt at describing appropriate appraisal interview behaviour, there will be, inevitably, some problems which remain for the participants. Some of these issues are in the nature of dilemmas, for which there is no definitive guidance.

One of the key issues is whether or not there is a place for criticism from the appraiser. The existing research evidence is conflicting.

Meyer et al (1965), found that criticism in an appraisal interview had a negative effect on subsequent goal achievement. In a review of the limitations of traditional methods, Riley (1983), suggests discussing only those areas in which the employee performs well, with no discussion of weaknesses. It is argued that a judgemental approach evokes defensive reactions that may block constructive search for ways of improving. Lusty (1981), found that:

> Negative feedback not only fails to motivate, but can cause him to perform worse. Only those employees who have a high degree of self esteem appear to be stimulated by criticism to improve performance.

On the other hand, Alapander (1980), outlines an approach to handling poor subordinate performance which involves training appraisers to criticise constructively. In a study in the Civil Service, Fletcher (1973), found that not only did discussion of the weaker areas of the individual's performance seem essential to the full effectiveness of the appraisal in giving accurate performance feedback and generating action; but that is also appears to be an acceptable, even desirable, element of the procedure from the appraisee's standpoint. Diffey (1991) found that potentially sensitive topics of performance weakness can be discussed without abandoning a joint problem solving orientation. When criticism was specific, constructive, and sensitively presented, this did not result in any noticeable deterioration in the relationship. In fact greater depth of insight and self-awareness often followed. The absence of any criticism may be worse – a one-sided, sterile and rather bland encounter, perhaps. Thus, when interviews are carefully handled, there ought not to be any tension between adopting a supportive, developmental approach, and the raising of contentious issues.

However, appraisers are faced with a conflict of roles. As line managers they are responsible for the work of their staff, and their contribution and effectiveness in relation to the needs of the *institution*. In certain circumstances – for example when promotion is at stake or when redundancies need to be recommended to the Governing Body – appraisers will be required to make judgements about the performance of their staff. The appraisal process is an invaluable source of data, which, even if desirable, it would be impossible to ignore when difficult decisions have to be made. At the same time, appraisers have a legitimate concern with the professional and personal welfare and development of their staff as *individuals*. Whilst in many situations organisational needs and individual needs may be complementary, it does not necessarily follow that they will always be – particularly as perceived by the appraisee. This difficulty has been recognised elsewhere:

> Inevitably, every leader of and in an organisation must at some time, come face-to-face with the potential dilemma of reconciling their responsibility for the welfare of the staff of that organisation with their responsibility for the continuing development and improvement of its work.
>
> Phillips (1984)

> One of the reasons the goal of employee development has not been achieved under many appraisal systems in the past is that the skills required for maximum attainment of these objectives are in conflict with the ongoing system of management practices in those organisations. That is, asking a manager to evaluate a subordinate's performance and recommend positive changes (judging) while simultaneously emphasising the need to be employee centred and supportive (helping) would demand a reconciliation of two incompatible systems of management.
>
> Burke and Wilcox (1969)

Wight (1985), explores the difficulties managers face during an appraisal interview when they try to play – simultaneously – the roles of counsellor, ('what the employee needs'), and judge, ('what the employee requires'). He advocates a procedure which deals with both aspects in different phases of the interview.

Uncertainty about whether teacher appraisal is going to be judgemental ('hard'), or developmental ('soft'), has bedevilled its introduction. The evidence of the six pilot studies, and the recommendations of the National Steering Group, all point very clearly to the conclusion that formative appraisal with a supportive, developmental, counselling interview style is the most effective.

Summary

An appraisal interview is not conducted in a vacuum. This description of good practice has made reference to necessary preconditions. These include an appropriate organisational context; an awareness that the interview has affective, functional, and relational dimensions; and a commitment to the necessary preparatory and follow-up work.

In an effective interview the behaviour of appraisers and appraisees have certain general characteristics. These features can be thought of as the 'outcome' of the application of process skills. For appraisers in particular, these skills include the ability to:

(a) Establish rapport;
(b) Manage the interview;
(c) Attend sensitively;
(d) Use questions appropriately;
(e) Give feedback properly; and
(f) Apply reflective skills.

Most importantly, there must be an awareness of the fact that interaction is essentially transactional, and that behaviour in the interview should be modified to meet objectives.

Interaction process skills and necessary preconditions are inextricably linked. The experience of the appraisee in an appraisal interview is holistic. It is a function of *both* his or her and the interviewer's behaviour, and the institution's policies. The style of the interview reflects the style of the organisation:

> Appraisal is not so much a management technique as a management philosophy.
>
> Beveridge (1975)

To be effective, an appraisal interview has implications for appraiser behaviour and the nature of relationships and communication throughout the organisation. Important though it is, there is more to appraisal training than interactive competence alone:

> Given time, however, most of the skills of appraisal can be taught. These include setting a climate based upon mutual trust, and setting objectives which are clearly defined, agreed to be feasible, with an agreed priority, and a time target.
>
> Performance and measurement criteria must both be understood. The skills involve writing meaningful job descriptions and the skills of listening – reflecting feelings, paraphrasing, leading, acknowledging, using silence.
>
> Trethowan (1985)

In Lewinian terms, behaviour in an appraisal interview is very much a function of 'person' and 'environment'. Person factors include the skills and attitudes of the participants. Environmental forces comprise the organisation context or suprasystem in which the interview takes place.

The essence of good practice in an appraisal interview is when interactively skilled participants are able to combine a developmental interview style with a complementary organisational culture.

4.3 Interviewing

4.3.2 Counselling interview

Bob Cooper

Introduction

A great deal has been written about the job of a manager in all kinds of organizations. All the texts agree that the successful manager is one who can influence and motivate others, and who is able to achieve results through other people. It has become a truism that the most important resource in any enterprise is the people involved, but in practice, both in industry and in schools, the job satisfaction of the staff and what Hertzberg identified as hygiene factors are often ignored. This is particularly true at the present time when so much emphasis is being placed upon the efficient and effective use of finance and other material resources. There is a real danger that the introduction of appraisal interviewing into schools may be seen by some teachers as another example of this emphasis, and not as an opportunity to improve teachers' job satisfaction by helping to develop their effectiveness and expertise.

One way in which many managers in industry and in the public services have responded to this challenge of improving morale and motivation is by making use of counselling skills, both during appraisal interviews and on other less formal occasions (de Board, 1983; Reddy, 1987; Sidney and Phillips, 1990). These skills have been used both because the managers are genuinely interested in the people they are managing, and in the interests of improving the quality of work done within the organisation. There are not only altruistic reasons why managers should be prepared to listen to what members of their staff have to say. There are also highly practical and economic reasons why it makes sense. The quality of work being produced by anyone can be very much affected by purely personal and emotional factors.

This is not to argue that an appraisal interview is the same thing as a counselling interview. The two types of interview have very different purposes, and because of this the 'contract' between the interviewer and the interviewee is different. In a counselling situation the initiative is normally taken by the interviewee or client, who is seeking the help of the counsellor. The process is a personal one, and the counsellor will not normally have a managerial responsibility for the client. The counsellor can be more objective, and will be concerned solely with the welfare of the person who has sought help. The appraisal interview on the other hand will be part of an organisation's management process, and will have been prearranged by the interviewer. This interviewer will have some kind of management responsibility for the person being interviewed and will, as a manager, be greatly concerned with the interests of the organisation which pays his or her salary. The objective of the counsellor is to help the client manage their own life problems more successfully, making use of the client's own resources. The objective of the appraiser is to help the person being appraised to develop their own abilities in the interests of the greater effectiveness of the organisation to which both belong. The two objectives are not incompatible, however, and the appraiser can learn much from the skills and the techniques employed by the counsellor.

The interviewer in an appraisal interview can make use of counselling skills without being a counsellor. There are occasions when some people may need professional counselling with problems of one kind or another. If this is the case, the appraisal interview may be a time when the problem is identified and the possibility of further help suggested, but it should not be used as a full-scale counselling situation. That is not its function, and the training for an appraiser is not the same as the extensive training undertaken by a counsellor. However, the manager in a work situation is well placed to notice individual problems developing, and may be in a good position to use informal counselling skills either to prevent problem situations from escalating, or to refer the person to someone who can provide professional help at an early stage.

Some managers are unwilling to intervene in personal problems, either because they fear that it will undermine their authority, or because they feel that it is not part of their job, or perhaps because they feel that they do not have the time for this kind of thing. However, time spent in helping a colleague to overcome a problem will probably save time in the long run, and will be fully repaid in terms of increased quality of the work done.

Counselling process

There are a number of different theories about counselling which lead to slightly different procedures being adopted, but the one most widely accepted is based upon the work of Carl Rogers. In essence it is not something which is new or unusual, and indeed it is highly likely that many people have already experienced the process in one form or another. What Rogers did was to identify and set out the elements of successful counselling. The process is essentially one of empathic understanding. The counsellor attempts to see and understand the problem from the client's point of view, and to share the client's experience of the world, in order to make the problem more explicit. The process of clarifying the problem often enables the clients themselves to suggest solutions and to see the need for a change in behaviour, and because they have been involved in the process, the clients are more likely to be motivated to carry through the necessary actions to resolve the problem.

The counselling process essentially consists of three major stages:

1. Clarifying the problem.
2. Exploring solutions.
3. Implementing the decisions.

These stages are not, of course, absolute and inviolable, and often merge with one another. It may not always be necessary to go through the whole procedure; sometimes the first stage of clarifying the problem is sufficient in itself to enable the client to undertake the other two stages without further help from the counsellor.

1. ***Clarifying the problem***

This stage of the problem can be broken down further into three aspects:

(a) Recognising the real problem.

(b) Discovering the reasons why it is a problem.

(c) Exploring feelings connected with the problem.

(a) Recognising the real problem When someone approaches a counsellor or is referred to a counsellor, it is because they have a problem of some kind. It may be a personal problem, or connected with the person's job, or more likely it is both at the same time. The first part of the counselling process is to define as precisely as possible the nature

of the problem. In order to do this the counsellor must first establish a rapport with the client. This means that the counsellor must show respect and warmth towards the client, and the individual and the problem must be treated with seriousness and consideration. At this stage the counsellor needs to employ advanced listening skills, in order to convey to the client that their problem and their viewpoint are worthwhile, and to attempt to understand the real nature of the problem. There are occasions when the latter is buried beneath a layer of other surface problems, and it is the function of this phase to attempt to clarify just what it is which is causing distress.

In order to probe the nature of the problem, the counsellor makes use of a range of personal skills. Many managers will already employ these skills to a greater or lesser degree in the course of their work with staff, and they can enhance these skills with special training. Perhaps the three essential personal qualities for the counsellor are

Empathy,

Acceptance, and

Genuineness.

Empathy is essentially the capacity to imaginatively project oneself into a situation in order to understand and appreciate how the other person is thinking and feeling. Only in this way can one pick up the whole of the message which the person is trying to convey. Some people seem to have this ability to a greater extent than others, as a part of their total personality. It is something, however, which can be improved by training.

Acceptance involves accepting both the client and the client's problem as they are, and not becoming impatient. In situations when someone is telling you their problem, there is a great temptation to immediately think of your own troubles and to then concentrate upon them. Acceptance of the client does not mean that you have to agree with the client or their behaviour, but at this stage the counsellor is trying to understand the nature of the problem from the client's point of view. This involves respect for the client and their viewpoint, and the ability to convey to the client that you value them as an individual. To a large extent, this means a suspension of judgement on the part of the counsellor. This can often be difficult for the manager in a counselling situation, but it is nevertheless very important if a full understanding of the nature of the problem is to be achieved.

Genuineness means being true to oneself, sincere and open about everything, and not attempting to cover up or fake feelings and emotions. To a large degree it involves not playing a role for the sake of effect. It is also sometimes difficult for the manager, because it is so easy to hide behind role behaviour. It does not mean that managers have to come out of their managerial role in order to counsel a subordinate – indeed, the manager would not be genuine if he or she did, and would be pretending that the situation was different from reality. However, what should not be role played is a genuine interest in the person and an acceptance of their problem.

The object of this first stage in the counselling process is to discover the reasons why the problem is a problem to that individual. The importance of active listening has already been mentioned, and this ability cannot be too highly stressed. It is perhaps the core skill in this stage of the process, and indeed throughout the whole encounter. Its purpose is to encourage the client to reveal both to the counsellor and to themselves their thoughts and their feelings about the particular worry they have. The client will already have done a great deal of thinking about the problem before they reach this stage, but everyone has a great capacity to hide things from themselves. It is part of the counselling function to make things more articulate. The counsellor attempts to draw this from the client by actively listening to what they are saying. There are occasions when the mere articulation of the problem helps in itself to provide a solution, as has already been mentioned.

The counsellor will make use of a number of devices to draw from the client the whole story. They may reflect back to the person what they have understood them to say or what they understand to be the feelings involved. They may summarise what they have understood so far. They may check with the client and clarify what has been said. They may perhaps echo some of the client's words in order to let the client hear their own words. They may get the client to amplify a part of what has been said, either to increase their own understanding or to encourage the client to go more deeply into a particular aspect.

Listening in this phase is not a passive skill. It involves a real awareness on the part of the counsellor, and an ability to intervene or to ask an appropriate question at an appropriate time.

(b) Discovering the reasons why it is a problem Having clarified the problem as far as possible, the counsellor will attempt to probe further and go deeper into the problem, in order to try, with the client, to understand the reasons why this particular problem is a problem. The counsellor is not at this stage attempting to fit the problem into any particular theoretical framework. The purpose is to try to find the cause of the client's problem from the client's point of view. What seems to be an insurmountable difficulty to one person is the merest trivia to another, to be taken in one's stride.

Again, the counsellor must make use of empathy to try to understand the reasons behind the client's problem, and must encourage the client to extend their own exploration of the problem beyond the point they have reached in their own thinking.

The counsellor will make use of a variety of skills at this point in order to move the process along. The kinds of questions which are asked are important, as is the time at which they are asked. Examples may be sought from the client to clarify and to verify any tentative conclusions which may have been reached in this joint venture.

Throughout this aspect of the process, the counsellor will attempt to summarise the progress made. The whole process takes time, and it is important that this analysis is not hurried. There is a tendency for the inexperienced counsellor to either jump in too soon at this stage without allowing the client the opportunity to explore in depth, or alternatively to wait too long before checking the joint understanding and so perhaps missing some of the vital detail.

(c) Exploring feelings connected with the problem An important part of the whole process is the feeling and the emotion involved. Emotion tends to cloud clarity of thought, but usually when a person has had an opportunity to express their feelings, then they begin to think more clearly and more rationally.

A major part of the training of a counsellor is an exploration of feelings so that they can become more comfortable both with their own emotional reactions and with those of others. Some managers are reluctant to become involved in any kind of counselling situation simply because it might involve them in an emotional situation. However, managing people will inevitably at times involve a consideration of feelings, and all managers need to come to terms with this.

A common reaction to an emotional situation is the desire to do something about it. This is often the result of an embarrassment in the face of deep feelings, or a wish to withdraw from the situation as soon as possible. This is perhaps particularly the case in our culture, which has almost created a taboo on the expression of emotion. At this stage, the counsellor has to learn that because you are with someone who is experiencing strong emotion, it is not automatically necessary to do something about it. In most cases trying to do something about the client's feelings in the first instance is premature. The feelings will be there as part of the situation: this is inevitable. It is enough at this stage to acknowledge that they exist and to try to understand and clarify that they are an integral part of the total problem. Later in the counselling process it may be necessary for the counsellor to attempt to persuade the client to face their feelings, or to challenge the appropriateness of a particular emotional reaction, but at this stage it is usually unprofitable.

2. *Exploring solutions*

In the second stage of the counselling process the counsellor takes a much more active and challenging role. Challenge, indeed, is central to this aspect of the whole process. If the counsellor is attempting to help a client to overcome a particular problem, it is important that once the problem has been clearly defined they are encouraged to move further in their thinking. The counsellor attempts at this point to add something to the situation, to contribute to or to change the client's picture of the situation, and to bring the client to the point where they are capable of challenging themselves. It has been suggested that self-challenge is the only worthwhile challenge, and that it is the counsellor's job to use their skill to help the client reach the point where they are able to challenge their own assumptions.

The counsellor will again make use of a range of skills to bring the client to the point where they are ready for this challenge, and are able to take responsibility for his or her own problem. Empathy is still involved, active listening is still essential, but the counsellor becomes something more than a mirror reflecting back to the client their own view of the world. The counsellor will now attempt to bring out into the open some of the aspects of the case which have perhaps only been implicit up to this point. The client might have been vaguely aware of some of the implications, but now is being forced to face the issues squarely. The nature of the counsellor's summaries may change. Instead of simply restating what has been said, the counsellor may begin to combine certain points in order to challenge the client to see things in a slightly different light. The counsellor may wish to highlight certain themes which appear to be running through the whole case, or may wish to point out what appear to be conclusions following on from what the client has said.

It may be necessary at this point to confront the client in some way. Confrontation in counselling does not have quite the same connotations as it has in ordinary speech. It does not mean that there has to be a stand-up row, but it does involve some kind of direct challenge to the client's thinking. This may involve the counsellor taking a risk. A rapport has been carefully built up, perhaps over a period of time. The client has come to trust the counsellor and to recognise that they will be listened to sympathetically and with understanding. However, there may come a time when the counsellor will have decided that this is not enough, and that if progress is to be made the client needs to confront the issue head-on. Usually the challenge can be made carefully and even tentatively, and of course it is better if the counsellor can persuade the client to confront themselves on the issue in hand. However, at some point in this stage of the process, confrontation is necessary in order to make progress.

The purpose of the challenge to the client is to enable them to see that in any situation there are a range of possible options open to them, and that to resolve a particular problem it is necessary to make a decision and to follow it through with some kind of action.

At the end of this stage the counsellor will have explored with the client a number of possible alternative ways of resolving the difficulty, and will have come to the point where there is a tentative agreement about a course of action. Like all other aspects of the counselling process, this should not be rushed. Part of the counsellor's skill is being able to recognise when the client is ready to move on to the next step; and when the client needs more time and more support to move their own thinking forward.

3. **Implementing the decisions**

Throughout the three stages of the counselling process the counsellor needs to be active in different ways. During the first stage the counsellor needs to actively listen to the client, to establish the necessary trust and rapport with the client and to attempt to come to an understanding of the client's real problems. During the second stage the counsellor will be rather more proactive and will be challenging the client to analyse the problem and suggest possible solutions. The third stage is reached when the client has fully accepted and agreed the necessity for a particular course of action to be undertaken by themselves, and a new 'contract' is then drawn up.

The third stage may very well involve both the client and the counsellor in action and activity, depending on what has been decided. In some cases the counsellor may only need to monitor how things are going, to provide encouragement and support, and may at this stage provide help and advice. Up to this point, the counsellor may very well have been reluctant to give advice. The problem about giving advice at too early a stage is that often the advice offered is the obvious solution, and it is the very one that for some reason the client is refusing to admit to themselves. The whole point of the counselling process is to enable the client to work out for themselves their best course of action. If this can be achieved, it is much more likely that the client will be committed to it and will be motivated to see it through to the end. If the counsellor were merely to advise a course of action and something went wrong, the client would feel justified in blaming the counsellor, and would have a perfect excuse for not persevering. The purpose of the counselling process is to enable the client to reach a point where they are themselves able to see a way forward, and are motivated to take the necessary steps to improve the quality of their own lives.

At this stage, the counsellor may also be asked to provide further resources or information to enable the client to fulfil the chosen course of action. In some cases it may be necessary to pass the client on to further specialist helpers for either technical or personal help of a kind which the counsellor is not qualified to give. This, however, will have been decided and agreed by both client and counsellor at the end of stage two of the process. In some cases this stage of the process is a comparatively short one; in other cases it may take some time and the counsellor's active supporting role may continue.

Counselling in schools and colleges

The third stage of the counselling process is the one which is most likely to be of interest to managers, whether in schools or in industry. A manager's job is to be concerned with the performance of those staff for whom they have a responsibility, and if there are problems which are affecting the quality of the work being produced, it is up to the manager to ensure that there is a change in behaviour which will bring about an improvement in overall performance.

In many cases there may be some conflict between the interests of an individual and the interests of an organisation. There may well be occasions when the problems of the individual are partly or wholly caused by membership of a particular organisation. The manager in both industry and in schools needs to ensure that as far as possible the conflicts are minimised, and that staff feel that their own interests and those of the organisation to which they belong are largely one and the same.

Schools and colleges are very much concerned with helping their pupils and students to develop any talents and abilities they might have, and in motivating them to work well. In the course of their work in the classroom, a teacher may well make use of counselling skills to help pupils to develop and to learn. Managers in schools and colleges are themselves teachers, and need recourse to these same skills in the course of their work with their adult colleagues.

4.3.3 Target setting

David Trethowan

Origins of target setting

The whole purpose of staff appraisal is to set targets to improve performance in the present post or in a future one. Appraisal without target setting is like a parliament which debates but never enacts: it is a shotgun without a cartridge. If targets are not formed or are set in place inappropriately or are ineffectively reviewed, then the whole process of appraisal falls into disrepute and fails. Handling the process of target setting and review is an essential skill of appraisal management.

Target setting is not new in the field of human endeavour. From earliest times leaders have clarified their aim, their purpose, their objective. It was built into a management system after World War II based upon the philosophies of Peter Drucker and later, George Odiorne. Revolutionary in its day, the concept is that the destiny of an organisation need not be left entirely to chance, but that an organisation which sets itself and its staff reasonable objectives is more likely to succeed than one which waits for fate to come a-calling. Sometimes seen as a system of cascading objectives down from the top to employees, it operates at its best as a participative process of joint goal setting between the manager and the managed: joint setting of goals; joint identification of responsibilities; joint agreement on the results to be achieved; joint identification of the criteria by which success is to be determined; and joint review of actual achievements. Specifically, therefore, targets must be agreed in advance of the performance and reviewed afterwards: it is the joint processing of both which gives power and direction to the work.

But the management style needed to implement target setting is an advanced one to handle. It requires a participative, sharing, encouraging, supporting style in the setting of objectives. During the period of their achievement, in areas where competence is agreed, the manager's style must allow the worker to operate in his or her own way but must be available for discussion and advice when either party feels there is a need. In practice too many managers fall into the trap associated with each style. They prefer to impose objectives rather than to agree them, they replace coaching with directing or they mistake abdication for delegation.

What target setting has learned from management by objectives is that it is more than a process, it is a management philosophy. Its effective use implies a particular attitude towards people – that people like to have some say in their work planning, want to work in a successful team, want to make a significant contribution to the overall effort and will perform better if they have a means of measuring their own progress. It is because many schools are beginning to believe that this management philosophy is an appropriate one to use to lead professionals, that the practice of target setting is growing at such a pace in British education.

Source of the target

What is the source of the target when target setting is used in schools? Eighteen years of experience in educational target setting has shown me that in over ninety per cent of instances the originator of the target is the person who is to carry it out. It is the teacher understanding well his or her own work and that of the team and offering to achieve a specific task to improve performance or prospects in at least one of them. It is the teacher asking the organisation, 'Can this be my target next year?'

Why would a teacher want to take on a target? Performance improvement is one reason. Teachers who can see a means of raising the standard of what they achieve or of reaching the same standard more efficiently with reduced input will often offer their ideas as a target. Personal development is another reason. Though much of the development of a teacher takes place through unplanned learning, the strongest case is for planned learning. Courses, seminars, conferences, self-directed learning, flexitime study, distance learning, special assignments, additional responsibilities – all are possible personal development targets. Improving the quality of team performance is another reason for target setting – preparing internal assessments for Key Stage 4 to be used by the whole department might well be offered as a target by a team member. In each of these cases, it is likely to be the teacher who, in order to raise performance standards, or to simplify working conditions or to develop new skills and experiences, proposes the target.

In an important minority of cases the target is proposed by the school or by the immediate team in which the teacher works. For example, a school may wish to give new impetus to its policy on the development of Information Technology across the curriculum and may ask appropriately skilled members of staff to take on the target of tutoring their colleagues. Similarly, in a department which wishes to raise awareness of giftedness and its associated pedagogical problems, the leader may ask selected individuals to turn key strategic moves into individual targets.

In short, targets may originate with the individual or with the team. The key feature of targets, however, is that they cannot be forced: they must be agreed. Even in the special case which we examine later, of the teacher who does not perform the basic task satisfactorily, the teacher is left with a choice. Forced targets exhibit a manipulative appraisal interview technique, ruin relationships and almost inevitably fail. When a target is initiated by an organisation the correct phrasing for the leader has to be a variation of 'Will you undertake this task?'

Boundaries within which the target must fall

The likelihood that most targets will be offered by the teacher who will undertake them may give the impression that any target which catches the fancy of a teacher will suffice. Far from it. Prerequisites of target setting are that the school must have a vision of itself in the future and have begun to tune its spirit – its ethos, its organisation, and its people – towards achieving that vision. The school must have a strategic plan against which any target proposed by a teacher, a team, or even the school can be validated: as a touchstone is used to test gold. Targets which do not move the school towards its vision have to be skilfully modified or discarded. Insensitive rejection may not only lose the leader an opportunity to attune the teacher to the school's strategy but can demotivate even the most enthusiastic supporter. 'How can we adapt what you are proposing to further the development of our school?' is the question the leader legitimately presents to the teacher – and together they discuss, persuade, negotiate until the target and the strategic plan are both congruent with the vision.

Comparison of target setting with the basic task

From what has been said about the practice of target setting it is clear that there must be another part of the task of a teacher which is basic, compulsory and fundamental to allowing the school to function satisfactorily. In most schools this task is laid out in a job description. In well organised schools it is identified as 'that level of individual performance which is the lowest the head can accept and still deliver a school which attracts customers' Elsewhere I have often called this level of performance *the basic task of the teacher* (Trethowan 1987). It reflects the whole of the task of a teacher: it touches every key result area. It is a continuous function. It changes only slowly, as society requires the role of education to change.

Distinct from the basic task is a target. A target is a particular aspect of specifically nominated work which is raised to a high priority for achievement within a set period. It does not reflect the whole of a teacher's task: it concentrates upon a few areas of temporarily high priority – a new skill to be acquired; a key contribution to be made to the department; a colleague to coach or support. Targets are set for a predetermined period only: they change frequently as personal, professional, team or organisational priorities change. The limits on target setting are not those agreed between unions and employers as with the basic task: the limits in target setting are those of the individual teacher. Targets become my opportunity to show myself and others how good I am.

Target setting criteria

The criteria for target setting are merely applied common sense. They are:

1. *Clearly define what is to be achieved*   It will help to ask 'How will I know when I've done it?' What will have changed when the task is complete?

2. *Clarify the criteria within which the task is to be carried out*   especially:

    (a) *time*   'By when will it be achieved?'
    (b) *quantity*   'How much or how many are needed?'
    (c) *quality*   'To what known standard?' or 'Whose judgement counts?' 'What level of performance is considered to be 'satisfactory' or 'good'?'
    (d) *cost*   'Within what budget do I work?'

3. *Confirm that leader and teacher both believe the targets to be achievable.*

4. *Show trust and understanding* by for example: stating willingness to revise targets if conditions should change.
5. *Agree how the target will be monitored and fix a review date.*

The likelihood of there being disagreement on target achievement is minimised if due time is spent on jointly answering the question 'How will I know when I've done it?' Sometimes the criteria involve a subjective professional judgement and the parties are well advised to agree beforehand whose judgement counts. Use all possible collectable, related, objective evidence to inform the subjective professional judgement. If the target was, for example, to raise the level of interest of a Year 9 class in a particular subject, related objective criteria might be pupil success in assessments, the number of positive and negative comments received from parents, the percentage of the class choosing the subject in Year 10 etc. Subjective criteria might be the opinion of the teacher or that of the departmental head. If there is disagreement on target achievement, the chief lessons to learn from it are the role of prior clarification of performance criteria and the importance of a continuous appraising relationship (Trethowan 1991b).

How to form effective targets

Select targets which:
1. Meet real needs;
2. Fall into priority areas; and
3. Are practical not idealistic.

Express targets:
1. Clearly and as unambiguously as possible;
2. Singly: compound targets cause confusion; and
3. As results not as processes

Agree targets:
1. To be achievable, not aiming too high nor too low;
2. Which have their own specific criteria for measuring success; and
3. Which relate to the professional development of the teacher.

Make targets:
1. Time bonded;
2. Less than six in number per annum; and
3. With an indicated order of importance for achievement.

Adapt targets:

1. To stretch the target holder personally or professionally;
2. To suit the person; and
3. If circumstances change during the target period.

Implications of target setting

A phrase I learned working with IBM was 'High but achievable targets'. The implication within IBM seemed to be that professionals were expected to agree to a target which stretched them, but the company made sure that the target was never unattainable. Target setting for teachers has a similar aim.

When a teacher's target is agreed with the leader, what are the implications for both parties? On the teacher's part the expectation is that the targets, once agreed, will be achieved. Though not a component of the basic task of the teacher, the target has been agreed between professionals and written into the expectations of the organisation. A target is a professional promise – a promise to produce a departmental mark scheme, to acquire a skill in negotiating, to coach a colleague, to produce a play. Accepting a target also implies a willingness to review its progress or the lack of it: to seek professional advice, criticism and support and not to see this as personal weakness. It also implies an entitlement to the acknowledgement and credit which successful target achievement merits.

On the organisation's part the very fact of agreement implies its approval, concern and interest and its belief in the importance of the target to the teacher and the school. These features concerning the target the leader is expected to convey in his or her day-to-day relationship with the target holder. Next, the organisation is expected to do all that it promised when targets were agreed – funding for that special assignment, space for that additional reference material, time for that learning experience outside work, opportunity to practice that newly acquired skill. Finally, there is an obligation on the organisation to contribute to an informed, professional review in such a way that leaves the teacher motivated to take more targets again in the future.

Target documentation

Targets are not an attempt on the part of the school to screw more work from its staff: in fact, the target work may well have been undertaken whether or not a system of target setting was in place. Target setting aims to improve the conditions in which these high but achievable challenges are performed. By acknowledging them the school is agreeing to resource them, guaranteeing that they do not conflict with the aims of the organisation and promising not only support but credit for their achievement. The chief opportunity for formally acknowledging target success comes when targets are reviewed – and the review can only be fair if both parties have the same perception of what was to be undertaken. The importance of accurate recording is clear. How frustrating for me if I spend months preparing work for the department resource pool only to be told that I have misunderstood the nature of the work required and that my efforts are virtually useless. The key features of the target which needs to be recorded on any documentation (*See* also Trethowan, 1983) are:

1. *Target description* What do I want to accomplish in the forthcoming academic year?
2. *Priority* Completion of which of these targets is:
    (a) Essential;
    (b) Quite important; and
    (c) Desirable.
3. *Criteria* How will I know when I have achieved the target?
4. *Target date* By when must the target be completed?

Experience shows that the target holder is the best person to begin drafting most targets. Expect the teacher to bring to the appraisal interview his or her hopes for their work of the next academic year expressed in the form of draft targets. Refine and develop them together – teacher and appraiser – in the interview. When they are agreed have the targets typed and distributed to those concerned with their achievement. A usual distribution might be the teacher, the team leader and the head teacher[6]. I have found the target sheet of individual teachers an excellent basis for the annual 'leapfrog' or 'grandparent' interview between teacher and head teacher. The ensuing discussion not only gives the teacher opportunity to be shown appreciation but enables the head to be continuously and closely in touch with developments from a new perspective. 'Management by walking about' is well supported by 'managment by talking about'.

Problems with target setting

The chief problems with target setting, together with suggested solutions, are:

1. *Too many targets* Help the teacher reduce the number to six or less. Never allow people to build stress into their lives by setting unachievable tasks. Target setting is meant to reduce teacher stress not increase it.
2. *No targets* Accept it. What the teacher *must* do is perform satisfactorily the basic task of teachers in the school. What the teacher *may* do is to set targets in addition to this. Most teachers will seek these additional challenges every year, but if one of them – possibly newly appointed to a post and wanting no further challenge than making a success of that post or maybe, although well established in the school, foreseeing major personal problems at home – chooses not to offer any targets, my advice is to respect that decision and to support it in a positive manner.
3. *Targets conflict with the organisation* Ask the teacher how the proposed targets can be adapted to fit in with the strategic plan of the school. Help the teacher to make the adaptation. Few people want to waste energy achieving targets which the school does not want or value.

    For those who still wish to pursue targets which conflict with the organisation advise them that these cannot be accepted by the school as targets with all that that acceptance implies in resourcing and support. An illustration would be the production of a workscheme for mixed ability groups in a department which pursued only strict setting.

    Let the teacher pursue them as a hobby at home: if the school does not want the proposed targets it should not accept them.

Unsatisfactory performer – a case for compulsory targets

A special case for target setting is created by the teacher who is unable or unwilling to perform the basic task satisfactorily. For this teacher, who does not control classes, fails to mark work regularly, or who regularly skips departmental meetings a target has to be set which closes the performance gap between what is being achieved and what must be achieved to produce a satisfactory performance in the basic task of teachers at the school. Once again, the target is better proposed by the teacher who will work to achieve it, but if it is not forthcoming then the leader must be willing to tell the teacher what is required and, using the established target setting criteria, set it in the form of target.

If the cause of the poor performance is lack of knowledge or skill, the target will involve coaching and support. If the cause is an unwillingness to perform the target may involve a warning of the consequences of failing to deliver the professional performance for which the school is paying. (*See* Trethowan 1991a for a fuller treatment of this subject.)

Virtues of target setting

Target setting brings its advantages to the teacher, to the school and offers value for money to those who fund our education system.

For teachers, target setting is the means of changing, developing and improving individual performance by agreement with the leader. It requires staff to be aware of the aims and strategic plan of the school, at least in relation to the area in which the teacher works. It encourages the teacher to search for self-monitoring practices. It encourages purposeful activity towards the group objective and provides an opportunity to give credit for good performance. The sense of 'control over task' it gives the teacher invariably acts as strong and positive motivation.

For the school it reinforces the need to be aware of its aims and direction, so that proposed targets can be validated. Targets offered by teachers pinpoint the spots where organisational change appears to be needed and at the same time provide a means of managing that change. It tends to encourage a healthy organisation in which development is encouraged as are supportive relationships. It gives the school an opportunity to show that it respects the judgement of all staff and to identify and tackle problems in an open way. It gives a sense of common purpose to all its teachers.

But target setting is no management luxury. Target setting makes the best use of scarce and expensive resources – the teaching staff. It seeks ways of measuring output. It builds better relationships within teams and between teams and the top management. It encourages identification of training needs and makes the training programme more effective by allowing teachers to influence the programmes provided. Finally, it encourages the most cost effective, powerful form of management training – training 'on the job'.

In short target setting has a powerful and fundamental effect upon all aspects of the culture of an organisation – its ethos, its organisation, its people and, most strongly of all, upon its relationships.

SECTION 5: ISSUES

5.1 Appraising management competences

Bertie Everard

Introduction

Comparable in significance to the 1988 *Education Reform Act* and similar legislation elsewhere, is the political movement to reform vocational education and training in the UK (Figure 5.1.1). Stemming from the *New Training Initiative* (MSC 1981), this has been led by the Training Agency and subsequently the Training, Enterprise and Education Directorate (TEED) of the Department of Employment, assisted by the National Council for Vocational Qualifications (NCVQ) in England and Wales and by the Scottish Vocational Education Council (SCOTVEC) in Scotland. In New Zealand a single such authority ensures consistency between secondary school and post-school qualifications (New Zealand Qualifications Authority 1991).

Competency movement

No longer are British vocational qualifications up to and including professional level to be based on norm-referenced examinations.

THE POLITICAL CONTEXT

Aim

The provision of a competent workforce

Instruments

The National Training Initiative (MSC, 1981)
White Paper, *Working Together—Education and Training* (1986)
White Paper, *Employment in the 1990s* (1988)

Structure

Secretary of State for Employment

Training, Enterprise and Education Directorate

National Training Task Force

Training & Enterprise Councils (local oversight of training)

Occupational Standards Branch → NCVQ (vets awarding bodies approves NCVQ awards)

NCITOs
NSTOs, ITBs (sectoral oversight)

Lead Bodies for each occupational category (e.g. management; training and development; education)

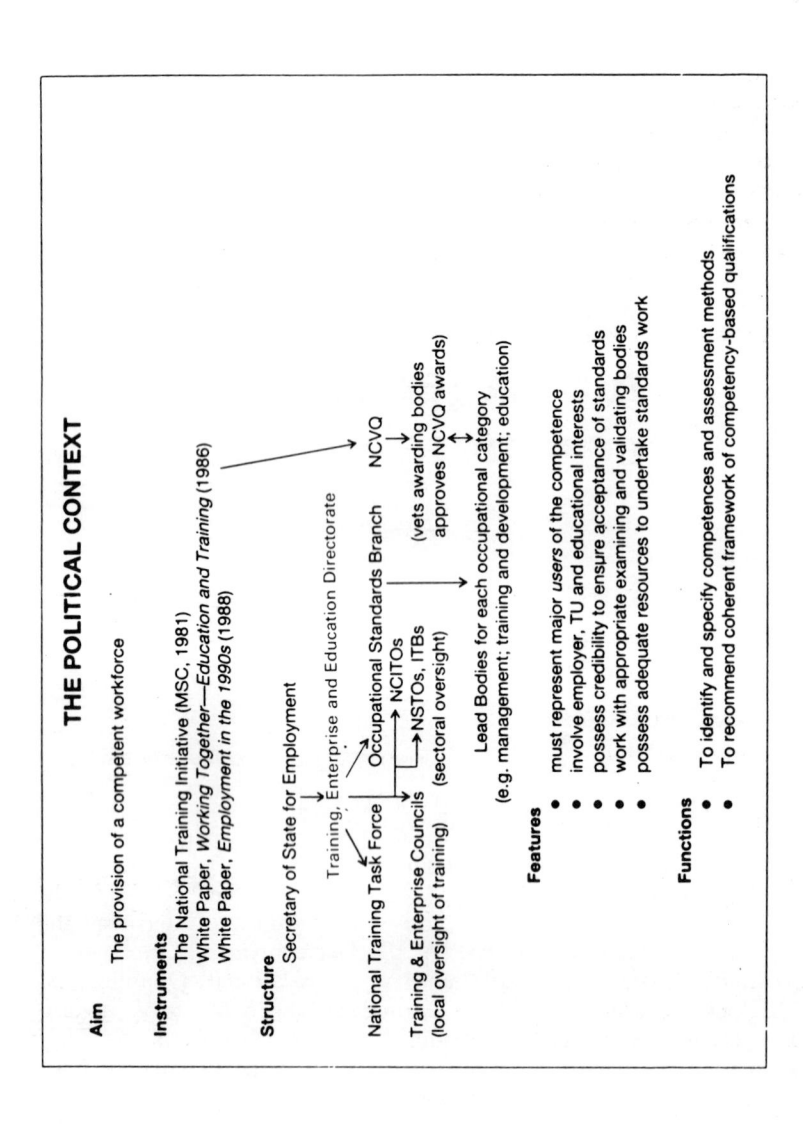

Features
- must represent major *users* of the competence
- involve employer, TU and educational interests
- possess credibility to ensure acceptance of standards
- work with appropriate examining and validating bodies
- possess adequate resources to undertake standards work

Functions
- To identify and specify competences and assessment methods
- To recommend coherent framework of competency-based qualifications

Figure 5.1.1 Political movement to reform training in the UK

Instead, they are to be grounded in occupational standards of competence, which describe what employers and employees think effective performance means in every occupation. The UK government's target is to have 80 per cent of the entire workforce covered by these standards by the end of 1992. By early 1991 TEED had designated 170 'lead bodies' to develop the standards in all sectors of employment and in cross-sectional occupations such as management, customer service, and training and development. With the exception of outdoor education, which is covered by the Sport and Recreation Lead Body, educational occupations are among the very few that by mid 1991 were not included. This is because the Secretary of State for Education and Science, rather than for Employment, is ultimately responsible for the competence of teachers in the public sector of education.

Notwithstanding this lag and gap between education and other occupations, it is highly probable that eventually the competency movement will materially influence teacher appraisal, accreditation and training, both initial and in-service, and already there are competency based programmes of study, training and qualifications on offer for teachers and lecturers (e.g. Blackpool and the Fylde College, 1990)[7]. TEED have funded a consortium, School Management South, to adapt the national standards for managers for use in schools. The College of Preceptors is examining ways of introducing competences into its qualifications, as are the RSA, BTEC and City and Guilds. It seems that the competency approach is a movement whose time has come in the UK and in other parts of the Commonwealth. If so, we can expect teacher performance to be appraised and accredited increasingly against predetermined standards of competence.

Approaches to competency in non-educational organisations

Developments in the USA pre-date those in the UK. There the competency movement has been around for over 20 years in education (Tuxworth 1989) as well as outside. Although not all plain sailing, there are some acknowledged successes, especially outside education. For example, the application of the competency approach to management by the consultancy firm McBer under the sponsorship of the American Management Association (Boyatzis, 1982) and independently by Byham and another firm of consultants, DDI (Byham, 1982), is now well established and has spread to the UK. A number of leading UK firms have embedded the McBer and/or DDI approaches into their human resource management, with such success as to give them substantial competitive advantage in the market place. One such firm is ICI, which has spent several million pounds in doing so over the last ten years (private communication). They are helping a group of head teachers in Cleveland to apply it to the identification of competences for heads. ICI uses competences for five main purposes:

1. As a development tool, for use in training and self development;
2. As a selection tool, both for recruitment and promotion;
3. For the annual performance review process; which is competency-based;
4. As a predictor of potential;
5. To provide a common language for international career pathing.

TEED Approach

The approach taken by TEED and NCVQ in the UK differs significantly from the successful practices imported from the US by several leading commercial organisations (Everard, 1990). The thrust in the UK is heavily geared towards promoting NVQs, and tax incentives are in place to support this. In the USA and in UK firms following their own approach, the thrust is more towards improving performance on the job. Moreover, there is a crucial difference in the accepted meaning of the word competence (or competency). In the UK it is defined as 'the ability to perform work activities to the standards required in employment' (NCVQ, 1988: the Training Agency produced a similar definition), whereas in the USA a competency is 'an underlying characteristic causally linked to superior performance on the job (Boyatzis, 1982). Thus the Americans admit personal characteristics like predispositions, and they focus on those features that distinguish superior from average performance (see Figure 5.1.2).

The result is a shorter and more manageable list, compared with a British list of every threshold condition necessary for average competent performance. A candidate for an NVQ must provide evidence that he or she possesses every element of competence, as demonstrated by specified performance criteria. The pass mark is 100 per cent and no one can meet the standards with distinction, for they are criterion referenced, not norm-referenced. The guidelines on the use of occupational standards of competence are summarised in Figure 5.1.3.

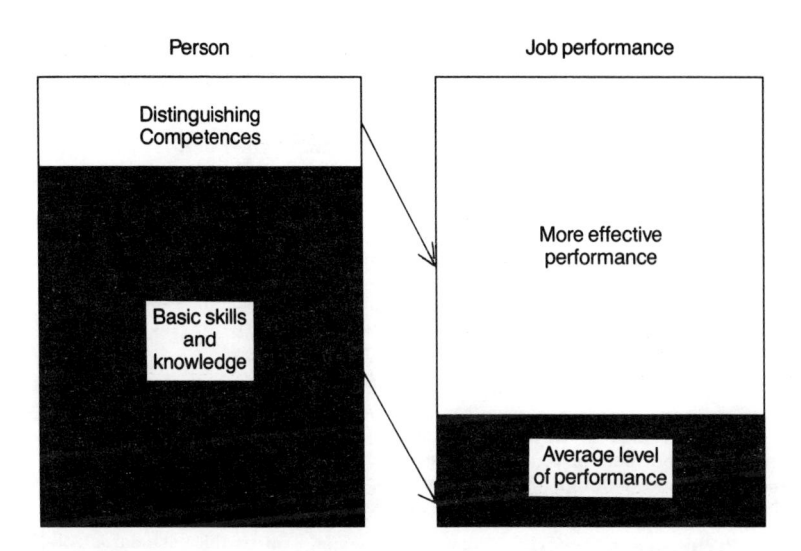

Figure 5.1.2 Competences and superior performance

Development of competences

The political aim of the standards approach is to help provide a competent workforce ready for entry into the single European market at the end of 1992. The application of this to the provision of competent head teachers and other senior managers in school and colleges is depicted in the flowchart in figure 5.1.4. Competence standards can be used to specify the manager's job and (especially if the American definition is used) the type of person required to fill it. Assessment centres can be used to establish whether candidates match the job; one LEA uses them and one polytechnic offers them. Standards can play a useful part in the induction of new appointees, by specifying exactly what they are expected to be able to do. However, since there are insufficient paragons to fill all positions adequately from the word go, and since in any case environmental demands evolve, a development process is needed to bring performance up to the level required. The competence standards can provide useful benchmarks in this process.

As part of the school's appraisal system, performance can be assessed against the agreed standards; and where it meets them, it can be accredited towards a qualification that attests to competence. Where it falls short, coaching, monitoring, counselling, training, self-develop-

1. **Standards** will form the prime focus of training and the basis of vocational qualifications.

2. Standards will be *based* on: the needs of **employment**; the concept of **competence**; and the **skills, knowledge** and **levels of performance** relevant to the work activity. They must be **assessable** and **endorsed** by the relevant employment sector or profession.

3. **Competence** is defined by TA (NCVQ definition is similar) as: *the ability to perform the activities within an occupational area to the level of performance expected in employment.* This embodies the ability to transfer skills and knowledge to new situations, and includes *personal effectiveness.* Competences should define **achievement** in terms of **outputs.**

4. Competence is made up of a number (20–100) of **elements** (cf. 'learning outcomes'), or descriptions of what can be **done**, clearly **relevant** to work, i.e. an **action, behaviour** or **outcome** that can be **demonstrated, observed** and validly, reliably and objectively **assessed,** or the demonstrable possession of underpinning **knowledge** or **understanding.** All elements specified **must** be directly assessed (i.e. no sampling or pass marks).

5. **Performance criteria** define the essential, observable standards of performance required for the successful achievement of an element of competence; all elements must have such criteria. Performance in the **workplace** should, where feasible, be the basis of assessment.

6. **Units** of competence comprise one or more (4–5) elements representing a discreet aspect of, or primary subdivision of, competence, which may be certificated independently as a **credit** towards an **award.** They should be concerned with the **application** of knowledge, skills and understanding, and be broad in concept. Units are **not assessed**—only elements.

7. **A (NV) qualification** is a statement of competence, in the form of the **title,** (5–20) **units, elements** and **performance criteria.**

8. **An award** is given to an individual by an **approved** (against 7 criteria) **awarding body** for the attainment of a qualification.

9. **Accreditation** of a qualification attests to its recognition (against 8 criteria) by the NCVQ as based on a statement of competence agreed by an industry or professional body.

10. **The NVQ framework** is intended to **rationalise** provision, facilitate career **progression** through (1–5) **levels** and cover **all significant occupations** and work activities.

Figure 5.1.3 Guidelines for occupational standards of competence

ment and other measures can be implemented to bring the person's competence up to the desired level. In other words, gap theory is being systematically used as a vector for continual improvement.

An illustration from outdoor education

Pending the establishment of a lead body for education, and to illustrate what occupational standards of competence in education will look like once they are written and nationally adopted, it is necessary to take an example from outdoor education. The key purpose of an occupation with a title such as OE teacher has been defined by the Sport and Recreation Lead Body as:

> To support individual development through safe management of outdoor experiences which enable self-discovery, personal enrichment and awareness of the outdoor environment.

By detailed analysis of many such jobs, seven key functions have been found necessary to fulfil this purpose, of which one is to 'Deliver the experience'. Under this heading there are eight units (or clusters) of competence, one of which, C2, is described in Figure 5.1.5, and is made up of two elements of which the first is defined also in the figure. This

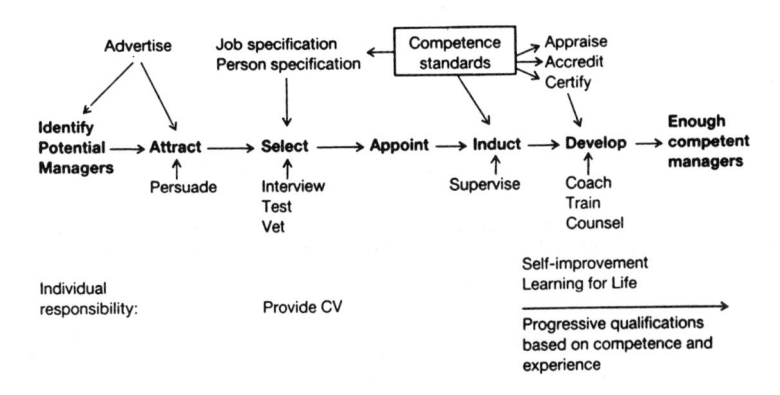

Figure 5.1.4 Competence and the development of staff

This is the element of competence. Elements described the functions or activities a candidate will have to carry out to achieve the unit.

This is the unit of competence to which this element belongs. Units are the smallest parts of a qualification which will receive separate accreditation.

Occupational Standards for Outdoor education, Training and Recreation

Unit C2. Encourage Personal and Social Development

The candidate should be able to:

Element C2.1 Encourage Group Formation and Social Development

Performance Criteria

The candidate should consistently ensure that:

C2.1.1 group cohesion is developed through the use of tasks, projects and activities which demand communication and co-operation for a satisfactory outcome;

C2.1.2 Opportunities for social interaction and development are provided where this is consistent with the aims of the session;

C2.1.3 participants are made aware of the effect of their actions on the other members of the group and are encouraged to modify their behaviour where this has an adverse effect on individuals or the community as a whole;

C2.1.4 where necessary, attention is focussed on interpersonal skills and communication and the contribution these factors can make to the successful completion of tasks and the learning process;

C2.1.5 the successful completion of group tasks is not achieved at the expense of the needs of the individual;

C2.1.6 encouragement given is related to the aims of the session and the needs and progress of the group.

Range Indicators

a) *Encouragement through:* tasks; projects; activities; example; demonstration; explanation.

b) *Groups:* motivated and unmotivated groups; special needs; male female; children; young people; adults; participants from UK European and ethnic or cultural minority groups; participants with and without social and domestic disadvantage.

c) *Group size:* large and small.

Outdoor Education, Recreation and Training Occupational Standards, Final draft: Phase 1, April 30. Prepared on behalf of the Sport and Recreation ILB by MainFrame Research and Consultancy Service. Crown Copyright 1991.
Page 96

These are performance criteria They indicate the standard which the candidate should consistently demonstrate in order to achieve the element of competence.

These are range indicators. They describe the range of circumstances within which a candidate should carry out the element of competence.

Figure 5.1.5   Competence element

illustration is taken from the 300 page long draft manual of standards in outdoor education (Sport and Recreation Lead Body, 1991). It shows how this element is described and identifies the six performance criteria which the job holder must be able to demonstrate consistently in order to be judged competent, within a defined range of circumstances. The manual also specifies for each element the sources and forms of assessment evidence, and the underpinning knowledge and understanding required to perform the job competently.

A head of department using this manual to appraise a teacher would look for evidence that the relevant performance criteria were being met, and would no doubt ask the teacher to assess himself or herself against the criteria. By discussing particular incidents and adopting a coaching mode, the appraiser could guide the teacher in the development of the competence in question.

It would, of course, be impracticable in an appraisal interview of normal duration to discuss performance against all the 100-odd elements included in this standards manual, so the appraiser would doubtless develop some means of ranking them in order of importance at a particular time and situation. The appraisee might well have views on which elements it would be most fruitful to discuss.

Competences and staff appraisal

The formal use of competences in staff appraisal is not yet a well-established practice in management, least of all in the education sector where there is no tradition of systematic appraisal and no agreed occupational standards of competence (even in OE it is a new approach).

There are, therefore, no published guidelines grounded in the collated experience of many schools. Appraisers who have been through assessment centres or who have been trained as assessors or verifiers by one of the examining and validating bodies such as RSA, are likely to be better equipped to apply the competence approach to appraisal than those who tackle the problem without prior training. Especially in the latter case it would be prudent to engage an appropriately qualified consultant or adviser before introducing a competency based appraisal scheme into a school.

Further reading

There are no books on the application of the competency approach to appraisal in education.

Competency Based Education and Training is a useful introduction edited by John W. Burke (1989).

Developing Managerial Competences G. Boak (1991) describes assessment well; it is largely based on the experience of the Northern Regional Management Centre.

The Assessment of Management Competences CNAA/BTEC Project Report (1990) contains a useful literature review.

Management in Education (1989, 1990, 1991). Bertie Everard is contributing a series of articles on competence in education management to the BEMAS magazine.

5.2 Handling poor performers

Brian Fidler

Introduction

This section has been written in general terms because poor performance can come from any of the employees of the school – teachers, clerical, technical, caretaking or cleaning staff. It can be expected that all schools will have procedures for providing help to any poor performers. Whilst these may be codified in professional support procedures for teachers, similar principles should be applied to other employees, thus, the suggestions contained in this section should be of some help in dealing with any poor performer. Where there are no formal appraisal procedures for staff, recognising and dealing with poor performance will require specific initiation procedures although they should arise as part of the process of managing staff.

The regulations (SI 1511, 1991) specifically see one of the aims of appraisal as being to:

> help school teachers having difficulties with their performance through appropriate guidance, counselling and training
>
> (para 4.(3))

Although appraisal procedures 'shall not form part of any disciplinary or dismissal procedures', information from appraisal statements may be taken into account by head teachers and LEA officers in making decisions about discipline or the dismissal of teachers.

The Circular (DES, 1991) warns about ensuring that governors taking part in any appeals procedure in connection with discipline or dismissal must not have been involved in any previous action in connection with that employee. Thus a chair of governors who had done more than see an appraisal statement in advance of the appeal should not take part. Any appeals procedure should be quite independent of previous stages in disciplinary procedures.

Appraisal and poor performance

The managerial process of appraisal has both evaluative and developmental components. The most basic and implicit evaluative component in the process is the overall judgement of the work performance of the appraisee as competent/not competent ([figure 5.2.1). This is an overall judgement on competence not one of individual aspects of performance. The basic question is 'Is this person performing the job to a generally acceptable standard over most of the important areas within the job?'. For a teacher this would involve a consideration of their teaching with most of their groups. Inevitably there will be points of improvement, but this first question is concerned with the standard of teaching with most of the groups taught and its general adequacy.

For the vast majority of personnel in most schools and colleges most staff will be judged competent and the appraisal process moves into its developmental aspect (figure 5.2.2).

However, the case of the 'not competent' is more complicated. Such people require development but it is of a more intensive and remedial kind (figure 5.2.3). Further, this activity has to be time bounded to

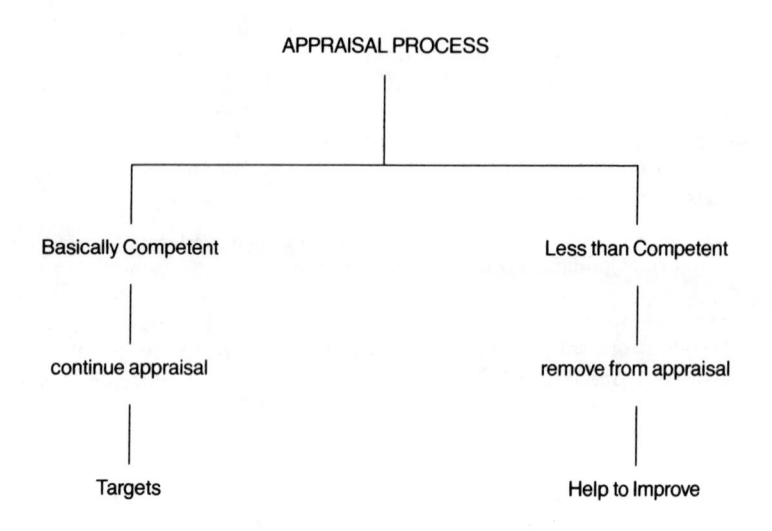

```
                    APPRAISAL PROCESS
                           |
           ┌───────────────┴───────────────┐
           |                               |
    Basically Competent              Less than Competent
           |                               |
           |                               |
    continue appraisal             remove from appraisal
           |                               |
           |                               |
        Targets                      Help to Improve
```

Figure 5.2.1 Basic competence decision

ensure that the planned development is sufficiently rapid. This activity is the equivalent of the 'professional support procedures' as adopted by most LEAs.

Where schools and colleges are confident that support procedures have been invoked for any poor performers, then the appraisal process can be wholly concerned with the development of the competent. Although there still may be cases come to light of temporary severe poor performance because of some individual or contextual difficulty.

Poor performers and poor performance

The term 'poor performers' is used here for the group of less than competent employees. Others are basically competent but individual aspects of their work performance need improvement. Such individual aspects of poor performance are probably best tackled in a joint problem solving mode and this section should be a useful source of ideas for investigating the causes, and ways of improving, such aspects, e.g. dealing with paperwork, time management, improving techniques with particular groups etc.

```
                    BASICALLY COMPETENT
                            |
              ┌─────────────┴─────────────┐
              ▼                           ▼
       Good Performers              Patchy Performers
              |                         /      \
              ▼                        ▼        ▼
    Development Targets &           Some      Some Targets to
    Training for New Skills      Development       Raise
                                   Targets       Competence
                                        ▼        ▼
                                         Training
```

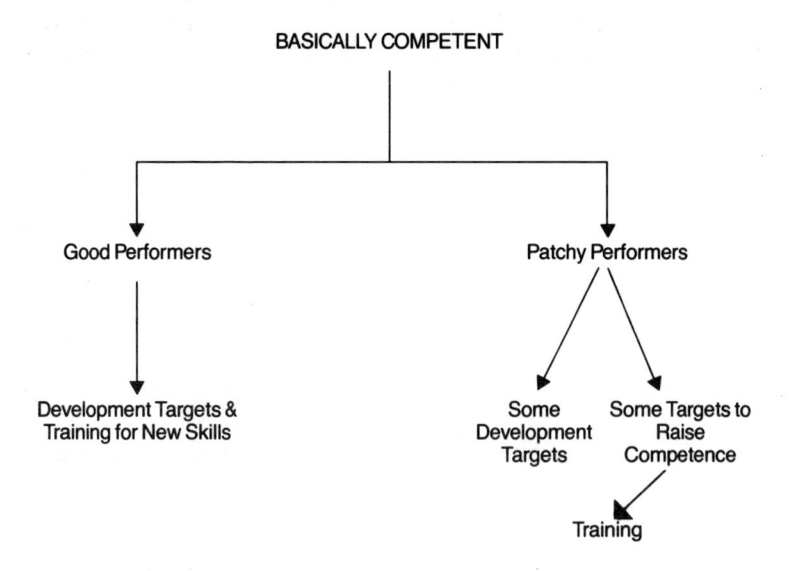

Figure 5.2.2   Development of the competent

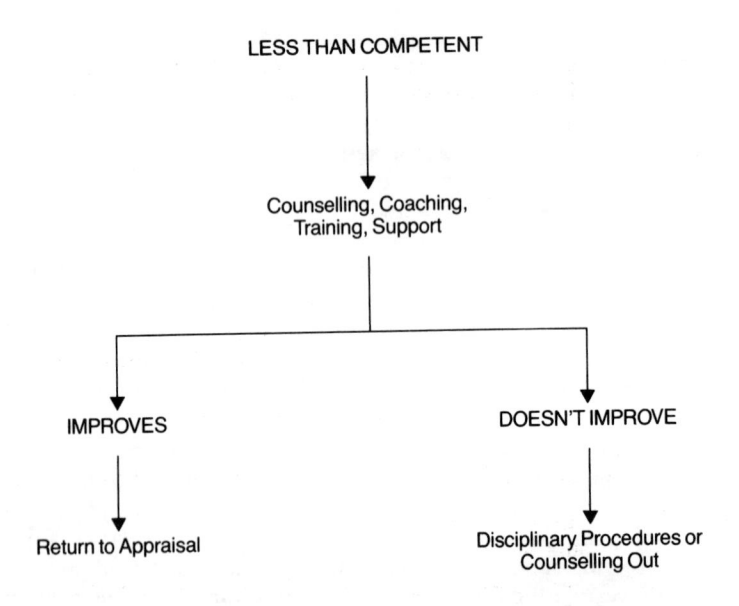

```
                    LESS THAN COMPETENT
                            |
                            ▼
                   Counselling, Coaching,
                    Training, Support
                    _____|_____
                   |                 |
                   ▼                 ▼
                IMPROVES        DOESN'T IMPROVE
                   |                 |
                   ▼                 ▼
            Return to Appraisal   Disciplinary Procedures or
                                     Counselling Out
```

Figure 5.2.3 Support procedures for poor performers

Need for action

The first formal round of staff appraisals will prove to be a fateful time for the small number of teachers who are not basically competent and have not previously received support. They will have major shortcomings which have been known about informally for some time but for a variety of reasons no effective action has been taken.

There are three reasons why such performers present a greater problem than in the past:

1. Delegated budgets mean that the school in which they teach is wasting resources on an ineffective teacher which could be deployed in other ways;
2. Changes brought about by ERA are likely to have exacerbated the problems of poorly performing teachers by increasing the demands upon them; and
3. The first round of staff appraisal provides a watershed for action.

The choices are either that they receive a satisfactory staff appraisal perhaps with some targets to improve or that their weaknesses are fully recognised and effective action is taken. This is a watershed because if poor performers are described as satisfactory then it becomes much more difficult in the future to take action if the problems are no worse or only marginally worse.

> The longer an employee remains in post, the more difficult it becomes to argue that he is incompetent. It is vital, therefore, that indicators of incapability are investigated immediately.
>
> (Drummond, 1990: p. 85)

Inevitably the introduction of staff appraisal will be a sensitive time when many conscientious and competent teachers will be anxious about the outcomes of such a process. There will be a great temptation to smooth the difficulties and conspire to overlook the poor performers in the name of good staff relations. However, in the longer term this will do more harm than good.

Among the principal reasons why action is needed are the following:

1. Further groups of children will be denied their fair share of educational opportunities;
2. Staff generally expect that something will be done about those who are failing to do a proper job;
3. Parents and the general public will lose confidence in the basis of the appraisal process if it does not adequately tackle those who are known not to be doing an adequate job.

If it is accepted that something must be done, then the real issues are related to how to tackle the problems fairly and considerately to all concerned.

It must be an act of faith that those who are not doing a good job cannot really enjoy their work and may only persist in teaching because they are trapped. There is life outside teaching and it is possible to be very successful outside schools and colleges.

If this sounds rather final and pessimistic this is only because it should be faced at the outset that for a small fraction out of the small number of teachers who are poor performers it may be in everyone's long term best interest for them to leave teaching. It is a sign of good management if this can be accomplished firmly but with the minimum of pain and anguish.

Whilst this may be the ultimate destination of the very few, this should only happen after genuine and positive efforts have been made to investigate and solve the problems of poor performance. Not only is this required of ethical managers but it is also backed up by employment legislation.

Conscientious managers will wish to ensure that they are getting a true picture of the performance of their staff, that they fully consider the reasons for any poor performance, and that they engage with the poor performer in a positive and firm but supportive way in tackling the poor performance. This section aims to provide help in each of these actions.

Legal aspects

To satisfy an industrial tribunal following dismissal the employer must prove that (Drummond, 1990):

1. Dismissal was based upon a fair and thorough investigation;
2. Correct procedures were observed and proceedings were conducted in accordance with natural justice;
3. Decision was a reasonable one given all the circumstances.

The three rules of natural justice are:

1. The employee must know the full case against him or her
2. The employee or his or her representative must be given an opportunity to explain
3. Those conducting the hearing must be impartial. The person hearing the case must be unbiased. Bias is defined as holding an adverse view or prejudging the issue. Impartiality must also be seen to be done.

Dismissal for poor performance may either be because:

1. The employee is incapable of performing his or her duties; or
2. Although the employee possesses the requisite skills and abilities, he or she fails to exercise them.

Incapability means that training, exhortation or encouragement would not enable the employee to perform the job. The incapability could be either because of incompetence or ill health.

Any poor performance should receive a warning, and training and support. Only if this fails should dismissal be considered. The employee must understand what is required and the standard of performance. Any deficiencies should be identified, the reasons established and remedial actions agreed. Such action plans should have a timescale and a review period. This should all be confirmed in writing to the employee.

At a review meeting either performance is satisfactory which should be confirmed in writing or if still not satisfactory then either the review period should be extended if there is good reason (e.g. partial progress) or proceed to disciplinary or other action.

If incapability is due to ill health, dismissal is admissible where there is no prospect of an employee's health recovering sufficiently within a reasonable time for him to continue in the job. Dismissal in these circumstances is not a disciplinary matter and should be approached sympathetically in consultation with the employee.

Where incapability arises because of a change in technology or working methods and the employee, through no fault of his or her own, is unable to learn new skills or adapt, this can be treated as redundancy from the previous position or incapability from the new. Training and help to adapt must be provided. Some scheme of voluntary severance could be offered.

Whilst the law deals with poor performance by the employee, as Drummond points out, 'Many problems attributed to employee performance actually reflect poor management' (p. 62). Much of this section examines such other factors which contribute to poor performance.

Stages of process

Whilst the legal aspects of dealing with poor performers are given above, the remainder of the sections deal with more informal management processes to deal with poor performance, however, some of these may comprise part of the above legal procedures.

Whilst some evidence of poor performance will come to light during the appraisal process, the efforts which should be made with poor performers go far beyond those of appraisal alone. The additional processes are:

- Diagnosis;
- Counselling;
- Help to improve; and
- Voluntary departure or dismissal if this fails.

Throughout the accent should be on **evidence** and not on opinion or, even worse, prejudice. As in appraisal, if the process of gathering evidence and agreeing the evidence can be separated from the drawing of inferences from the evidence then this provides a sound foundation for all future efforts.

Few managers can relish the prospect of tackling poor performers and those who do are the ones for whom the checks and balances of employment legislation were intended. The law provides protection against arbitrary treatment and unfair dismissal.

The vast majority of school managers will be apprehensive of having to tackle such problems and wish to ensure that they are being scrupulously fair and reasonable to all concerned including those who are suffering as a result of poor performance. The advice and guidance provided here should provide reassurance both about correct procedures but more importantly try to provide the flavour of a firm determination to tackle the problem whilst trying to be positive and helpful to all the people involved. The process is all the more painful when the condition has become habituated and this is all the more reason to tackle it early.

All problems are individual and it is important to beware of stereotyping. Moreover it is important to be aware that there are many causes of poor performance only some of which the individual employee is able to overcome.

Diagnosis

This involves studying the problem behaviour and beginning to analyse its possible causes. The causes may lie with the:

1. Employee;
2. Job and its context; or
3. Way in which the employee has been managed.

There is no easy answer to 'how poor the performance should be to warrant this treatment'. This is a matter of judgement. Questions to ask oneself suggested by Stewart and Stewart (1982) are

1. Exactly what behaviour is it that I am objecting to?
2. How does this behaviour adversely affect our work?
3. Would any other manager be likely to see the same poor performance as I see and interpret it in the same way?
4. Am I over generalising on too little evidence?
5. Could I defend my judgement at an industrial tribunal?

Attribution theory

There are dangers of misperception of both behaviour and its causes. An article by Mitchell and Green (1983) looks at attribution theory to gain insights into how poor performers are diagnosed and the perceived causes. A systematic attribution process consists of:

(i) Observe action;
(ii) Infer intentionality;
(iii) Make attributions about internal or external causes of the action; and
(iv) Respond in light of the attribution.

The causes may lie within the individual (internal) or they may lie in the job or its context and surroundings (external). Any solutions proposed will differ depending upon whether an internal or external attribution is made. An internal attribution should lead to changes in the individual whilst an external should lead to attempts to change the job or environment.

Three kinds of information are used to assist in diagnosing whether the causes are internal or external:

Distinctiveness	comparison of differential poor performance in this task compared to others, is more likely to lead to external attribution;
Consistency	how does performance change with time? – more likely to be internal if it is a similar pattern; and
Consensus	is performance similar to other people doing the same job? If so, an external attribution is likely.

In addition to internal/external a further distinction is between stable and unstable causes, i.e. whether there is a clear pattern over time. For an internal attribution, if the pattern is stable then the cause is likely to be seen as lack of ability whilst an unstable pattern is likely to point to lack of effort. For an external attribution, a difficult task would cause a stable pattern whilst bad luck might be seen as the cause of an unstable pattern.

There are two systematic biases to beware of when making attributions:

Actor/observer bias	this assumes that other people have internal causes of poor performance whilst external factors affect oneself;
Defensive attributions	this assumes that one's successes are due to personal internal factors and failures are due to external factors and *vice versa* for other people.

Some social factors also appear to affect attribution for example:

Leader – subordinate relationship if the poor performer is similar to the leader or the leader is familiar with the job then the cause is more likely to be attributed externally whilst if failure reflects on the leader then an internal cause is more likely to be attributed.

There is some evidence that the separation of behaviour and its effects is difficult. If the same behaviour has disastrous consequences then more extreme actions are likely to be taken than if the consequences were small, e.g. carelessness with matches leading to a smouldering waste bin compared to the school burning down.

Internal causes are generally diagnosed and seen as easier to change than external ones. Mitchell and Green (1983; p. 513) conclude:

Leaders are likely to attribute the cause of subordinate failure to internal motivational causes.

They suggest that this is frequently an incorrect attribution and suggest that understanding the attribution process can lead to more correct diagnoses.

Latham et al (1987) point out some other biases to beware of when observing and rating performance:

Contrast effect is concerned with the tendency to rate performance in comparison with that of others rather than on absolute performance in the specifics of the elements of the job. This leads to inaccurate assessment when the others are either very good or very bad.

Halo effect leads to over generalisation about performance based upon one aspect which is either very well or badly done. Each individual part of the job performance needs to be considered individually and independently.

Similar-to-me error involves the tendency to inflate the assessment of performance of those who are similar to oneself in outlook and attitudes and underrate those who are very dissimilar.

Diagnosis involves gathering evidence. This may be hard data but it may also be soft data – impressions, hunches and surmises. Both kinds are valuable but the softer kind should always be regarded as provisional until adequately confirmed. The evidence of behaviour should be accumulated over as long a period as possible so that present performance can be seen in context. This may show a sudden drop or a gradual fall or a more systematic pattern in some parts of the job being poorly done in comparison to others. It should also indicate some areas of good performance which may be the starting points for positive future developments.

Causes of problems

There is an initial tendency to assume that any cause of poor performance must reflect on the individual but the insights into attribution above have opened up the possibility that the causes may be internal to the individual or external to the individual.

There is a further useful subdivision of internal causes – those that affect poor performance in a particular job and those which are related to behavioural characteristics which are likely to affect job performance in most jobs (and possibly social life generally) and may mean that whilst technical performance in a job is satisfactory, the ability to get on with other people is impaired. This latter group will be called 'difficult people' (Bramson, 1981). This group will be considered last as they are only partially related to poor performance. They will, however, be difficult appraisees.

It is worthwhile to further divide external causes into those that are situational – the job and its context – and those that are process related – how individuals are managed. This section considers external factors first since these should be taken into account or eliminated before the individual is considered.

Job and its context

It should be faced as a possibility that not all jobs can be done satisfactorily. Where a job has been done by previous incumbents satisfactorily and providing the job has not changed and the previous occupant was not so specially talented, then there may be no doubts about the job. However, where the job is a new one or has substantially changed, the possibility of an 'undoable' job should be considered. The crucial question is 'How do I know that this job can be done to the standard that I consider satisfactory?'. Many teachers' jobs have changed as a result of the *Education Reform Act* and thus individuals are being asked to do jobs in ways which they have never previously been done. Many middle managers' jobs have had additional tasks accreted along with a growing recognition of how much more there was to the original job. Thus to do a new job to what is increasingly recognised as an appropriate but higher standard, is setting new levels of competence and these may be unattainable for previously competent performers without other adaptations, e.g. more time in which to carry out the duties or more clerical or other assistance.

Most jobs have elements to them that are difficult either by their very nature or because time pressures make them so. An organisation which is constantly striving to do better should be constantly on the look out for such elements which can be made less demanding by redesigning the jobs in some way. There is no merit in making life difficult on the basis that previous groups have surmounted such obstacles and that this is in some way meritorious. There are enough real problems without artificially adding to them ones which can be prevented or designed out.

Mager and Pipe (1984) suggest considering whether there are features in the context of the job which militate against good performance. They suggest considering such questions as:

Is performance punishing?

Is non-performance rewarding?

Does performance really matter to them?

These really revolve around the proposition that individuals may well operate in their own best interests as they interpret them in the context of the particular job. It really is quite unreasonable to expect anyone, even teachers of great professionalism, to be able to calculate what is best for the school and to carry this out when all the effects of carrying out the particular job in its context are unpleasant or appear punishing or that not doing the job is more pleasurable. Getting some teachers to do more of a demanding job can be to make good performance a punishment and to let off those who find some aspects of the job a struggle is to reward non-performance. Completing paperwork on time is a typical example. This is not to suggest that those with a natural ability for a task should not be given more of it to do, but rather to suggest that this should be seen as an explicit trade-off for being relieved of some other work.

The basic principle is that the organisational messages whilst carrying out the job should be clearly reinforcing successful performance rather than ambiguous. Clearly delegated jobs for which individuals are correctly prepared and equipped and for the performance of which they are accountable and rewarded provides the basis for performance mattering to individuals.

Management

The way in which individuals are managed in the job can have a profound effect on their performance. Whilst an element of this is the elusive capacity to motivate other people there are much more mundane, but nevertheless important, processes such as induction, coaching, training, communcation and praise which are vital to the successful performance of others.

Thus in cases of poor performance the operation of these processes should be considered to see if their lack or poor operation is a major contributory cause of poor performance. Clearly any lessons should be learned for the future. It is much more difficult to change habituated poor performance than to ensure that appropriate standards of performance are started and maintained when a new employee starts or an existing employee starts a new job. Induction, training, coaching and supervision are the essential ingredients to starting an employee in a job successfully.

Where good management practices are operating – suitable people have been selected for jobs; they have been appropriately inducted and have begun to work competently – diagnosing cases of subsequent poor performance is much simplified. Any fall-off in performance can be recognised as a change from previous practice and the range of possibilities is likely to be reduced to personal changes affecting the employee or possibly changes in the job. Any personal factors affecting the work performance of the employee should be picked up and appropriate counselling procedures used.

The individual

When other possibilities as whole or partial contributory causes of poor performance have been considered there remains the contribution of the employee. As indicated earlier it should not automatically be assumed that the problem only lies with the employee but few problems do not have an employee component.

The first big distinction to be made is between those problems which represent a deviation from previously satisfactory performance and those which have a long history of poor or difficult performance.

Recent effects If the employee has been performing satisfactorily until recently then the more profound causes of poor performance considered in the next section are unlikely to be serious contenders and the most likely cause is some social or emotional effect on the employee. The cause of these effects may lie at work or more likely outside work.

Stress can affect performance considerably either directly by a failure to concentrate on the job or more indirectly by reducing the importance of work compared to the cause of the stress.

There are two kinds of severe psychological disorder – neurosis and psychosis (Stewart and Stewart, 1982). Neurosis is when the patient knows they are ill (and is more common). Typical conditions are anxiety, depression and obsession. Psychosis is when the patient does not realise they are ill but other people often do. Typical conditions are paranoia, delusions and withdrawal. The cues to psychosis are –

sudden changes, inactivity, capriciousness, sudden increase or decrease in speech, extreme emotionality, tremor or persistent sweating. A change in these is a better indicator than the actual level of them since there are differences in individual's base levels of these behaviours. In such cases and also for alcoholism and drug abuse Stewart and Stewart recommend that all the manager should do if any of these are suspected is to create the circumstances for a talk and create an awareness of the need for professional help.

Long-standing effects In the cases where the poor performance has been the condition for some considerable time or the person is new to the job and has not demonstrated satisfactory performance then the considerations need to be much more penetrating. It should not be taken as self-evident that the person has the appropriate intellectual and other skills for the particular job.

It may be that the original selection process was flawed. The whole purpose of the selection process is to identify those individuals with the intellectual and behavioural skills appropriate to a particular job. In the main, any evidence for these skills relates to a different job in a different context and so it is a matter of inference that the person will be able to do the present job satisfactorily. These judgements may be just plain wrong. Any evidence for a misappointment should come from the induction process and follow-up. The appropriate question to ask to examine whether this is a possible cause is 'Could they do the job if their life depended on it?' (Mager and Pipe, 1984). Where a misappointment was made a long time ago things are very difficult. In hindsight such problems should never have been allowed to happen, but as Honey (1980; p.6) relates:

> the substantial ones almost slip into being. They develop over a period of weeks, months or even years. Initially the problem does not seem worth bothering about and, before we know it, it has settled down into a predictable pattern that looks obstinately permanent.

If the answer to the question is that the person is capable of doing the job then the two possibilities are that they don't know how to do the job or that they don't want to do the job. The first case is a training/induction/coaching problem whilst the second is a motivational problem. Stewart and Stewart (1982) point out that for new employees there may be very basic needs which require satisfying, such as feeling secure and obtaining satisfactory accommodation, before the newcomers can really wholly concentrate on the job.

Taking action

When poor performance has been diagnosed it is essential to involve the poor performer. This is important at the ethical level 'Nobody should be identified as a poor performer without his being told.' (Stewart and Stewart, 1982: p. 93) and also for the very practical reason that 'it's difficult to improve really poor performance...by stealth' (p.93). Although this generally means an individual interview with the poor performer, Stewart and Stewart suggest that if more widespread poor performance is evident on taking over a managerial role from someone else then a standard setting exercise for everyone is a useful precursor. In this way everyone knows the new standards of performance which are required and this eliminates any possibility of ignorance of the standard of work that is required of everybody.

Counselling interview

Unless the poor performance is caused by wilful disobedience of known rules then a disciplinary interview is inappropriate. The most useful meeting is one which sets out to identify the problem and examine possible solutions. The elements of a basic framework are suggested by Stewart and Stewart:

Agree standards;

Agree that there is a gap;

Agree size of gap;

Agree responsiblity for gap;

Agree on actions to reduce the gap;

Agree measures and time to reduce gap; and

Set time for follow-up.

Stewart and Stewart offer some useful suggestions about the approach to this interview.

Make it easy for the person to do what you want do not let the interview degenerate into a contest.

Handle the problem not the person deal with behaviour and not with personality. Not only can this be done more objectively by agreeing on the evidence but it is easier to change behaviour and it is only behaviour at work which ethically a manager should wish to change. This approach is more likely to succeed since then the poor performer is not under attack as a person.

Deal with behaviour and results since the 'right' behaviour may not be producing the desired results for some reason.

By adopting a problem solving approach it is less likely that the poor performers' response will be (Latham et al, 1987)

Deny it	This is a natural first reaction and managers should be prepared to confront it and encourage a more positive approach.
Hide it	Covering up is the second response when denial would be pointless.
Justify it	The next stage is to seek to justify or rationalise the behaviour.
Allocate it	The problem is allocated to someone else or to external causes.

Since most problems are multicasual the difficulty is to know where to start on formulating a solution. Stewart and Stewart suggest 'Find the knot that is easiest to undo, and start there' (p. 8).

Solutions

Plainly any solution must be individual to the particular problem, however, it is worth considering the range of possible components in addition to the traditional ones identified by Honey (1980):

1. *Denying the problem or any solution;*
2. *Pep talk* telling the person to pull their socks up;
3. *Coaching, counselling and appraising* this requires accurate diagnosis of the problem, appropriate skills from the manager and a lot of time;
4. *Sending poor performers away for training* this can work if there are identifiable skills which are lacking but not if the problem is part of the work situation which hasn't changed;
5. *Punishing poor performers* if this works it is only in the short term and may have undesirable side effects; and
6. *Getting rid of poor performers.*

As Stewart and Stewart (p. 72) observe, although frequently used, training is often not the answer:

Some people benefit from training; some are unscathed; and some come back worse than they went.

The range of solutions above concentrate on the poor performer but as has been shown earlier the cause of problems may lie outside the employee and so other solutions which should be considered, if the cause lies there, are:

Job redesign;

Changes in supervision;

Transfer to another job;

Demotion;

Professional counselling; and

Medical treatment.

Where the problem lies with the employee and the undesirable behaviour is attitudinal or motivational, Stewart and Stewart stress the importance of peer group pressure either formal or informal.

For this type of problem Honey (1980) suggests behaviour modification.

Behaviour modification This consists of analysing the undesirable behaviour and identifying the cue which sets it off and the pay-off or reward which the undersirable behaviour gives. The second stage is to identify desirable behaviour to replace the previous behaviour and to devise a new trigger for this behaviour and a suitable pay-off or reward for this new more desirable behaviour. This represents a form of conditioning and Honey is conscious of the ethics of using such techniques but concludes that since there must be a satisfactory outcome for both parties and since the active cooperation of the other person can be used, the worries on that score can be overcome.

Difficult people

These people are not necessarily poor performers in a cognitive sense but are poor performers behaviourally when they work together with other people. Bramson (1981) has identifed seven stereotypes. Actual examples are composites of these seven.

Hostile-aggressives who bully and overwhelm by bombarding others, making cutting remarks or throwing tantrums when they do not get their own way.

Complainers who gripe incessantly but never try to do anything about it either because they feel powerless or will not accept responsibility.

Silent and unresponsives who are monosyllabic.

Super-agreeables are often very personable, funny and outgoing individuals. They are reasonable, sincere and supportive whilst you are there but left to themselves they don't deliver.

Negativists will pour cold water on any new proposal.

Know-it-all experts are those people who think they have superior knowledge and wish others to recognise it. They are condescending if they have genuine expertise and pompous if they don't.

Indecisives are those who stall on major decisions until they have no choice or who hang on for the perfect solution.

Bramson maintains that such people have possibly unconsciously learned these behaviours as a means of manipulating others. They all have the effect of putting others at a disadvantage. The aim of the techniques summarised below is very modestly set at 'coping' so that the business in hand can be accomplished rather than hoping to bring about a transformation of the problem.

Briefly the analysis and suggested coping strategies for each are:

Hostiles can either be very obvious in their intimidation of others or can use criticism like a rapier to achieve the same effect much more subtly. They are driven by the need to demonstrate that they are right. The effect on others is confusion or flight.

The essence of the coping strategy is to stand up for yourself and be assertive but not return the hostility. Do not show intimidation and deflect any aggression. Insist on stating your personal point of view. Be ready to be friendly at the first opportunity.

Complainers can pick on real problems but do so in ways which are unlikely to lead to solutions. They have a strong sense of how others should behave and complain when they do not do so. Generally they are powerless to do anything about it and so the exercise is futile and demoralising for others listening to the depressing catalogue.

The key to successful coping is to break this self-confirming cycle of passivity, blaming others and powerlessness by adopting a problem solving approach. The first step is to listen attentively, this allows the complainer to let off steam and to feel that they are being taken seriously but it also allows awaiting the cue to move on the next step.

Acknowledge what has been said without necessarily agreeing with it and try to make the point more accurate since originally it may be rather hyperbolic. Then move on to trying to formulate the nature of a soluble problem related to the original complaint. If all else fails ask the complainer how they would like the conversation to end.

Silent and unresponsives

Won't or can't talk when you need conversation with them. It is often difficult to understand what this means as it is likely to be different on different occasions and certainly with different people.

Ask open ended questions with a friendly, silent stare – a quizzical, expectant expression. Don't break the silence except to comment on what has happened and the non-response. Try to help the 'clam' out by asking helpful questions about the (silence) problem. Listen attentively.

Super-agreeables

Always tell you things you want to hear but often let you down. Promises are made in good faith but not kept. Avoidance of conflict is the highest priority but can only be done in the short term. Eventually when choices have to be made someone will have to be disappointed.

Make honesty non-threatening. Try to get them to be honest. Don't allow them to make unrealistic commitments. Reassure them about their value as people. Be prepared to compromise providing it gets the job done. Listen to the humour are there hidden messages?

Negativists

This is not the considered verdict which is a useful warning of an unsound idea but a blanket reaction to any suggested change. 'It won't work'. 'We tried it once and it didn't work.' The acid test is to ask if there are any solutions to the identified problem – to the negativist there never are any. They truly feel dispirited and defeated. 'Negativists, with their steadfast, rational communication of helpless resentment, can touch that potential for depression in each of us and induce in us that same sense of being blunted'.

(Bramson, 1981: p. 105)

Try not to get sucked in. Try a positive breakout. Try problem-solving. Try to find courses of action worth trying. Spend time analysing the dimensions of the problem and asking questions. Present a moving target. At forebodings examine the worst consequences of the course of action to show that it is less dire than imagined. Use negativists constructively and use their warnings for contingency planning. They can also prevent over optimism. Be prepared to act alone if that is the alternative to increasing depression.

Some highly analytical people may act negatively until they have fully understood a situation so do not rush them.

Know-it-all experts

Some have genuine expertise and are confident they alone have the right answer (bulldozers). Others are blustering phonies with scraps of information and use these to impress (balloons). Though difficult to differentiate without corresponding expert knowledge they should be treated differently.

Bulldozers require preparation of facts and a questioning technique moving from conceptual to concrete without direct confrontation. At the concrete level a more adequate judgement of the ideas by others is possible.

Balloons seek admiration and respect. Alternative points of view and facts can be presented providing their face is saved.

Indecisives

Appear to agree and have made a decision but later change their mind or fail to implement the decision. The primary wish is to be helpful to everybody and hurt nobody. Some postponed decisions go away but maybe at a longer term cost. They have a strong internal desire to be honest.

Any hints of indecision must be investigated. Try to make honesty easy and help problem solve, reducing the number of alternatives to no more than two if possible. Concentrate on the solution which has humanitarian or quality benefits. Try to follow-up and support the decision to ensure no further change of mind. Fix a deadline for the final decision. Beware of forcing overloaded stallers into making decisions because they may make irrational decisions and be unwilling to reconsider.

Summary and conclusion

Poor, marginal and unsatisfactory performance will officially come to light as a result of the first round of formal staff appraisals in a way that has never happened before. Before any attempt is made to justify or rationalise not doing anything about this situation, there should be a consideration of the effects on the 'victims' of the poor performance – children being disadvantaged and other staff being demoralised.

Having decided that the problems need tackling, the emphasis should be on gathering evidence in an open minded way in order to form a clear picture of the situation. The job that the poor performer is carrying out and its context should be studied to see if there are features which make it especially difficult. The way in which the person is, and has been managed, should also be considered to discover how far he or she will have been made aware of any poor performance and received help to improve. Finally, the individual and their abilities and skills should be carefully considered in the light of the previous evidence.

Following this drawing together of the evidence by the manager, either as part of the appraisal process, or in advance of the institution of an appraisal scheme if handling poor performers first is the chosen strategy, the poor performer should be drawn into discussions. Such discussions should focus, firstly, on shared perceptions of the standard of work performance and the adequacy of this. Jointly collected further evidence and the judgements of others may be needed to make the case of poor performance compelling. When the poor performance standard has been accepted by the employee, the causes can be identified and plans drawn up which aim to improve performance to an acceptable level.

Such plans should commit resources and management effort for coaching and support for an agreed but limited amount of time before the results are reviewed. These plans should have the whole-hearted support of both the poor performer and manager. They should have a realistic and high chance of being successful. As the plans proceed, the closeness of working between the two people should lead to early indications of whether the plans are working. If they are working the problem should be solved, on the other hand, if there are increasing indications that they are not then efforts should be made to discover other more radical solutions which involve the poor performer leaving the school or teaching. Any examination of alternative solutions should be with the full support of the manager and the school. The school should be willing to commit resources to help find a joint solution.

It takes a great deal of courage to tackle poor performers of long standing but it is possible to do this positively and fairly by following the spirit of the suggestions made in this section.

5.3 Performance related pay

5.3.0 Performance related pay in local government and public sector organisations: lessons for schools and colleges

Brian Fidler

Introduction

The present pay structure in schools relates pay to the work to be done and the particular *post* but not to how well the *individual* is performing the job. Ironically, good performance may be rewarded by promotion to a new job where the person may or may not be successful. In recent pay settlements there have been moves to reward individuals who are performing well but such efforts have been largely subverted into pay for the job for a variety of reasons, one of which is associated with the difficulty of identifying good and superior teaching. As the Pay Review Body chaired by Sir Graham Day reported:

> Very few appear to have been awarded solely because the teacher concerned has demonstrated outstanding ability as a classroom teacher – only around 1.5 per cent on HMI's evidence
>
> (DES, 1992; p.21)

Such evaluative approaches to Performance Related Pay (PRP)

elsewhere, such as merit pay schemes in the US, have had little success. However, a new approach to PRP, target-setting, in an appropriate performance management culture may overcome previous difficulties.

That pay should be related to:

(a) the effort expended on the job;
(b) successful performance in the job; and
(c) extra performance in the job

are generally appealing ideas, though there are important differences in principle between them. There is also the relationship between pay and effort or performance to be considered. Should the relationship be a continuous one or should there be additional pay above a threshold?

A further point is whether such possibilities should be open to all or only restricted groups and whether such payments could and should genuinely be potentially available to all who satisfy some given criterion or whether their availability should be competitive.

Over and above the merits of PRP on rational grounds, its emotive political appeal should not be overlooked. The general public and politicians are far more likely to accept higher pay for better performance than to sanction higher pay with no such returns (Cohen & Murnane, 1985).

However, the discussion of PRP should not rest only at the point of principle since what scheme is taken up and how it is operated can make the difference between a measure which has more benefits than disadvantages compared to one which has major disadvantages. A failure to engage in the discussion may lead to others passing down a scheme which may not be the best available. Thus an analysis of the potential benefits of different PRP schemes is worthwhile. In addition there is evidence from a number of sources about how various schemes work in practice.

Also thinking strategically (Fidler, 1989; Fidler, Bowles & Hart, 1991) there are two further reasons for seriously investigating PRP when setting up a scheme for staff appraisal. The experience of PRP in local authorities is that adequate preparation is needed before introducing such schemes. Part of this is concerned with designing and obtaining commitment to the scheme but part is derived from skills gained from operating a staff appraisal scheme without PRP. The second point is related to this. It would be quite counterproductive to launch an appraisal scheme which was quite incompatible with PRP and had to be radically revised to accommodate PRP. Thus is would be prudent to set up a scheme of staff appraisal which was compatible with good practice in PRP. The requirements of this emerge at the end of this section.

Objections to PRP

In addition to political difficulties of acceptance of PRP by teachers' unions, there are an array of further difficulties. These relate to:

1. Matters of principle involving a service ethic, appropriate pay for professionals and pay as a motivator;
2. Matters of practice involving the difficulty of assessing performance, the devolution of staff payment decisions to lower levels in organisations; and
3. An unhappy historical legacy, 'payment by results'.

These objections could be discussed at length and be quite inconclusive at the level of argument, however, there is empirical evidence from other organisations employing professionals with a service ethic which demonstrates that PRP is acceptable to such groups (LACSAB, 1990a). Evidence on how to deal with the practical matters is also contained in the same evidence and is discussed later in this chapter. This leaves pay as a motivator and 'payment by results' to be discussed.

Pay as motivation

To some people it is evident that performance related pay is a nonsense because the conventional wisdom is that pay is not a motivator. It is odd that such views prevail when common experience during the 1980s and 1990s is of increasing levels of pay across a wide sweep of occupations and particularly chief executives of commercial organisations (often of a performance related nature). There are a number of possibilities – such payments are not intended to motivate; they are misconceived; or else some groups are motivated by pay and teachers are not.

In many cases the turning point for arguments about pay as motivation is heavily influenced by acquaintanceship with Maslow's Needs Hierarchy Theory of motivation and Herzberg's Motivation Hygiene Theory which appear to come to this conclusion. Above some very basic level of pay other needs are more important motivators than salary (Miner 1980).

The first thing that should be said is that theories are just that. They are intended to be summaries of experience and to make predictions which should be checked against reality. As will be seen in the first chapter of this book, the empirical support for these two theories is not strong and so it is particularly unwise to rely on their predictions. Although these theories have become among the best known in school management, they are not the only theories of motivation nor are they regarded as being among the most promising.

The second thing to say is that the concept of pay requires some further analysis. There is an important distinction to be drawn between absolute pay and relative pay. Judgements about the actual amount of pay received are rare compared to comparisons between the pay in one organisation compared to another and between the pay of one person and another in the same organisation.

A further distinction is between pay to attract the appropriate person into a job or prevent their leaving and pay to motivate those already in a job. Taking the first situation, although some organisations have been attracted to PRP as a way of boosting general salaries in order to overcome recruitment and retention difficulties, there has been a dissatisfaction with it as a solution. In this case it is the job which should be rewarded adequately. For the second situation, it is the performance of the job holder which should be rewarded as an incentive to continue high performance.

If the relatively small amounts of extra pay resulting from PRP are seen as symbolic of the recognition of good performance then they can be seen as motivation by esteem rather than by pay. In achievement motivation theory pay is seen as a token of achievement rather than the money itself being motivational.

The important point about financial rewards as distinct from other rewards of esteem such as praise is that money is not unlimited. If money is given then this has to be prioritised and each sum can only be given once unlike praise which is unlimited. Attaching even relatively small amounts of money to the process of giving esteem to good performance attaches a greater significance to the act than if no money were attached. Thus the process of recognising good performance is taken that much more seriously.

If the money is associated with the setting of targets then those targets will be more seriously negotiated and their achievement more closely scrutinised than if the process was carried out without money being involved.

Payment by results

As usual in education there is some previous history the very name of which precludes rational discussion – namely the infamous 'payment by results' set up by Robert Lowe in the *Revised Code* of 1862. It may be said that since this was so long ago it has no contemporary relevance, however, there are points of principle which are worth abstracting and also it is worth perhaps trying to set the record straight and debunking some of the mythology of this episode.

Standards in schools at the time were very low. This is evidenced both by accounts of work in schools and also by the failure of Mechanics Institutes to provide technical education post-school largely because of a lack of the basic skills of those who wished to develop further the skills of their trade. The effect of 'payment by results' was to raise standards albeit on a narrow and restricted curriculum. School attendance, as measured, also rose. Although the means of measuring the results – attendance of pupils and performance on basic skills – can be faulted, such inadequacies of methodology are unlikely to undermine the basic conclusions about the efficacy of the exercise. Thus as a measure of its time it had some benefits (Fletcher, 1972, 1981). However, the point of principle for the discussion here is that payment to the managers of the school was based on *the performance of children*. And it was from this income that teachers were paid.

Thus it was the manifest unfairness of paying teachers on the basis of crude measures of pupil success which can legitimately be criticised in 'payment by results'. The major objection is about whose results determined the pay of teachers rather than payment by result *per se*. It is the indirect connection between the efforts of the teacher and the performance of individual children which so discredited 'payment by results' from the point of view of rewarding teachers.

One key finding, therefore, from this episode is that if teachers are to be paid by results at all, it should be on the basis of as direct a measure of their own efforts or performance as possible.

There are further experiences to learn from. There is the experience of American schools and 'merit pay' and also there is the growing volume of experience in non-educational organisations of performance related pay.

Merit pay in the US

This is a scheme to improve the quality of teaching by which better teachers receive additional pay. The quality of teaching is to be assessed during classroom observation as part of staff appraisal. On the basis of a rating on a checklist of features of high quality teaching a teacher could become eligible for merit pay. Thus this is an evaluative scheme on predetermined criteria of effective teaching.

The points to note are that 'effective teaching' has to be defined and although different states in the US claim to have identified this 'by research' there are differences in what emerges. Thus 'effective teaching' is an administrative concept rather than a rationally defensible measure. What emerges from the critical research literature is that there are no universal truths and that teaching is rather more contingency based even for cognitive learning let alone any more subtle and ill defined learning in an affective domain. Thus the basis for the judgement of merit is flawed.

Further it should be noted that the whole of the appraisal process is evaluative and there are direct financial consequences of the evaluation. However, the system is not a linear one but operates on a threshold by which only extra pay and not basic salary depends on the rating.

Whilst the above represents the general reaction to merit pay in the US, Cohen and Murnane (1985) carrying out research in the early 1980s discovered, to their surprise, quite a number of school districts with long established schemes. They identified four strategies which made merit pay acceptable in these schemes:

1. Extra pay for extra work;
2. Politically decided criteria for the award of merit pay;
3. An effort to minimise discrimination by making the payment small or by giving it to nearly everyone; and
4. Keeping a low profile by making the scheme voluntary.

Each of the six districts studied in detail used a combination of these strategies. In assessing the impact of such incentives on performance, Cohen & Murnane (p.22) concluded that:

> On the one hand, there is no evidence that the money had an appreciable or consistent positive effect on teachers' classroom work. On the other hand, there is a fair amount of evidence that it did encourage some teachers to do the sorts of work outside the classroom that many educators consider important. There is some evidence that the evaluation requirements associated with some merit pay plans were useful to some teachers. In addition there is quite consistent evidence that these merit pay schemes helped many teachers to feel better about their work because the schemes seemed to express support for good teaching.

The other effect that they noted was the justification which merit pay provided to those who sought finance for education in justifying extra spending.

Non-educational organisations

Whilst it is tempting to assume that payment for performance is easy in non-educational organisations since one only has to count the number of widgets produced, the reality is more complicated but also more instructive. Whilst 'piece rate' payments are well established for certain simple productive tasks these are not without their problems, whilst in most non-profit making organisations and managerial jobs in just about any organisation there are no such simple measures to relate pay and performance.

PRP is quite widespread in non-educational organisations and has been gaining ground in public services. Most of the 400,000 civil servants are now covered by such schemes and over a quarter of local authorities had some employees covered by a form of PRP (IDS, 1989). There is a clear commitment in the Conservative Government's 'Citizens' Charters', announced in 1991, to expand the coverage of PRP as a way of improving public services.

Features of schemes in the public sector

PRP is particularly significant in public sector organisations because of

1. Service ethic;
2. Difficulty in measuring performance; and
3. Little devolved authority.

The service ethic meant that there had not been a great emphasis on measuring performance. This was both because of a different culture and also because of the difficulty of measuring performance in diffuse jobs. There has generally been an absence of financial measures on which to pin performance and there has also been a lack of delegation of managerial authority to manage staff including their remuneration.

More authority has recently been devolved as in education and determined efforts are being made to measure performance. The hope is that the service ethic will be enhanced.

There is a wide variety of schemes which can loosely be described as performance related. Some have tried to erect a distinction between 'merit pay' schemes whereby progress through salary increments is dependent on performance; and performance related 'bonus' schemes involving non-consolidated bonus additional to normal salary which is dependent on performance (IDS, 1989). However, there are crucial differences which are not elucidated by such nomenclature and so we shall not follow this classification. The variety of schemes makes discussion of PRP particularly difficult since what may be found ineffective in one scheme may not be the case in another. The crucial differences cover the:

1. Basis of performance assessment;
2. Basis of the payment made; and
3. Cultural context of the scheme.

From the LACSAB (1990a) report on 17 case studies of local authority schemes for PRP some important pointers to successful schemes emerge. The research concluded (p. 2) that some schemes:

> were more likely to reap the benefits of significant improvements in individual and organisational performance.

It is from the perspective of directly improving performance that the schemes will be viewed. Although there may be other indirect effects to be gained in recruitment it is generally agreed that PRP is no substitute for appropriate basic pay. The main effect of PRP should be in 'leveraging' performance (Brading and Wright, 1990)

1. Basis of performance assessment

Although there were a number of variants, in terms of the degree of sophistication employed in making the assessment, there were two basic types of assessment:

(a) *Merit rating* based upon some general assessment of all or parts of job performance; and

(b) *Performance against targets* based upon the extent to which pre-agreed targets had been achieved.

The merit rating schemes were generally 'home grown' and reduced the exercise to an evaluative one and ran into a series of problems in devising valid criteria against which to assess performance. In the LACSAB survey few authorities had schemes of this kind and they were more likely to generate problems.

The target-setting schemes were more promising since they:

(a) could be incorporated into appraisal schemes;
(b) retained a balance between development and evaluation; and
(c) built upon the advantages of target-setting.

Performance is assessed against a number of work targets. The targets can be more or less sophisticated. In an elaborate system, each year agreement was needed on:

(a) *principal accountabilities* half dozen or so core features of the job which only vary if there is a fundamental change in the nature of the job;

(b) *key tasks* at least one key task or objective will be agreed (related to organisational objectives);

(c) *performance indicators* or agreed measures used to assess the accomplishment of the key task(s) (deadlines, costs, feedback from clients etc.); and

(d) *possible constraints* such as might hinder the completion of the key task(s). These are in preparation for assessing the reasons for any partial failure to complete the key task at the year end.

As a result of the review overall performance is graded on seven grades from (1) inadequate to (7) faultless. The number of categories varies from 3 to 7 with 5 and 6 being most prevalent.

The translation of a review of target attainment into a single performance rating is the most error prone of the whole process and could deteriorate into assigning a grade on general criteria unrelated to target attainment.

(LACSAB, 1990a: p. 38)

2. The basis of the payments made

Again there is a wide variety in the type of payments made. Some organisations had taken this opportunity to completely rethink their salary scales and incorporate PRP, others had made minimal changes by adding a performance bonus payment. The three types of payment were:

(a) *Cash bonus* this was not consolidated into basic pay and had to be earned each year. A further variation is the level of performance at which the bonus becomes payable and the size of the bonus for different levels of performance.

(b) *Incremental progression* performance determined the rate of progression up a fixed scale. This could be supplemented by (a) for those at the top of a scale.

(c) *Salary matrix* complex arrangement whereby there is in effect a salary scale for each level of performance and there is differential progress on the scale depending both on performance and position on the scale (higher increases below the mid-point of the scale). This depends on job evaluation and the comparison of pay for similar jobs in other organisations. It requires yearly updating and generally involves the work of expensive consultants.

The most widely used was the cash bonus.
There are two further decisions to be made:
   (a) Size of payments; and
   (b) Who will be eligible to receive payments.

(a) Size of payments There are two views about the size of PRP bonus payments. One argues for substantial sums that are noticeable. A rule of thumb for incentives for manual workers is that they need to be about one third of basic salary to have a marked effect. In the LACSAB survey the highest payment was 20% of salary and this was quite exceptional, most were under 10%.

The other view (p. 44) is that the sums do not need to be large as they are tokens of recognition:

> It was argued, for example, that the key to motivation was the recognition of performance and not its reward and that this could be achieved through a relatively modest sum of money combined with the praise and thanks of the employee's manager.

(b) Who will be eligible for payments Here there are real dilemmas. The most obvious one is the size of the total extra salary bill if, say, 5% extra salary was to be paid to a majority of employees. Out of a fixed salary budget this would argue for up to 5% fewer employees.

But there are equally cogent arguments against the most obvious means of seeking to reduce this sum. If PRP is not to be open to all employees then those who are exempt (except by their own choice) can be expected to be demotivated. If PRP is open to all but payments will be made only to the highest levels of performance then most employees are likely to be unaffected in terms of increased motivation. If payments are to be made to an arbitrary fixed proportion of employees then those who do not rate highly their chances of being in that group can be expected to be unaffected by the scheme.

Thus the scheme has to be open to all and all members have to have a genuine and realistic opportunity (dependent on their own efforts) of receiving some payment.

In the first instance a sum has to be budgeted to cover the likely cost based on reasonable but flexible assumptions about the proportion of employees who are likely to be awarded payments. After one year's experience more accurate estimates can be made from this base of a slightly rising proportion of employees receiving payments each year.

3. Cultural context of the scheme

The launch of PRP schemes in the public sector has generally been associated with other trends, most notably, the delegation of decision making and budgetary authority to lower levels in organisations; a greater focus on performance and outcomes of the organisation as a whole; and a desire for improved performance from all employees. These have been called the performance management culture.

Many organisations which had begun to move in this direction before taking on PRP reported that the performance management culture was already providing benefits. It was suggested by some of those in the LACSAB survey that the attachment of money concentrated attention on performance rather than directly motivating it.

Thus the performance management culture seems to be an essential pre-requisite to successful PRP

> PRP will only be successful if the necessary attitudes, systems and skills are in place prior to its introduction
>
> (LACSAB, 1990a: p.12)

PRP contributes to performance management by:

(a) Requiring managers to discuss objectives and required performance standards with their staff
(b) Requiring managers to assess the performance of their subordinates and reward good work
(c) Providing incentives and recognition for achievement it would stimulate initiative and lead to more proactive work.

Clearly managers and staff have to be committed to performance management before PRP is introduced. The steps to prepare for the successful implementation of a PRP scheme are discussed in the next section.

There is a further tension in embarking on a PRP scheme of this kind. There will be a natural wish by senior managers to ensure that staff are treated equitably and appropriate performance standards are being used by all managers, however, there is a real problem here. This will have to be carried out with great sensitivity if this is not to undermine the principle of delegation of authority on which performance management depends.

Steps in the introduction of PRP

1. Develop a performance management culture;

2. Gain experience with a target-setting appraisal system;
3. Consult widely on the design of a PRP scheme for the particular organisation both to formulate a good scheme and develop a sense of ownership;
4. Communicate the principles of the scheme widely to further develop a sense of ownership;
5. Provide training in target setting skills;
6. Gradually introduce PRP to small groups to gain experience and be prepared to modify the scheme; and
7. Implement, monitor, and evaluate the workings of the scheme.

Unions or professional associations can be drawn into such discussions if they are not opposed in principle to PRP. Their involvement can lend authority to the scheme and prevent difficulties later. In local government the largest union, NALGO, was opposed to PRP in principle and suspected it of being a means of circumventing collective bargaining. Some schemes have been approved locally where an appeals scheme has been included and the union was given information about the general distribution of payments as reassurance about its equity. Some schemes were pushed through by direct appeal to employees.

Implications for schools and colleges

1. PRP can reinforce a performance management culture and experience in local government is generally positive with more acceptance than had been originally envisaged.
2. The adoption of a target-setting approach to staff appraisal is an important preparation for PRP. Experience of target-setting will be very important and is best gained before money hangs on the result.
3. Local government personnel departments generally found the preparation and monitoring of PRP required considerable extra effort. Within schools and colleges, senior management are likely to have to pick up these functions.
4. Without an earmarked budget for either PRP or staff salaries, finding resources to implement PRP will be invidious. Money to finance PRP will be a direct trade-off to purchasing extra books for children, for example.
5. If payments are to be both nominal and have an impact then the sum should be paid as a lump sum rather than as a small monthly

supplement. At current rates, a payment of £500 or so might be the lowest to meet both these requirements.

6. Within secondary schools, colleges and large primary schools, PRP will create major problems when those who have delegated staff management responsibilities do not have an associated delegated staffing budget out of which to finance PRP. Grouping departments into larger faculties and allocating such larger units a notional staffing budget may offer a solution.

7. The present salary structure is dysfunctional for economic decision making. Long incremental scales distort cost benefit decisions. For example, an experienced school teacher at the top of the basic scale costs considerably more to employ than an experienced teacher half way up a scale but doing basically the same job. Is it sensible to try to graft on PRP 'bonus' payments to such a structure?

In conclusion, the available evidence suggests that PRP has much to offer if it is associated with a performance management culture. This culture has to be built up systematically over a period of time and has to extend to all those in a management position within the school or college. Merely paying existing staff more or imposing a PRP system on an unprepared staff are both likely to be ineffective.

5.3.1 Experience of performance related pay in an education department

David Cracknell

Introduction

This chapter offers a personal perspective on the experience of one education department which has introduced performance related pay. A key development in changing the culture and management of many LEA education departments over the last three or four years has been the introduction of various forms of more systematic Performance Management (PM). In some departments this has been associated with performance related pay (PRP). The experience of LEAs will be of interest across the service both for LEAs and within schools and colleges. A case study of East Sussex county council, where the local authority has operated a PRP scheme since 1988 draws out some of the practical challenges of this approach. The East Sussex initiative is set in the wider context of local government performance management and some general themes which emerge from the experience are proposed.

Performance related pay in context

A helpful working definition of systematic PM within local government is:

> an integrated set of planning and review procedures which cascade down the organisation to provide a link between each individual and the overall strategy of the organisation.
>
> (Rogers, 1990)

PRP has been seen by many local authorities as an important element in effective PM and a growing number now operate a PRP scheme. Arguably PRP helps to 'sharpen the focus' for managers.

For local government, PRP is an individualised system of payment linking all of the reward of each employee to his or her performance in the job and it commonly uses rating scales or comparison of achievements against objectives (LACSAB, 1989), a definition which may be of wider value. PRP is distinct from group incentive schemes, profit sharing and market pay supplements. It is easy to confuse PRP with merit pay systems which have operated in local government since the 1950s. PRP is less subjective and does not focus on behavioural and personality issues. It has a clear association with performance objectives.

At best PRP has played a part in enabling local authorities to improve their strategic management and the quality of their services – at worst PRP has been a painful and expensive experience (Brading & Wright, 1990; LACSAB, 1990a; Spence, 1990; Wills, 1988). Industrial models have been available to local authorities (e.g. IBM, John Lewis, Nissan, Alliance and Leicester, Legal and General, and Hanson) but the transfer of business methods and technology to public service has been far from straightforward.

PRP in East Sussex

Experience of introducing PRP has demonstrated the importance of developing a scheme which is tailored to the specific needs of the business or organisation concerned (Brading & Wright, 1990). There is, therefore, no single 'package' of PRP to be taken from the shelf. Until LACSAB became active in this field and published guidance from 1989, the main sources of advice to local authorities setting out on the path to PRP were consultants with experience of business schemes and the pioneers amongst county and district councils. So when the County Management Team of Chief Officers in East Sussex decided in April 1986 to seek committee approval to pursue PM, they did so against a general national interest but with little readily available outside experience upon which to draw. It was agreed that consultants (Kinsley Lord) should undertake a feasibility study which was completed in 1987 and the consultants were also asked to support the initial process of job evaluation for senior managers. PRP was introduced for approximately 90 chief officers, deputies and senior managers across all council departments in April 1988 and their performance was assessed against targets in 1989, 1990 and 1991. During 1989 work was undertaken to extend the PRP scheme to approximately 280 middle managers across all departments. Job evaluations were handled by four panels of senior managers chaired by deputies. PRP was extended to middle managers in April 1990 with the first assessment of performance completed by April 1991.

The senior and middle managers' schemes differ in some details, such as car leasing arrangements, but essentially they both operate as follows:

- Emphasis is on PM and so PRP is seen as subordinate and complementary.
- Focal event of the PM process is the Annual Review Day (in April) which gives county councillors a first opportunity to review the previous year's performance for each service/department, based on the Chief Officer's Commentary.
- Chief Officer's Commentary and an associated business plan incorporates a statement of service objectives for two to three years which reflect countywide objectives and, in the Education department, have been built up during an annual planning cycle involving staff throughout the department.
- In January each year a period is set aside especially for departmental planning during which service objectives are worked up into more detailed targets and performance indicators within and across all of the major sections and teams in the Department.
- Targets from sections and departments form the basis for individual targets and performance assessment.
- Focal event of the PM process for the individual is a performance management interview which takes place in February/March with each person's manager but there are also short briefing and updating sessions when changes in circumstances and agreed targets can be recorded during the year.
- Interview gives an opportunity to: review individual performance and set a reward for the past year; establish targets for the next year; and agree a development plan for the individual manager.
- Interview is structured around a set of simple forms; it is initiated by the individual who makes an initial assessment of performance and drafts the targets; the outcomes are moderated by the manager's manager ('grandparent'); and the process is kept under general review by the Chief Executive and County Personnel Officer.
- Managers are asked to select one or four performance ratings and an appropriate performance pay reward (see Figure 5.3.1.1).
- Pay scales in 1990, for example, provide for six increments

(of approximately £500–1,000) on each of the four senior and five middle manager bands which have all been developed locally following surveys of other local authorities and national scales.

– Review and flexible interpretation are seen to be essential features of the scheme – the process should not become unwieldy but be sufficiently light and well focused to allow an open review 'so that we can improve what we are doing and how we are doing it'.

(ESCC, 1989)

Performance Rating	Within Scale	Scale Maximum
EXCEPTIONAL	3 or 4 increments	8%–10% lump sum
GOOD	2 increments	5%–7% lump sum
SATISFACTORY	1 increment	NIL
UNSATISFACTORY	No increment	NIL

Figure 5.3.1.1: East Sussex performance rating and reward scale

It is difficult to separate the impact of PRP from other initiatives in which the county council and the education department have been engaged over the last four to five years. An emphasis on better communications, on service quality and on being more responsive to customer needs have been associated with a general extension of delegated management and the introduction of service level agreements between departments. In 1988–89 there was a distinct feeling of 'innovation overload' in East Sussex. PM has, however, been consistent with the thrust of these other initiatives, reinforcing a more systematic approach to managing change and sharpening the focus of activity. In retrospect the various changes in management style and structure now look more coherent and PM is welcomed by most managers. The PRP element in these PM developments has, however, been more contentious.

Evaluating the East Sussex experience

The responses from senior and middle managers in the East Sussex Education Department to a questionnaire on PM and PRP in July 1990 illustrate the issues which have emerged:

1. Most managers had been enthusiastic in 1987 although several

were less happy about PRP. One manager was strongly opposed to PRP ('Money will buy no more hard work from me') from the outset. PM was seen by most as a valuable complement to service planning – it helped to focus on priorities, reducing over ambitious targets, and defended staff somewhat against the unplanned accretion of tasks. It brought managers together to produce better communications and more thinking time. PM set the work of individuals within the wider context of what the county council and the rest of the department were trying to achieve. In some cases the practice had not quite matched the theory with priorities being overwhelmed by the 'morass of day-to-day work'. Looking back over the experience of PM and PRP in East Sussex, most of these managers continued fully to support the initiative but recognised that it needed 'constant care to preserve the right atmosphere'. An initial opponent of PRP was dissatisfied on a personal basis and convinced even more of the demotivating effects of PRP and these views were echoed by another manager.

2. Although it was too early to come to a clear judgement, there were signs that PM was helping to improve services – being prepared for change, responding to customer needs and using performance indicators. PM was seen to be as much about style as technique and effective services depended upon a whole range of management action. Improvements to services had come with better cross-departmental understanding but there was still a danger of the PM process being marginal to the continuing challenge of day-to-day management.

3. Generally the introduction of PRP into the Education Department was not seen to have improved staff motivation, recruitment and retention. Some felt it had positively harmed motivation through specific decisions about job evaluation and ratings for senior managers and unresolved reservations of principle from middle managers and NALGO. PM still attracted a great deal of support but for some 'PRP is a side issue which potentially distorts the whole PM process'.

4. Performance management interviews were generally seen to have great value. They made it easier to see key success factors, to set priorities and stick to them. They enhanced morale, informed personal development and through praise and positive criticism helped to motivate. For some it corrected an over pessimistic self-evaluation. Managers identified a number of ways in which the interviews could be improved:

> Both managers and managed need to give sufficient time to preparation and the interview itself;

> More honesty is needed in setting criteria and in assessing outcomes;
>
> Timetable for the process needed to be set well in advance;
>
> More training in interviewing and counselling was essential; and
>
> More emphasis on interim discussions should exist to ensure that the decisions reached in the annual interviews were vigorously acted upon.

5. Most dissatisfaction was felt about the arrangements to decide PRP ratings for individual senior managers. There was a perceived failure to moderate the first year's ratings across departments and although most managers saw the second year as much improved, there was concern about delay in informing managers, returning claim forms and securing comparability across departments. Although the terms used in the rating were defined for managers there was unease about the category 'satisfactory' which was felt not to match adequately a performance which was on target.

6. The education department had used for some years an annual management development interview for senior staff which the PM interview incorporated. Some newly appointed managers, without this background of experience in East Sussex, were happy with the staff development element in the interview. Most other managers, however, could see little or no evidence in 1990 that there were tangible improvements in staff development following the introduction of PM. It may be too early to judge since a new formal management development programme only became available to senior managers in 1990. However, there was a feeling that staff development was taking a lower priority as the department's focus switched to performance and that staff were not aware of training opportunities or receiving the development they needed.

East Sussex reached the stage in 1990 where it was considering whether it should modify its PM arrangements and, in particular, if and how it should extend PRP to other categories of staff. It was already evident that different approaches to job evaluation might be needed, in particular for those staff who did not see themselves as primarily general managers but offering a professional or advisory service. It may be that different frameworks for PRP ratings and rewards are appropriate within one organisation.

Learning from the PRP experience

The *Handbook on PRP* (LACSAB, 1990b) offers helpful and practical advice but it is not for the faint hearted.

> While many organisations believe that PRP helps to clarify the intentions of management and motivate staff, some have found it inappropriate or hard to get right.

A majority of PRP schemes are perceived to have failed, i.e. lost their focus on performance such that the wage bill is inflated without securing any benefits. Some local authorities like Coventry have recently abandoned PRP schemes and others like Suffolk have, after careful investigation, not introduced the scheme. This should not come as a surprise since:

> The history of performance appraisal has, in some local authorities, been an unproductive one, with a life cycle...of only two to three years, during which time a scheme is designed, never fully implemented and supported and gradually withers away as a result of direct opposition, or of simple neglect, or because it did not produce the performance results anticipated
>
> (Rogers, 1990)

For an organisation which is heavily committed to PM and PRP, the message is not necessarily that it too should withdraw but that the lessons of experience should be rigorously applied:

1. **We need to be sure why we want PRP**

It is not always clear how PRP is intended to promote quality improvements in a public service operating within a democratic framework. Account must be taken of the political dimension of local government. PRP is primarily about individual and organisational performance but some schemes have been introduced to improve recruitment and retention. East Sussex, in a competitive market for staff, was undoubtedly influenced in its early interest in PRP by recruitment worries. Anyway it is misleading to draw a sharp distinction between performance and recruitment/retention – the one depends heavily on the other, especially in public service. However, improved performance expressed in service terms must be regularly reinforced as the primary driving force for PRP if it is to retain its edge as an effective tool of management.

2. **We need to be clear about every job in the organisation**

Job evaluation in East Sussex was a difficult but productive exercise. A growing number of local authorities are moving towards 'Hay-MSL' type job evaluation systems and have had to come to terms with the investment in time and training which these require to be effective. PM and associated planning arrangements to set shared objectives across the department have helped to build a better understanding about the complementary nature of managers' jobs.

3. **We need to get better at defining performance**

It has been recognised (Brading & Wright, 1990) that defining and communicating an objective assessment of performance is one of the most difficult aspects of PRP. Loose or muddled thinking about performance is readily exposed as PRP sharpens issues and highlights inconsistencies. PRP increments in one local authority are awarded to chief officers for 'corporate endeavour' which is not defined and in another these are awarded on a basis which has no explicit linkage to an appraisal system. In East Sussex the department has worked hard to involve managers in setting more precise but manageable service and individual objectives and to identify linked performance indicators. Good and convincing performance indicators are elusive in many areas of work in an Education Department. Members were involved in East Sussex but schools, colleges and other 'clients' had not been drawn in systematically to help set performance criteria. These are likely to be important disciplines for PRP in the future.

4. **We need to defend stability in the organisation and continuity of purpose**

PRP can tempt managers to set targets and reward achievement where change is occurring and not sufficiently in areas of essential business maintenance. Indeed some appraisal systems linked to PRP explicitly focus on a limited area of marginal change. Performance is rarely just about managing new initiatives – it is important that performance in the rest of our work is not allowed to go by default. 'Short-termism' has been used to describe attitudes in industry (Kinder, 1990) which have led to an unhealthy weakening of strategic objectives by succumbing to short-term payoffs. Such attitudes are not unknown in local government and can be encouraged by PRP if the focus is too narrow. Relating PRP to a three to five year vision ought not to dismay us.

5. **We need to continue to emphasise non-financial recognition**

Some managers believe that it is inappropriate and ineffective to use marginal changes in pay as a reward or recognition for good performance – for them it is demotivating. This scepticism is healthy if it leads to reappraisal and to the evolution of more effective approaches to PM but it risks degenerating into damaging cynicism. The search for more and different forms of recognition and reward (particularly the kind that make it easier for individuals to do their job) must be extended. The introduction of PRP should not be seen as an excuse for assuming that this continuous search need no longer preoccupy the effective manager.

6. We need a scheme that operates fairly and openly

Equity and justice are not, in the East Sussex experience, matters requiring vague assurances and they are continually relevant in the operation of PRP. Staff want to know that they will be treated equitably across the organisation, that equal opportunities criteria will be rigorously applied and that the administrative machine will not be allowed to grind on with scant attention to individual needs.

> But perhaps the most problematic area is the degree of inaccuracy which may be exhibited by appraisers when making evaluations and rating performance. Inaccurate assessments naturally create feelings of injustice and quickly lead to a deterioration in the perceived value of the scheme....there is ample evidence that appraisers consistently make errors when rating performance.
>
> Rogers, 1990

East Sussex experience demonstrates how difficult it is to resist being secretive about some aspect or other of a PRP system. It also shows that PRP will not, in itself, resolve long-standing problems of grading and comparability.

7. We need to minimise the divisive potential of PRP

Having made considerable efforts to reduce historical divisions and to weaken hierarchies, it was galling for senior managers in the education department to be faced with a PRP scheme which was to be introduced, no doubt for good reasons, on a phased basis from senior management 'down'. There was also some concern that the emphasis on the individual would undermine team unity but so far this has not been apparent. Typically, the full involvement of trades unions has not been given great emphasis in introducing PRP. In the longer term this may well weaken its chances of success.

8. We need to maintain a strong staff development focus in PRP

A significant weakness of the PM scheme operating in the East Sussex education department is that it failed up to 1990 to give sufficient priority to implementing the development plans which it was intended should form an integral part of the process. This is ironic given that the roots of the present PM system lay in a management development process and that East Sussex successfully pioneered school focused staff development. PM will succeed or fail in the eyes of some managers to the extent to which it integrates organisational objectives and staff development needs.

9. We need to communicate better and train more

If managers and staff at all levels are to be committed to PM and PRP, PM will need to be given more senior management attention. East Sussex operated *team briefing* and the department had reviewed its internal and external communications. All these channels need to be fully exploited to sustain the impetus for making effective use of PM. Training for PRP was better for middle managers in East Sussex than for senior managers but there is a clear need for continuing preparation of individuals and teams of staff if the process is to be effectively embedded in the management of the department.

10. We need to see PRP in its wider context

This chapter began with a reference to 'sharpening the focus' of the work of managers – a visual metaphor which highlights the contribution that PM and PRP have made to management thinking. Periodically, managers need stimulation to see things from another perspective. PM has certainly helped to do that in local authorities like East Sussex. However, PRP seems to some managers in education departments to be a dispensable sub-set of PM. Linking pay to performance has the advantage of showing that the organisation really does recognise good performance and that it sees performance generally as important but it runs the risk of creating unnecessary tensions.

> Pay is important and must be got right but it is a means to the end of improved performance not an end in itself.
>
> (LACSAB, 1990b)

PRP may be, for some organisations, a valuable step along the road to making PM stick but it is by no means evident that it is a necessary step. That conclusion is relevant to appraisal systems in schools and colleges as well as in local government departments.

5.3.2 Performance related pay for head teachers and deputy heads

David Turley

Introduction

This review looks at the motivation for performance pay, offers an overview of the writer's experience at the Royal Borough of Kensington and Chelsea, considers performance pay in the education sector, comments on some key factors, and summarises some of the benefits of performance pay as seen.

Motivation for performance pay

Amongst the various factors which contributed to the introduction of performance pay in the Royal Borough of Kensington and Chelsea, some were internal – wanting always to make ourselves more effective, others were external – our need to bring more flexibility into the reward structure. These were some of the issues

Improving performance. More than four years ago, we embarked on a long term plan to introduce individual performance review (or 'appraisal') processes. Our objectives were, and still are, quite wide. They included more systematic work planning and review processes, healthier communication between managers and their staff, and greater attention to individual development needs and opportunities. Put another way, more focus for manager and employee alike.

Improving retention and recruitment. Like most other local authorities and south eastern employers, Kensington and Chelsea had been suffering from a high staff turnover. We recruit in a competitive labour market. We needed a remuneration policy which supported our aims of encouraging good people to join and to stay, and to perform well whilst with us.

Fair rewards and genuine incentives. An increasing number of people believed that, whilst highly prescriptive pay arrangements had shown advantages of being open and consistent, they failed to distinguish adequately between those who performed particularly well and those who are barely acceptable.

Overview of our experience

In 1987 we embarked on a major review of our reward policy at management level. Consultants were asked to direct this – particularly for the benefit of their wider perspective, together with the comparative data they have on the salary market – though the project was resourced internally. As a result of that examination the council introduced a new remuneration package. In outline:

1. We used the consultants' proprietary job evaluation scheme (more relevant to higher management levels than the scheme we had previously operated) and carried out a comprehensive and objective assessment of all senior management roles in the organisation. Each position was scored and ranked according to its relative weight.
2. Drawing on the consultants' market survey data, we considered how our jobs fared compared with going rates in our area for jobs of similar weight.
3. We dropped national salary points, and constructed new salary ranges. Each followed the same principle – a wide range where the maximum possible salary was 30 per cent greater than the minimum.
4. No fixed salary or incremental points were set: there could be any salary (to the nearest £100) provided it fell within the range.
5. Progression within these ranges would be entirely dependent on performance. An individual would be eligible for an annual merit based increment, its size relating to his or her assessment. Because an individual's salary would reflect his or her performance assessment, we adopted a policy of keeping pay information confidential.
6. A cost of living increase would be given by the council each year, over and above an individual's performance based increase.

We offered these new arrangements to existing managers on the understanding that each could decide whether or not to accept. There was no pressure to change over, but almost all did, even though there was no general increase offered as an inducement. What the new contracts meant for most was an opportunity to progress further, by performance, over the coming years. Previously the majority of staff had been stuck at the maximum of very short salary scales. Currently in the order of 10 per cent of our total workforce is engaged on these local arrangements.

In 1989, we started to develop a new reward and retention package for other staff. The overriding objective was to stem staff turnover. Our aim was to introduce greater flexibility and scope for individuals to progress, and thereby encourage more employees to pursue longer term careers with us. We have recently introduced a new grading structure for these administrative and professional staff. It involves fewer but wider salary ranges – five in total – based on, though replacing, 13 national grades. It keeps within the national agreement, using national salary points, but it frees things up, and offers scope for staff to progress to higher rates, based on a combination of performance and duties.

Performance pay in the education sector

With regard to the education service, Kensington and Chelsea has of course only relatively recently become an education authority. Senior education staff have been recruited by the Royal Borough on the same performance contracts as other managers in the organisation.

We have been giving considerable attention to the question of performance pay in the education service and, in particular, we commissioned two major assignments covering head teachers. One extremely interesting project, which was led by consultants but included head teachers and a governor on the working group, has identified – following detailed and structured analysis – those factors which distinguish the most effective performers. To use the current jargon: *competencies*.

Head teachers and deputies

We also have had a major study into the desirability and scope for performance pay for head teachers and deputies. Following extensive research and consultation with all concerned, we concluded that:

1. A performance pay scheme was both viable and desirable. Most important, we should regard it as an integral part of performance management and the school's development plan. The scheme envisaged has two fundamental parts:
   (a) professional development of the head teacher, and
   (b) effective performance and management.

2. Whilst a number of approaches were considered, the one chosen would be to assess performance against achievement of previously established and agreed objectives. This would be supported by careful regard to relevant quantitative and qualitative indicators.

3. The appraisal should be approached on an integrated basis involving the three relevant parties – the head, the chairman of governors, and the chief education officer.

4. A system of merit salary increases would apply, this being similar to, and based on, the council's existing management pay provisions. Appointment would be onto a range which contains the national scales, but would allow progression based on performance into the higher part of the range over and above the national maximum.

5. Participation in performance pay would be voluntary for existing head teachers and deputies.

These policies were adopted, and new contracts were offered to head teachers and deputies in April 1991. Eighty four invitations were made and, as at May 1991, 49 have chosen to switch to the new arrangements.

The local ranges will be reviewed in line with the national pay award for head and deputies and progression within the ranges will follow a local pattern of assessing achievement against targets, with five levels of assessment:

AA	*Exceptional*	consistently exceeds expectations
A	*Highly effective*	standards for objectives exceeded
AB	*Effective*	targets achieved
B	*Less than effective*	some objectives met
C	*Unacceptable*	less than half objectives met

It is intended that the local scheme will keep to the set national increments and this is reflected in a matrix which translates the assessment into increments.

Assessing performance

So how can the performance of head teachers be assessed? As a senior colleague in the education service said:

> I know the job I am doing, it all seems to be going well, so why should I write it all down for someone to scrutinise? In fact, the job couldn't really be written down – it was very complex, and every day was different. How could the outcomes be measured, especially when we work as a team.

That same person was asked to set down all the things that were done in her role, and then to say how she measured the effectiveness of the service. She was also asked to review the future work programme and define a plan for the coming year.

She said afterwards that was probably the best thing she ever did. It not only explained to other people what she and her team did, but it gave a measure of how they did it, and provided the vehicle to analyse the work, to question priorities, to ask herself how she was doing. Most especially, it gave the chance to look forward so that changes could be planned, and projects and goals identified.

This mirrors the experience of many managers who have entered the scheme. Not only does it require them to look afresh at their priorities and refocus their efforts, but it also provides a regular opportunity to discuss progress with their own managers. It is only too easy for both these exercises to go 'by the board' with the pressure of day-to-day service delivery.

It is easier to identify tasks and goals than may at first be imagined. For a start, every head teacher has a job description: there is a clear summary of what a head teacher's responsibilities are. Then there is the LEA's plan which, together with the National Curriculum, gives further key pointers and objectives. Thirdly, schools are producing individual development plans, to formulate plans for the delivery of the National Curriculum as well as other aspects of school life.

These form the basis of a personal task list, from which it is straightforward to identify specific projects and goals – in other words, here are the objectives which the head teacher has for the coming year. They should be expressed in terms of end results and, when these are clear and explicit, the process of reviewing performance is relatively easy – it is apparent to all parties what has been achieved.

Personal development targets are vital. Relating to an individual's professional development needs and aspirations, it is right to expressly state what is on the agenda for that individual's growth in the coming year.

In my view, a good set of objectives covers a range of topics relevant to that person and their current job. I would say that there should be at least half a dozen targets (fewer means that the whole job is not being covered), though much more than ten is too much (it no longer provides a focus for priorities).

Of course some measures are more objective than others. Quantifiable indicators have a useful part to play, and obviously they are the least subjective, but sometimes the availability of figures and hard data may be limited. In the education sector, the sensitive and proper use of quantitative performance indicators (e.g. attendance, pupil attainment) seem likely to be relevant.

Qualitative evaluation would appear to be similarly useful. This might include the outcome of monitoring and evaluation by the inspectorate. School performance reviews would be useful, with indicators such as what is being done in the way of staff development, or parental and community involvement.

I believe the best approach to performance assessment is going to be one which concentrates on specific objectives, but which is supported by a careful and suitable regard to personal skills and quantitative and qualitative indicators.

Assessment of head teachers and deputies

Assessments are to be carried out on an annual basis. At the same time targets and objectives for the following year are agreed.

From 1 April 1991, the responsibility for the assessment of performance of the heads and deputies rests with the council's Director of Educational Services and will, usually, be carried out by the inspectorate. Where the head of an LEA school agrees, another person experienced as a head teacher may take part in the appraisal. Where the head and governors of a Voluntary Aided school agree, the governors may nominate another appraiser. Where the head and governors of any school agree, the chairman of governors may be an active participant in the process.

The assessment of deputy heads opting into the local scheme would be carried out by the head teacher in consultation with the Director of Educational Services. The deputy head will be entitled to have another deputy head present as an observer. In the case of a deputy of a school where the head teacher has elected not to be associated with the scheme, the assessment will be the responsibility of the Director of Educational Services.

A full review of the effectiveness of the scheme is to take place in October 1992.

Some key factors in the introduction of performance pay

Looking back on our experience of introducing performance pay, there are a number of points or considerations which I would identify as important, including:

1. *Evolutionary approach.* It has been greatly beneficial to have introduced performance processes gradually and carefully. We have been introducing appraisal over a period of several years, and performance pay has followed this and also come in stage by stage. This has made it easier to support the changes with plenty of discussion. Over a period of time, we have become more accustomed to the process of target setting and reviewing performance. As an organisation our skills have improved as we form new habits and routines and we have been able to fine-tune our procedures in the light of experience.

2. *Communication and training.* At every stage, we provided for discussion, and invited people to raise their questions and concerns. As well as briefing people about the new procedures, we concentrated on training in technique – the techniques of setting objectives, how performance can be measured, advice on conducting such meetings, and so on.

3. *Involvement.* Whilst many of the initiatives were led by the personnel department and consultants, we sought to involve as many line managers as possible. For example, we equipped selected line managers to lead seminars on appraisal processes.

4. *Monitoring* We have established careful processes to monitor, guide and support the new arrangements. In the longer term we may be able to relax the controls and safeguards we have built, as confidence grows. But, for the present, we are monitoring things closely.

5. *Administration.* If there was one thing which we probably did get wrong, it was to underestimate the changes in personnel administration which would follow. It is not that the administration is particularly complicated or difficult, but it does require new processes and requirements. It's important to plan for these.

Whilst acknowledging that the practice of performance pay is new, different and, perhaps, even threatening to some, many managers have expressed strong support for the move. They say, firstly, that they are not shy of being judged on their performance and, secondly, that operating performance pay sends a favourable impression to staff and would-be staff that the organisation is serious about performing well.

A view has sometimes been expressed that performance pay means managers getting paid for their workers' efforts. This is true to the extent that managers are paid to get results through others, but objectives and targets must be meaningful, and these must measure a manager's performance and effectiveness.

Some also say that performance pay is divisive. But systematic performance review or appraisal is becoming the norm for all staff. Much of what is involved in appraisal and performance pay is similar – objective setting, and ensuring that staff are given a focus, and feedback.

Others reason that performance pay is not applicable to their group, usually on the grounds that their job is not measurable. But performance pay is about systematic planning and objective setting. It offers staff focus, and the chance to review achievements and results, and it means reward and recognition. These considerations are as valid for one worker as another.

Benefits

In my organisation, we are four years into a long term plan of introducing more systematic objective setting and performance review processes, in the context of trying to influence quality and effectiveness. In many senses, these are still early days: there are growing pains and discomforts. We are also trying to update our reward system, aiming at performance and recognition – as well as responding to the ever tightening and costly employment market.

But we have laid a number of important foundations. Although there is a lot that is fragile, we are evolving new processes which have a secure and sound logic to them. We have tried to avoid superficial quick-fix approaches.

We are providing our staff with a better focus, and a clarification of what is expected of them. Most people like that. We are giving feedback, and being more systematic and structured as to how we address an individual's development.

SECTION 6: OVERVIEW AND ACTION PLAN

6.1 Overview and guide to the process

Brian Fidler and Bob Cooper

Introduction

Staff appraisal is an integral part of the management of staff. It is an important part but not the whole of staff management, thus preparation for the introduction of staff appraisal should be seen as one aspect in the context of improving the management of staff and improving the quality of management generally within the school or college. Management should be concerned with leading, supporting and resourcing staff so that they can fully contribute to the achievement of the aims of the school.

The appraisal process will only be fully functional when it takes place within an overall framework for the management of the whole organisation. This begins with a strategic view of where the school or college is heading (Fidler, 1989; Fidler, Bowles and Hart, 1991). When this is clear and other structures and processes are in place, staff appraisal can help both individuals and the organisation as a whole achieve their aims.

Organisational context

If the appraisal process is to help the school or college achieve whatever are the institution's medium term goals then it is vital, particularly for appraisers, to have clear understanding of both these goals and the resources, and other constraints within which these goals have to be pursued. If all appraisals were carried out by the head teacher, these requirements would be most easily achieved but except in the smallest of primary schools this would not be desirable. Not only would the head teacher be overloaded by appraisal interviews but this would intervene in the on-going relationship between middle managers and their staff. However, delegating appraisal to middle managers then requires those middle managers to combine a sectional and a whole school view of organisational goals when appraising their staff. For example, a head of maths appraising one of the maths staff who has tutorial and public relations responsibilities in addition to teaching maths, has to take a whole school view rather than a partisan maths point of view when helping the maths teacher to resolve conflicting priorities on his or her time, to choose development opportunities and consider career decisions. This will require a great deal of development of middle managers.

There is much evidence that the appraisal system which is introduced must be consistent with the culture of the organisation and that all those operating the process must feel a sense of ownership of the process.

The appraisal process must be carried out in the same style as the everyday operations of the school or college. If the style is, for example, informal and non-hierarchical then the appraisal process should be carried out in that spirit not taking on a formality and a corresponding artificiality which lend it an air of being unrelated to the on-going day-to-day work which it should facilitate. This is not to deny that the process is a serious one and should be given due weight but that it should be in keeping with how the school or college works for the rest of the year.

Following from this is that the appraisal scheme should be tailored to the particular institution and that the individuals within it should see the process as operating for them and the institution and not as an imposition from outside which is being carried out for someone else. The largest source of dissatisfaction with the working of an appraisal scheme in other organisations has been shown to be when those engaged in appraisal feel themselves to be carrying out the process for someone else. Thus ownership of the particular scheme which is set up in the school or college is vital.

Many staff can be expected to be diffident if not anxious when appraisal is first introduced. Appraisal is a combination of evaluation and development. Although it should be clear that the appraisal process provides a number of safeguards for appraisees:

Job description is the basis for the appraisal process;

Documentation and explicit procedures exist;

Teaching is sampled;

Context can be explored – hurdles and blocks;

Comments can be added to the appraisal statement;

'Grandparent' reporting;

Appeals procedure;

Agreed support and discipline procedures;

Grievance procedure; and

Employment legislation

Perhaps the greatest safeguard is the development of a management culture which includes a recognition of a responsibility for facilitating high performance work by teachers and lecturers.

Where any poor performers (see section 5.2) have already been assisted by professional support procedures before the appraisal process starts, appraisal can be genuinely launched as a developmental process although it will still have its evaluative aspects in identifying any minor areas in need of improvement, however, where there are poor performers who have not received such help there will be a dilemma. Appraisal procedures are going to generate the evidence to show such cases are in need of more urgent and more demanding assistance than can be provided by appraisal. Where there are no other evaluative processes diagnosing those in need of professional support procedures, the appraisal process has to carry out this function and it would be disingenuous to pretend otherwise. The alternative would be to undermine public confidence in appraisal if such cases of poor performance proceeded through the appraisal process, received inadequate help and were not seen to improve.

Appraisal of middle managers

The *Education (School Teacher Appraisal) Regulations* (SI 1511, 1991) require that all school teachers be observed teaching on two occasions and thus their teaching performance should form some part of the appraisal process. However, for those who have a major managerial responsibility within the school it should not form the main part. Their major contribution to the success of the school is their managerial efforts and it is these that should be the main focus of attention in the appraisal process. A key component in such managerial activities is the management of staff and this should be an important element to be appraised. A substantial indicator for the management of a member of staff is his or her appraisal statement and thus these should be important sources of evidence in the appraisal of those who manage staff.

This has implications for the order in which staff are appraised. Junior staff need to be appraised first so that their appraisal statements are available as evidence in the appraisal of their appraisers (*see* section 1.2 p.20). The regulations require that a copy of the appraisal statement is made available to the head teacher and so if the appraiser of middle managers is the head teacher no confidentiality is being breached, however, where the line manager of a middle manager is not the head teacher it will require agreement within the school for the appraisal statements to be released to the 'grandparent' appraisee or appraiser of middle managers. It would be in the interests of junior staff to have their appraisal statements released in this way since it provides them with an additional safeguard against being unfairly managed and appraised since such treatments would be apparent in the appraisal records.

There may be a case for not following this order of appraisals for the first cycle of appraisals since in this case where those carrying out appraisals have never previously been appraised it may be more important for them to experience the appraisal process *before* they appraise their staff.

Appraisal process

The stages of the process are the following:

 Informal self-appraisal;

 Initial planning meeting;

 Collection of evidence;

 Classroom observation and feedback;

 Self-appraisal;

 Interview;

Written statement;

Follow-up action;

Review meeting (following year); and

Next cycle.

Informal self-appraisal

The starting point for both appraisee and appraisee is an informal self-appraisal of the appraisee so that both can come to the initial planning meeting with some considered ideas about what should be included in the appraisal of the particular teacher.

Initial planning meeting

This is the short but vital meeting which plans out the whole process for the particular teacher. Any special features or specific focus for any part of the process are agreed here. Plans for classroom observation and the collection of other data including reports from other people are discussed.

This is a negotiating session. There will be many possibilities from which any choice is made. Both appraiser and appraisee need to feel that their principal wishes have been met.

The meeting should cover three areas:

1. Reassurance of the appraisee about the process;
2. Special features for observation and data collection; and
3. Timescale of the components of the process.

Collection of evidence

Most teachers do not carry out work which is the responsibility of only one manager, particularly in secondary schools and in colleges, thus there is a need to collect evidence on these other dimensions to their work.

For each individual appraisee there will be a need to agree at the initial planning meeting:

From whom?

In what form?

About what?

should data be collected.

The scheme of appraisal applied within the particular school or college will need to contain general policies dealing with the ethics of data collection so that it does not require each appraisal to agree basic rules. Such rules should cover the general form in which data should be collected – verbal or written – and how far the appraisee should have access to all such evidence.

Where teachers are in a matrix organisational structure and their work is almost equally split between two managers there may be a case for conducting one subsidiary appraisal interview with their secondary manager and allowing the results of this interview to contribute to data collection for the main appraisal interview. For this one of two or more managers would have to be designated principal appraiser and other evidence and interview results would be fed into the appraisal interview with the principal appraiser. Although this would have many advantages, the main disadvantage would be the extra time which would be required. Whilst this would not be appropriate for all appraisees, for a small number who have substantial responsibilities to two managers this may be worthwhile.

Classroom observation and feedback

All school teachers except head teachers must be observed teaching on two separate occasions by their appraiser. Since these represent two 'snapshots' from a whole year's teaching programme, the two occasions need to be chosen with care. One or both could be chosen to concentrate on some particular feature of the appraisee's teaching.

There needs to be agreement on classroom visits which covers:

> To what groups?
>
> When?
>
> To see what?
>
> For what purpose?

The pilot schemes have found it valuable to identify three parts to the observation process. The:

> Choice of lesson;
>
> Context for the lesson; and
>
> Precise focus of the observation

should be agreed at the **observation preparation** session. Following the **observation** and within two days there should be an **observation feedback** session.

The observation should lead to detailed notes of evidence about what happened in the particular areas of interest. There should be no judgements at this stage. From such evidence there can be discussion about why such events occurred and whether any changes would be of value.

Self-appraisal

The completion of a formal self-appraisal document is both worthwhile in its own right and also helps provide a common component of the agenda for the appraisal interview for all appraisees. Whilst it is a common component, the particular responses of the appraisee begin to identify any further major areas of discussion which are especially relevant for a particular appraisal interview.

A self-appraisal document which is designed to be appropriate to a particular school or college can provide the stimulus for a structured review of the past year, some prompts to formulate plans for the future and to devise putative targets for the coming year.

This completed self-appraisal document should be passed to the appraiser some days before the appraisal interview so that he or she can also undertake the same sort of private review of the appraisee's work and future and compare this with that of the appraisee.

Interview

The interview is the major part of the whole process. It brings together all the evidence from the stages already completed – self appraisal, observation of teaching and other data collection – and moves on to plan for the future. An agenda should include discussion of the following:

1. Review of the past year;
2. Praise for achievements;
3. Any improvements needed, training required to improve or organisational problems which impede performance;
4. Check job description;
5. Career plans;
6. Professional developments for the coming two years, including training, job changes or development projects; and
7. Precise targets for action for the coming two years.

Such a discussion should be conducted:

> in conducive surroundings;
> without interruptions; and
> in a problem solving mode.

There is clearly a long agenda particularly for some appraisees and it may not be possible to complete the interview in one session. In such a case, or where additional information or discussion with others is required in order to make progress on an issue, there should be an agreement to meet again to continue the interview at a convenient time in the near future: The discussion to that point should be summarised and notes made and also the remaining points to be discussed should also be recorded.

The appraisal interview will incorporate reference to the observation of teaching and other evidence which has been collected at appropriate points during the interview.

Finally, it should be borne in mind that the appraiser and appraisee may meet together every day in the normal course of their work and much of the agenda may be formalising and bringing to a conclusion wide ranging previous discussions. **All managerial communication for two years does not have to be packed into one appraisal interview!** Although in the first interview, if there has not previously been this kind of in-depth opportunity to concentrate on the work and future of each member of staff, there may be pent up demand for a comprehensive discussion on a wide range of issues.

Review of the past year The work of the past year should be reviewed to highlight successes and sources of satisfaction and areas in need of improvement or development. The importance of genuine praise and encouragement for work well done should not be under estimated. Teachers receive too little praise and can be unduly self-critical. The few who are not sufficiently self-critical should be posed questions, based on evidence, which challenge any complacent assumptions which they may hold.

Any teachers who are not operating at a basically competent level should already be receiving support procedures to help them improve (*see* section 5.2 p.281). Where such cases have not previously been recognised, the appraisal process will paint a picture of problems too great to be tackled as small improvements and remedial targets appropriate to the appraisal process. Instead professional support procedures are the proper course of action with intensive assistance over a relatively short timescale to help them improve.

For any teachers who in the past have been competent but are showing signs of distress or temporary poor performance, some form of counselling in addition to the appraisal process may be necessary. The appraisal interview provides an excellent opportunity for managerial counselling (*see* section 4.3.2 p.252) in order to discover the most appropriate form of more professional counselling.

Such cases as the last two paragraphs have considered will be the exception for most appraisals but where they exist they have to be recognised and relevant action taken rather than continue with an appraisal process that is inappropriate to their needs. For the overwhelming majority of teachers who are basically competent but who have some areas of their work in need of improvement, the remaining sections of the interview are particularly appropriate.

Improvements and developments There are two distinct ways of improving the service given to children and young people by teaching staff:

1. Improving personal performance standards; and
2. Developing the job.

Improvements involve the raising of personal performance standards for an individual teacher for some aspect of the job whilst the job remains unchanged, e.g. getting to classes on time, marking and returning work within a set time period. Developments, on the other hand, involve changing and improving the task to be done, e.g. devising new ways of grouping children in class leading to improved learning, devising a new teaching scheme for a particular aspect of the curriculum as shown in figure 6.1.1.

For most appraisees the outcomes of appraisal should be a mixture of improvements and developments. There is a tendency to implicitly use a deficit model of performance by which all departures from some notional 'ideal' are regarded as areas to be improved. There are three dangers of this approach:

1. Not all departures from a high level of performance are equally important:
2. Changing aspects of the job may yield far larger improvements to pupils than improving personal performance in an unchanged job; and
3. A deficit model encourages a failure mentality since most individuals will fall short of the 'ideal'.

These follow from an unreasonable and unrealistic expectation of performance.

Performance standards To prevent the adoption of a deficit model it is important to identify appropriate standards of competent perform-

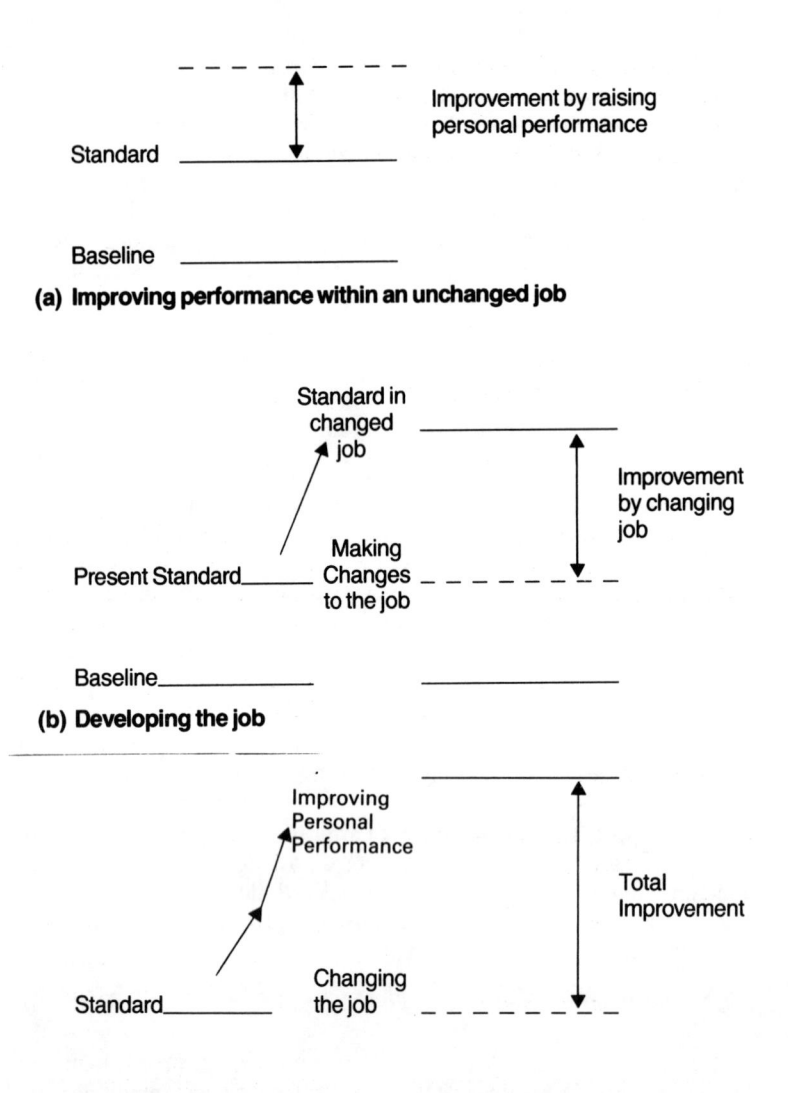

(a) Improving performance within an unchanged job

Standard — Improvement by raising personal performance

Baseline

(b) Developing the job

Present Standard / Making Changes to the job → Standard in changed job

Improvement by changing job

Baseline

(c) Improved performance in changed job

Standard / Changing the job → Improving Personal Performance

Total Improvement

Baseline

Figure 6.1.1 Improvement of performance and development of the job

ance – what can reasonably be expected of all staff day in and day out when they work in a well-motivated but sustainable way. Much discussion will be required at institutional level to tease out such standards and to define policies which reflect appropriate expectations of how staff in the school or college will operate. Carrying out whole institutional discussion of such issues helps to ensure that all appraisers are applying consistent standards and appraisees know what is expected of them.

Organisational problems The appraisal interview is also an opportunity for appraisees to raise any organisational problems which obstruct their work. These can range from relationships with other staff, lack of resources, or a lack of commitment from their appraiser. Where the appraiser recognises an obligation, as part of his or her staff management responsibility, for the successful performance of the appraisee, he or she will be seeking to meet all reasonable requests and jointly work towards the solution of problems. The appraiser will wish to know how they can be of greater assistance to each of their staff.

Check job description As appraisal interviews are only held every two years and much can have changed in the school or college in the meantime, the appraisee's job description should be checked to examine how far it describes the current job and to amend it if it has changed or to amend it if as part of the appraisal targets some change to the job has been made. This also provides a convenient opportunity to reappraise priorities between different aspects of the job and make some of these targets for the coming period if that is appropriate.

Career plans Any developments which take place as a result of appraisal need to be a combination of making progress for the school or college and also for the individual. For most staff such progress will be associated with career developments thus the career plans of the appraisee should be discussed so that the appraiser can give advice and feedback and developments can be considered which further realistic career plans of the appraisee.

Targets The targets are in addition to the normal ongoing more routine work thus they should be few in number – probably not more than five at most and may be:

Remedial	bringing an aspect of the job back to an acceptable level of performance;
Developmental	developing an aspect of the job;
Problem solving	finding a way of overcoming some problem aspect of the job; and

Personal development   identifying some temporary task which contributes to personal development but which may not be part of the enduring job description.

The targets can be expected to change regularly. Many will be completed in one year. Targets should be:

Challenging but achievable;

Precise as possible; and

Worthwhile to the organisation and the individual.

Questions to ask to help identify and firm up on targets:

1. How will you know when it is achieved?
2. How will you know you have done it well enough?
3. What is the challenging component (e.g. time, quality, innovative, uncertainty)?
4. What help and resources are needed from others in order to achieve it?
5. When should it be completed?
6. What are the potential sources of failure?
7. Are there any milestones or sub-targets along the way?

A successful appraisal interview should both involve a beneficial process and also lead to worthwhile outcomes.

Written statement

The appraiser is required to write an appraisal statement in consultation with the appraisee. Thus as soon as possible after the interview the appraiser should draft a report covering the main features of the interview discussion and including any conclusions reached and any targets for action. This should be shown to the appraisee and any differences of emphasis or opinion should be negotiated. In most cases agreement should be easily reached. Where there is no agreement, the appraiser should write the report whereupon the appraisee would be entitled to add comments or to complain about the appraisal statement.

The appraiser must show a copy of the final appraisal statement to the appraisee who then has 20 days in which to add comments in writing. Where there is a complaint from the appraisee about the statement, a review officer is to be appointed who did not take part in the original appraisal (SI 1551, 1991; para 11) to conduct a review of the appraisal with wide powers including the amendment of the statement or the ordering of a new appraisal under a new appraiser.

The targets within any appraisal statement are to be in a separate annex so that these can be circulated independently of the remainder of the statement. Targets requiring training or development are to be made available to both school INSET co-ordinators and to appropriate LEA advisers. The targets are also to be made available to the chairperson of governors upon request.

Follow-up action

At the appraisal interview and in the report there will be references to plans and targets. These may involve

- Attendance at training courses;
- Coaching;
- Work shadowing;
- Change of job;
- Extra resources;
- Developments to the job; and
- Personal development.

Some of these may involve negotiation and require the sanction of others or the deployment of resources from limited funds. In which case, at the time of writing the report these may be provisional or even speculative. At the earliest opportunity any such tentative plans should be confirmed or altered so that as soon as possible feasible and reasonably precise plans can be agreed.

All parties should play their part in helping to realise the plans. What has been agreed by the school and manager should be delivered to facilitate the efforts of the appraisee. There should be brief but regular follow-up to discuss the achievement of progress on the plans. If any major event occurs which throws the targets into doubt, the plans should be renegotiated at the earliest opportunity rather than wait until the review meeting in the following year to rather limply discover that no progress had been made due to circumstances outside the appraisee's control.

Review meeting

The review meeting during the early stages of the following year is the formal opportunity to review progress on the plans and targets.

Any agreed changes to the plans and targets made at the appraisal interview should be recorded in the appraisal statement. The fact that the review has taken place and its date should be recorded on the statement.

Next cycle

Having completed one two-yearly cycle much valuable experience will have been gained with which to begin the next cycle. And in addition there will be progress to review on the plans and targets which were set at the first appraisal interview. This is the pattern for the future – it is the first cycle which is the unusual one when there are no plans to review at the first appraisal interview and a whole range of pent up issues which have never been discussed before.

6.2 Formulating an action plan

Bob Cooper and Brian Fidler

Introduction

The object of this book has been to discuss a range of issues which it is necessary to consider before an attempt is made to introduce a system of appraisal into a school or college. It has also brought together in the form of case studies some of the accumulated experience of those who have already travelled some way along the path, and have set up systems of appraisal. The stage has been reached where the formal appraisal of school teachers is a statutory requirement and that of college lecturers is agreed. Therefore all educational institutions will have to face a number of these issues if they have not already done so. The nature of the education system in this country at present is such that individual institutions have a great deal of freedom to initiate systems which, in the professional judgement of the staff, are appropriate for that school or college at this moment in time. The *Education Reform Act* 1988 has given schools and colleges more freedom to manage but within a more prescriptive overall framework imposed from central government.

In the case of grant maintained schools, appraisal fits into this framework quite straightforwardly in that the school governing body is the appraising body and is charged with setting up an appraisal scheme for the school, within the National Regulations, which is appropriate for that school. The situation is less satisfactory for county and voluntary schools. Here the LEA is the appraising body. However, Circular 12/91 (DES, 1991) makes it quite clear that schools should have freedom within the regulations to tailor any LEA scheme to meet the needs of the school:

Subject to their own responsibilities, appraising bodies will wish to give schools scope within the Regulations to put in place arrangements for appraisal. It would be appropriate for the governing body to approve the school's arrangements.

(para. 5)

There is now a great deal of accumulated wisdom about both the introduction and the ongoing process of appraisal in educational organisations. It is still considerably less than the experience of industry in this regard but it is nevertheless significant. If this knowledge and experience can be shared it will undoubtedly prove to be of value.

This last section attempts to bring together some of the facts and some of the ideas which have been discussed more fully elsewhere. The attempt has been made to put together an action plan, a model which incorporates the stages of an implementation strategy. At each stage the range of possibilities is briefly discussed. Like all models it is inevitably simplified and abbreviated but it is hoped that this will provide a suitable summary and conclusion to this book.

Climate and culture

The importance of a good general climate of staff relations has been stressed in almost all of the articles in this book. For a staff appraisal scheme to be effective it needs to be set in a climate of mutual trust and confidence. The introduction of an appraisal scheme into a school or college is part of the general management of a developing institution; it should not be something which is merely bolted on in response to external pressures. It will only succeed if it is seen to be an integral part of the existing management practice. Because of this the form and the style of the scheme adopted should vary from one institution to another just as the management and leadership style will inevitably vary from one institution to another. Even if the procedures for appraisal are standardised by a local authority, individual schools and colleges will need to discuss how best to adapt those procedures to fit into the existing management framework. If the general management style is bureaucratic then it will probably be more appropriate to introduce a standardised and rational system. If the management style is more collegial, or what Handy (1985) calls a 'person culture', then the form and the procedures may have a looser, more democratic nature. Whatever form or style is adopted the channels of communication between the senior management and the staff need to be effective. Information needs to be shared and staff need to feel able to discuss the issues freely and openly

Institutional plans

One of the factors which all the successful organisations investigated by Peters and Waterman (1982) in the USA and Goldsmith and Clutterbuck (1984) in the UK had in common was that they had clear objectives and a shared sense of where the firm was going. Educational institutions need a similar sense of common purpose or strategy. Of course the essential purpose of any educational institution is the education of its students, but the way in which that purpose is to be achieved needs to be discussed and agreed by the staff concerned (Fidler, Bowles and Hart, 1991). There needs to be a shared sense of where the institution is going and the means by which the objectives are to be attained. Once some kind of agreement has been reached about objectives then it is possible to discuss ways in which the resources available to the institution can be employed to meet those objectives. This will include looking at the most valuable resources available – namely the human resources. A policy can be agreed about staff development needs in the light of the discussion concerning objectives. The general staff development policy can then be further refined at departmental and sectional level.

All staff development should be seen in the light of both institutional and individual needs. If the institutional policy is agreed first then the necessity for some system to identify individual needs in the light of this policy becomes obvious.

It is also important at this point to fully establish the many constraints which inevitably surround all development activities. All institutions have financial constraints and have to make economic choices. The financial constraints on education at the moment are particularly severe and individual teachers need to be made fully aware of the reality of the situation which individual schools and LEAs have to face. There are also constraints upon the institution in relation to time and the availability of expertise. In an ideal situation the school or college may want to send one of its staff on a particular course which would be of benefit to both the individual and the institution, but it may not be able to do so because that member of staff's expertise cannot be replaced at this moment.

Once a need has been identified it is right that action should be agreed to meet that need, but the action must also take fully into account the various constraints which have to be considered. There is no doubt that the introduction of a staff appraisal system generates expectations about in-service opportunities. This indeed is one of its functions. The longer term success of any scheme introduced will depend on how those expectations are fulfilled. Many writers of case studies have spoken of the honeymoon period which occurs at the beginning of a new headship or on the introduction of a new scheme. Nothing can ruin a honeymoon faster than expectations not being realised! If all parties in the appraisal process are aware of the background against which decisions have to be made then it is possible to ensure realistic expectations.

Consultation

Appraisal is an emotive subject for many teachers and lecturers, and everyone needs time to adjust to new ideas and new situations. Means must be found if a new system of appraisal is to be introduced into a school or college to provide opportunities for the staff to talk about the ideas and to discuss their individual concerns and their worries. This cannot always be done in large open meetings, in which many staff are diffident about speaking in front of large numbers of colleagues. The consultative process takes time but there is a large amount of evidence, not least from Japanese industry, to testify to its effectiveness. This process needs to be managed. Time is required for individuals to come to terms with new ideas but there should be a continuing sense of purpose and direction during this period rather than stagnation. There should be a timetable of meetings and activities which whilst it has a relaxed timescale also has a sense of progression.

Part of the process may be to invite visiting speakers who have already introduced a system of appraisal, to talk about their experiences. Another part may be to go through the very necessary preliminary process of job analysis and the development of job descriptions. These activities inevitably involve staff and enable them to feel part of the decision making and planning procedures.

Planning

Scheme design

Whilst a natural focus when setting up appraisal is on the appraisal of individuals, it should also be borne in mind that an appraisal scheme is also a means of improving the running of the school or college and so there is an important institutional dimension to the design of the appraisal scheme.

Strategy Appraisal should be consistent with the overall strategy of the school or college and have been incorporated into the strategic plans of the institution (Fidler, Bowles and Hart, 1991). This is especially important as it:

1. Is such a huge process;
2. Consumes resources;
3. Takes large amounts of time;
4. Represents an enormous opportunity to improve communication and gain commitment; and
5. Can improve motivation and climate.

Organisational structure A suitable organisational structure is critical both to facilitating the strategic direction of the school or college and also for being the framework within which appraisers and appraisees have an ongoing relationship (*see* section 4.1 p.197). Thus the organisational structure should be reviewed before appraisal is implemented and may well need further change after the first cycle of appraisals since much new data will have come to light in addition to the practical experience of having worked with a revised structure.

Staff management Appraisal should take place within the context of staff management (*see* sections 1.1 p.1 and 2.1 p.38). Work will be needed with managers to clarify expectations of the task of leadership and management which include how appraisal fits into these. In particular, managers have to see the benefits of appraisal to staff management in order for it to remain a 'live' activity rather than a dull bureaucratic imposition from someone else.

Practical steps

Once agreement has been established in principle there are a range of issues which need to be discussed and upon which decisions need to be taken. Many of these issues are discussed more fully in Sections 1, 2, 4 and 5 of this book. For those in colleges, a useful set of discussion papers has been assembled by Field (1987).

It is generally appropriate to establish a working party or a series of working parties with clear terms of reference and with a definite timetable to produce firm recommendations for the staff as a whole. The working parties should have a clear brief to bear in mind all the various resource implications and constraints when they are making their reports.

In particular the costing of the time required for all aspects of the process will need to be given careful attention. This should include any administrative or secretarial requirements in addition to the time of teaching staff.

Some of the issues upon which decisions need to be made are as follows. These are not prioritised in any way. Some of these decisions need to be taken in the light of the National Regulations and any LEA framework.

1. What is the purpose and style of appraisal? The broad aims of appraisal which we identify are to:

(a) Carry credibility with the public as a check on the quality of work in schools and colleges;

(b) Lead to improvements in the learning experiences of pupils and students; and

(c) Lead to greater job satisfaction of all those who work in schools and colleges.

What priority is to be accorded to each of them? On the accountability–development display on p.4, where should the proposed system be placed? How far should the process be a professional dialogue between peers and how far should it be a dialogue between superior and subordinate, or manager and managed? Is an objective of the system really to be the improvement of the performance of every teacher? Answers to these questions will reflect the values of the organisation and the style of management into which the appraisal process must fit. Agreement on these fundamental issues has implications for many of the subsequent more detailed questions.

2. Who is to be appraised and who is to do the appraisal? Decisions will need to be taken about the overall comprehensiveness of the scheme. Will it include every member of staff or will it be voluntary in the first instance? The appraising body has to ensure that half the teachers for whom it is responsible begin the process by 1st September 1992, and all have begun by 1st September 1994.

In addition to appraisal by superordinate, is there to be subordinate or peer group appraisal? Will there be any part played in the appraisal by 'grandparent' (*see* section 6.1 p.334–35) – that is appraisal not by the immediate superior, but by the person one above him or her in the hierarchy? How will the appeal procedure work? Is the head teacher going to appraise all the staff? How is the head or the principal to be appraised? How is appraisal by line managers to operate? Are there clear line managers for each member of staff? Are the line managers – that is, in general, heads of department – aware that they have that kind of management responsibility? Will the appraisal system include non-teaching staff? How are part-time staff to be fitted in?

3. Collection of information and confidentiality Decisions will need to be made about the confidentiality of some of the discussions which will take place as part of an appraisal system. An agreed system will need to be worked out concerning the nature of the records themselves, what information is to be written down, where the completed records are to be kept, and who is entitled to see those records. All successful systems of appraisal depend upon the cooperation of staff. If a member of staff is concerned that the things he or she says as part of the appraisal process may be used against them at a later date, there is little chance that there will be a full and frank exchange of views which is the essence of the whole appraisal process.

The Regulations (SI 1511, 1991) state that the head teacher shall receive a copy of the appraisal statement, and if an LEA school, the CEO or nominated officer, any review officer and any new appraiser after the start of the cycle. The chair of governors may request a copy of the targets. The head teacher should keep a copy of the statement for at least three months after the end of the appraisal cycle. They may be retained longer and two cycles may be an appropriate length of time. Information from the statement may be used in discipline or dismissal proceedings (see section 5.2 p.280).

The Circular recommends that all those with access to statements 'should treat them as confidential'. Except for court or tribunal proceedings or a police investigation, statements should not be disclosed without the permission of the appraisee. All documents produced for the appraisal process other than the statement should be destroyed after the statement has been finalised.

Annex A to Circular 12/91 presents guidance and a code of practice for the collection of information other than through classroom observation. The general principles suggested convey a tone of trust, sensitivity, and lack of bias in the process.

The appraiser and appraisee should agree about the information to be collected at the initial planning meeting including any specific aspects on which information should concentrate.

Information

(a) Appraisers will need copies of relevant school policies, the appraisee's job description and to appreciate national and LEA policies and requirements in addition to the school context for the appraisee's job (paras 12, 13 and 14)

(b) Information should be sought and presented in an objective way and where personal opinion is sought (for example reactions to a change) this should be made clear (para 23)

(c) Information provided should be fair and considered and those making comments should be prepared to acknowledge and substantiate them (para 20)

(d) Any general comments should be supported by specific examples (para 6)

(e) Those making critical comments should be asked to discuss them directly with the appraisee before they are used (para 22)

(f) Information should relate only to the professional performance of the appraisee (para 9)

(g) Anonymous information should not be used (para 8)

Interviews

Any interviews used to collect information should be one to one and the purpose and the way in which information should be treated should be made clear (paras 7 and 19)

Written submissions

Any written submissions should remain confidential to the author, appraiser and appraisee (para 21)

4. *Form of the documentation* There needs to be an agreed job description which includes a statement about standards of performance as a prerequisite to any appraisal interview. A point to bear in mind when considering the documentation which will result from the appraisal is that no system can ensure that there will be continuity from year to year in the pairings of appraiser and appraisee and if there are inadequate records it means starting from the beginning again with someone new.

In practice most schemes have devised some form of self-appraisal checklist, together with a form of record of decisions which can be agreed by both parties at the end of the interview.

The self-appraisal document should cover most of the areas for discussion at the interview. Thus it should look back over the previous year and identify high points and low points, it should reflect the professional context of the appraisee's work and any organisational problems, it should consider career aspirations and developments, training and development needs, and finally any targets for action in the coming period.

The appraisal statement following the interview is to be in two parts. The major part is an account of the appraisal interview and the areas covered within it. Any targets for action are to be recorded separately so that they can be available to the chairperson of governors and staff development coordinator of both school and LEA.

5. *Venue and timing* Not least among the decisions which have to be made are those concerning where and at what time of the year the interviews are to take place. In some cases this may be no problem because one person will be doing almost all of the appraising and that

OVERVIEW & ACTION PLAN

person will have an office available which can be used for the purpose. In other cases, where it has been decided that the task of appraising should be spaced among the middle management as well as the senior management, there may well be problems of both time and place which have to be addressed. If heads of department and section heads are to do this as part of their management responsibility, then this needs to be fully acknowledged. Time should specifically be allocated within working hours for this purpose and suitable office accommodation free from interruptions by pupils or telephones needs to be found.

Should appraisals be a biennial event for all? Or should they be at different frequencies for some? Should there be more than one interview per year? And by different appraisers?

6. *Referral system* From time to time there will inevitably be differences of opinion about certain aspects of a review. In some cases it may be that the appraisee feels that he or she is being unfairly treated in some way. In other cases the appraiser may feel that he or she is not completely competent to deal with the issues raised. In some cases there may be a genuine clash of personalities which cannot easily be resolved by the two parties concerned. There is a need to establish and to agree some form of referral system through which the two parties, either separately or jointly, may refer certain aspects to a different authority. This is more difficult to arrange if the head teacher is undertaking all of the interviews.

The Regulations recognise that there may need to be some adjustment for individuals of their appraiser and that an appraiser can be changed at any stage of the process by the head teacher.

There is a right of appeal against an appraisal statement. Any comments can be added by the appraisee within 20 working days of having access to the statement. There is also an entitlement to complain about the statement. The Regulations require a review officer to be appointed who has not been involved in the original appraisal. He or she is appointed by the head teacher unless the head carried out the original appraisal in which case the appraising body appoints a suitable person.

After taking evidence from the complainant, the review officer has wide powers which range from

> Allowing the appraisal statement to stand;
>
> Adding comments;
>
> Amending the statement with the agreement of the appraiser; to
>
> Ordering a fresh appraisal and statement under a new appraiser.

7. *Classroom observation* What form it should take and the extent of training in observation techniques, all need to be discussed.

Whatever is decided it is important that as part of the process of appraisal the appraisee should receive adequate feedback about their performance as a teacher from someone who knows the particular context and the special difficulties of that school or college. The object of the whole exercise is the improvement of performance, and one of the best ways of improving one's own performance as a teacher is to receive informed feedback about that performance.

The Regulations require that teaching shall be observed by the appraiser on at least two occasions. The Circular expects that the period of observation will total at least one hour and that the observation will normally be discussed with the teacher within two working days.

Are any other forms of data on classroom performance to be used as the basis for the appraisal interview?

8. Standards of performance Some general guidelines which address the notion of expectations of professional standards within the particular school or college will be found very helpful by both appraisers and appraisees alike. These will inevitably reflect the values and approach of the whole organisation. Their articulation will be a very valuable exercise in communication in order to develop further a shared culture within which appraisal is easier to operate.

9. Outcomes What mechanisms are to be used to collate staff development needs identified through appraisal? How are training needs and other developmental opportunities to be co-ordinated across the organisation? How is feedback on individual staff development plans to be given?

What mechanisms are to be used to feed into the management structure, organisational problems which are identified as a result of one or more individual appraisals?

What contingency plans should there be to cope with any poor performers who are identiied as a result of appraisal? What resources does the school or college have to provide advice, counselling, coaching and support for those who may need them?

Confirming the decision

When the working parties have completed their work there will be a need to share their recommendations with the staff as a whole and to confirm further proceedings. It is essential to ensure the commitment of all staff as far as possible, but of the line managers or heads of departments in particular if they are to operate the scheme.

The case studies (*see* Section 3) in general confirm what has been found elsewhere that, if there has been a full and thorough debate on all the issues, and staff have had opportunities to examine the arguments, there will by that time be a high level of commitment on the part of some staff which will be to some extent counteracted by the mere acceptance of the inevitable on the part of others.

Additionally an opportunity may need to be found for a more wide ranging discussion among the staff as a whole on questions of value and the assumptions behind the management models which are being advocated. These matters are discussed in Sections 1, 4 and 5.

Training

The next stage in the process of introduction will be to arrange the form of training. This may take a variety of forms and its extent will vary according to the needs of any particular institution. In addition to training in the essential interpersonal skills which are part of the interview process and which are discussed in Sections 4.3.0, 4.3.1 and 4.3.2 there may be a need to consider general management processes in the institution as a whole.

Initial training in interview skills, classroom observation skills and other identified skills will be required but there will be ongoing maintenance training required to develop and improve these skills once the appraisal system is working.

If middle managers are to carry out the appraisal of members of their teams and they are to be expected to carry out a greater managerial role, then some consideration should be given to their management training needs as a whole since **an appraisal system is only as good as the managers who have to operate the system.**

Training will not only be required for appraisers but also teachers who are to be appraised. They need to understand the system fully and to have realistic expectations of their role within the process so that they can both contribute and benefit.

Implementation

Issues

1. *Awareness and ownership* These must be present before implementation begins.

2. *Other systems in place* The organisational structure, systems for

delivering adequate training and development and job descriptions need all to be in place before implementation.

3. *Appraisal manager or co-ordinator*   In a medium or large school or college the whole appraisal process needs managing both initially and as the process continues. A person is needed to have an overview and to track and monitor the progress of each appraisal.

4. *Appraisal evaluator*   Particularly for the first cycle of appraisal because it is such a large process, is so important and there may be so many anxieties it may be worthwhile appointing a fairly junior member of staff as an appraisal evaluator to put together a picture of how the process is working quite independently of those managing the process (*see* section 3.3.2).

5. *Whole school review*   One way of beginning thinking about the appraisal process and ensuring that it is clearly tied to institutional improvement is to begin with a whole school review. This sets the tone and also generates much useful data.

6. *Job descriptions*   Where adequate job descriptions do not yet exist another preparation for appraisal is to hold interviews to negotiate job descriptions.

7. *Pilot some appraisals*   Before appraisals are to begin for large numbers allow volunteers to pilot the process and report back.

Working party

It is as well to give the people concerned with the interviewing the opportunity to undertake an interview at an early date following the training process. There are often a number of fears and apprehensions which can be overcome through the first real experience of conducting an appraisal interview. One can take part in simulated situations during the training process but it is never quite the same as facing a colleague as part of the real thing. A working party can then fine tune the process.

Monitoring

Following the first interview situation it is often advisable to create the chance for those who have been acting as appraisers to come together to discuss any problems encountered and to assess the experience. This sharing of experience is a further part of the training process and is itself a development activity.

Completion of interviews

It is important to try to ensure that all the interviewing is completed by the end of the academic year so that the cycle of appraisal which is of course a continuous one, can have some kind of shape and symmetry.

Allocation of resources

The appraisal interview has a review stage, a diagnostic stage, and a commitment to action stage. Having obtained that commitment to action on the part of individual members of staff the school or college as a whole has to find the resources to facilitate that action. How this is done will vary from one institution to another. A number of schools and colleges now have a senior member of staff identified to make these decisions. In smaller institutions it may well be the head teacher who makes the final decision. In some larger schools and colleges there is a staff development committee which has a wide and representative membership, and whose terms of reference are to make recommendations in the light of the institutional plan. However the decisions are made it is important that they are fair and are seen to be fair by staff.

Ideally the decisions on training and other developmental resources should be taken as close to the appraisal process as possible – both in terms of time and the people taking the decisions. If there are funds for training and development devolved to and within the institution, the feedback and accountability of the decisions should be facilitated.

Evaluation

Like other aspects of the work of a school or college the appraisal scheme, once it has been set up and is running, will need to be evaluated. This can either be done through a form of self-evaluation – asking the various participants in the scheme for their views on the process and the outcomes of the system – or alternatively some kind of external audit might be set up. This could take the form of inviting an outside consultant, either a local adviser or inspector or someone from a local college or university to critically evaluate the effectiveness and the efficiency of the whole.

Revision and further training

Whatever form of evaluation is set up the results need to be carefully considered by all those involved in the scheme and then changes made in the light of that evaluation. Teachers are constantly evaluating and appraising the work of their students and attempting to bring about changes in behaviour as a result of that appraisal. On the whole teachers are less good about undertaking systematic evaluation of the school as an organisation and then acting upon the results of that evaluation. Polytechnics and colleges whose courses have been validated by the CNAA are very used to this way of developing courses and have benefited from the process a great deal.

Conclusion

The costs in terms of professional time required to operate an effective appraisal system are high as has been pointed out throughout this volume. They cannot adequately be met within present resources and will require additional funding from central government beyond that already committed. The major costs are not the start-up and training costs but the ongoing costs year after year plus the resourcing of the increased expectations of training and development. This would show a commitment to higher standards in a very positive way.

Like all innovations, appraisal can either be regarded as an opportunity to be seized or as an imposition to be endured. Unless staff appraisal is seized as an opportunity by which the organisation and the individual can both benefit there is a danger that the result will be the imposition of a bureaucratic assessment system which will be inimical to a profession dedicated to development and improvement.

We believe that opportunity is best seized at individual institutional level as part of the management process. As a guiding principle for the implementation of any appraisal system we end with our three overall aims for a staff appraisal system which should:

1. Carry credibility with the public as a check on the quality of work in schools and colleges;
2. Lead to improvements in the learning experiences of pupils and students;
3. Lead to greater job satisfaction of all those who work in schools and colleges.

Contributors

Keith Barnes is Deputy Head at The Emmbrook School, Wokingham, with a brief that includes INSET and staff development. He steered the work on appraisal through its development and participated in the trial by appraising a Head of Faculty. He has a scientific background and teaches physics to A level.

Vanessa Champion was involved as a trainer in Cumbria LEA for the duration of the National Appraisal Pilot and has worked extensively in training for appraisal at all levels in both schools and colleges. She is currently Director (Appraisal Training Team) Charlotte Mason College, Ambleside.

Bob Cooper was formerly the Head of the Education Management Department at Crewe & Alsager College of Higher Education. For the past two years he has been coordinator of a DES funded research project looking at Profiles for Teachers, and has been the Secretary of the Consortium for Education Management Development.

David Cracknell is Group Director Education Services for Cheshire County Council but until the end of 1990 he was Deputy County Education Officer in East Sussex. He has taught in schools and in a college of education and worked as an education officer in Warwickshire, Leeds and Wakefield. Alongside a number of national commitments, he is active in the Society of Education Officers, particularly in the Industry Committee.

Peter Delaney has been Head of St Edmunds RC Primary School, Salford, since 1972. He has contributed at the highest level to a wide range of in-service initiatives related to school management in general and appraisal in particular. His appraisal courses for senior staff in primary schools are well established at Manchester University. He has also lectured at conferences and courses organised by the Industrial Society, BEMAS, Manchester Polytechnic and the North West Educational Management Centre at North Cheshire College.

Keith Diffey is Deputy Head teacher, Southway Comprehensive School, Plymouth. He has recently completed research into the nature of interaction in teacher appraisal interviews. He has taught in Africa and the USA as well as a number of secondary schools in this country.

Ian Duckett teaches English and communications across a wide range of courses at Barnet College of Further Education, where he is currently involved in a number of curriculum development projects, chair of the Staff Development Committee of the Academic Board and a flexible learning adviser. He is author of *Piloting Appraisal* and an Open College publication on appraisal in FE.

Bertie Everard is the former Education and Training Manager of ICI. In 1982 he wrote the first of three books on school management and became a

Visiting Fellow of the University of London Institute of Education. He has assisted in producing competency frameworks for three lead bodies and two examining bodies.

Brian Fidler is Senior Lecturer in Education Management at the University of Reading. His main interest is the management of educational institutions. He is course leader for the MSc in School Management. He is Treasurer of BEMAS and chair of the Education Management Development Committee. Previous publications include *Staff Appraisal in Schools and Colleges*, *Effective Local Management of Schools*, and *Planning Your School's Strategy*.

Dallas Hackett was recently Adviser, Salford LEA. Dallas taught in secondary schools and worked as deputy and head teacher in Salford before joining the appraisal project team participating in national pilot work. She led Salford's implementation of teacher and head teacher appraisal and is now active in appraisal training and consultancy work.

Iain Johnston was the head teacher of Arnside National School, Cumbria. The school was one of the first in Cumbria to participate in the National Pilot Study into school teacher appraisal and Iain was amongst the first group of head teachers to be appraised. Iain is currently working for the LEA to support the implementation of statutory appraisal.

Dr Chris Kyriacou is lecturer in Educational Psychology at the University of York, Department of Educational Studies. He is a former teacher of mathematics in secondary schools, and has published widely on aspects of teaching, particularly effective teaching, teacher stress, and teacher appraisal. He has written two books, *Effective Teaching in Schools* (Blackwell, 1986) and *Essential Teaching Skills* (Blackwell 1991). He has regularly run workshops in schools on teacher appraisal.

Barry Mountford has been a change agent inside and outside the school and college system. He is currently Principal Lecturer at Crewe & Alsager College of Higher Education. His particular interests are in educational issues relating to values, school/college quality assurance systems and the management of change.

Kevin Quinlan is Development Officer, Cheshire Local Education Authority. Kevin trained as a further education teacher and taught at a College of Further Education and a Tertiary College for eight years before joining Cheshire LEA where, for the past five years, he has been working across a wide range of education and organisation developments.

David Trethowan works currently as a management and training consultant from his home at Gorwydd Farm, Llanddewi Brefi, Dyfed. His clients include LEAs, individual schools, universities and colleges as well as international companies. He has 25 years of experience of education management, fifteen of them as headteacher of a successful comprehensive school in Sussex.

David Turley is Director of Personnel for the Royal Borough of Kensington & Chelsea. His experience covers appointments in both public and private sectors, and also includes a period in a line management role. He is a Fellow of the Institute of Personnel Management.

Mike VaughanEdwards is Deputy Head, Birchwood Community High School. After working in the theatre Mike VaughanEdwards completed a PGCE at Manchester Polytechnic. He has taught in a range of schools in

Cheshire. His current responsibilities include curriculum, INSET and staff development. He is completing an MSc dissertation on the effective use of school development plans.

John West-Burnham is Development Officer: Teacher Performance for Cheshire LEA. He taught in schools, further and adult education before teaching education management in higher education for five years. He is now responsible for supporting the implementation of teacher appraisal in Cheshire schools.

Notes

National agreement

1. In June 1991 the National Joint Council concluded an agreement on staff development, training and appraisal (NJC, 1991). This proposes a National Framework within which there will be local schemes agreed at LEA or college level. The scheme has to be agreed by 31 August 1992 and all staff have to have completed one year of a two year cycle by 31 August 1994. Although this is not a statutory agreement, the reference book for lecturers' conditions of service has been modified to require them to participate in an agreed local scheme. The National Framework for the appraisal process is similar to that for school teachers with the following differences:

    A recommendation for institutional or departmental review preceding individual appraisal; and
    Positive promotion of equal opportunities.

    The National Framework has appraisers determined by the governing body of the college and subject to approval by the LEA. The requirements for appraisers in terms of their position in the organisation imply that they should normally be line managers although the need for credibility and flexibility is recommended. It is recommended that appraisers carry out no more than eight to ten appraisals in a year and less than that if they also carry out teaching or task observation in addition.
    The National Framework for the appraisal process consists of:

    Initial meeting;
    Self appraisal;
    Evaluation of the facilitation of learning;
    Collection of other data:
       information from college or departmental reviews,
       job description,
       outcome of evaluation of teaching or other activity, and
       previous appraisal record;
    Appraisal interview; and
    Agreed record.

    The evaluation of the facilitation is likely to involve the observation of teaching for those with a major teaching contribution. This may be carried out by someone other than the appraiser. This can both reduce the load on appraisers and ensure that the evaluator has appropriate teaching expertise. The outcome of this evaluation has to be provided for the appraisal interview. The agreed record is expected to contain targets for the coming period and a range of recommended staff development activities.

2. Subsequently the pilots have informed the *National Framework for Staff Development, Training and Appraisal* (NJC, 1991).

3. This was prior to the implementation of compulsory appraisal in September 1992.

4. In the light of the National Framework this seems to be the case.

5. In this respect it is disappointing that the NJC has opted for compulsory appraisal.

6. National appraisal regulations correctly make these three people mandatory recipients whilst copies go to the CEO and chair of governors on request only.

7. The Further Education Unit has undertaken field trials of the Training and Development Lead Body standards to establish their relevance to staff in FE.

References

ACAS 1986 *Teachers' Dispute: Report of the appraisal training group.* London:. ACAS
Adair J 1983 *Effective Leadership.* Pan
Alpander G 1980 Training supervisor to criticise constructively. *Personnel Journal* March, 1980
Banks C G & Murphy K R 1985 Towards narrowing the research– practice gap in performance appraisal *Personnel Psychology* **38** (2) 335–45
Banner D K & Graber J M 1985 Critical issues in performance appraisal. *J. Management Development* **4**(1): 26–35
Barber & Klein 1983 Merit Pay and Teacher Evaluations. *Phi Delta Kappan* Dec. p.247–251
Barnet College 1989 *Pilot appraisal scheme working party: notes for guidance*
Beer M 1986 Performance Appraisal. In Lorsch, J W (ed.) *Handbook of Organizational Behaviour.* Prentice Hall Inc., Englewood Cliffs, NJ pp.286–300
Bell L (ed) 1988 *Appraising teachers in schools? a practical guide.* Routledge
Benne K D & Sheats P. 1948 Functional roles of group members. *Journal of Social Issues* **4** (Spring 1948)
Bernardin H J & Klatt L A 1985 Managerial appraisal systems: has practice caught up to the state of the art? *Personnel Administrator* November 1985, pp.79–86
Beveridge W 1975 *The interview in staff appraisal.* George Allen and Unwin
Blackpool and the Fylde College 1990 *7307 Further and Adult Education Teachers Certificate: Handbook and Record of Achievement.* Blackpool and the Fylde College
Blumberg A & Greenfield W 1980 *The effective principal; Perspectives on School Leadership.* Allyn & Bacon. Boston
Boak G 1991 *Developing managerial competencies* Pitman.
Bollington R Hopkins D West M 1990 *An introduction to teacher appraisal.* Cassell
Boyatzis R E 1982 *The competent manager* Wiley. New York
Brading L & Wright V 1990 Performance-Related Pay. *Personnel Management* Factsheet 30, June 1990
Bradley H et al 1989 *Report on the evaluation of the school teacher appraisal pilot study – report to the national steering group, Cambridge.* Cambridge Institute of Education
Bramson R M 1981 *Coping with Difficult People.* Bantam Doubleday Dell. New York
Brannen R Holloway D & Peeke G 1981 Departmental organisational structures in further education. *Journal of Further and Higher Education* **5**(3): 22–32

Bridges E M 1986 The incompetent teacher. Falmer Press
Brown A F et al 1982 Changing promotion criteria; cognitive effects on administrators' decisions. *J. Experimental Education* **52**(1): 4–10
Buckler T 1989 Teacher appraisal – the Cumbria experience. In Evans A & Tomlinson J (eds) (1989) *Teacher appraisal: a nationwide approach.* Jessica Kingsley
Bunnell S (ed) 1987 *Teacher appraisal in practice.* Heinemann
Burke J W ed. 1989 *Competency based education and training.* Falmer
Burke R & Wilcox D S 1969 Characteristics of Effective Employee Performance Review and Development Interviews. *Personnel Psychology,* **23**
Buzzotta V & Lefton R 1979 Performance Appraisal. *Industrial Engineering* (Jan. 1979)
Byham W C 1982 Dimensions of Managerial Competence. *Monograph VI* DDI Pitsburgh, Penn.
Cava R 1990 *Dealing with difficult people.* Piatkus Books
Cave R and Cave J 1985 *Teacher appraisal and promotion.* R and J Cave Ltd
Child J 1982 Professionals in the Corporate World: Values, Interests and Control. In Dunkerley D & Salaman G (eds). *The International Yearbook of Organization Studies 1981.* Routledge and Kegan Paul.
Child J 1984 *Organization: a guide to problems and practice.* (2nd edn). Harper & Row
Clarke K 1991 Speech delivered at the North of England Education Conference, Leeds, January
CNAA/BTEC 1990 *The assessment of management competencies.* CNAA
Cohen D K & Murnane R J 1985 The merits of merit pay. *Public Interest* **80** (Summer 1985): pp.3–30
Cooper R 1991 *Management Development Profiles for Teachers: Conference Report.* CEMD North Cheshire College
Cowling A G & Mailer C J B 1987 *Managing human resources.* Edward Arnold
Cumbria County Council 1985 *Submission for Education Support Grant.* Cumbria County Council
Cumbria County Council 1989 *Opening Doors a report by the Teacher Appraisal Working Party on the findings of the Cumbria Appraisal Pilot Study.* Cumbria County Council
Darling-Hammond L Wise A E Pease S R 1983. Teacher evaluation in the organisational context: a review of the literature. *Review of Educational Research* **53**(3): 285–328
Day C 1989 Issues in the management of appraisal for professional development. *Westminster Studies in Education* **12**: 3–15
de Board R 1983 *Counselling people at work.* Gower
De la Bedoyere 1989 *Managing people and problems.* Wildwood House Ltd
Dean J 1991 *Professional development in school.* Open University Press
Delaney P 1988. Staff Appraisal. In Fidler B & Cooper R. (eds.). *Staff appraisal in schools and colleges.* Longman
DES 1983 *Teaching quality* **Cmnd 8836** HMSO
DES 1986 *Better schools – evaluation and appraisal conference.* HMSO
DES 1987 *School Teachers' Pay and Conditions of Employment: The Government's Proposals.* DES

REFERENCES

DES 1989 *School teacher appraisal: a national framework.* HMSO
DES 1991 School teacher appraisal (**Circular 12/91**). DES
DES 1992 *School Teachers' Review Body: First Report 1992.* HMSO
Diffey K 1991 *The teacher appraisal interview* unpublished PhD thesis. The Open University
Drucker P 1989 *The new realities.* Harper & Row
Drummond H 1990 *Managing difficult staff: effective procedures and the law.* Kogan Page
Duckett I 1990 *Piloting appraisal – the Barnet College experience.* B.C. Publications
Duckett I 1991. Promoting appraisal through an active staff development programme. *School Organization* **11** (2)
Duckett I Nash E & Smith D (1992) *Appraisal in FE: into action.* Open College
East Sussex County Council 1989 *Performance Management Guidance Notes.* ESCC
Erault M 1986 Friends or Foes. *Times Educational Supplement* 5 Sept.
Everard B 1989 Competences in education and education management. *Management in Education* **3**(2): 14–20
Everard B 1991 The Competency Approach: Part 3: Are Standards Valueless!. *Management in Education* **5**(2): 29–30
Everard K B 1986a *Developing management in schools.* Blackwell
Everard K B 1986b Staff appraisal: lessons from industry. *Coombe Lodge Reports* **18**(8): 393–401
Everard K B 1990 The Competency Approach to Management Development. *Management in Education* **4**(2): 19–22
Everard K B & Morris G (1990) *Effective school management.* PCP
Fidler B & Bowles G (eds) (1989) *Effective Local Management of Schools; A Strategic Approach.* Longman
Fidler B & Cooper R (eds) 1988 *Staff appraisal in schools and colleges: a guide to implementation.* Longman
Fidler B 1989 *Appraisal as staff management: a managerial approach to staff appraisal.* Paper presented at BEMAS Annual Conference 1989, 15–17 September 1989, University of Leicester
Fidler B 1989 Strategic Management in Schools. In Fidler B & Bowles G (eds) *Effective Local Management of Schools; A Strategic Approach.* Longman
Fidler B Bowles G & Hart J 1991 *ELMS Workbook: Planning Your School's Strategy.* Longman
Field M 1987 Preparing for staff appraisal. *Coombe Lodge Reports* **19**(10): 661–89
Fletcher L 1981 A further comment on recent interpretations of the revised code 1862. *History of education.* **10**(1): 21–31
Fletcher L 1972 Payment for means or payment for results: administrative dilemma of the 1860s. *Journal of Educational Administration and History* **IV**(2): 13–21
Fletcher C 1973 Interview style and the effectiveness of appraisals. *Occupational Psychology* 47
Fletcher C 1984 What's new in ... performance appraisal. *Personnel Management* **14**(2) Feb. 1984

Fletcher C & Williams R 1985 *Performance appraisal and career development.* Hutchinson
Florida Dept of Education 1983 *Domains of the Florida Performance Measurement System.* Office of Teacher Education. Tallahassee
Freemantle D 1985 *Superboss: the A–Z of managing people.* Gower Press
Fullan M 1982 *The meaning of educational change.* OISE. Toronto
Further Education Unit 1992 *TDLB standards in further education.*
Gane V L 1989 The appraisal of headteachers. In Evans A & Tomlinson J (eds) (1989) *Teacher appraisal: a nationwide approach.* Jessica Kingsley
Georgia Dept of Education 1984 *Teacher performance assessment instrument.* Division of staff development. Atlanta
Giegold W C *1978 Performance appraisal and the MBO process: a self-instructional approach.* McGraw-Hill. New York
Gill D 1977 *Appraising performance.* IPM
Gitlin G & Smyth J 1989 *Teacher evaluation: education alternatives.* Falmer
Glogg M & Fidler B 1990 Using examination results as performance indicators in secondary schools. *Educational Management and Administration* **18**(4): pp.38–48
Goldsmith W & Clutterbuck D 1984 *The winning streak.* Penguin
Gray J 1982 Publish and be damned? The problems of comparing exam results in two inner London schools. *Educational Analysis* **4**(3): 47–56
Haefele D L 1981 Teacher Interviews. In Millman, J (ed) *Handbook of Teacher Evaluation.* Sage Publications
Hall D 1984 Effects of three principal styles on school improvement. *Education Leadership* Feb. 1983
Handy C 1984 *Taken for granted? Understanding schools as organizations.* Longman
Handy C 1985 *Understanding Organizations.* Penguin
Handy C 1990 *The age of unreason.* Arrow Books
Harling P 1984 *New directions in educational leadership.* Falmer Press
Hayes M 1984 One company's experience with performance appraisal. In Kakabadse A and Mukhi S (eds) *The Future of Management Education.* Gower
Hendry W D 1975 a general guide to matrix management. *Personnel Review* **4**(2): 33–39
Hewton E 1988 The appraisal interview. Open University Press
HMI 1985 *Education observed 3: Good teachers.* DES
HMI 1987a *Education observed 5: Good behaviour and discipline in schools.* DES
HMI 1987b *Primary schools: some aspects of good practice.* HMSO
HMI 1988a *The new teacher in school.* HMSO
HMI 1988b *Secondary schools: an appraisal by HMI.* HMSO
HMI 1989 *Developments in the appraisal of teachers.* DES
HMI 1990 *Standards in education 1988–89.* DES
Honey P 1980 *Solving People-Problems.* McGraw-Hill
Hopkins D & Bollington R 1989 Teacher appraisal for professional development, a review of research. *Cambridge J.Education* **19**(2): 163–182
Hoy W K & Miskel C G 1991 *Educational Administration: Theory, Research and Practice* (4th Edn). McGraw-Hill. New York

REFERENCES

Hughes M 1985 Leadership in Professionally Staffed Organisations. In Hughes M, Ribbins P & Thomas H (eds.). *Managing education: the system and the institution.* Cassell

Hunt J W 1987 *Managing people at work: a manager's guide to behaviour in organizations* (2nd edn.). McGraw-Hill

IDS 1989 *Paying for performance in the public sector: a progress report.* Income Data Services and Coopers & Lybrand

IMTEC (1983) *International movements towards educational change – institutional development programme.* Dalin and Rust. through NFER

Jaques E 1990 In praise of hierarchy. *Harvard Business Review* **90**(1): 127–33

Johnson T J 1972 *Professions and Power.* Macmillan

Kinder J R (1990), Short-termism as a recurrent British theme. *Financial Times*, p16, 7 Aug. 1990

Knight K 1976 Matrix organisation: a review. *Journal of Management Studies.* May 1976, pp.111–130

Koontz H & O'Donnell C 1978 *Essentials of management* (2nd edn). McGraw-Hill. New York

Kyriacou C (1986) *Effective teaching in schools.* Blackwell

Kyriacou C 1991 *Essential teaching skills.* Blackwell

LACSAB (1989) *Performance related pay – an update.* LACSAB

LACSAB 1990a *Performance related pay in practice: case studies from local government.* LACSAB

LACSAB 1990b *Handbook on Performance Related Pay.* LACSAB

Landy F J & Becker W A S 1987 Motivation Theory Reconsidered. In Cummins L L & Staw B M (eds.). *Research in Organizational Behavior* Vol 9. JAI Press. Greenwich, Conn. US

Latham G P & Locke E A (1979) Goal setting – a motivational technique that works. In *Organizational Dynamics* **8**(2): 68–80 (Reprinted in Steers R M & Porter L W (eds.) 1987 *Motivation and Work Behavior* (4th edn) McGraw-Hill). New York [pp 120–33]

Latham G P & Yukl G A 1975 A review of research on the application of goal setting in organizations. *Academy of Management Journal* **18**(4): 824–45

Latham G P, Cummings L L & Mitchell T R 1987 Behavioral strategies to improve productivity. In Steers R M & Porter L W (eds.) *Motivation and work behavior* (4th edn.). McGraw-Hill. New York.

Latham G P, Mitchell T R & Dossett D L 1978 Importance of participative goal setting and anticipated rewards on goal difficulty and job performance. *Journal of Applied Psychology* **63**(2): 163–71

Laycock N 1987 Appraisal at ICI Plant Protection Division. In Cooper, R & Fidler, B (eds.) *Appraisal in Schools and Colleges 'What can be learned?' and 'The Way Forward?'.* Crewe and Alsager College

Lessem R 1991 *Total Quality Learning.* Basil Blackwell

Locke E A & Latham G P 1990 *A theory of goal setting and task performance* Prentice-Hall. Englewood Cliffs, NJ

Locke E A 1968 Towards a theory of task motivation and incentives. *Organizational Behavior and Human Performance* **3**: 157–89

Locke E A, Latham G P & Erez M 1988 The determinants of goal commitment. *Academy of Management Review.* **13**(1): 23–39

Locke E A, Shaw K N, Saari L M & Latham G P 1981 Goal setting and task performance: 1969–1980. *Psychological Bulletin.* **90**(1): 125-52

Long P 1986 *Performance appraisal revisited.* IPM
Lorsch L 1977 Organizational design: a situational perspective. In Koontz et al (1980). *Management: a book of readings.* McGraw-Hill. New York
Lusty M 1981 *Staff appraisal schemes in secondary comprehensive schools – a study* Unpublished MSc dissertation, University of Surrey
Mager R F & Pipe P 1984 *Analysing performance problems: or you really oughta wanna* (2nd edn.), David S Lake Publishers. Belmont, Cal.
Maier N R F 1976 *The appraisal interview: three basic approaches.* University Associates Inc. La Jolla, California
McMahon A et al 1984 *Guidelines for review and internal development.* (1) *GRIDS: primary school handbook*), (2) *GRIDS: secondary school handbook*). Longman
Meyer H Kay E & French J 1965 Split Roles in Performance Appraisals. *Harvard Business Review* **43**
Miles M B 1971 *Learning to work in groups.* Teachers College Press. New York
Miner J B 1980 *Theories of organizational behavior.* Dryden Press. Hinsdale, Ill.
Mintzberg H 1979 *The structuring of organizations.* Prentice-Hall. Englewood Cliffs, NJ.
Mintzberg H 1983 *Structure in fives: designing effective organizations.* Prentice-Hall. Englewood Cliffs, NJ.
Mitchell T R & Green S G 1983 Leadership and poor performance: an attributional analysis. In Hackman J R, Lawler E E & Porter L W (eds.). *Perspectives on Behavior in Organizations* (2nd edn). McGraw-Hill. New York
Montgomery D et al 1985 *Evaluation and enhancement of teaching performance: a pilot study.* Middlesex Polytechnic
Morrisey G L 1976 *Management by objectives and results in the public sector.* Addison-Wesley. Reading, Mass.
Morrisey G L 1983 *Performance appraisals in the public sector.* Addison-Wesley. Reading, Mass.
MSC 1981 *The new training initiative.* HMSO
Murgatroyd S & Gray H L 1982 Leadership and the effective school. *School Organisation* **2**(3): 285–95
NATFHE 1989 *Pilot Schemes in FE.* Branch Circular, Oct. 1989
NCC 1989a *Mathematics: non-statutory guidance.* NCC
NCC 1989b *Science: non-statutory guidance.* NCC
NCC 1990 *English: non-statutory guidance.* NCC
NCVQ 1988 *The NVQ criteria and related guidance.* NCVQ.
NDCSMT 1989 *Towards a national framework for appraisal.* Consortium of Teacher Appraisal Pilot Schemes. Newsletter Mag.
Nemeroff W & Wexley K 1979 An exploration of the relationships between performance feedback interview characteristics and interview outcomes as perceived by managers and subordinates. *Journal of Occupational Psychology* **52**(1)
New Zealand Qualification Authority 1991 *Designing the framework.* NZQA. Wellington, New Zealand
NJC 1989 *Pilot appraisal schemes in MFHE: general principles agreed by NJC working party, 1989*

REFERENCES

NJC (1991) *Agreement, commentary and employer advice on staff development, training and appraisal.* LGMB
Nuttall D 1986: What can we learn from research on teaching and appraisal? In Dockerall B et al (eds.) *Appraising appraisal.* BERA.
Oldroyd D & Hall V 1991 *Managing staff development.* PCP
Osborn R N, Hunt J G & Jauch L R 1980 *Organization theory: an integrated approach.* John Wiley and Sons. New York.
Paisey A 1981 *Organization and management in schools.* Longman
Payne B 1989 Appraisal in the inner city. In Evans A & Tomlinson J (eds.) (1989). *Teacher appraisal: a nationwide approach.* Jessica Kingsley
Peaker G 1986 Teacher management and appraisal in two school systems in the southern USA. *Journal of Education for Teaching,* **12**(1): 77–83
Peters T J & Waterman R H 1982 *In search of excellence.* Harper & Row. New York.
Phillips A 1984 Grasping the nettle – one school's attempt at teacher assessment. *The Journal of Evaluation in Education.* Issue No.7, (April 1984).
Pratt K and Stenning R 1989 *Managing staff appraisal in schools.* Van Nostrand Reinhold
Randell G 1974 *Staff Appraisal.* Lonsdale
Randell G Packard P & Slater G 1984 *Staff appraisal: a first step to effective leadership.* IPM
Reddy M 1987 *A manager's guide to counselling people at work.* Methuen
Reynolds D (ed.) 1985 *Studying school effectiveness.* Falmer Press
Richardson W 1987 A perspective from industry: industrial staff training and career development panacea or pitfall?. *School Organization* **7**(1): 13–18
Riley M 1983 Better Performance Reviews. *Office administration and automation* (July 1983)
Rogers S 1990 *Performance management in local government.* Longman.
Routledge M D & Dennison W 1990 Introducing appraisal – what has been achieved?. *School Organization* **10**(1): 51–56
Rowbottom R & Billis D 1987 *Organisational design: the work-levels approach.* Gower
Salford LEA 1991a *Appraisal and the school managers' handbook.* Salford Education Dept
Salford LEA 1991b *Appraisal and You.* Salford Education Dept
Sayles L R 1976 Matrix organisation: the structure with a function. *Organizational Dynamics* Autumn 1976. pp.2–17.
Schon D 1983 *The reflective practitioner.* Basic Books. New York
Schuster F E & Kindall A F 1974 Management by objectives – where we stand today. *Human Resource Management* **13**(1): 8–11
Sidney E & Phillips N 1990 *Counselling skills for managers.* Pitman
Sidney E Brown M & Argyle M 1973 *Skills with people: a guide for managers.* Hutchinson
Skitt J & Jennings J 1989 Raising morale through an active staff development programme. *School Organization* **9**(2)
Solem A R 1960 Some Supervisory Problems in Appraisal Interviewing. *Personnel Administration* XXIII
Spence P 1990 Performance Management. *Local Government Employment* pp.14–15 Feb. 1990

Sport and Recreation Lead Body 1991 *Occupational standards for outdoor education, training and education.* Main Frame Research and Consultancy Services

Statutory Instrument 1991 *The Education (School Teacher Appraisal) Regulations 1991 (SI No 1551).* HMSO

Steinmetz L L 1985 *Managing the marginal and unsatisfactory performer* (2nd ed.). Addison Wesley. Reading, Mass.

Stenning W I and Stenning R 1984 The assessment of teacher's performance: some practical considerations. *School Organization and Management Abstracts* **3**(2): 77–90

Stewart V & Stewart A 1983 *Managing the poor performer.* Gower Press

Stewart V and Stewart A 1977 *Practical Performance Appraisal.* Gower

Stodolsky S S 1990 Classroom Observation. In Millman J & Darling-Hammond L (eds.). *The new handbook of teacher evaluation: assessing elementary and secondary school teachers.* Sage. Newbury Park, Cal.

Strauss G A 1972 Management by objectives: a critical view. *Training and Development Journal.* **26**(4): 10–15

Suffolk LEA (1985) *Those having torches. Teacher appraisal: a study.* Suffolk Education Department

Suffolk LEA 1987 *In the light of torches teacher appraisal: A further study.* Industrial Society

Sumner R 1988 Formal teacher appraisal: why and how, not if. In Fidler B & Cooper R (eds.). *Staff appraisal in schools and colleges: a guide to implementation.* Longman

Trethowan D M 1983 *Target setting.* Industrial Society

Trethowan D M 1987 *Appraisal and target setting: a handbook for teacher development.* Paul Chapman Publishing

Trethowan D M 1991b *Managing with appraisal: achieving quality schools through performance management.* Paul Chapman Publishing

Trethowan D M 1991a *Improving the unsatisfactory teacher performance.* The Industrial Society

Trethowan D 1985 ... to appraise teachers, not to bury them. *The Times Educational Supplement* 8 March

Tubbs M E 1986 Goal setting: a meta-analytic examination of the empirical evidence. *Journal of Applied Psychology* **71** (3): 474-83

Turner G Clift P 1987 *A second review and register of school and college based teacher appraisal schemes.* Open University

Turner G Clift P 1988 *Studies in teacher appraisal.* Falmer Press

Tuxworth E 1989, Competence based education and training: background and origins. In J W Burke (ed). *Competence based education and training.* Falmer Press

Ungerson B 1983 How to write a job description. IPM

Weindling R & Early P 1986 How schools manage change. *School Organization* **6**(3): 327-38

Whyte J B 1986 Teacher assessment: a review of the performance appraisal literature with special reference to the implications for teacher appraisal. *Research Papers in Education* **1**(2): 137-63

Wight D 1985 The split role in performance appraisal. *Personnel Administrator.* May 1985

Willis M 1989 Piloting teacher appraisal in an outer London borough. In Evans A & Tomlinson J (eds.). *Teacher appraisal: a nationwide approach.* Jessica Kingsley

Wills J 1988 Linking pay with performance. *Local Government Chronicle.* pp. 17-18. 20 May 1988

Wise et al (1985) Teacher evaluation: a study of effective practices. *The Elementary School Journal.* **86**: 61–121

Wood C J & Pohland P A 1983 Teacher evaluation and the 'hand of history'. *Journal of Educational Administration.* **21**(2): 169-81

Wragg E C 1987 *Teacher appraisal: a practical guide.* Macmillan

Wright P M 1989 Test of the mediating role of goals in the incentive-performance relationships. *Journal of Applied Psychology* **74**(5): 699-705

INDEX

accountability 3
appraisal
  career plans 345
  collection of evidence 339–340
  confidentiality 354–355
  definition 2
  documentation, form of 356
  improvements and developments 343
  information collection 354–356
  managing 105–106
  of middle managers 337
  organisational problems 345
  outcomes 358
  performance standards 343–345, 358
  process 338
  purpose and style 354
  referral system 357
  theory of 4
  upward 17
appraisal in education, problems of 27–38
  appraisal and line managers 35–36
  difficulty of assessing teaching 31–32
  essential features of appraisal system 38
  heads of institution 37–38
  lack of infrastructure 34–35
  lack of time 34
  line managers in education 36–37
  management of professionals 27–29
  rewards and performance related pay (PRP) 30–31
  results unclear 29–30
  setting standards 32–33
  too many bosses 33–34
appraisal follow-up 347
  change of job 347
  extra resources 347
  job development 347
  personal development 347
  training courses 347
  work shadowing 347
appraisal review meeting 348
appraisal process 77–86

classroom observation and feedback 80–81, 106–108, 97–98, 128–129
  collection of evidence 79–80
  follow-up 85
  informal self-appraisal 77–78
  initial planning meeting 78–79
  interview 81
    agenda 81
    career plans 84
    frequency of 17
    job changes 84
    job description check 82
    general discussion 82
    organisational changes 84
    style of 17
    targets 82–83
    training and development 83–84
  next cycle 86
  review meeting 85–86
  statement 84–85
appraisal systems
  evaluative and developmental 3, 43–44
  non-educational organisations 21–26
    appraisal document 22
    interview 22
    main weaknesses 23
    purpose of appraisal 21–22
    reasons for failure 25–26
    some particular systems 23–25
  organisational culture 20, 45–48

change, implementation of 66–74
  conceptual understanding 69–71
  interpersonal skills 72
  intuition and techniques 67
  managing the change 68
  technical knowledge 68–69
  theory for change 66–67
Child, J. 199, 202, 203, 210, 211
Civil Service 23
classroom observation 69, 76, 108, 132, 218–31, 340–341, 357–358

INDEX

choosing appraiser 220
conducting lesson appraisal 222
  discussion and decision re which lesson 222
  feedback 222
  how observation is carried out 222
  self-appraisal 222
  documentation of lesson appraisal 222–23
  target setting 223–25
climate and culture 350
confidentiality 354–355
consultation 352
counselling interview 253–61, 295–296
  counselling in schools and colleges 261
  process 255
  implementing decisions 260–61
    personal qualities of counsellor 256–57
      acceptance 256
      empathy 256
      genuineness 256–57
    problem, clarifying the 255
      discovering why it is a, 257
      exploring feelings connected with the, 258
      recognising the real, 255–57
county and voluntary schools 349

decision, confirmation of 358–359
development 3, 109, 115–116, 129–132, 151, 173–174, 183, 186–187, 193–195, 325, 345, 347, 366
development, staff 53–65
  appraisal and 53, 54–56
  career plans 345
  criteria for effective 53
  evaluation 64–65
  managing appraisal linked to 56–57
  managing outcomes of appraisal process 60–64
  strategy 58–60

evaluation 361

further education colleges
  Barnet College 153–62
    scheme 153–54
    appraisal in practice 160–62
    appraisal in theory 156–60
      appeals procedure 158, 159
      designing the scheme 154–56
        acceptance 156
        background 154
        decision to participate 155
        design 155–56
  further education colleges' pilot schemes 148–52
    appraisal meeting 150
    appraisal procedures 149
      agreed action follow up 149
      preparation 149
      review meeting 149
      teaching/task observation 149
    further recommendations 152
    implementation 151–52
      preparation for appraisal 152
    observation of non-teaching tasks 150
    appraisal meeting 150
    observation of teaching 149–50
      teacher-trained observer 149
    relationship of other college structures 151
      appraisal of senior management 151
      staff development 151

goal theory 5–7
  implications for school management 7
  monetary incentives 6
  participation 6
grant maintained schools 349

head teachers, appraisal of, 129
  Cumbria's experience 138–42
    issues 139–42
      appraisers of head teachers 139–40
      head teacher appraisal and assessment 141–42
      size of appraisal exercise 140–41
  pilot schemes 134–37
    appraisal interview and follow-up 136
    appraisers 135
    data gathering 136
    introduction 134–35
    resourcing 137
    training 135
  Salford's experience 143–47
    appraisal work 145
    conclusions 147
    learning experiences 143–44
    pilot work, outcomes of 145
    training 146–47

ICI 23–24, 274
initial planning meeting 339
institutional plans 350, 351–352
interview 341–342

job descriptions and organisational
  structure 198–217, 345
  concepts 199–211
    job descriptions 214–217
      features of 216–217
      objectives 216
      targets 216
        developmental 216, personal
          developmental 216, problem
          solving 216, remedial 216
    organisational design 211–214
      horizontal structure 212
      schools and colleges 214
      vertical structure 212
    organisational types 200–204
      bureaucracy 200
        collegial structure 202
      matrix structures 208–211
        complex work 208
        matrix 209–211
          co-ordination 210, equal
            210, secondment 210
      professional bureaucracy 204–207
        line manager 207, middle line
          206, operating core 206,
  span of control 207, strategic apex 205,
          support staff 206–207,
          technostructure 206, unity
          of command 207
    organisational design 211–214
      horizontal structure 212, vertical
        structure 212, schools and
        colleges 214
      policy making and executive action
        200
      structural context, schools & colleges
        212–214
institutional evaluation 2
interviewing 232–237
  interview
    conclusion 237, definition 232,
      guidelines 233, phases 234–235,
      questions, types of 235–237,
      types of 232–234
job description 16, 76, 214–217, 109, 96–97
job evaluation
  Hay MSL system 322–323
Joseph, Sir Keith 188
LEA pilot appraisal schemes 177–179
  design 178
  documentation 178
  implementation 179
  organisation 177–178
  records and confidentiality 179

Cumbria's experience 180–187
  development 186–187
  implementation 182–184
    individual appraisal 183,
      individual development 183,
      whole school self-evaluation
      183
  initiation 181–182
    individual career reviews 181,
      participative whole school
      review 181
  pilot group 184–185
  special features 187
  training for all
    feedback and evaluation 185,
      secrecy 185, teacher
      involvement 185
Salford experience 188–197
  development 193–195
    availability of detailed
      documentation, 193
    consultation: LEA–teacher
      associations 193
    difficulties experienced 194
    personal support to schools
      193–194
  implementation 191–193
    appraisal introduction 192
    schools chart course 192
    LEA support 192–193
    preparation and training 192
    readiness of schools 191–192
  initiation 189–191
    approach in practice 191
    LEA's approach 190–191, role 190
    mechanics 189
    principles 189–90
      benefits to institution 190, to
        teacher 189
  special features
    links with INSET provision 196
    funds for institutional
      development 196
    teaching analysis and support 195
    whole school evaluation 195–196
Legislation and Regulations ix
  Conditions of Service (DES 1987) ix
  1986 Education Act (No. 2) ix
  National Framework (DES 1989) ix
  National Scheme (DES 1991) ix
  Regulations (SI 1511, 1991) ix

management by objectives (MBO) 4–5, 7,
  16

INDEX

management competences, appraisal of 271–280
  competences, development of 275–277
    outdoor education 277–279
    and staff appraisal, 277–280
  competency movement 271–274
  TEED approach 274–275
Mintzberg, H. 205–207

national agreement on staff development, training and appraisal (NJC 1991) 366

organisation 336

performance
  data 16, 76
performance appraisal, goals of 14–15
  benefits to individual employee 14–15
  potential conflict 15
  reducing conflict 15–16
performance related pay (PRP) 303–315
  education department, experience of 316–326
  head teachers and deputy heads 327–334
    benefits 334
    motivation 327
      fair rewards and incentives 328
      performance improvement
        retention and recruitment improvement
    overview of experience, Kensington and Chelsea 328–329
    performance assessment 331–332
      head teachers and deputies 332
    performance pay in education 329
      head teachers and deputies 329–330
    key factors in introduction 333–334
  in context 316–317
  introduction of, steps in 313–314
  & performance management 316–326
    East Sussex experience 317–321
      evaluation of 319–321
    learning from the experience of 322–326
      certainty of need for PRP 322
      communication improved 325
      continuity of purpose 323
      divisive potential minimised 324
      evaluation of every job in organisation 322–333
      fair and open operation of scheme 324
      non-financial recognition 323–324
      performance, improved definition 323
      PRP wider context 325–326
      stability in organisation 323
      staff development, emphasis 325
      training increased 325
  public sector schemes 309–313
    payment basis 311–312
      cultural context of 313
      eligibility for 312
      size of 312
    performance assessment, basis of 310–211
      merit rating 310
      performance against targets 310–311
  schools and colleges, implications for 314–315
  teachers, objections to 305
    merit pay in US 307
    pay as motivation 305–306
    payment by results 306–307
planning 352–358
  organisational structure 353
  scheme design 352
  staff management 353
  strategy 352–353
pilot schemes in schools 87–91
  appraisal interview and target setting 89–90
  appraisal and school development 90–91
  classroom observation 89
  LEAs taking part 87
  preparation and data gathering 88–89
  training 87–88
poor performers, handling of 281–302*
  appraisal and poor performance 282–284
    poor performers and poor performance 283–284
  diagnosis 288
    attribution theory 285–290
  difficult people 297
    complainers 298
    hostiles 298
    indecisives 300–301
    know-it-all experts 300
    negativists 299–300
    silent and unresponsives 299

super-agreeables 299
legal aspects 286–287
need for action 284–286
problems, causes of 291
  job and its context 291–292
  management 292–293
  individual employee 293–294
process, stages of 287–288
solutions 296–297
taking action 295–296
  counselling interview 295–296
target setting 269–270
management and poor performance 18–20
primary schools
  Arnside National School Cumbria 101–112
    appraisal conference 108–110
      aims and targets 109
      classroom observation 108
      current year 108–109
      follow-up 110–111
      improvements 109
      job specification 109
      professional development 109
    classroom observation 106–108
    managing appraisal 105–106
    preparing for appraisal 105–106
    training for appraisal 101–102
    whole school review 103–105
  St Edmunds RC School, Salford 92–100
    introducing the scheme 94–99
    school description 93–94
      creating favourable climate 94–95
      implementing the programme 96–99
        appraisal interview 98–99
        feedback discussion 98
        initial meeting 97
        job description 96–97
        planning meeting 98
        summary record 99
      planning the programme 96
      preliminaries to introduction 95
    school description 93–94

resources, allocation of 361
revision and further training 362
secondary schools
  Birchwood Community High School, Cheshire 125
    development 129–132
      changes in interview pattern 130–131
      classroom observation 132
      future developments in INSET 131–132
      mid-year interviews 129–130
      special features 132–133
    implementation 126–129
      classroom observation 132
      first interviews 126–128
      head's appraisal 129
      meeting training targets 128
    initiation 125–126
    school description 124–125
  Emmbrook School, Berkshire, 114–123
    appraisal trial 117–118
    development 115–116
    initiation 114–115
    self appraisal document 118–119
      future of 119
      job specification 119
      review of past year 119
      target setting 119
    subsequent developments 121–12
    trial in practice 120–121
professional and management development
  Cheshire Education Management Programme (CEMP) 163–176
    case studies 175
      further education 176
      sixth form college 176
    CEMP process 166
      action learning plan 167
      evidence of achievement 168
      induction 166
      personal review 167
      preparation 166
      recognition 168
    development 173–174
      CEMP into industry 174
      initial teacher training
      whole organisation professional development 173
    evaluation 170–171
      coaching by manager 171
      issues 170
      managers, who are the? 170
      reviewers 171
      workbased management learning 170–171
    initiation 163
      needs analysis 164–165
      specification 164–165
      what is CEMP? 165–166
    introduction 163
    issue of time 172

INDEX

managing the process 172

self appraisal 76, 77–78, 118–119, 222, 339, 341
staff appraisal system, overall aims
  credibility with public 362
  pupils improved learning experiences 362
  job satisfaction improval 362
staff management 7–13, 39–52
  appraisal and, 7–10, 40–52
  culture of school 45–48
  evaluative and developmental appraisal 43–44
  introducing appraisal 50
  leadership 48–50
  managerial approach to appraisal 44–45
  motivation theory 10–13
  organisation structure 40
  process of 8–9, 41–43
  reward systems 40
  selection criteria 40
  summary, D. Nuttall (1986) 52
  teachers 50–51
  training 40

target setting 262–270
  boundaries of 264
  comparison with basic task 264-265
  compulsory for poor performers 269–270
  criteria for 265–266
  developmental, job 345
  personal 346
  documentation of 267–268
  effective requirements for 266–267
  implications of 267
  origins of 262–263
  problem solving 345
  problems with 268–269
  remedial 345
  source of 263–264
  virtues of 270
teacher appraisal interview 238–252
  characteristics of 241–247
  introduction 238
  preconditions for
    climate setting for 239
    planning and follow-up 240
    recognition of dimensions of 239
      affective 239
      functional 239–240
      relational 240
  skills needed for 242-247
    attending 244-245
    control, exercise of 243–244
    feedback 246-247
    interaction 247-249
    moods,.values, 'halo effect', attribution, allowing for 245–246
    questioning 246
    rapport, establishment of 243
    reflection 247
  style, appraiser 249–251
teachers, basic task of 264–265
teaching, craft or profession 27–29
training 359